INTERCULTURAL UTOPIAS

A BOOK IN THE SERIES

LATIN AMERICA OTHERWISE

Languages, Empires, Nations

SERIES EDITORS:

Walter D. Mignolo, *Duke University*

Irene Silverblatt, *Duke University*

Sonia Saldívar-Hull, *University of
Texas, San Antonio*

Intercultural Utopias

PUBLIC INTELLECTUALS,

CULTURAL EXPERIMENTATION,

AND ETHNIC PLURALISM

IN COLOMBIA

Joanne Rappaport

DUKE UNIVERSITY PRESS

Durham and London

2005

© 2005 DUKE UNIVERSITY PRESS
All rights reserved
Printed in the United States of America
on acid-free paper
Designed by Amy Ruth Buchanan
Typeset in Minion by Keystone Typesetting, Inc.
Library of Congress Cataloging-in-
Publication Data appear on the last
printed page of this book.

FOR MIMI

CONTENTS

Latin America Otherwise is a critical series. It aims to explore the emergence and consequence of concepts used to define "Latin America" at the same time exploring the broad interplay of political, economic, and cultural practices that have shaped "Latin American" worlds. Latin America, at the crossroads of competing imperial designs and local responses, has been construed as a geocultural and geopolitical entity since the nineteenth century. This series provides a starting point to redefine Latin America as a configuration of political, linguistic, cultural and economic intersections that demands a continuous reappraisal of the role of the Americas in history, and of the ongoing process of globalization and the relocation of people and cultures that have characterized Latin America's experience. *Latin America Otherwise: Languages, Empires, Nations* is a forum that confronts established geocultural constructions, that rethinks area studies and disciplinary boundaries, that assesses convictions of the academy and of public policy, and that, correspondingly, demands that the practices through which we produce knowledge and understanding about and from Latin America be subject to rigorous and critical scrutiny.

This book is about dreams: dreams of belonging to and participating in a new Colombia. The dreamers are part of an indigenous movement in the province of Cauca—an extraordinary one that builds on the many knowledges and talents of native and nonnative women and men. Their vision is insistently inclusive, incorporating the insights of intellectuals and cultural planners from different ethnic backgrounds; it is also insistently communicative, forging dialogues between indigenous communities and across them to representatives of larger regional and national groupings.

We learn about building dreams and attempts at realizing them and about the complex roles of public intellectuals in that process. We learn about intercultural engagement and the transformative discourses that ensue. But,

most astonishing, we learn from an extraordinary dialogue between indigenous thinkers and the anthropologist whose participation in this movement
for an all-embracing nationalism is inseparable from her ethnography of
the movement. *Intercultural Utopias* is engaged anthropology at its best, providing us with "otherwise" perspectives on cultural practices—perspectives
rooted in indigenous knowledges, indigenous inclusiveness, and an advocacy
anthropology.

ACKNOWLEDGMENTS

The research on which this book is based was conducted during the summers of 1995–2002 in the cities of Popayán and Bogotá and in various rural communities in Cauca, Colombia. It began in 1995, when David Gow and I were asked by the Instituto Colombiano de Antropología to conduct an exploratory study of the Nasa of Tierradentro, who had been displaced in 1994 by a massive series of earthquakes and avalanches and resettled in distant territories. From 1996 to 1997 we were supported by a grant from Colciencias, the Colombian scientific research agency, to the Instituto Colombiano de Antropología for a team project on new social movements in which David and I participated; I thank María Victoria Uribe, director of ICAN, Claudia Steiner, then director of social anthropology in ICAN, and María Lucía Sotomayor, coordinator of the research team, for the opportunity to participate in the project. In 1998, 1999, and 2001 I received summer research support from the Graduate School of Georgetown University, for which I am grateful. In 1999, I was awarded, together with Myriam Amparo Espinosa, David Gow, Adonías Perdomo, and Susana Piñacué, an International Collaborative Grant from the Wenner-Gren Foundation for Anthropological Research, which provided a critical arena for discussion of the issues brought up here; the grant was renewed in 2001 with the participation of Tulio Rojas Curieux in place of Myriam Amparo Espinosa, who was involved in other projects. The National Humanities Center, through a fellowship funded by the National Endowment for the Humanities, provided me in 2002–2003 with a stimulating environment in which to write this book. I am particularly grateful to the fellows with whom I had the privilege to interact and exchange ideas and to the NHC administration, librarians, copy editors, and computer specialists who keep this wonderful place running. I am particularly beholden to Kent Mullikin, director of the fellowship program, to Eliza Robertson, director of the library, and to Joel Elliott, the resident computer wiz. I also received a Georgetown University Senior Faculty Fellowship in 2003, for which I am very grateful.

The conversations of the collaborative research group in which I was privileged to participate have enriched my perspectives on indigenous cultural experimentation and have widened my appreciation of who can do ethnography and how it should be accomplished. Although I mine the transcripts of our discussions for ethnographic material in the following chapters, I do not consider our conversations to have been a strictly ethnographic experience, nor did my Nasa colleagues play the role of informants. To the contrary, the exchange that transpired during the course of the grant—and which continues to the present—constituted a critical arena for analysis, much as do university seminars and panels at professional meetings. Most of the chapters, in some form or other, received thoughtful commentary from members of the team.

The willingness to converse and the hospitality of the leadership of the Bilingual Education Program (PEB) of the Consejo Regional Indígena del Cauca (CRIC) made my research project possible, despite the fact that I continually probed their feelings of insecurity and weakness; had the CRIC team not been so politically mature, such conversations would not have been possible nor as fruitful as they proved to be. In particular, I would like to thank PEB members Hermes Angucho, Álvaro Cabrera, Mélida Camayo, Alicia Chocué, Rosalba Ipia, Yamilé Nene, Mauricio Parada, Benjamín Ramos, Alba Simbaqueba, Manuel Sisco, Luís Carlos Ulcué, and Luís Yonda for their patience and support. I am particularly indebted to Graciela Bolaños, Abelardo Ramos, and Inocencio Ramos for their friendship, their conversation, and their hospitality. Graciela and Abelardo invited me to collaborate with them on a history of PEB, which not only opened further windows into the ethnography of indigenous cultural planning, but provided me with insights into how to analyze my materials, besides constituting a concrete venue in which I could participate in the organization. Inocencio and his then *compañera*, Claudia Inseca, were constant and insightful interlocutors at their home in Popayán and on trips to rural localities. The Ramos brothers never allowed me to travel alone to increasingly dangerous rural areas and invited me to shamanic rituals for further protection.

My family and I were made to feel at home in Popayán by Ana Ruth Mosquera and Rubiela Estrada Mosquera; our extended family grew to include Beto Estrada Mosquera, Nancy Charrupí, and their daughter, Isabela, as well as Juan Diego Castrillón, Costanza Valencia Mosquera, and their children. Cristóbal Gnecco, Cristina Simmonds, and their daughter, Isabel, also provided us with a home away from home. In Tóez, we were enveloped in the hospitality of our *compadres* Felipe Morales and Mercedes Belalcázar, as we were in San José del Guayabal by our *comadre* Lucía Musse and her parents, Jesusa Dicue and Mario Musse, with whom I had lived in the late 1970s when conducting dissertation research in Tierradentro. Fathers Antonio Bonanomi and Ezio Roattino of the parish of Toribío opened the doors of their convent to us, providing us with intense discussion and debate, as well as warm hospitality. In Bogotá, we were always welcome at the home of Graciela Bolaños and Pablo Tattay, where intense discussion and hard work were combined with congenial meals and the friendship of their adult children, Libia and Pablito.

Many individuals, in the academic world and beyond, provided critical insights into identity formation, law, and the rise of intellectuals, for which I am deeply thankful: Antonio Bonanomi, Lisandro Campo, Mauricio Caviedes, Waskar Ari Chachaki, Henry Caballero, Antonio Chavaco, Lucho Escobar, Marcelo Fernández Osco, Herinaldy Gómez, Jorge Eliécer Inceca, Jean Jackson, Diego Jaramillo, Jon Landaburu, César Maldonado, Carlos Mamani Condori, Omaira Medina, Manuel Molina, Marco Tulio Mosquera, Bárbara Muelas, Jessica Mulligan, Luz Mery Niquinás, Alfonso Peña, Gildardo Peña, Alcida Ramos, Ezio Roattino, Stuart Rockefeller, Cristina Simmonds, Carol Smith, Libia Tattay, Pablo Tattay, Esteban Ticona Alejo, Benilda Tróchez, Odilia Tróchez, Julio Tróchez, Taita Floro Alberto Tunubalá, Arquimedes Vitonás, Kay Warren, James Yatacué, Angel María Yoinó, and the students of CRIC's Licenciatura en Pedagogía Comunitaria. Carlos Ariel Ruiz, Leoxmar Muñoz, and Donna Lee Van Cott engaged me in insightful conversations regarding customary law and indigenous special jurisdiction; Carlos Ariel and Donna also provided me with copies of key decisions by the Constitutional Court, without which the final chapters would not have been possible. Daniel Mato and Walter Mignolo continually cautioned me on the need to read anthropological writings coming *from* Latin America, not only analysis *of* the region, although I must admit, I took their admonitions a step further, seeking out the work of indigenous intellectuals in particular. Earlier drafts of several of these chapters were presented to meetings of bilingual teachers, community activists, indigenous intellectuals, and professors of ethnoeducation, as well as to our research team; their commentaries helped me to rethink a number of critical issues.

I thank Magdalena Espinosa, Stella Ramírez, and Libia Tattay for their transcriptions of interviews and team meetings. Libia was also an engaging interlocutor, who not only transcribed team meetings but shared her impression of team dynamics with me.

Preliminary versions of various chapters and the seeds of some of my arguments were presented at several symposia and speakers' series. I thank the following individuals for inviting me to try out my ideas in these venues and providing me with constructive criticism and avenues for further interpretation: Jaime Arocha (Bogotá, 2002); Ryan Calkins (New Haven, 2004); Manuela Carneiro DaCunha (Chicago, 2000); Jeffrey Gould (Bloomington, 2000); Rosana Guber and the late Hernán Vidal (Buenos Aires, 1996); Sally Han (Ann Arbor, 2002); Jean Jackson and Kay Warren (Cambridge, Massachusetts, 1999); Adriana Johnson (Irvine, 2004); Bruce Mannheim (New Orleans, 2002); Daniel Mato (Caracas, 2002); Andrew Orta (Urbana, 2004); João Pacheco de Oliveira (Rio de Janeiro, 2002); Gyan Pandey (Baltimore, 2000); Deborah Poole (New York, 2000); Gustavo Lins Ribeiro (Brasília, 2002); Carol Smith (Davis, 1996); María Lucía Sotomayor (Quito, 1997); Mark Thurner and Andrés Guerrero (Gainesville, 1999).

Portions of chapter 5 appeared in my article "Redrawing the Nation: Indigenous Intellectuals and Ethnic Pluralism in Colombia," in Mark Thurner and Andrés Guerrero, eds., *After Spanish Rule: Postcolonial Predicaments of the Americas* (Durham, N.C.: Duke University Press, 2003, pp. 310–346). Portions of chapter 7 appear in Spanish in my article "Imaginando una nación pluralista: Intelectuales y la jurisdicción especial indígena," published in Bogotá in 2004 in the *Revista Colombiana de Antropología* (vol. 39, pp. 105–138). The epilogue appears in my 2004 article "Between Sovereignty and Culture: Who Is an Indigenous Intellectual in Colombia?" in the *International Review of Social History, Supplement* 12 (vol. 49, pp. 111–132).

Henyo Barretto, Graciela Bolaños, Román de la Campa, Gloria Castro, Jan French, Charles Hale, Aurolyn Luykx, Bruce Mannheim, Daniel Mato, Diane Nelson, Andrew Orta, Yoshinobu Ota, João Pacheco de Oliveira, Abelardo Ramos, Gustavo Lins Ribeiro, Mart Stewart, Mark Thurner, Kay Warren, and the members of my fall 2001 Autoethnography seminar at Georgetown University provided stimulating commentary on parts of this manuscript. In addition to mapping out the salient points of the many Constitutional Court decisions concerning conflicts between collective and individual rights among indigenous people, Lucas Izquierdo was a stimulating interlocutor for the chapter on customary law and an insightful reader of the book as a whole. The commentaries of the reading group we formed at the National Humanities Center—Kathryn Burns, Ginger Frost, Grace Hale, Susan Hirsch, Teresita Martínez, Paula Sanders, Moshe Sluhovsky, Erin Smith, Faith Smith, and Helen Solterer—were also critical to this book, providing me with thoughtful reflections on my writing and insightful suggestions that have enhanced my arguments; Helen, Moshe, and Susan gave me penetrating comments on a number of chapters beyond the one that I presented to the reading group. Rob Albro magnanimously volunteered to read the entire first draft of my manuscript and returned to me an extensive set of astute and penetrating commentaries that I fear I cannot do justice to. I was fortunate to have two unusually perceptive reviewers at Duke University Press. One of them, Les Field, prodded me into incorporating more thoroughly into certain chapters my intention of interweaving life narratives of utopian individuals caught up in conflict. He also reminded me, through his commentaries and through his own work, that it is possible to do serious anthropology and at the same time maintain a political commitment. The other, Jean Jackson, has always stood as an example to me for her long-term commitment to Colombianist anthropology and Colombian anthropologists. Of course, notwithstanding the contributions of all of these readers, what is written here is my own responsibility.

This is my second experience working with Valerie Millholland of Duke University Press. By building Duke as a major site for Latin American studies, she has played a crucial role in defining what a theoretically engaged area studies might be. She has also been a friend over the past few years. It is an honor to have the continued opportunity to work with her. I also thank Valerie for placing me in contact with Linda Huff, who did a wonderful job on the map and illustrations.

I thank Irving and Betty Rappaport for their constant support over the years. This was my first field experience in which I conducted research with family members. David Gow was a member of our collaborative team and has been a constant interlocutor and an unrelenting critic. Many a dinner hour in our home has been taken up with conversations and arguments about politics in Cauca, the tensions of balancing political and academic commitments, and approaches to the analysis of indigenous movements. Working with David has made this project entirely different from the more individualistic research endeavors I had undertaken before. The accompaniment of our daughter, Miriam Rappaport-Gow, who first visited Cauca at the age of six months, made our research considerably less solitary and infinitely more complex. Mimi's friendships with Nasa children, who learned words in English to communicate with her while she learned to respond to them in Nasa Yuwe and in Spanish, as well as her intimacy with children in Popayán—some of whom are now political refugees—humanized our field stays in a generally tense and conflict-ridden Cauca.

A NOTE ON THE ORTHOGRAPHY
OF NASA YUWE

Nasa Yuwe, the language of the Nasa, has over time been written in various alphabets, beginning with the 1755 dictionary, grammar, and catechism of Fr. Eugenio del Castillo y Orozco (1877 [1755]), parish priest of Tálaga, Tierradentro. However, it is only in the last decades of the twentieth century that the Nasa themselves began to employ various orthographic systems in the educational sphere. The first of these alphabets (Slocum 1972), based largely on the Spanish alphabet but also to some degree using borrowings from English, was created by the Summer Institute of Linguistics (SIL), an organization of evangelical missionaries whose objective was to translate the Bible into indigenous languages and to convert indigenous peoples to evangelical Protestantism. Until recently, the SIL alphabet was employed not only by Nasa Protestants, but also, in slightly altered form, by Roman Catholic missionaries from the Apostolic Vicariate of Tierradentro and those Nasa intellectuals engaged in educational planning within the Vicariate's schools (García Isaza 1996). As a result of advanced linguistic training at the Universidad de los Andes received in the mid-1980s by several Nasas affiliated with the Consejo Regional Indígena del Cauca (CRIC), a more rigorous alphabet was developed (CRIC n.d.c) to account for the complex phonology of Nasa Yuwe; this alphabet has been used in most of the CRIC publications, with the exception of the earliest ones, which employed a variant of the SIL's orthography.

Beginning in the 1990s, attempts were made to create a unified alphabet for Nasa Yuwe (Various n.d.), bringing together proponents of the CRIC alphabet with advocates of the SIL orthography and with representatives of the Apostolic Vicariate in Tierradentro. To some degree, the positions of the three parties owed to distinct appreciations of how Nasa phonology should be written, particularly concerning the necessity of following Spanish orthographic conventions. However, the differences across the three positions were largely political, given that each of the three groups espouses a distinct vision of the nature and objectives of the indigenous movement. By 2000, a single alphabet was agreed upon (Abelardo Ramos and Collo 2000). For the most part, I have chosen to privilege the new unified orthography by substituting it in quotations in the place of earlier alphabets. Its rules are reproduced below, adapted from Abelardo Ramos (2000, 52–53).

CONSONANTS

Basic

p t ç k m n b d z g l s j y w r

Ç has a hard sound, like the letter *k* in English. *J* is pronounced as in Spanish. These were concessions to Spanish orthography. Consonants *b*, *d*, *z*, and *g* are prenasalized; in the SIL alphabet, these consonants were preceded by the letters *m* or *n*.

Palatalized

px tx çx kx nx bx dx zx gz lz sx jx fx vx

Occlusive silent aspirated

ph th çh kh

Occlusive silent aspirated palatalized

pxh txh çxh kxh

VOWELS

Oral

a	e	i	u
a'	e'	i'	u' (glottalized)
ah	eh	ih	uh (aspirated)
aa	ee	ii	uu (long)

Nasal

â	ê	î	û
â'	ê'	î'	û' (glottalized)
âh	êh	îh	ûh (aspirated)
âa	êe	îi	ûu (long)

Nasal vowels can be written with the following diacritics: â, ä, or ā.

ABBREVIATIONS OF
COLOMBIAN ORGANIZATIONS

Indigenous Organizations, Programs, and Political Parties

ACIN   Asociación de Cabildos Indígenas del Norte del Cauca (Association
        of Indigenous Cabildos of Northern Cauca)

AICO   Autoridades Indígenas de Colombia (Indigenous Authorities of
        Colombia)

ASI   Alianza Social Indígena (Indigenous Social Alliance)

CECIB   Centro Educativo Comunitario Intercultural Bilingüe (Intercultural
        Bilingual Community Educational Center)

CETIC   Comité de Educación de los Territorios Indígenas del Cauca
        (Education Committee for the Indigenous Territories of Cauca)

CRIC   Consejo Regional Indígena del Cauca (Regional Indigenous Council
        of Cauca)

CRIT   Consejo Regional Indígena del Tolima (Regional Indigenous
        Council of Tolima)

MAQL   Movimiento Armado Quintín Lame (Quintín Lame Armed
        Movement); also called Quintines in this book

ONIC   Organización Nacional Indígena de Colombia (National Indigenous
        Organization of Colombia)

PEB   Programa de Educación Bilingüe, CRIC (Bilingual Education
        Program, CRIC)

Peasant Organization

ANUC   Asociación Nacional de Usuarios Campesinos (National Association
        of Peasant Users)

Guerrilla Groups

ELN   Ejército de Liberación Nacional (National Liberation Army)
FARC   Fuerzas Armadas Revolucionarias de Colombia (Revolutionary
         Armed Forces of Colombia)
M-19   Movimiento 19 de Abril (19th of April Movement)

Paramilitary Organization

AUC   Autodefensas Unidas de Colombia (United Self-Defense Forces of
         Colombia)

Nongovernmental Organizations and Research Institutes

CINEP   Centro de Investigación y Educación Popular (Center for Popular
         Education and Research)
FUCAI   Fundación Caminos de la Identidad (Roads to Identity Foundation)
FUNCOP   Fundación para la Comunicación Popular (Popular
         Communications Foundation)
La Rosca La Rosca de Investigación y Acción Social (Circle of Research and
         Social Action)
TDH   Terre des Hommes

State Organizations and Mainstream Political Parties

CNK   Corporación Nasa Kiwe (Nasa Kiwe Corporation)
DAI   División de Asuntos Indígenas (Division of Indigenous Affairs)
ETI   Entidad Territorial Indígena (Indigenous Territorial Entity)
INCORA   Instituto Colombiano para la Reforma Agraria (Colombian
         Institute for Agrarian Reform)

INTRODUCTION

Colombia, as we know from media coverage, is a land riven by almost fifty years of civil war. Torn apart by guerrilla violence and paramilitary terror fueled by money from the sale of illicit drugs, Colombians are heirs to a feeble state, one of whose few effective institutions is an armed forces with deep links to ultra-rightist paramilitary forces. Colombian citizens, particularly those living in rural areas, do not always benefit from the basic services that a state is supposed to provide; in some regions there is virtually no state presence and the territory is occupied by leftist guerrilla organizations that, though not as bloodthirsty as the paramilitary, are guilty of numerous abuses of human rights and of local sovereignty.[1] In this complex mix, only 2 percent of the 42 million Colombians identify themselves as indigenous or live in a *resguardo*, the communal territories designated for native peoples and administered by *cabildos*, or traditional indigenous authorities. So why, then, write a book on native-inspired intercultural utopias, when Colombia is only marginally indigenous and is hardly a place known for its utopian dreams?

Indigenous People and the Colombian State

Despite its small aboriginal population, slightly more than a quarter of the Colombian national territory is in indigenous hands, constituting more than a million square kilometers of communally owned resguardo lands. Eighty percent of Colombia's mineral resources are to be found in these territories. Indigenous lands are also home to some of the most intense conflicts in modern Colombia, which many times revolve around competition for resources and for agricultural land (Valbuena 2003, 14). Therefore, although Colombia is not similar to Bolivia or to Guatemala in terms of the statistical weight of its indigenous population, the distribution of native peoples across certain critical regions lends them a significance that transcends their demographic impact.

Indigenous political discourses also weigh heavily at the heart of Colombia's moral conscience because of the strength of its ethnic organizations. The first of these to appear was the Regional Indigenous Council of Cauca (CRIC), one of the most consolidated of the nation's indigenous organizations, founded in 1971. CRIC conceived itself as a council of cabildos representing various ethnic groups in the southwestern highland province of Cauca, including the Kokonukos, Guambianos, Nasas, and Yanaconas.[2] CRIC's original platform revolved around land claims, the reconstitution of cabildos, and the promotion of indigenous culture (Avirama and Márquez 1995; Gros 1991); CRIC's program followed the demands laid out in the first half of the twentieth century by the Nasa political leader Manuel Quintín Lame (Castillo-Cárdenas 1987; Castrillón Arboleda 1973; Rappaport 1998b). Since CRIC's founding, a plethora of local, regional, and national indigenous organizations has entered the Colombian political stage, many following the CRIC model. In Cauca, new indigenous organizations sprang up in the late 1970s, including a network of cabildos coalescing around Guambiano leadership, which would ultimately be called AICO, or the Indigenous Authorities of Colombia (Findji 1992). AICO grew out of Guambiano critiques of CRIC's land claims strategy, which in the early years centered on the establishment of government-supported cooperatives; AICO, in contrast, advocated the reincorporation of reclaimed lands directly into the resguardo structure. Undoubtedly, AICO also developed out of a centuries-old rivalry between Guambianos and Nasa, resulting in a Guambiano-dominated AICO opposed to a Nasa-influenced CRIC. In the 1990s, a group of Nasa cabildos with largely evangelical Protestant leaderships constituted what they called a "nonaligned movement," which remains independent of CRIC and AICO, although its demands echo theirs. This constellation of organizations, and their counterparts in other regions of Colombia, is what I call the "indigenous movement." The movement has proven itself to be a major contender for political space in Colombia, belying the fact that it is so diverse and represents such a small sector of the national population.

By the 1990s, CRIC celebrated twenty years of existence, dedicated to the highly successful recovery of native lands usurped from resguardos in the colonial period and the nineteenth century and to the reconstitution of indigenous political authority in regions where cabildos had been liquidated or coopted by mainstream political parties. During the course of its first two decades, the leadership of the organization shifted from militant agriculturalists trained in the various leftist movements that operated in the region throughout the century, to schooled and cosmopolitan leaders who erupted onto the national scene with a sophisticated critique of neoliberal government policy and dreams of building an ethnically pluralist nation (Gros 1991, 2000; Jimeno 1996). Correspondingly, CRIC's objectives were repositioned from a focus on rural land claims to an active intervention in regional and national affairs. The militancy of indigenous organizations, particularly in areas marked by conflict among armed actors, had forced the Colombian government to take native peoples into account during the two decades of peace negotiations that marked the close of the twentieth century (Leal Buitrago and Chernick 1999). Native leaders were propelled into the legislative arena as participants in the drafting of the 1991 constitution, which recognizes Colombia as a pluriethnic and multicultural nation (Van Cott 2000a), forcing Colombians to reimagine themselves as a society free of the myth of racial and cultural homogeneity that permeated postindependence nationalism throughout Latin America (Gould 1998). In this sense, Colombia's indigenous movement mirrors developments in Ecuador (Pallares 2002; Selverston-Scher 2001) and Mexico (Collier and Stephen 1997; Hernández 2002; Nash 2001; Stephen 2002) in its advocacy of new notions of ethnic citizenship, the insertion of indigenous demands into those of other popular sectors, and the opening of a dialogue among equals between members of the dominant society and indigenous citizens.

Collaborative Research

I began my research career in the Nasa heartland of Tierradentro in the late 1970s, combining ethnographic research on how historical memory was encoded in the topography with archival work on the transformations of Nasa leadership over the centuries. After completing my dissertation research, which I initially wrote up in Spanish, I left Cauca for a time in response to the violent conflicts taking place there between an indigenous guerrilla organization, the Quintín Lame Armed Movement (MAQL), and the Colombian army. I gravitated toward the study of indigenous organizing at the grassroots level, conducting fieldwork along the Colombia-Ecuador border among descendants of the Pasto ethnic group, who have harnessed their historical memory to the repossession of lands usurped by large landowners in the nineteenth century (Rappaport 1994). I had always sought a collaborative relationship with indigenous organizations, but in the 1970s my advances had been rebuffed by a CRIC distrustful of foreign scholars or, indeed, of anything that smacked of the United States. I returned to Cauca in 1995, when the Colombian Institute of Anthropology asked me to do an ethnographic study of Tierradentro communities that were displaced by a landslide and earthquake in 1994 (Rappaport and Gow 1997). Upon my return I discovered that CRIC was now open to dialogue; those activists affiliated with its bilingual education program, some of whom had read my Spanish-language publications, made overtures in the hopes that I would share my historical analyses with them. Thus began a long-term collaboration, in which ethnographic research merged with participation in CRIC seminars, workshops, and meetings, leading to joint research on the history of the organization's efforts at bilingual education and to numerous instances in which I was invited to teach and to facilitate workshops in communities. Thus, the fieldwork that I have conducted since 1995 is unusual for a foreign scholar, insofar as it combines scholarly research with advocacy, not on an international level, but in the local and regional arenas.

My dialogue with CRIC was complemented by participation in an international and interethnic research team, composed of U.S. scholars, Colombian academics, and two Nasa researchers, one affiliated with CRIC and the other an advocate of the "nonaligned movement." The purpose of our team was to share our interpretations of contemporary ethnic politics in Cauca, with the objective of establishing a mutual dialogue emerging out of three different subject positions—foreign researcher, national scholar, indigenous intellectual—each with a distinct agenda and methodology.[3] Most of the issues and conceptual categories I use in this book come out of these parallel conversations with CRIC and with the interethnic research team. My intention is to privilege these categories in an effort to engage in an anthropology whose agenda not only reflects the issues currently in vogue in the North American academy, but also revolves around the concepts with which indigenous intellectuals are grappling. Perhaps the best way to get at how I merge these overlapping approaches, one transnational and academic, the other activist, is to mine the issues at stake in the title of this book: *Intercultural Utopias: Public Intellectuals, Cultural Experimentation, and Ethnic Pluralism in Colombia.*

The Notion of the Intercultural

Multiculturalism has gained a great deal of currency during the past few decades in North America and other parts of the developed world, where minority groups fight for a piece of the action not only in the state and civil society (Kymlicka 1995; Povinelli 2002) but also in the academic world (Turner 1993). Among Latin American activists, however, it is interculturalism, the selective appropriation of concepts across cultures in the interests of building a pluralistic dialogue among equals (López 1996), which has been harnessed as a vehicle for connecting such domains as indigenous bilingual education to the political objectives of the native rights movement. The philosophy of interculturalism is framed by a critique of multiculturalism, the latter being seen by Latin American educators as fostering tolerance but not equality. Interculturalism is a central discourse for CRIC, affording indigenous educators ways of critically absorbing ideas and practices from the dominant society, including the technology of literacy, pedagogical methodology, the analytical insights of linguistics, and theories of ethnicity from anthropology and society. Out of the cultural insights gleaned from intercultural research CRIC politicians construct elements useful in a proposal for ethnic pluralism in the political realm, drawing on those grassroots sectors that have been organized politically through experimental schools, intervening in the construction of local systems of justice, participating in constitutional reform, and entering electoral politics under independent platforms.

As my collaboration with CRIC and my conversations with the research team deepened, I came to appreciate the ways interculturalism operated in the indigenous organization. I began to focus on how translation furnished a strategy for the appropriation of concepts across cultures. I discovered that native linguists who had translated pertinent articles of the 1991 Colombian constitution into the Nasa language had harnessed translation as a tool for reconceptualizing key political terms—state, justice, authority—from a Nasa point of view, thus going beyond the creation of neologisms to pose indigenous-inspired alternatives to existing models of nationality and citizenship. Translation was also key to the appropriation of ideas outside of the constitutional sphere, serving as a means of making sense of external pedagogical and social theory, proposing new regional administrative structures in the educational sphere, and discovering new ways of synthesizing the values of indigenous cultures that the movement sought to emphasize and propagate.

I began my research with a desire to write an ethnography of indigenous intellectuals in Cauca, focusing at first on the members of CRIC's bilingual education program: young, schooled indigenous researchers, mostly Nasas, engaged in educational planning and in ethnographic and linguistic inquiry. I found that my dialogue with them was to become an intercultural exercise, in which I shared ideas originating in anthropological and cultural theory and, in turn, absorbed some of what drove their own agenda. Among the ideas that I could share with them, I discovered that W. E. B. Du Bois's (1989 [1903]) notion of double consciousness, which conceptualizes the tensions between ethnic identity and national belonging in discriminatory societies, was quickly latched onto and reinterpreted by Nasa intellectuals; they were also intensely interested in anthropological debates over essentialism. But, in turn, they had a great deal to share with me. I came to appreciate the political and intellectual utility of describing cultural projects as indigenous activists do, in terms of the movement between cultural "insides" and "outsides," conceptual boundaries that permit indigenous militants to distinguish groups on the basis of their relative adherence to distinct cultural logics or, perhaps even more important, culturalist projects. For the indigenous intellectuals with whom I was in dialogue, cultures are not delimited as geographically based things. Instead, "inside" and "outside" constitute metaphors through which the cultural values that the movement aims to construct and instrumentalize are imagined. That is, their dichotomy does not delimit existing or bounded constellations of culture, but instead, furnishes signposts for conceptualizing politicized notions of culture that are in the process of creation. In this sense, the "culture" in CRIC's interculturalism does not derive from realist anthropology but from a political imaginary in which culture is a vehicle for negotiating diversity and is, consequently, always in flux.

As my research progressed, I was struck by the multiplicity of the indigenous movement, whose variability is apparent not only in the range of political positions that its component organizations take, but also in the heterogeneity of its participants. CRIC is an organization that folds various ethnic groups into a common platform, thus laying the foundations for an intercultural dialogue among subordinated groups. But even within those groups, there are varying commands of native languages, political discourses in conflict, different modes of appropriating the cultural values of the dominant society, and distinct ways in which indigenous cultural forms are accentuated. In part, this heterogeneity closely follows regional lines. As I show in the course of this book, northern Cauca, a militant area where CRIC was founded, is a space in which the values of the dominant mestizo society and of leftist organizations merge with Nasa mores and Afrocolombian cultural forms to a much greater degree than in the less politically active and more traditionalist Tierradentro, where key elements of Nasa culture, particularly language, have been conserved. These differences, which are the basis of regional rivalries within CRIC, result in different approaches to the politics of culture. So "Nasa culture" is by no means monolithic. The intracultural diversity of Nasa activists is further crosscut by differences between regional activists and local leaders, who appropriate external concepts and movement discourses in radically distinct ways, suggesting that cultural variety should not only be sought at the grassroots, but must also be found in the ways localities construct their identities in dialogue with overarching political organizations.

Finally, I discovered that the fact that CRIC is part of an *indigenous* movement does not mean that all of its militants are members of native ethnic groups.[4] To the contrary, the day-to-day work of the organization is carried out by intercultural teams that include not only Nasas, Guambianos, and Totoróes, but also leftist intellectuals from urban centers who have dedicated themselves to indigenous politics and who bring much-needed skills to the movement. Some of the most fruitful ideas developed at the regional level come out of conversations between indigenous activists and nonnative sympathizers (whom I call *colaboradores*, as they call themselves). Interculturalism does not, then, consist exclusively of the process of appropriation of external ideas within the indigenous movement, but is an essential component of everyday social interaction in CRIC, a kind of a political microcosm in which pluralist practice can be imagined.

Interculturalism thus encompasses three interwoven threads. First, it constitutes a method for appropriating external ideas, connecting the diverse network of activists, colaboradores, and occasional supporters of the indigenous movement into a common sphere of interaction. Second, it is a utopian political philosophy aimed at achieving interethnic dialogue based on relations of equivalence and at constructing a particular mode of indigenous citizenship in a plural nation. Third, it poses a challenge to traditional forms of ethnographic research, replacing classic thick description with engaged conversation and collaboration.

As I became aware of the significance of these three meanings of interculturalism, I began to reconsider my initial objectives, which confined the scope of my project to a relatively narrow sector of regional activists. Instead, I found that my understanding of who is an intellectual and what is a social movement were problematized, leading me to expand the scope of my ethnographic attention. As I began to view the indigenous movement as a complex bundle of interethnic networks and not as a homogeneous entity, I also came to realize that the conceptual framework within which activists operate is not essentialist. The notions of inside and outside that they use to make sense of the multiple identities at play in ethnic politics furnish, instead, penetrating conceptual—and political—tools for making sense of cultural diversity and for proposing new kinds of political practice in a divided nation. In short, my attention was turned away from the construction of an ethnography of a monolithic movement with a homogeneous set of actors, and toward an examination of how ethnic politics emerges out of the negotiation of a broad network of political and ethnic identities, a process that includes not only regional indigenous intellectuals, but less cosmopolitan local actors as well, a web of affiliations that also encompasses individuals not attached to indigenous communities, such as colaboradores, anthropologists, and state functionaries.

Forging Utopias

CRIC and other indigenous organizations are in the business of formulating utopias. For Caucan native activists, utopias are not impossible dreams, but objectives toward which they strive, sometimes in the long term. Their ultimate objective—to live as indigenous people in a plural society that recognizes them as equal actors who have something to contribute to the nation—has been only partially realized as a result of their efforts over the past thirty years. Indigenous organizations have successfully reclaimed the bulk of those traditional lands that were once in the hands of large landlords, integrating them into the communal regime of the resguardo and affording former indigenous sharecroppers a space in which to farm; that is, they have laid an economic and political basis for enacting pluralism from an autonomous position. Indigenous organizations have persuaded the dominant society that ethnoeducation must be a primary national concern, permitting communities to build bilingual schools in which indigenous cultural identities can be strengthened. They have made the first steps toward official recognition of Colombia as a pluriethnic nation, both in the text of the 1991 constitution and in the legislature, where indigenous people are entitled to two seats in the Senate. They have achieved recognition of native legal systems at the local level.

But Cauca's indigenous people are still mired in poverty, forced to migrate to urban areas as markets contract and the foodstuffs they produce bring in ever diminishing earnings, or to grow coca or poppies on the hillsides in hopes of eking out a livelihood. While urban migration pulls apart the social, cultural, and political fabric of resguardos, drug cultivation subjects communities to the dangers of U.S.-sponsored aerial fumigation and diminishes the land base on which food can be grown, fostering malnutrition. Freedom of movement has been restricted by guerrilla groups, paramilitary organizations, and the Colombian army, all of whom periodically occupy indigenous territory, sometimes blocking the transport of food and people. For example, the United Self-Defense Forces of Colombia (AUC) paramilitary has limited residents of the resguardo of Las Delicias-Buenos Aires, in northern Cauca, to less than $20 of goods that individuals can bring into the community each time they visit the markets of Piendamó, Mondomo, or Popayán.[5] This deprives resguardo residents of access to food and critical supplies, placing them in great danger should the limited number of roads that lead to the community be closed by armed conflict. Numerous massacres have been perpetrated by armed actors within Cauca's resguardos, sometimes aimed at dampening indigenous self-determination and sometimes focused on appropriating native lands. One of the most egregious examples was the 1991 massacre of scores of Nasa and Afrocolombians in the Naya region of Cauca at the hands of the AUC, whose members then occupied these lands. Leaders of many communities have been singled out by armed groups and murdered, particularly by AUC and by the guerrilla groups FARC (Revolutionary Armed Forces of Colombia) and ELN (National Liberation Army). Indigenous youth are frequently rounded up by guerrillas and forcibly recruited, or they are offered monthly wages if they join the guerrillas or the paramilitary.

Yet peaceful utopias, and not violence, are the central trope that comes across in indigenous political discourse. At the many meetings called to address the most recent wave of violence, which began in the mid-1980s and has intensified at the turn of the millennium, one hears little about armed aggression and much about the need to strengthen native cultures, to build grassroots authorities, and to relegitimize shamanic practice and authority.[6] The ubiquity of utopias, and not talk of violence, in the Caucan indigenous movement led me to follow a course that might seem unusual to North Americans, who are anxious to learn more about the Colombian conflict. My friends in CRIC and on the intercultural research team were more interested in how I see their education projects as contributing to an intercultural future. They requested that I give workshops on the history of their culture heroes whose traces can be found in the archival documentation of the eighteenth century. They expressed interest in my ethnographic analyses of the gap between regional militants and local activists. In short, they are more concerned with my interpretations of their utopias than with an analysis of the activities of the armed actors that surround them. They want to be seen as actors, not as victims. And because they are unarmed, their agency emerges through their dreams and plans, not through military action.

Quite obviously, indigenous utopias run up against the objectives of those who seek to control indigenous lands as corridors for transporting troops or as reservoirs in which illicit crops can be grown to sustain armed struggle. Indigenous utopias also come at loggerheads with forces bent on controlling native hearts and minds. So violence is an essential component of my story. But in this book I intend to privilege the strengthening of community author- ity, as much in the cultural arena as in the legal and political orbits, because it functions as an antidote to the violence of outsiders. The construction of an indigenous cosmology and the relegitimization of shamans are as essential to this objective as are the introduction of civic guards in localities and the building of an indigenous legal system to judge and punish violent offenders, because the movement can survive only if it engages in a process of identity formation that promotes the construction of novel strategies for survival. Otherwise, theirs would be a peasant movement and not an indigenous move- ment. This distinction is crucial in Colombia, where indigenous communities and, increasingly, Afrodescendants identify themselves by culture and eth- nicity, and not by an economic positioning within Colombian society, as do peasants. In other words, "indigenous" and "peasant" are seen by the move- ment, and increasingly by the state, as categories that do not overlap.

Public Intellectuals

Indigenous utopias are constructed by intellectuals. My own understanding of what constitutes an intellectual grows out of the work of Italian communist theorist Antonio Gramsci (1971), who did not confine his analysis to the lettered classes that produced learned writings, but argued that intellectual work is the province of the many and involves much more than production of scholarly research, a literary canon, or the erudite essays of social commenta- tors. Instead, Gramsci rooted his argument in the historical contexts in which intellectual work of all sorts maintains the hegemony of certain social classes or fosters the emergence of new sectors. Gramsci's notion of the intellectual was not so much focused on individuals as on the relationship between intel- lectuals or groups of intellectuals and the social sectors in whose name they speak. Their role is to create new cultures or maintain existing ones. Gramsci distinguished between those whom he called traditional intellectuals who work within existing hegemonic sectors in order to maintain them—teachers and priests are good examples—and organic intellectuals who nourish the imaginings of emergent working-class groups. For Gramsci, the notion of organic was not confined exclusively to those intellectuals who emerge from a given class. Instead, he emphasized that what is at stake is the creation of organic relationships within a class in the course of a struggle for hegemony. In this sense, the creation of intellectuals involves not only fostering their emergence within a particular class, but also assimilating traditional intellectuals into that group, thus transforming them into organic intellectuals.[7]

The people with whom I originally planned to conduct my research, the activists in the bilingual education program of CRIC's regional office in the provincial capital of Popayán, are organic intellectuals who come out of resguardos and whose activist aspirations led them to Popayán to pursue political and cultural activities in the organization's regional headquarters. Many cultural activists are Nasas who come from areas characterized by subsistence farming and the use of indigenous languages, places like the resguardos of Caldono on the western slopes of the Central Cordillera, a few hours from Popayán, or from the isolated communities of Tierradentro, four hours of hard travel to the east.[8] Correspondingly, they tend to define "indigenous" according to the cultural characteristics of their home communities, where the native language is Nasa Yuwe, where shamanism provides a widespread alternative to Western medicine, and where the majority of the population supports the cabildo. Having received the bulk of their training as apprentices in the indigenous organization, their task is to produce a cultural discourse and to create an educational infrastructure in which this discourse can be operationalized at the regional and local levels. This dual task involves a combination of community organizing with ethnographic, educational, and linguistic research. Given their objectives, such activists are intellectuals only to the extent that they remain conscious of their ethnic identity, because this is what distinguishes them from those members of indigenous communities who have acquired university degrees and become professionals at large in the dominant society.[9] In addition, CRIC educational activists are intellectuals so long as they participate in the organization, in cabildos, or in other similar institutions, because it is through their identity as members of a group that they function as intellectuals. The objectives of the organic intellectuals of CRIC thus revolve around their identity as native people and their service to the movement. Their work is not harnessed to the creation of academic knowledge, but to promote local activism infused with a contestatory and culturally oriented indigenous ideology. This is achieved by encouraging local schools to function as organizing venues and, simultaneously, as a base from which an ethnic ideology that originates from below can be articulated in dialogue with regional cadres.

Cultural activists employ discourses that diverge significantly from those of indigenous politicians, who are much less apt to make recourse to cultural forms and are more motivated to cast their objectives in a universal political language that is comprehensible to their allies in other social movements and to the state officials with whom they negotiate. CRIC's most forceful political leadership springs from northern Cauca, where in the early and mid-twentieth century, Nasas migrating from insular areas like Tierradentro sought employment on cattle ranches and sugar plantations, and where Nasa lifeways have taken on the cadences of urban Colombian culture, given their proximity to the metropolis of Cali and the small city of Santander de Quilichao. While many of these leaders maintain a strong indigenous identity, they have opted for a regional organizational culture and discourse, as opposed to local ones. Thus, many of these men—for their ranks are largely male—are highly pragmatic social actors not as apt to speak in the culturalist discourse of their colleagues. In fact, CRIC's cultural activists see themselves as the cultural conscience of the movement and are constantly seeking to instill in the political leadership a deeper appreciation of the nuances of cultural difference. It is important to note, however, that cultural activists, like indigenous politicians, are intensely political, wedded to organizational strategies and CRIC's program of land claims, defense of the resguardo system, and support for cabildos. What is different about the two groups is the discourse that each employs to achieve these common objectives and the political space in which each moves.[10] Clearly, the work of indigenous organic intellectuals is not confined to educated writing, but to the creation from below of an activist politics of identity.

True to their calling as cadres who emerge from the native sector, indigenous public intellectuals in Cauca are generally loath to call themselves by such an elitist epithet. Lacking the traditional status and tools of the trade of those deemed by the dominant society to be intellectuals, they prefer to see themselves as activists who are engaged in intellectual concerns. That is, they consciously dissociate themselves from those who identify as intellectuals in Colombia, and whom Gramsci would call traditional intellectuals.[11] Beyond the obvious members of the Popayán elite—a city known for its poets, historians, and national politicians—whose job has been to mediate between a bourgeois civil society and the state (Castañeda 1993; R. Ortiz 1998; Sarlo 2002; Yúdice

1996), traditional intellectuals include local priests, particularly in Tierra-dentro, who are wedded to mainstream political parties and who in the early years of the indigenous movement strove to dampen its emergence. There are still a few *tinterillos*, or unschooled grassroots lawyers, whose livelihoods are sustained by the ignorance of legal procedure and indigenous rights among many rural people. There are local powerholders, both indigenous and nonna-tive, who cling to the clientelistic politics of the mainstream parties, the Lib-erals and the Conservatives. There are many schoolteachers, both nonnative and, increasingly, indigenous, who reject politicized claims to indigenous identity and conform to national curricula that "other" native peoples.

But beyond the obvious candidates in Popayán who vie for the status of traditional intellectual and who are seen by indigenous public intellectuals as the antithesis of what they hope to become, I also met university professors who work closely with native activists in the various indigenous organizations and whose intellectual priorities have merged with those of their Nasa or Guambiano colleagues, resulting in a relationship that has shifted the para-digms used in the academy. This has especially occurred in anthropology, marking Colombian social science as different from its northern counterparts. But the relationship of these metropolitan intellectuals to the indigenous movement is uneasy, as they are outsiders to indigenous communities and to the political discipline of the indigenous organization. Furthermore, the theo-retical discourses that they employ, though frequently of interest to indigenous intellectuals, emerge from and are most pertinent to academic agendas and are geared not toward promoting activism but with an eye to producing academic writings—which, for many indigenous activists, makes academics essentially untrustworthy, almost cannibalistic. Academics are traditional intellectuals who are not organic to indigenous organizations, but are sympathetic to them; they could almost be said to be in transition between traditional and organic status, given that in the Gramscian model, traditional intellectuals could po-tentially be absorbed within the cadre of organic intellectuals.

More active interlocutors are the colaboradores who work full time for ethnic organizations, whose everyday lives transpire in an indigenous milieu, and who submit to the rigors, the dangers, and the discipline of ethnic organi-zations. Many of the most prominent members of this group function as interlocutors who stimulate discussion in the organization, but they rarely publish their ideas in formats other than internal documents and reports. This sector is almost totally ignored in the academic literature, perhaps because colaboradores do not fit neatly in the essentialist models that we have created for analyzing indigenous organizations. I also came across radical priests ready to give their lives for the indigenous cause and open to mixing Christian dogma with native cosmologies. These men are torn between the discipline of their religious calling and the exigencies of the movement they have chosen to serve, leading them to be at odds with both their own hierarchies and indigenous political leaders.

All of these actors are organic to the indigenous movement. However, despite the adherence of such outsiders to organizational objectives, their discourses only partially mirror those of indigenous intellectuals, for the conceptual models that they employ originate in part in the worlds from which they have come, just as do those of academic interlocutors. In fact, their origins outside of the resguardos and their use of external ideas mark their ambivalent membership in the movement as "outsiders-within" (Collins 1991, 11). But in spite of their close association with indigenous intellectuals, they are not, in any sense of the word, a vanguard of the sort that intellectuals in leftist parties hoped to constitute. Colaboradores see themselves as adherents to an existing movement, playing an equal role alongside the cabildos and the indigenous activists that form its backbone, although as native activists become more and more cosmopolitan, colaboradores find themselves occupying a subaltern position in indigenous organizations. Furthermore, their political goals frequently transcend those of the indigenous movement to encompass more global demands on the national level. Although for the most committed, and although it would be painful to disengage from the indigenous movement, there are many other organizing venues in which they can incorporate themselves and further their political agendas, unlike the indigenous intellectuals who recognize that their very survival as indigenous people is what is at stake in the movement.

Colaboradores and university-affiliated supporters of the indigenous struggle are intellectuals who are, in many senses, in the process of becoming organic to the indigenous movement—colaboradores more so than academics, as the latter's interests are less likely to be subsumed by the exigencies of the movement. Gramsci's theory of intellectuals is useful in making sense of how these outsiders are able to play an internal role in indigenous organizations. In fact, if we are to take Gramsci to heart, we cannot study the indigenous movement without paying attention to the role of outsiders within it. But notwithstanding the utility of the Gramscian distinction between traditional and organic intellectuals for making sense of the relationship between indigenous intellectuals and colaborador outsiders, Gramsci does not supply us with sufficient conceptual tools to contend with the internal complexities of intellectual work in Cauca, nor, I suspect, in other locations.

The category of the organic intellectual provides a key to comprehending the interactions of the organization with external actors but does not shed light on negotiations internal to CRIC or between the regional office and the local sphere of action, where a multiplicity of indigenous organic intellectuals operate, frequently at loggerheads with one another. There are considerable differences in the discourses employed by the indigenous intellectuals of CRIC's regional office and affiliated teachers or cabildo members working in local venues. Whereas the former look to leftist theorists, particularly those writing about bilingual education or grassroots development, to stimulate their construction of indigenous proposals, the latter are more concerned with fostering an exchange with other indigenous groups and with subordinated minorities, such as Afrocolombians, in the peasant sector. It is within the dynamic that unfolds between regional and local indigenous intellectuals that ethnic projects are constituted, not in the imposition of one sector on top of another.

There is, moreover, another significant group of local intellectuals, the shamans—in Nasa Yuwe they are called *thê' walas*—whose discourses are rooted in an exchange with the spirit world and not with the dominant society and whose knowledge provides a potent language for the construction of politicized cultural forms. I call these individuals *sabedores* or "knowers," in acknowledgment of the recognition that the movement has given them as the source of the organization's cultural imaginings and their role as brakes against what the movement perceives as its ideological colonization by external forces. Despite their considerable influence, shamanic language and methods stand in such a stark contrast to other indigenous intellectuals that they must be considered separately from other activists.

So, while Gramsci's contribution helps us to conceptualize the differences between the articulation of intellectuals with social movements and the mediating function that Latin American intellectuals have filled between civil society and the state, we need to go beyond Gramsci to make sense of the multiplicity of organic intellectuals in indigenous organizations and to explore how the very heterogeneity of this group presents fertile ground for the construction of a native political ideology. One of the most useful tools I have encountered is the distinction between culturalist projects and discourses of sovereignty (Albert 1995; Chadwick Allen 2002; Field 1999): between an inward-looking emphasis on the revitalization of cultural specificity and a stress on transnational languages of minority rights that discursively and practically link the indigenous movement to other progressive social sectors and make possible negotiation with the state. It is at the intersection of these two discourses that the articulation of the indigenous cultural project with the movement's political objectives can be most fruitfully explored. This calls for a comparative analysis of the positioning of indigenous intellectuals in local and regional venues, as well as an understanding of the fluidity of their discursive practices within the diverse political contexts in which they operate. Accordingly, what I hope to do in this book is to explore the alliances, dialogues, and disjunctures among the indigenous cultural activists who move in the regional sphere, regional and local indigenous politicians, sabedores, colaboradores, and academic interlocutors. Although their ultimate aim is to construct a movement that speaks to the dominant society in what appears in the course of mobilizations as a single voice, their objectives emerge out of a heterogeneity of agendas, methodologies, and discourses.[12]

The Scope of Ethnic Pluralism

Despite the political violence that characterizes its recent history, Colombia is not an arena of ethnic strife. Seemingly in contradiction with this assertion, indigenous and Afrocolombian communities have, in relation to their numbers, borne the brunt of armed attacks because they inhabit marginal territories that are of interest to the armed contenders. In fact, almost half of the displaced in Colombia are Afrodescendants (Ng'weno 2002), and in areas along the Pacific coast, many are indigenous. But the sorts of ethnic conflict that have recently been known in Europe, Africa, the Middle East, and South Asia are not part of the violent mix in Colombia, nor are they pertinent to the rest of Latin America, where ethnic minorities have chosen instead to participate in reconstructing the state by pushing it toward a radical brand of pluralism in which minorities are viewed as important interlocutors in the construction of civil society—a utopian project, if there ever was one, but a goal whose first steps have already been taken.

CRIC and other Caucan indigenous organizations share this pluralist objective. It marked the participation of three native Colombians—one of them Nasa and the others Guambiano and Embera—in the Constituent Assembly that drafted the 1991 constitution. It colors the policies of Taita Floro Alberto Tunubalá, a Guambiano leader who, until recently, was the governor of Cauca. It influences the dynamics of the broad coalition of popular and ethnic organizations that periodically blocks the Panamerican Highway in Piendamó, to the north of Popayán, with the aim of demanding that the state provide adequate social services to rural communities and to the marginal fringes of the cities; in fact, Tunubalá was chosen as a candidate and his campaign was run out of that intercultural and interorganizational milieu. Pluralism is something that the indigenous movement projects out into popular sectors and the nation.

But at the same time, it is something that must be constructed within the indigenous world. Take the resguardos of northern Cauca, for instance. Here, Afrodescendants have always held cabildo office; they, together with landless Nasas and peasant sharecroppers, were instrumental in unleashing a wave of land occupations in the 1980s that ultimately led to the reconstitution of the resguardo of Corinto, whose status had been lost in the early twentieth century. Even in the heartland of Tierradentro, where at least half of the population is Nasa, relationships are being forged between indigenous authorities and their Afrocolombian colleagues through joint participation in cabildo-sponsored development plans. In the resguardos that line the Panamerican Highway between Popayán and the Cauca Valley, Nasas live side by side with Guambianos and with peasants, some of whom participate in cabildos, while others do not. This state of affairs necessitates a novel approach to the construction of autonomy.

When the Guambianos began a process of land claims in the early 1980s, they organized their demands around metaphors of reciprocity—*mayeiley*, or "there is enough for all"; *latá-latá*, or "equality"; and *linchap*, or "accompaniment" (Findji 1992, 127; Vasco, Dagua, and Aranda 1993, 38–41)—all of which convey Guambiano appreciations of the need for pluralism in the construction of an indigenous movement. The first publication of the Guambianos was the *Manifiesto Guambiano* (Guambía 1980), which proclaims in its title, "Ibe namayguen y nimmereay gucha": "This belongs to us, but it's for you." In the Guambiano translation of the 1991 constitution, "autonomy" is glossed as "nømtø isua ashá marøpelø," or "acting within one's own culture" (Muelas et al. 1994, 171), which suggests that there is room for the coexistence of and dialogue across various cultural approaches within the Colombian political system. Similarly, the Nasa translation reads, "peekx ûushu yaakxnxi," or "thinking or feeling from one's own heart" (Abelardo Ramos and Cabildo Indígena de Mosoco 1993, 115), which does not preclude the coexistence of alternative modes of thinking but suggests that by engaging in this exercise one is better equipped to cross cultural boundaries.[13] What these glosses tell us is that political pluralism is not only a matter of fostering tolerance, coexistence, or even equality, but that it is only possible once minority groups learn to "act from within their own culture" and to "think from their own hearts." It is the cultural planning that nourishes this utopia that is the province of the public intellectuals with whom I am concerned in this book.

The Cast of Characters

Unlike many of the well-known studies of Latin American ethnic movements (Alvarez, Dagnino, and Escobar 1998; Brysk 2000), my study employs ethnographic methodology as a central tool for exploring the nuances of indigenous political imaginings, following the pathbreaking work on Guatemala by Fischer (2001), Nelson (1999), and Warren (1998a). In the following pages, I interweave the stories of individuals with an analytic appreciation of the history of CRIC and, to a lesser extent, of other indigenous organizations. In fact, the entire book revolves around individuals who make up the various groups of intellectuals with whom I am concerned—regional indigenous activists, colaboradores, anthropologists, local teachers, indigenous authors, shamans, and native politicians—moving through these different positionings in an effort to comprehend what they mean in practice.

I open the book with organic intellectuals from CRIC's regional office, whom I have heard call themselves "frontier Nasa" because they feel they are precariously balanced on a frontier between Nasa culture and the dominant society. These are people like Susana Piñacué of our interethnic research team, who has spent a large part of her life in Popayán and, on the basis of her disciplinary specialization in linguistics, is working with several of CRIC's experimental schools in the development of their primary-level language curricula. Susana works alongside Inocencio Ramos, who, like her, is from Tierradentro and speaks Nasa Yuwe. Inocencio has functioned in a supervisory capacity in the organization, coordinating CRIC's bilingual education program and heading up a coalition of resguardo-based educational planners. But despite the considerable contributions that Susana and Inocencio have made to indigenous education in Cauca, they see themselves as inexorably divorced from the everyday life, what they call the *vivencias*, of those based on the "inside," in the isolated communities of Tierradentro. In this chapter I interweave conceptualizations of the relationship between frontier Nasa and the rural grassroots that they serve with life stories of regional organic intellectuals that illustrate both the alienation they feel and the ways their frontier position enables their cultural work. In the course of the chapter, I explore the meanings of "inside" and "outside" for CRIC militants and inquire into the usefulness of such constructs for external scholars.

Graciela Bolaños, originally from the southern city of Pasto, Bogotá native Henry Caballero, and Ezio Roattino, an Italian priest, are some of the colaboradores who have dedicated their lives to the Caucan indigenous movement. Graciela was among the founders of CRIC's bilingual education program, coming to indigenous organizing via INCORA, the Colombian agrarian reform agency that in the late 1960s sought to organize peasants in the Cauca Valley. She has worked in CRIC for over thirty years and, although she is well aware that she is not indigenous, does not feel that she is any longer an outsider. Nor does Father Ezio, the former parish priest of Caldono and now resident in Toribío. Through his work in inculturation, a Catholic evangelizing practice that merges Christianity with indigenous cosmologies, Father Ezio senses he has absorbed Nasa lifeways and that his experience is no longer separable from that of his flock. But Henry Caballero, formerly a member of the Quintín Lame Armed Movement and until the 2003 gubernatorial election a functionary in Taita Floro Tunubalá's provincial government, perceives himself as never quite having fully closed the gap between colaborador and indigenous militant, in spite of the efforts he has made.[14] The second chapter explores the quandaries of colaboradores, how they, like the frontier Nasa, balance on a frontier between inside and outside and how they strive to reconceptualize indigenous organizing as pluralist, not only in its demands but in its very composition.

As a foreign anthropologist, I am firmly based in the outside. I was born in the United States, educated there, and reside there now, but my contacts with the Nasa go back to the 1970s. Like my fellow nonindigenous team members, I have striven through collaborative research to become an interlocutor, if not a colaboradora, with the indigenous movement, to forge a conversation between inside and outside that is cognizant of our differences and our similarities. The third chapter explores the extent to which such a dialogue is possible, inquiring into the legitimacy of external researchers in relation to the organic intellectuals of the movement and the contradictions that arise between us and our constituencies as we seek to shift the terms on which our research is based. Here, I examine the ways that Latin American social scientists have tried to engage indigenous activists and situate the activities of our interethnic team in a Colombian intellectual trajectory. Individual narratives, particularly those of the Nasa and Colombian academic team members, inter-woven with my own personal reflections, further explore how a frontier joins and divides us.

The frontier between inside and outside looms between the frontier Nasa and their colaborador allies, on the one hand, and local teachers and activists, on the other. The philosophy of interculturalism, as I have already mentioned, is appropriated in quite distinct forms by the two groups, with the latter turning their sights toward neighboring indigenous groups while the former engages in dialogue with leftist intellectuals from the dominant culture. The history of CRIC's bilingual education program sheds considerable light on how this internal frontier emerged as the organization moved away from the no-tion of the school as an instrument for political organizing, toward an em-phasis on pedagogy and on schooling in the more literal sense. The informa-tion I use in the fourth chapter originated in the collaborative research that I conducted with members of CRIC into the oral history of their education program. Here, the major actors are local activists like Hermes Angucho of Totoró, who has been involved in coordinating a network of representatives of cabildos to create an educational policy on the regional level. I also look at individuals like Roberto Chepe, who was recruited in the early years of CRIC to become a bilingual teacher in the resguardo of La Laguna on the basis of his activist experience and not his schooling.

But while I employ this information in the fourth chapter to develop my own analysis of CRIC history, the militants with whom I worked on the history project—Graciela Bolaños and Abelardo Ramos, a Nasa linguist from Tálaga, Tierradentro, educated in the M.A. program in ethnolinguistics at the Univer-sidad de los Andes in Bogotá, and who is, besides, Inocencio's brother—have written their own interpretation of their history with my collaboration (Bo-laños, Ramos, Rappaport, and Miñana 2004). The fifth chapter inquires into the theoretical underpinnings of this enterprise: the development of a priv-ileged analytical perspective articulated by organic intellectuals. I move be-tween an examination of the creation of culturally specific theoretical vehicles in the writings of the Guambiano history committee, a grassroots group work-ing under the aegis of the cabildo of Guambía, which has employed the metaphor of the spiral as a trope for retelling their past, and the analysis of discourses of sovereignty as they are appropriated by Nasa activists researching CRIC history. The two approaches, an inward-looking culturalist vision and an outward-looking sovereignty perspective, are equally significant in the indige-nous movement. They must, moreover, be examined not only as forms of writing, but in relation to the organizing potential of the collective research methodologies that organic intellectuals employ. By juxtaposing these two approaches, I argue that we must go beyond writing to comprehend how organic intellectuals function in practice and to understand what is at stake in their enterprise.

Perhaps the most innovative example of collective research conducted by native peoples in Cauca is the far-ranging study of cosmovision that Manuel Sisco—a Nasa activist, a student of shamanism from Pueblo Nuevo, and a sometime anthropology undergraduate at the Universidad Salesiana in Quito—undertook with almost two hundred shamans from Tierradentro. A synthetic origin story emerged out of the individual contributions of the shaman-scholars, a narrative used in workshops and seminars across indigenous Cauca. Shamanic research is tactile and highly personal, interpreting bodily signs to engage the spiritual world in dialogue. This is a methodology that is quite distinct from ethnographic research as it is practiced by external anthropologists, or even by frontier Nasa. Chapter 5 inquires into the incommensurability between the results of shamanic research and their translation into a movement discourse used in educational workshops, as well as into the differences between how cosmovision is articulated by regional intellectuals and its appropriation by local activists. Although regional activists have in large part rejected Christianity as a philosophy relevant to their cultural utopias, local people continue to engage in syncretic practices in which Nasa and Christian philosophies merge. They have been supported by leftist priests, most notably Father Álvaro Ulcué, a Nasa cleric from Pueblo Nuevo who served as parish priest in Toribío until his untimely death in 1984 at the hands of a rightist death squad. The struggle between purist notions of cosmovision as articulated by regional intellectuals and the Christian inculturationist philosophy of the Consolata Fathers of Toribío provides a context for my interpretation in chapter 6 of the appropriation of shamanic knowledge in activist circles.

I end this book with a look at Nasa politicians and their appropriation of the culturalist discourses of regional activists in the construction of customary law. Since the 1991 constitution, Colombian indigenous communities have been obliged to conduct judicial procedures according to their own uses and customs, instead of sending the accused to the national justice system. The movement has gone to great pains to adapt the dispersed and highly localized legal practices that in the course of almost five centuries of colonial domination never fully disappeared from the local sphere, to a regional context of confrontation with armed actors and with a state that prizes ethnic pluralism in its constitution but neglects to implement it through legislation. In the course of this process, the cosmological investigations of organic intellectuals that constitute the logic of Nasa legal uses and customs have been read against indigenous forms of resistance to the predatory actions of armed actors, and indigenous philosophies have been essentialized by the well-meaning Colombian jurists who have decided recent legal cases arising out of the implementation of customary law. Chapter 7 inquires into how an indigenous movement that demands that the state become pluralist takes on the attributes of the state while redefining its scope and its logic.

As I move across these constellations of biographies, I hope to complicate matters by teasing out the conceptual and political confrontations that arise when one group of intellectuals enters into dialogue with another. Thus, this is an ethnography that does not take a place or a discrete group as its focus but, instead, roves across the activist networks that have expanded the localized scope of the indigenous community, so that it impacts on region and nation and, simultaneously, has successfully channeled external ideas so that they can be reinterpreted on the inside.

CHAPTER 1

Frontier Nasa / *Nasa de Frontera*

The Dilemma of the Indigenous Intellectual

Two years ago, Susana Piñacué told me that she was a *nasa de frontera*, a frontier Nasa. Susana is a key player in the elaboration of indigenous cultural policy in Cauca, a member of the bilingual education team of the Regional Indigenous Council of Cauca (CRIC). Currently engaged in research for her M.A. thesis in ethnolinguistics at the University of Cauca and an avid reader of feminist literature, Susana is fluent in Nasa Yuwe, the Nasa language, which her family speaks almost exclusively in their home in the city. Susana comes from a family of prominent local and national politicians: her brother, Jesús Enrique, served as president of CRIC in the 1990s and is now in his second term as a senator in Bogotá, and her father, Victoriano, is a well-known leader in the locality of Calderas, Tierradentro. Her own affiliation with CRIC and her family connections have placed Susana in constant contact with an indigenous urban network that encompasses members of indigenous organizations, rural schoolteachers, and nonnative sympathizers with the indigenous movement. At the same time, she is fiercely committed to work with the grassroots, spending several weeks at a time working on curricular matters with local teachers in the village of Juan Tama, a resettled community originally from Vitoncó, Tierradentro. Susana has been instrumental in creating a network of Nasa women, both those belonging to the burgeoning crop of female political leaders who are assuming local cabildo office, and elderly women who Susana feels have been overlooked in the drive to organize the Nasa.

However, Susana views herself as standing on the frontier of the Nasa community. She discriminates between cultural workers like herself, who, she says, "talk about culture from the vantage point of Spanish" and who address cultural themes in the "past tense," as opposed to members of rural communities, who "live culture in the present."[1] "Living culture in the present" is commonly glossed by Susana and her colleagues as a *vivencia*, which might be translated as a lived experience that is constitutive of an individual's character, although the English version does not capture the self-conscious and politicized significance of the term as it is employed by Nasa public intellectuals. Paradoxically, it is precisely these intellectuals, who speak in the past tense and who Susana claims "do not believe in what we are saying and writing," who are engaged in forging a cultural future for the rural Nasa. As a result, reasons Susana, cultural workers reconceptualize the rural population as "others," while they consider themselves to straddle what she calls a "frontier."

The borderlands to which Susana refers are both ideological and geographic, encapsulating and idealizing communities that have retained certain key attributes, such as language and shamanism, in contrast to other indigenous localities that are more firmly embedded in the regional culture and produce foodstuffs for the market. Traditionalist localities are singled out as recipients of the planning efforts of urban indigenous cultural workers. Bound by their inadequate command of the Spanish language and their unfamiliarity with the academic and political terminology bandied about by intellectuals, the local bearers of culture are inadvertently excluded from the planning process, "othered" in relation to regional activists. Susana asks if indigenous intellectuals are creating their own discrete identity, a kind of "theoretically Nasa" subject position that never quite embraces Nasa lifeways, because in the course of the organizing process, political activism and ethnographic research function not only as supports for grassroots cultural renovation, but as vehicles for intellectuals' own process of self-discovery. Although Susana questions such attitudes, she recognizes that cultural activism affords her a context in which she can revitalize (*recuperar*) her own cultural roots, thus validating her participation in the movement ("se reivindica con el proceso cultural").

Inocencio Ramos, another of CRIC's cultural workers, goes yet further in emphasizing the uncomfortable liminal character of the members of his political world. Like Susana, Inocencio hails from Tierradentro, but his is a Protestant family from the resguardo of Tálaga. He and his two brothers, Abelardo and Benjamín, all work in the bilingual education program of CRIC; one of his sisters is a shaman and served in 2002 as lieutenant governor of Tálaga. Inocencio is an intensely perceptive man, with a remarkable capacity for synthesizing complex issues. He is a talented and visionary administrator who moves with ease between regional and local circles. But Inocencio perceives his own contributions to cultural planning as superficial, mediocre, and colonized, and believes that only the thê' wala, the shaman, working from within the rural community, possesses the knowledge and the methodology to speak authoritatively about culture "in the present tense." Nevertheless, he, like Susana, is in search of a way to be Nasa in the rarified atmosphere of the urban indigenous organization, always asking himself "if what I plan to do is in accord with the intentions of the culture." He attempts continuously to decenter Western culture through an insistence on incorporating traditional procedures into hybridized proposals for cultural planning, focusing particularly on the investigative strategies of thê' walas, centered in the ritualized reading of bodily signs. He cannot, however, verbalize the practical implications of such a combination, because the two systems are incommensurable.

For Inocencio, as for many of the Nasa cultural workers with whom I have spoken, the thê' wala is the only true Nasa intellectual:

> *JR:* What do you think is the role of the indigenous intellectual?
> *IR:* Well, I've never really thought about what an intellectual would be like, and I don't understand the concept of the intellectual.
> *JR:* Well, someone who is producing knowledge . . .
> *IR:* Well, if that is what intellectual means, then we could say that the shamans are the [only] ones who deserve [to belong in] that category and that if you want to philosophize you can do so, but it isn't legitimate. I'd say that it's legitimate when it's someone who has all that experience [*vivencia*], the trajectory, all of what goes into a process of creating knowledge. And people who understand that whole structure of knowledge, who are reevaluating knowledge, [they] would be the true intellectual[s]. But, then, those of us who more or less approach the culture superficially, even if you're indigenous, well, you make the problem very superficial. That's ideological colonization, as I already said. I don't know the culture [simply] by virtue of being indigenous. So this is our challenge. . . . That is the dilemma.

While he is conscious of the value of shamanism, Inocencio questions whether he, an educated and urban Nasa, can possibly adopt those values that he sees as "natural" in rural communities but that for urban activists are products of self-conscious cultural reflection.

In this chapter, I explore the ambivalences of identity construction among regional indigenous intellectuals in Cauca, focusing in particular on the uncomfortable position in which they find themselves vis-à-vis their rural counterparts. While these activists foster cultural revitalization among members of native communities, given the discourses they employ to project themselves within Colombian political space, they feel they cannot lay claim to cultural authenticity. Instead, cultural activists redirect their self-identification in such a way as to heighten their particular form of sophisticated otherness, which is what permits them a privileged analysis of Colombian society. Indigenous intellectuals identify as Nasa and feel that they live according to Nasa cultural precepts in what they explicitly recognize as a heterogeneous process of modern indigenous identity construction. But at the same time, they feel the need to employ a strategically essentialized definition of culture in their political work to distinguish themselves and their constituents from the dominant society. Consequently, they experience the sensation of approaching Nasa culture from somewhere beyond its boundaries, which leads them to question their commitment to their cultural heritage.

Indigenous Public Intellectuals

Who are the indigenous intellectuals to whom I refer? In recent years, anthropologists have begun to explore the emergence of an indigenous Latin American intelligentsia associated with cultural movements in Bolivia (Stephenson 2002; Ticona Alejo 2000), Guatemala (Fischer 2001; Fischer and Brown 1996; Nelson 1999; Warren 1998a), and Mexico (Campbell 1994, 1996; Gutiérrez 1999; Hernández Díaz 1996). In these countries there are extensive teacher training programs and institutions dedicated to bilingual education, linked with state-sponsored *indigenista* policies, and full-time university study is available to a wide range of indigenous people. Indigenous movements have a long history in these countries. The critical mass afforded by the fact that a substantial percentage of the national population considers itself to be native has contributed to the growth of a group of urban-based, university-educated, indigenous professionals associated with a range of private research institutions, universities, and government agencies. These are individuals who might be seen as constituting an indigenous middle class, more in the sense of their positioning in national society than in terms of income (Campbell 1996; Warren 1998b). They are the indigenous intellectuals whom we meet at international conferences and in graduate programs in the social sciences, whose books are available in bookstores, who have won the Nobel Prize, who are increasingly being recognized as important players in the national political arena, and who have become the focus of scholarly interpretation.

Although similar to this sector in terms of their linking of intellectual production with political activism, the indigenous public intellectuals of Cauca have more modest backgrounds and the nature of their insertion into national society is distinct from that of their Guatemalan, Mexican, and Bolivian colleagues. Most of them are based in rural areas, working in local schools or cabildo associations; those attached to regional and national organizations located in cities spend a great deal of their time traveling to rural districts. Some of these people have trouble speaking Spanish correctly and only a tiny minority can write well. Most have degrees from high school, seminary, or normal school, a kind of secondary-level teacher's college. Many of them achieved these degrees through the *profesionalización* programs set up in the 1980s and 1990s to provide rural teachers with normal school proficiency training. A few received their training in the ideological seminars of the various guerrilla movements that have operated in Cauca since the 1970s, becoming well versed in indigenous legislation and introduced to Marx, Lenin, and Stalin. Few of the indigenous intellectuals I know have attended full-time university programs, with the exception of ethnolinguists studying in internationally supported programs in Colombia and Bolivia, although many are currently registered in the numerous long-distance programs that have sprung up in recent years, providing substandard training to rural teachers who are now being required to produce college degrees if they are to continue teaching. This is a far cry from the rigorous training received by the indigenous intellectuals I have met from other countries. As a result, Colombian indigenous cultural activists are considerably less oriented toward academic issues than are their peers in Guatemala and Bolivia.

Another significant difference between Caucan indigenous intellectuals and their colleagues in other Latin American countries is their refusal to affiliate themselves with institutions other than the indigenous movement. Marcos Yule, one of CRIC's linguists, put it this way:

> I have received many offers from outside, from universities [and] from institutions, but I have never aspired to that, it bores me. I worked for the CRC [Regional Corporation of Cauca, a regional development organization], but their scheme is different, their goals are different [from ours]. I am still working with the [Ethnoeducation Program of the] Universidad del Cauca, but you feel that their project is not the same as [ours] and you feel "disconnected." You feel better, even though you earn so little, [working] within a process in which you learn so much.

Thus, the identity of Caucan indigenous intellectuals has developed in a politically contestatory context that defines them by virtue of their ethnic and political loyalties and not their identity as intellectuals.

These are organic intellectuals in the Gramscian sense, who open paths of knowledge in the service of an emergent social sector. When I explained my usage to my Nasa interlocutors, however, I was told that they were not intellectuals because they neither enjoyed the working conditions nor had they received the elite education enjoyed by most Colombian intellectuals. Moreover, they did not want to be considered as different from other Nasa, as a kind of Nasa elite, although they fear that they are swiftly becoming one.[2] I found that many of these cultural workers were uncomfortable with the label of intellectual precisely because they were embarrassed by their own standing in relation to their ethnic compatriots, as well as their subordinate position relative to the intellectuals of the dominant society.

Unlike those whom we generally call intellectuals, indigenous or otherwise, the public intellectuals of the Caucan indigenous movement do not, for the most part, produce the book-length studies that attract national readerships and the attention of international scholars, which mark the indigenous intelligentsia of the other Latin American countries I mentioned. In fact, I can think of only two recently published books by native Colombians, an ethnography-cum-autobiography by U'wa author Berichá (1992), who has not been able to find a publisher for a second edition of her book, and the work of the Guambiano History Committee, written in collaboration with a Colombian academic (Dagua Hurtado, Aranda, and Vasco 1998). In part, there is an inhospitable atmosphere for indigenous-authored publications in Colombia. But more significant, Colombian indigenous intellectuals do not choose to intervene in the academic world. Most Caucan research is collective in nature; a great deal of it is unauthored—a list of those who contributed to the enterprise in any way, including logistic support and typesetting, is commonly included on the title page—and is based on themes chosen by organizations and community authorities, produced by teams designated by the political leadership. Much of this research is not published at all, but available only in manuscript form or self-published for internal use. A great deal of this work is not written, except as notes taken at workshops. Such contributions include local primary and secondary school curricula organized according to indigenous cultural criteria, cosmology workshops, games using terms in native languages, new alphabets for these languages, evaluations of educational planning projects. In the few cases in which the results are published as articles in academic venues,

they are frequently coauthored by outsiders, who incorporate the suggestions of indigenous researchers into the text, or they are transcripts of public
speeches. The only exceptions are the work of university-trained indigenous linguists (Muelas Hurtado 1995; Nieves and Ramos 1992; Yule 1995),
who employ technical discourse and direct their work toward an academic
audience.[3]

Notwithstanding its lack of academic character, this research is a form of
"autoethnography," in the sense that it reflects on the cultures of the authors
(Reed-Danahay 1997), engaging Western modes of interpretation in epistemological models arising out of indigenous worldviews (Pratt 1992). The melding
of indigenous and Western discourses by these indigenous intellectuals is
politically motivated, combining the international language of indigenous
sovereignty ("territory," "culture," "autonomy") with native cosmologies (Albert 1995), as is also the case with the writings of Native American intellectuals
in the United States (Cook-Lynn 1998; Landsman 1997; Medicine 2000). This is
not autoethnography in the sense generally used by those anthropologists who
have addressed the issue of "native" anthropology (Abu-Lughod 1991; Fahim
and Helmer 1980; Jones 1970; Limón 1994; Narayan 1993; Ohnuki-Tierney
1984; Page 1988; Wang 2002), who focus their gaze on university-educated
anthropologists writing in standard academic discourse for a professional
audience and publishing in academic venues. Marilyn Strathern (1987, 32)
distinguishes university-educated Papua New Guinean ethnographers from
nonprofessional English autoethnographers, in the sense that the former are
engaged in deliberate meditation, whereas the latter seek to contribute to a
store of personal self-knowledge. Caucan indigenous intellectuals are also
engaged in deliberate meditation, but for political, not academic, ends, which
is what makes them different from the academics of Port Moresby. Their intellectual activities are always qualified by their ethnic identity, because it is only
in the context of indigenous identity politics that they engage in such intellectual pursuits. In fact, as I describe later, the Nasa ethnographers who collaborated with me in a joint research project distinguished themselves as Nasa
from other members of the team, who were seen as anthropologists, pointedly
asserting that ethnicity takes precedence for them over disciplinary identity.[4]

Finding the "Inside"

For Nasa researchers, autoethnography involves a search for the "inside" of
indigenous culture, the construction of a Nasa essence. This is anathema to

academic anthropologists, "native" or otherwise. What Inocencio and Susana believe, in conjunction with most other Nasa cultural activists, is that there is—or perhaps better put, there should be—an inside, an untouched center of Nasa culture. In Nasa Yuwe, two paired terms, *ajxyu* and *ûyu*, are used to distinguish, respectively, locations "on this side" and "on that side" of a border. The dichotomy is highly contextual, so that a place is ajxyu or ûyu only in relation to the temporal and topographic context of the speaker, creating a momentary and highly relational inside. However, a geographic and cultural barrier is effectively constituted by the high swampy Andean plain, or *páramo*, that separates the Nasa heartland of Tierradentro, literally, "the inside land," from the Nasa communities of the western slopes of Colombia's Central Cordillera, sometimes called Tierrafuera, "the outside land" (Espinosa 1996). Until an unpaved highway was built in the second half of the twentieth century to connect Tierradentro with the series of valleys along the Cauca River, the páramo was held to be a spiritually dangerous and meteorologically inhospitable environment, a deterrent to the movement of people and agricultural products from Tierradentro to the urban centers of Popayán and Cali and to Nasa communities on the western slopes. In the distant past, ritual accompanied the first occasion on which an individual crossed the páramo: men made tiny corrals and women miniature looms to ensure that they would be hard workers during their adult lives (Hernández de Alba 1963). The páramo is also the home of the sacred precincts in which mythicohistorical culture heroes dwell, and where cabildos annually refresh their insignia of office (Rappaport 1998b). The communities on alternate sides of the páramo enjoy different growing seasons, so that when it is raining in Tierradentro, it is the dry season in Tierrafuera. Thus, there is a firm basis for distinguishing between the two sides of the Cordillera, providing the empirical grounds for the opposed categories of inside and outside.

For activists like Inocencio and Susana, the inside is buried deep within Tierradentro itself. But although Tierradentro is emblematic of the inside, only certain spots are actually designated as such, given that such large resguardos as Belalcázar, Mosoco, and Tóez are all ethnically heterogeneous, presenting varying mixtures of Nasa, mestizos, and Afrodescendants, some of whom participate in cabildo activities.[5] Speaking to Susana, Inocencio, and countless others, I learned that the inside is located in the isolated rural communities of Lame, Suin, Chinas, and San José (see map). Here, in the most inaccessible corners of Tierradentro, where there are still no roads or electricity and the majority of the population is Nasa—the kind of place that the

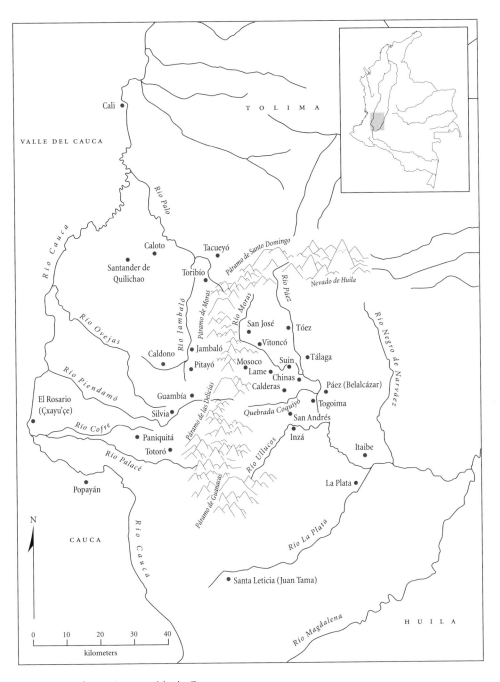

Map of Nasa Communities in Cauca

budding anthropologists of the 1970s, like myself, chose as appropriate for field research—Nasa Yuwe predominates over Spanish, people go to thê' walas instead of Western doctors, and there is a strong sense of community expressed through participation in ritual and in the cabildo.[6] These communities, however, are replete with return migrants, men who spent their youths in distant coffee harvests and women who were attached to urban Colombian families as domestic servants, given that Tierradentro's subsistence agriculture does not provide its residents with the cash they need to negotiate the modern world.

Many of the older people were displaced from these villages during the civil war, commonly called *La Violencia*, that raged throughout Colombia in the late 1940s and 1950s, pitting Liberals against Conservatives and turning landlords, powerful politicians, and priests against the peasant population.[7] La Violencia was particularly bloody in Tierradentro, a stronghold of the Liberal Party and thus a target for the Conservative-led military police; some Tierradentro communities had been the focus of Communist Party organizing in the 1940s, making them even more prominent targets of repression in this era. Hence, at midcentury, Tierradentro was a land with a peripatetic population. Today, a large and ever-growing proportion of the inhabitants of Tierradentro are evangelical or pentecostal Protestants, and the Catholics are heavily influenced by the politically and theologically conservative Apostolic Vicariate of Tierradentro, whose missionaries control myriad aspects of the life of the region. Whereas other Nasa communities, influenced in part by leftist ideologies, have rejected traditional Colombian party politics in favor of alternative forms of political action, the Liberal and Conservative Parties are powerful and active in the tiny towns that dot Tierradentro's mountainsides. Moreover, these lands provide an important corridor for guerrilla organizations, particularly FARC, the Revolutionary Armed Forces of Colombia. Young people are pressed into service to the armed movement, cabildos are subordinated to their demands, and the freedom of assembly and movement of the communities of the region is severely impaired. The people of Tierradentro, frequently with the encouragement of FARC, have been actively engaged in opium poppy cultivation, linking them to a clandestine global economy that Susana and Inocencio know only secondhand.[8]

Tierradentro is, therefore, an ambiguous inside. Ironically, it is in such inside places as Lame, Suin, Chinas, and San José that cultural activists working from the frontier labor to introduce policies of cultural recovery to ensure the survival of Nasa Yuwe, historical tradition, and shamanic practice. And it is by returning inside, primarily through activism and the rejection of Christianity, that these cultural workers seek to solve their inner conflicts as frontier people. The inside exists only conceptually with respect to the outside, where activists live and work. For them, Tierradentro is the heartland of Nasa culture, a kind of a cultural reserve. It is a place to which they travel to hold meetings, in which community participation is frequently confined to the cooking of meals and an *integración* (a party) at the end of the workshop. Tierradentro is the focus of consulting activities undertaken by indigenous activists and NGOs in the areas of education, development, and health. In fact, it is one of the least active zones within CRIC's sphere of operation. Representatives of the region have rarely occupied key posts on the regional executive committee and inhabitants frequently talk about the regional organization as though they were its clients, receiving the medical, educational, and legal services provided by CRIC programs.

Why, then, is Tierradentro so vital as an inside, when it is not only marginal to the political struggle but also manifests all of the marks of incorporation into global economic, political, and cultural flows, much as do other Nasa areas? In part, I suspect, this owes to the fact that many cultural activists are themselves from Tierradentro or from communities that immediately border it, so that the region provides them with a ready point of comparison with themselves. The Colombian state, moreover, constituted the region as a zone of alterity in the late nineteenth century, when Law 89 of 1890, the most extensive legislation on the resguardo system, was enacted. Under Law 89, Tierradentro was officially a *territorio de misiones*, a hinterland inhabited by people whom the state considered to be "primitive" and in need of the tutelage of the Catholic Church; this status only began to be transformed in the wake of the 1991 constitution, whose indigenous provisions overrode Law 89. It is in part due to Law 89 that Tierradentro represents an important zone of conflict for CRIC, given that the indigenous movement has struggled for decades here to wrest control, particularly in the educational sphere, from the Church. In addition, Tierradentro was exoticized by various generations of anthropologists, clearing a path for the politicized perpetuation of alterity by contemporary activists.[9]

Members of the communities of Tierradentro participate in the organizational discourse through which they are othered, assuming an oppositional Nasa identity to differentiate themselves from nonindigenous Colombians (*musxka*, in Nasa Yuwe), as well as from other Nasa. Their identity is as self-conscious as is that of frontier Nasa, although people in Tierradentro perceive themselves to be more "authentic" than the activists. While they understand and appreciate the work of cultural workers, urban intellectuals are seen as people who talk of Nasa identity but do not live it, thus mirroring the preoccupations of the activists themselves. For example, a woman from the resguardo of San José told me an ironic joke about how cultural activists encourage the maintenance of Nasa tradition, but they themselves live in the city and marry nonindigenous women, thus refusing to live this tradition. Ethnic exogamy functions as a significant trope for constituting inside and outside, because Juan Tama, the Nasa culture hero and historical hereditary chief, is said to have ordered his people to marry only within their ethnic group—a biting and painful criticism of the inauthenticity of urbanized cultural workers that ignores the social landscape in which they work and live. Thus, both those on the inside and those on the frontier define cultural activists as "inauthentic" because they fail to live up to the paragon that an idealized Tierradentro presents. For both groups, authenticity is breached by the ambiguous cultural positioning of urban intellectuals who celebrate Nasa culture but do not live it, in opposition to an unconscious lifeway (*una vivencia*) for those on the inside—despite the fact that the latter are as attentive to their indigenous identity and as politicized as are the frontier Nasa.

Between these not-so-opposite poles is the vast majority of Nasa, monolingual in Spanish or bilingual in Spanish and Nasa Yuwe, agricultural wage laborers and sharecroppers who have toiled for generations on nearby haciendas and restored them to cabildo control through land occupations in the 1970s and 1980s. These residents of Tierrafuera share their territory with mestizo peasants, Guambiano migrants, and Afrocolombian farmers. They have historically constituted the most fertile ground for the growth of the indigenous movement, as they did in earlier periods for various leftist organizations. In particular, we might speak of northern Caucan communities such as Caloto, Corinto, Las Delicias, Jambaló, Tacueyó, and Toribío, where CRIC was founded in 1971. The resguardo of Las Delicias, Buenos Aires, is a case in point. This community, located in the Western Cordillera in a mining region whose majority population is Afrocolombian, was settled in the past half-century by Nasas from Pueblo Nuevo, Caldono, and other centuries-old resguardos of Tierrafuera. Las Delicias has not yet been officially recognized as a resguardo although its cabildo is quite prominent in the municipality and in CRIC and its members are known to be very militant. Resguardo lands, which are communally held, are not continuous throughout the territory, as they are in other parts of Cauca, but are interspersed with private property not belonging to the resguardo. The cabildo, currently engaged in a long-standing dispute with black organizations over rights to a mountain rich in gold ore, is composed of both Nasa and Afrocolombians (Ng'weno 2002). Las Delicias, like its other Nasa neighbors in northern Cauca, demonstrates a cultural fluidity and a heterogeneous ethnic profile that do not correspond to the image most Caucans have of the resguardos of Tierradentro. Such populations, which form the backbone of CRIC, are seen, both from the standpoint of the "interior" and from that of the frontier Nasa, as balancing on the edge of a precipice: Nasa, but not quite as Nasa as we are, or not as Nasa as we *should* be.

The Nasa "ethnoscape," to appropriate Appadurai's (1996) terminology, is very much like the hypothetical topological construct known as the Klein bottle: "Most containers have an inside and an outside, a klein bottle is a closed surface with no interior and only one surface. It is unrealisable in 3 dimensions without intersecting surfaces" (Bourke 1996). The one-sided Klein bottle looks like a bottle, but it cannot be one, for its surface does not have two sides. Like the Klein bottle, the inhabitants of Tierradentro and Tierrafuera, along with urban activists, all occupy a single surface, although at first glance they appear to be located on distinct surfaces located inside or outside the vessel. The single surface is constituted by the common history and global connections that they all share, as well as by the political space created through ethnic organizing. However, the intersection of the multiple discourses and practices of the movement, the state, and metropolitan intellectuals cause them to be positioned differently, ostensibly balanced on different surfaces. It is significant that the definition I cited for the Klein bottle emphasizes the impossibility of such a construct in the three-dimensional Euclidean reality in which we live; we cannot really draw or make a Klein bottle because it is impossible to double a one-sided surface over itself. Likewise, the representation of a cultural inside standing in opposition to an inauthentic frontier does not stand up to reality, particularly given the fact that Tierradentro's relative isolation from the indigenous movement owes in part to its very insertion in global hegemonic discourses and practices of missionary religion, economic modernization, illicit agricultural production, and mainstream party politics, whereas those communities of Tierrafuera who have "lost their culture," as many activists would have it, are actively engaged in the very projects of cultural revitalization aimed at restoring their "authenticity." Clearly, given the heterogeneity, complexity, and ambiguities of the Nasa ethnoscape, it would not be fruitful to draw a polar distinction between metropolitan Nasa intellectuals and local indigenous actors, as would some analysts who see authenticity as pertaining exclusively to the local domain (Michaels 1994). It would be like attempting to pour *chicha*, the fermented cane juice drunk at Nasa festivities, into a Klein bottle.

Essentialism and Indigenous Intellectuals

The culturalist discourse of indigenous intellectuals and their search for the inside must be understood in a specific historical context. First, there is the influence of structural linguistics, which is studied by many Nasa intellectuals, and which can potentially lead to a series of essentializing approaches to culture. In fact, Jon Landaburu, the French linguist who introduced the first ethnolinguistics program in Colombia and who obtained scholarships for indigenous students to attend it, intimated to me that his native students found structuralism to be a tremendously appealing vehicle for linking language with culture and for inserting both in a coherent and self-enclosed logical model. But essentialist approaches also respond to the requirements of the state, which demands that indigenous groups define themselves according to a cultural essence in their preparation of development plans, bilingual curricula, and the codification of customary law (Gow 1997; Gow and Rappaport 2002). If indigenous communities are to assert their special rights as culturally different citizens, then they must focus publicly on the incommensurabilities—and not the fruitful dialogues—between the dominant society and themselves. The movement's own demands, which balance the celebration of cultural difference against the militancy of subordination and the utopia of sovereignty, are conducive to an essentialization of culture for some of the same reasons. Finally, the images through which Colombian national culture and its intellectual institutions have represented native peoples provide compelling templates for essentializing exercises on the part of indigenous militants.

Inocencio, Susana, and their comrades might easily be accused of essentialism, of describing Nasa culture as an enduring, monolithic, and homogeneous "thing" with clearly demarcated boundaries (Fuss 1989). However, the utility of such a critique of their work is highly questionable. Students of native rights movements (Friedman 1994) have argued that when we criticize these movements for their essentializing discourses, we do a political disservice to them by delegitimizing their objectives. Briggs (1996) suggests that constructivist analyses of indigenous cultural activism that critique essentialism from an academic standpoint are made possible only by the resources, prestige, and distance afforded by our comfortable positions in foreign universities, privileges that are not enjoyed by local actors.

A more fruitful option is to inquire into the specificities of the Colombian context in order to comprehend whether or not militants see essentializing discourses as appropriate political strategies for fostering pluralism. That is, we must inquire into how and why activists create such representations (Turner 2002) and, ultimately, evaluate whether these discourses are essentialist at all. Colombia is a country that has always imagined itself as homogeneous. Yet, most recently, the national society has grown to prefer a more liberal approach to ethnic diversity in the face of the rise of ethnic militancy of both native peoples and Afrodescendants, an option that fosters multiculturalism without upsetting the apple cart in terms of the redistribution or the reconfiguration of political power. Notwithstanding the tensions that exist in Colombia between proponents of radical pluralism and supporters of liberal multiculturalism, understandings of how cultural difference should be articulated contrast with those of industrialized English-speaking countries.

Unlike the Australian or U.S. experiences, where the state requires that aboriginal communities prove their cultural authenticity by demonstrating their resistance to change (Campisi 1991; Clifford 1988; Field 1999; Povinelli 2002), under the 1991 constitution the Colombian state does not judge the authenticity of native Colombians, preferring to authorize indigenous organizations to assume the helm in the construction of a "hyperreal Indian"—a simulated, culturally perfect "insider" whose attributes conform to the characteristics defining indigenous alterity that have always been deployed in the dominant society (Alcida Ramos 1998). The state has forced the indigenous movement to walk a cultural tightrope, to conform to age-worn notions of culture, at the same time that it provides the necessary wiggle room for communities to create or reintroduce those attributes that official policy forced them to discard in the past. In the contemporary Colombian political space, semiautonomous and culturally distinct indigenous communities are the only permanent authorities in a territory in which the state is an occasional, sometimes a marginal, actor. Indigenous cultures and their bearers thus emerge as a kind of "constructed essence" whose function is highly strategic for the state.

But when Ramos's notion of the hyperreal Indian is transported to Cauca, the lines of conflict and control are not as transparent as they are in Ramos's own analysis, which focuses on nongovernmental organizations and their more contained relationship with indigenous spokespersons in Brazil. Let us take the case of the resettlement of the Nasa displaced by a 1994 landslide that devastated northern Tierradentro (Rappaport and Gow 1997). The Corporación Nasa Kiwe (CNK)—Nasa Kiwe means "Nasa territory" in Nasa Yuwe—the

parastatal organization set up to relocate the displaced, promoted a resettlement policy that concentrated new communities in relatively isolated areas, far
from urban centers and distant (ostensibly) from zones of guerrilla activity, to
protect those whom they saw as Nasa rustics from the ravages of modernity. In
reality, however, most of the lands available for purchase were put on the
market by landowners who had tired of paying "taxes" to FARC or who had
been threatened by the guerrillas, so that resettled communities became
buffers between territories that are policed by the state and those that are not.
Thus, native peoples have become strategic pawns in military confrontations
and in the economic restructuring of the Colombian countryside. But they are
framed, as they have historically been cast, as bumpkins in need of state
tutelage who are placed in these marginal areas to "conserve their culture." The
CNK clearly interpreted the Nasa according to at least some of the stereotypes
that Alcida Ramos (1998) identifies as nourishing the image of the hyperreal
Indian: exotic, romanticized, and backward.

Nonetheless, the Nasa cannot be depicted as defenseless instruments of the
state or of the guerrillas. The CNK included members of CRIC on its executive
board, many of whom counted themselves among the displaced, and CRIC did
not articulate the hyperreal discourse in quite the same way as the state did.
Local resguardos and resguardo associations operating under CRIC's umbrella
resisted the CNK's policies and in response, founded settlements in regions
closer to urban centers to enjoy the comforts of modern life, including educational opportunities, transportation, and markets. At the same time, these
Nasa opponents articulated a culturalist discourse promoting bilingual education, indicating that they, like the CNK, held Nasa cultural survival as one of
their fundamental objectives. But they extended this culturalist discourse in an
unexpected direction, suggesting that the resettlement of the displaced in
northern Cauca, already inhabited by Nasa who were considerably more integrated into the regional culture, would help to disseminate Nasa culture
throughout the culturally impoverished populations of the north. The very
heterogeneity of the Nasa and the ways cultural diversity operates within CRIC
itself mitigated against the kind of essentialized vision promoted by the state.
In fact, the displaced communities' notion of culture, like that of the movement as a whole, contrasts in significant ways with an academic appreciation
of essentialism.

For indigenous activists and their supporters, culture is more of a political
utopia than a concrete and preexisting thing. Culture is a tool for delineating a
project within which people can build an ethnic polity protected from the

hegemonic forces that surround them, including drug lords, paramilitary units, and guerrilla columns. Culture also provides a vehicle for the reconstruction of lifeways that afford indigenous communities alternatives to the dominant values of individualism and consumerism, which militants perceive as endangering them. That is, essentializing constructs are more usefully understood as guides for disseminating cultural policy and engaging in political action than as totalizing truths; they are something to be continually questioned, redefined, and redeployed. The notion of strategic essentialism (Spivak and Grosz 1990), which posits that social movements and subaltern actors deploy essentialist constructs in response to wider political forces, is thus not all that useful for comprehending the specificities of how Caucan indigenous intellectuals and their colleagues across Latin America operate (Campbell 1994, 214; Hale 1997, 578). In fact, as Les Field (1999) has argued, indigenous ethnic discourse is neither essentialist nor constructivist in an academic sense. Indigenous activists frame their cultural analyses within their own appreciation of the dangers and benefits that the external essentialist gaze has conferred. The poles for them are not so much those of essentialism and constructivism as those of cultural revitalization and sovereignty. Thus, it might be more useful to frame indigenous culturalist logic through the notion of the instrumentalization of cultural difference (Alcida Ramos 1998), the modes through which apparently essentialized cultural elements are deployed as political tools at specific historical junctures. In Cauca, indigenous languages and the ideas and practices surrounding shamanism have been highly useful in asserting cultural difference vis-à-vis the dominant society and in promoting an acceptance of this discourse within communities.

In my dealings with Nasa intellectuals, I discovered that many of them found essentialism to be a fascinating topic of discussion and reading. None of those with whom I spoke saw themselves as essentialist at all, and when they caught a whiff of essentialism in the activities of their colleagues, they immediately criticized it. In fact, to the contrary, they saw the dominant society as essentializing *them*, as well as other minority groups. Abelardo Ramos once attended an academic conference in Bogotá with me that focused on indigenous and Afrocolombian issues. At the end of the week, when I asked him what he had thought of the papers, he noted that although many of the panelists had used the word "race," no one had defined precisely what they meant by it, but had accepted it as a given, an essence, conveying to me his own anti-essentialist sensibilities. Moreover, cultural activists ironically engage the essentializing stereotypes of the dominant society, deploying them with the aim of forcing their listeners to rethink once dominant ethnic categories; that is, when they become "inappropriate others."

The Inappropriate Other

Adonías Perdomo, a Nasa intellectual from the community of Pitayó, once told me that only "frontier Nasas can channel the Nasa voice to others, moving from the center to the periphery to lead inside and communicate with those outside." The transition to frontier status and, ultimately, to possible political leadership occurs when people abandon their communities to pursue educational objectives in urban areas, as well as for reasons of economic necessity or even adventure. But for Adonías, such movement is possible without any physical displacement, through reading, education, or work with external institutions. Crossing the frontier is not a physical displacement, but an ideological one. As Adonías told me, "The frontier is not singular. One must approach the frontier in the course of organizing a movement. It's a question of movement in thought and in identity, not a physical exit." Those who achieve this mobility and can use displacement as a vehicle for reflecting on matters of identity are organic intellectuals, travelers in the "contact zone," the space of interlocution between hegemonic and subaltern groups, those who bridge the frontier thanks to a hybrid discourse that articulates metropolitan forms of expression with indigenous cultural forms (Pratt 1992).

Adonías himself has crossed the frontier many times, in various capacities. The son of the first converts to evangelical Protestantism in Pitayó, he received religious training for a time at a seminary in Bogotá and returned to Pitayó to become a pastor, helping to establish considerably more churches than the U.S.-based Summer Institute of Linguistics missionaries had been able to achieve in their years in his community. Adonías embraces Protestantism as a potential escape hatch that holds the opportunity of freeing the Nasa from the control that Catholic priests have traditionally exerted on them. However, unlike most evangelicals in Colombia, he does not believe that Protestantism implies a deepening of his commitment to Christianity. In contrast, Adonías told me that he sees Protestantism among the Nasa as a step toward the total abandonment of Christianity, which will ultimately be replaced by Nasa religiosity; the belief system toward which he looks is based in shamanic practice, which he has observed firsthand through his mother, a thê' wala. In this sense, his adoption of Protestantism follows the trajectory of Ecuadorian indigenous activists, for whom religious conversion was only an intermediate step toward ethnic activism (Muratorio 1981). Adonías simultaneously inhabits a kind of spiritual outside in relation to his majority-Catholic compatriots and the non-Christian inside in the process of construction. Unlike many of the other cultural activists I have known, Adonías is also a long-standing cabildo member, having held significant posts over the years. He has been instrumental in his community's framing of itself as part of a "nonaligned movement" that shares many of CRIC's and AICO's objectives, but straddles the two organizations, thus placing him on another kind of frontier. Finally, Adonías is the founder of a Pitayó-based think tank, the School of Nasa Thought, which, over the years, has made Nasa culture an object of conscious reflection and interpretation, a stance that can be taken only if one moves back and forth across the frontier. Adonías is a kind of "inappropriate other."

The Vietnamese filmmaker Trinh T. Minh-ha uses the term "inappropriate other" to refer to those who refuse to identify themselves exclusively with one side or another of the frontier:

> The moment the insider steps out from the inside, she is no longer a mere insider (and vice versa). She necessarily looks in from the outside while also looking out from the inside. Like the outsider, she steps back and records what never occurs to her the insider as being worth or in need of recording. But unlike the outsider, she also resorts to non-explicative, non-totalizing strategies that suspend meaning and resist closure. (This is often viewed by the outsiders as strategies of partial concealment and disclosure aimed at preserving secrets that should only be imparted to natives.) She refuses to reduce herself to an Other, and her reflections to a mere outsider's objective reasoning or insider's subjective feeling. . . . Undercutting the inside/outside opposition, her intervention is necessarily that of both a deceptive insider and a deceptive outsider. She is this Inappropriate Other/Same who moves about with always at least two/four gestures: that of affirming "I am like you" while persisting in her difference; and that of reminding "I am different" while unsettling every definition of otherness arrived at. (1991, 74)[10]

The inappropriate other is an other who has not been appropriated by the centrifugal forces of the dominant society. This implies that she is not obliged to consider herself to be authentic, because criteria of authenticity are immaterial to the conditions under which she operates in the contact zone. Consequently, the inappropriate other does not need to follow exclusively the behavioral norms of her community (76).

Gayatri Spivak (1988) argues that the subaltern cannot speak for herself because once she tries to exercise her voice in the hegemonic society, she necessarily must assume the dominant discourse and, hence, no longer speaks as a subaltern, but as an organic intellectual. This dichotomy between those who employ hegemonic discourses and subaltern ones dissolves in the face of Trinh's argument, given that the inappropriate other consciously and simultaneously employs both discourses. Her strength (and her inappropriate character) originates in her ability to interrelate the two discourses, to juxtapose them with the objective of producing discomfort, obliging listeners to reflect on the fact that the speaker is (in the Caucan case) an *indio* (a derogatory term for indigenous) but highly sophisticated and worldly, that she is culturally different but not subordinated. This obliges listeners to rethink the meaning of *indio* and to reconceptualize the indigenous actor as someone who is culturally different and who, on the basis of this difference, engages in a productive dialogue with equal counterparts from the dominant Colombian culture, as opposed to being identified as subaltern and, therefore, powerless and inferior.[11]

In this sense, the best example of the inappropriate other is Taita Lorenzo Muelas, a member of the Constituent Assembly that wrote the 1991 constitution and a former national senator.[12] Taita Lorenzo wore his Guambiano attire in the halls of the Colombian Senate and openly spoke his language, using both his appearance and his idiom in the press and on television to emphasize his identity and to mark his inappropriate alterity, so that his interlocutors never forgot he was Guambiano and felt the weight of his indigenous discourse. Taita Floro Alberto Tunubalá, another former senator from Guambía and, until recently, governor of the department of Cauca, similarly wears his Guambiano attire at official functions. But Taita Floro, who is of a younger generation than Taita Lorenzo, uses his Guambiano identity to promote political objectives that focus beyond the indigenous sphere: he employs ideas and proposals from the indigenous movement as points of departure for constructing regional policy. Taita Floro proposes that what was once located at the margins of Colombian society can function as its conceptual center by importing practices, such as the Andean *minga*, or communal work party, as a metaphor for regional development (Cauca 2001), that might normally be seen as inappropriate in departmental administration and using them to redefine the aspirations of popular sectors of Caucan society. This strategy is fundamental in a country like Colombia, where the 1991 constitution recognizes the multiethnic nature of society, but where the indigenous movement must continually struggle to make ethnic pluralism not only a reality for native communities but also a proposal for a better Colombia for all of its citizens.

For the movement to achieve its pluralist objectives, indigenous intellectuals must maintain a consciousness of being inappropriate others. As Adonías Perdomo observes, they must continually reflect on crossing the frontier so as not to remain on the outside, cut off from their ethnic compatriots, a fear that Fanon (1963) articulated when he wrote that native intellectuals who returned to their people had to recognize their estrangement from them. Furthermore, intellectuals must constantly remind themselves of the porous and inclusive nature of the frontier so as not to appear before the dominant society in the guise of ethnic separatists. This reflexive process generates a sentiment of incommensurability between their position as frontier intellectuals and their identity as Nasas. It is the recognition of this contradiction and the continuing attempt to transcend it that is central to the work of Nasa intellectuals. It is what permits them to cross the gulf between inside and outside without falling to one side or another. A productive way of thinking about this task is provided by Eric Michaels (1994, 44) in his essays on Australian Aboriginal media. Here, the artistic practice of the Aboriginal television producer is founded on a back-and-forth movement, from in front of to behind the camera, blurring or complicating the polarity between "us" and "them" (or, to use the Nasa characterization, between inside and outside). African American feminist Patricia Hill Collins (1991, 11–12) calls this stance that of the "outsider-within," who can "draw on the traditions of both our discipline of training and our experiences as Black women but . . . participate[s] fully in neither" (18n). Chinese anthropologist Wang Mingming (2002) calls it a "third eye" and, as I elaborate below, African American sociologist W. E. B. Du Bois (1989 [1903], 2–3) called it "double consciousness."

The Return

Being an inappropriate other is dangerous business. Many of those who cross the frontier—particularly labor migrants, but also professionals—never return, but instead shed their identity and submerge themselves in popular sectors of the dominant society. As Adonías suggests, reflexivity and consciousness-raising are two strategies used by inappropriate others to achieve equilibrium on the frontier, having crossed it and returned. But how do indigenous public intellectuals ensure their return to the indigenous side of the frontier, or even their ability to perch precariously on its edge? What distinguishes them from the many migrants and the few intellectuals who adhere permanently to the mestizo identity of the dominant society? Most of the male public intellectuals with whom I have spoken cross the frontier unconsciously, but return consciously. Their life histories display their strategies of return that they inadvertently chance upon when they make contact with members of the indigenous movement who persuade them to join indigenous organizations and to reflect on Nasa culture.

Luis Carlos Ulcué is a leader of CRIC's bilingual education program and the former governor of the resguardo of Pueblo Nuevo, the son of Nasa migrants to the lowland Caquetá province who fled there to escape the ravages of La Violencia in the 1950s. He was brought up in a multiethnic colonist milieu, with little consciousness of his Nasa identity and only sporadic contact with other Nasa or with Nasa Yuwe. In Luis Carlos's opinion, he began to value Nasa culture in secondary school, under the tutelage of the Consolata Fathers. For several years, Luis Carlos taught school in Caquetá and then left for Bogotá to train for the priesthood and to study anthropology:

> I worked for two years as a teacher. It was very helpful for me to work with [Nasa] because until then, even in high school, [I was exposed to] colonialist perspectives that marked me from the start—the colonists, the environment, my education. The ideas one had in those days about indigenous people were totally negative. That is, when I was a student in primary and secondary school, I never identified myself as indigenous, I was never conscious of my identity. Finally, after two years I was given the opportunity to study in what was called the Missionary Institute of Anthropology [IMA]. That was in Bogotá. [The course of study] lasted more or less five years, [classes being held] during vacations. When I arrived there I found an array of indigenous people from different groups . . . from different parts of Colombia. That was when I began to become aware of different sorts of social commitments. . . . I began to meet people who sympathized with the indigenous movement. . . . That impressed me, because [at IMA] indigenous people were looked upon as very interesting, as the kind of people you would want to meet, to befriend, [they asked] where you were from, to which group you belonged, creating a very homey and friendly atmosphere, particularly the priests. You began to acquire a different perspective on yourself, on your lack of identity—*desidentidad*—if you could call it that. They awakened my identity and also, there I met Father Álvaro Ulcué.

Álvaro Ulcué was a Nasa priest, born in Pueblo Nuevo and assigned to the parish of Toribío, who organized his flock around issues of development and bilingual education and was in contact with CRIC. He was murdered in 1984 by assassins presumably connected to the police of Santander de Quilichao (Cauca's second city) and supported by local landlords. As a result of the profound impression Father Álvaro made on him, Luis Carlos returned to live in Cauca, learned Nasa Yuwe, and became active in CRIC. His acquisition of consciousness and his return from the frontier were lengthy processes, taking years, and, paradoxically, included a detour along another frontier, that of the priesthood. I purposefully define the priesthood as a kind of frontier because, after taking vows, there is a pull toward assuming the quality of "religious" as one's primary identity, regardless of the presence of other forms of identification, including ethnicity.[13] Immersed in the outside, Luis Carlos began to draw closer to the inside. Under the influence of Father Álvaro, his original vocation as a missionary mutated into a desire to be a parish priest in a Nasa community.

But this was also when Luis Carlos became conscious of the realities of the isolating daily routine of the parish priest, whose membership in the community comes only at the cost of a social distancing from his parishioners. Having once returned across the frontier, Luis Carlos realized that the very institution that had encouraged his reindianization was intent on restraining his insertion into the Nasa community, that the Church would require him to straddle a new frontier as a priest:

> When I began to realize the importance of culture and identity, I began [to experience] a compelling internal conflict between being indigenous and living that other reality from which I drew no strength . . . but with which I clashed over many behaviors . . . because I was in a religious environment. I lived with this internal conflict for a long time, sometimes committed, sometimes ready to escape. Finally, I said to myself, "Maybe what I have learned will be useful. [Even] if I don't become a priest . . . I'll probably get something out of my education." I began to reflect, then I said, "No. I want to work here in Cauca." Father Ulcué said, "Brother, if you want to work, that's what we have here." But he wanted to leave me to work in the parish, registering baptisms, leading workshops, and I was not happy with that. I wanted to be in the countryside, with the people, traveling, observing, questioning, trying to learn the language that came with that worldview.

Luis Carlos decided that from that moment on he would cross the religious frontier and participate more directly in the movement by becoming a bilingual teacher in the resguardo of Las Delicias:

I began to have contact with CRIC, with some leaders, particularly with the Bilingual Education Program, which is what interested me most. Then they asked me if I would like to be in a school, to get experience, to see reality as it is and to see how the people live. So I said, "Sure." I went to the school in Delicias-Buenos Aires. . . . I began to build a relationship on the inside. I liked . . . working closely with the cabildo, supporting them, helping write legal petitions, some documents, being available for any sort of assistance. So that dynamic helped me to understand how the people lived, what they felt, what they thought, how they were experiencing the political situation [*coyuntura*], [given that] they were reclaiming lands at the time I arrived [and I could see] how their authority system worked, how it was organized. Well, this helped me a great deal in situating myself, particularly with respect to the reality [they were living], the socioeconomic conditions under which they lived, at a time when being a schoolteacher meant earning no salary at all, no economic assistance—the Program only gave us bus fare to get there and the community gave us food. But when one has arrived from an environment [in which] one is ensured a place to sleep, [where there is] good food—a convent environment—and to have to eat what the people eat, well, this was rough, but it was even more rough to begin to think about the level of injustice, such as the family that gave us meals: the people ate with their children, a family of eight or ten children, eating manioc with salt for breakfast. You had to adapt to this reality, which led me to think, "Man, this is a very inhuman situation that the people are living in."

Father Álvaro opted, in the years before his death, for a different solution. He strove to erase the frontier between priest and community through Christian practice. A graduate of the seminary, with all its emphasis on Christian identity and its obligatory isolation from his Nasa upbringing, he had "whitened" himself, and now had to return to his roots. As Father Ezio Roattino, one of his successors in Toribío, told me, "Álvaro went through a second conversion. . . . He recognized that his people had their own project and that he could accompany it through the Gospel." That is to say, Father Álvaro grew to merge his Nasa identity with his identification as a priest and as a Catholic. He began to study Nasa culture, his aim the infusion of his evangelizing efforts with Nasa philosophy. As Father Ezio reflected:

Álvaro is called *Nasa Pal* [Nasa priest]. . . . I felt that he was a Christian and that it was possible to do this. And he was striving for his people to encounter the true Christ. . . . Álvaro rethought mission work, something that some missionaries accomplish, but for him, his mission was not to conduct marriages or to administer sacraments. . . . He took a critical view of evangelization. But what did he think of Christ? That He helped His people. A man who died, who died on the cross, a man who spoke of the poor, a man who respected the neglected. . . . How could he be an enemy of the Indians? He couldn't.

In contrast, Luis Carlos was "reindianized" only on leaving the cloister, coming painfully to appreciate what it meant to stand outside and reassume his Nasa identity. This allowed him to observe the movement from a frontier (and not an external) position.

In spite of the advantages that the frontier affords the reindianized subject, providing a simultaneous vantage point on both the outside and the inside, as the indigenous intellectual balances on the frontier and makes forays into indigenous and nonindigenous social spaces, he is obliged to struggle continuously to reaffirm both a native identity and an intellectual subject position. To decline this struggle is to remain on the outside. In the early 1980s, Father Álvaro studied anthropology at IMA, a long-distance university program for church workers in which ethnology is heavily infused with Catholic theology. At one point in his university career, along with seven other native students, some of them lay Nasa (among them, Abelardo Ramos) and some of them priests, Father Álvaro wrote the following letter to his superior:

> We, the native people present in the institute, wish to express with great affection what we have been feeling in the course of our study and we note the following:
>
> 1–*Eliminate* from the everyday language of the missionaries the possessive term: "our Indians," given that this term assigns us as belonging to someone and we consider that we are the property of no one. It is a terminology that makes us uncomfortable and leaves much to reflect upon.
>
> 2–The entire student body of IMA should be more concerned with the community in which it works: its needs and demands, as well as the written works generated here; we note the danger that we might fall into the same impropriety for which we criticize anthropologists and sociologists. We must remember the mysticism and the commitment we have here.
>
> 3–We have a series of questions and preoccupations regarding written work: In whose hands should these works remain? Who should use them? Who will benefit from them? Do they appear in the name of IMA or in the

name of the author who wrote them? We consider that even inside the institute one sites bibliographic sources. We demand that whenever one works on an indigenous community, one must deposit a copy with its authorities.

4–We demand that whenever indigenous people are brought to study at IMA, those who bring them must take a responsible attitude; this, in order to feel secure and to continue in future coursework. If this is not the case we would continue to feel we have been used. Some of us have felt uncomfortable because we feel that our reflections about the reality we live, feel, and think, are being restricted. We do not want to make a polemic, but to the contrary, wish to build ties of brotherhood in the interests of a better Christian coexistence in which no one feels superior to others. (Archivo de la Casa Cural de Toribío, Cauca [ACCT] 1982)

These very issues absorbed the interest of anthropology students throughout the country in the decade following the founding of the first indigenous organizations, particularly in Cauca, where CRIC served as a kind of beacon for scholars-cum-activists. But in the case of native Colombian anthropology students, such demands were enmeshed in a struggle to define their own ethnic identity and their position with respect to their nonnative cohorts.

Father Álvaro's demands surrounding the ownership of ethnographic information represented a radical innovation for the movement, given that at the time, organic intellectuals in organizations like CRIC rejected academic affiliations, university-style research programs, and even claiming authorship of their writings.[14] Indigenous researchers thus confronted the academy on different terms than did nonnative anthropologists, because their own identity as intellectuals was something that was at stake. Father Álvaro's confrontation with IMA over the integration of indigenous students in the program also represents his acceptance of his own reindianization process, which in his case was stimulated by his relations with CRIC, by the intense struggles going on in northern Cauca, and by his growing appreciation of the importance of native cosmologies as he dedicated himself to the linguistic study of Nasa Yuwe and its application in bilingual education (Ulcué Chocué 1981, 1983–84, 1984).

Double Consciousness and Ethnic Militancy

What the indigenous students of IMA felt, cloistered in a religious and paternalistic academic environment, was the sensation of standing, simultaneously, on the inside and on the outside of an exclusionary social system, what the African American sociologist W. E. B. Du Bois called "double consciousness":

> After the Egyptian and Indian, the Greek and Roman, the Teuton and Mongolian, the Negro is a sort of seventh son, born with a veil, and gifted with second-sight in this American world—a world which yields him no true self-consciousness, but only lets him see himself through the revelation of the other world. It is a peculiar sensation, this double-consciousness, this sense of always looking at one's self through the eyes of others, of measuring one's soul by the tape of a world that looks on in amused contempt and pity. One ever feels his twoness—an American, a Negro; two souls, two thoughts, two unreconciled strivings; two warring ideals in one dark body, whose dogged strength alone keeps it from being torn asunder. (1989 [1903], 2–3)

The notion of double consciousness arose out of Du Bois's experience as an African American intellectual living in the highly racist and polarized atmosphere of early twentieth-century North America. As a result of the contradiction he lived as an excluded member of society in the United States, Du Bois suggested that racial minorities might be privy to an intellectually privileged perspective on the world (which he called "second-sight").

Nahum Chandler argues that the concept of double consciousness presupposes a complex and heterogeneous experience: "Having no strictly delimitable site of origin or fixed sense of habitus, the African American subject is quite often 'both/and,' as well as 'neither/nor.' Remaining faithful to the problem of understanding the actual lives of the Negro people . . . , Du Bois was not only led to produce a description of an original sense of being in the world, but to elaborate a sense of being that in itself could not be reduced to some simple essence" (1996, 85). In Du Bois's view, then, heterogeneity can be thought of as a resource or a good, a gift (85). In the language of indigenous Cauca, we might substitute the term "ethnic pluralism" or "interculturalism" for "heterogeneity," thus underlining the fact that although second sight grows out of the experience of discrimination, it is most successfully harnessed in the course of politicized identity production, something that unfolds on the Colombian stage in a pluralist, and not a separatist, context.

The Du Boisian notion of double consciousness as it might be interpreted in Cauca was resignified for me during a week-long intensive course I taught to forty-odd Nasa university students in a university program in the village of Caldono set up by CRIC for bilingual teachers. We spent a day discussing the notion of double consciousness based on a rough Spanish translation of the

Du Bois quotation. Our conversation strained to extricate Du Bois's ideas from their North American context, and said much about the "outsiderness" of cultural activists and their special sensibilities deriving from their liminal condition. The students defined consciousness as "thinking and acting with clarity from within an identity" and as "thinking and acting within various cultural spaces." Double consciousness was, for them, a cultural-ideological process of "revaluing their own mode of thought as difference," which they experienced on the picket line and in the urban domestic employment some of them had held in the past. They perceived their role as educators as one of appropriating knowledge systems (*conocimientos*) within their own mode of thought (*pensamiento propio*), thus acting on a consciousness derived from a specifically Nasa experience of the world—in Spanish, *vivencia*, which they translated into Nasa Yuwe as *fi'zenxi*—and maintained through the adoption of a critical posture with regard to other cultures. That is, not only a position of continuous struggle, but also of continuous exchange with the outside. This positioning is framed by the notion of interculturalism, the productive dialogue across cultures in conditions of equality. Nevertheless, cultural difference operates, simultaneously, in an internal political matrix characterized by collective action. María Rut Peteche and Plinio Ciclos, teachers in the resguardo of Huellas in northern Cauca, suggested as much in their written work for the seminar. They argued that Nasa double consciousness can be comprehended only in its communal dimension, because for them, identity is not constructed on the basis of individual consciousness, but arises in a collective political practice founded on values of reciprocity and consensus. This is, indeed, a new twist on Du Bois, moving his ideas out of the polarized and individualized racial context of the United States, to apply them, instead, to the exercise of cultural consciousness, marked by belonging to a group and forming bridges with other groups.

In effect, the frontier provides fertile ground for a politicized construction of identity that differs from the Du Boisian notion of double consciousness in its appeal to cultural difference and its insistence on the primacy of the collective dimension. The Maya scholar Demetrio Cojtí (1997) gets to the root of this issue, distinguishing between various levels of consciousness and the ability of each sector to speak. Rural, illiterate Mayas, he argues, possess a consciousness as a people *en sí*, a literal translation of *en sí* being "in or by itself." In other words, they recognize themselves as Mayas and they realize that they are marginalized, but they have no sense of their power on a national level, nor do they comprehend the possibilities of organizing an ethnic struggle. Maya proletarians grouped into popular organizations in which ethnicity is not a defining element have an indigenous consciousness en sí and a class consciousness *para sí*, literally, "for oneself," here suggesting a more active or intentional consciousness. Schooled Mayanist activists have developed a consciousness as a people para sí: they are conscious of their situation as a colonized people and organize around cultural and political interests. This is precisely the sense in which Nasa students framed their definition of double consciousness, harnessing for political action the ambivalent feelings voiced by Susana and Inocencio. Because of their activism and their education, which differentiates them from the communities they serve, they see themselves as the bearers of a consciousness of being a people *para sí*, transforming them from simple outsiders into a special type of internal actor working on the frontier. In the words of Abelardo Ramos, they redefine the boundaries between inside and outside at the same time that they build bridges between these two positions.

A Gendered Frontier

Gender is crucial to the hall of mirrors that is the frontier. Frontier women do not always negotiate their position in the same way as do their male colleagues. My conversations with female intellectuals, both those in the central leadership of the movement and those working in grassroots settings, suggest that, on the one hand, the frontiers inhabited by women are more consciously seen as temporary positions, and, on the other, they are considerably more difficult to cross than are those traversed by men. Various women with whom I spoke had worked temporarily in domestic service, jobs that they intentionally sought for brief periods of time, either to earn money to pay for their education or to hide for a limited period from personal problems, such as abusive fathers and husbands or gossiping neighbors. For the vast majority of women, however, urban domestic labor generally does not lead them to opt for frontier positions. Some former domestics return to their communities after working in the city, resuming their lives as wives and agriculturalists, not as politically conscious fashioners of a new social imaginary; others remain in working-class social sectors in the city (Unigarro 2000).

Women intellectuals cite domestic service as a vehicle for the development of their double consciousness. Alicia Chocué, one of my students in CRIC's university program and currently governor of the cabildo of Pueblo Nuevo, worked for a time as a maid in Cali. She eloquently writes of double consciousness as a sensation of the "anguish over being indigenous, because of all of the implications of rejection we are subjected to and, at the same time, the pride in being different, with a clear and defined identity" (Chocué 2000, 14). She began to feel this pain during her stay in Cali as a domestic worker:

> In 1985 the Pope visited Colombia. During his visit he went to various cities, among them, the city of Popayán in the Department of Cauca. In this city many people gathered to hear the Pope's sermon. In the midst of the crowds were the indigenous peoples who still exist, among them, the Nasa, who are the most well known for their struggle to conserve the land, and the Guambiano, among others. In those times the struggle for the land was in full splendor.
>
> I don't know how they won the right in those difficult times, to [include] in the program a message from the indigenous people. When the *compañero* began to read his letter, almost immediately he was cut off in a brusque manner by the archbishop of Popayán. [The speaker's] name was Guillermo Tenorio, a Nasa from the *resguardo* of Toribío, located in the north of the Department of Cauca. I didn't know him at the time, but only figured out that he was Nasa because he wore a poncho and a hat; I came to know him later.
>
> At that time I was working as a domestic employee in the city of Cali and I was watching it all on television, when I saw that, and although I didn't understand what was happening, I only saw that the Monsignor gestured and said that the "document was not that one, it was another document." I don't know, but it made me feel a great deal of rage, made me shiver, and my blood ran hot, I was angry and sad all at once. I cannot describe the moment in words, neither oral nor written, and I couldn't understand why such a thing occurred. And to cap it off, the woman who employed me was there and she said, "What was that *indio* reading?" This made me feel even more useless, but I didn't say a word.
>
> Now, I understand why I had that reaction. However much we try to imitate the thought and feelings of whites, we are different [and] any aggression makes us react intuitively. (15)

In contrast with men, who begin their life histories with narrations of their adventures along the frontier, never reflecting on the importance of these experiences in their process of consciousness-raising, domestic service is considered by women to be a significant step in their reindianization. Whereas women's narratives emphasize that they came to this realization through their experience of discrimination, men generally describe their coming to consciousness as the product of an encounter with an activist. That is, even before they join the movement, women feel they inhabit a kind of frontier.

The woman intellectual walks an unbridgeable boundary, not only with respect to the dominant society, but also with regard to the indigenous community. Female intellectuals are viewed by the community as "inappropriate women," who have assumed obligations and who move in social circles that are not customary for Nasa women. For this reason, they frequently suffer marital conflicts, which are sometimes violent, or have trouble finding a permanent male companion, another set of motifs that comes up repeatedly in their narratives. They are frequently designated as "licentious" (*libertina*) when they choose to establish sentimental relationships more akin to those of their urban male colleagues. They find little solace in the organization when they go through marital difficulties, even when they are victims of spousal abuse. In effect, the female indigenous intellectual can be none other than an "inappropriate (woman) other" for the simple reason that to be an intellectual clashes with the gender values of her community of origin (Piñacué 2003).[15]

The condition of being "inappropriate" is of greater consequence for the woman intellectual, in comparison to her male colleagues. Diane Nelson (1999, chap. 5) has analyzed the circulation of jokes about Rigoberta Menchú, the Maya recipient of the Nobel Peace Prize. Such jests focus on her ethnic clothing and, consequently, on her "transvestite" nature: an indigenous woman who has assumed a masculine social position or, alternatively, as a *ladina* (mestiza) who is pretending to be indigenous. For Nelson, the jokes originate in the transgression of national, ethnic, and gender boundaries made possible by the development of the Maya movement, which has come to be embodied in an internationally known female spokesperson dressed in traditional clothing, a woman who has also become emblematic of such transgressions. At the level of the movement itself, both in Colombia and in Guatemala, such an ambiguous position is reflected in the subordination of female militants, who are concentrated in such "traditionally feminine" areas as education and who are hardly represented at all in the leadership of indigenous organizations, although they are increasingly assuming the helm of local cabildos. It comes through in their refusal to be called feminists, an apellation that, like "intellectual," is seen as adhering to elite status. It is also reflected in the silence that many of these female leaders exhibit at regional meetings. For example, at a 2002 regional assembly concerning a conflict of the cabildos of the municipality of Caldono with their mestizo mayor, Alicia Chocué, at the time lieutenant governor of the cabildo of Pueblo Nuevo, said nothing in the public discussion, although she had been instrumental in propelling the cabildos to entering the conflict. In comparison to what her male colleagues confront, the female indigenous intellectual encounters frontiers that are at once more numerous and of a specific nature.

Those indigenous activists who inhabit the frontier—women and men, urban migrants and rural dwellers—share their space and their anxieties with other frontier dwellers, in particular, the nonindigenous supporters or colaboradores who work in ethnic organizations. If, to recast Collins's (1991, 11) terminology, indigenous activists are "insiders-outside," then colaboradores are "outsiders-within," sharing many of the difficulties also faced by anthropologists. The indigenous intellectuals with whom I have been concerned in this chapter cannot be properly understood without making reference to their nonnative colleagues, who are equal players in the political process, working side by side with frontier Nasa on a daily basis and who have, to some degree, abandoned their identity as members of the dominant Colombian culture in favor of a commitment to indigenous politics. I turn to them in the next chapter.

CHAPTER 2

Colaboradores

The Predicament of Pluralism in an Intercultural Movement

Alongside "frontier Nasa" like Susana, Inocencio, and Abelardo there are full-time nonindigenous supporters working in CRIC. Since the organization's founding, colaboradores, as these individuals are called, have been among the organization's key activists, as well as occupying prominent positions on its roster of martyrs.[1] The earliest colaboradores came to CRIC in an official capacity as employees of the Colombian Institute for Agrarian Reform (IN-CORA). INCORA was an important point of entry into the rural communities of Cauca in the late 1960s because, as long-time colaborador Pablo Tattay told me, its regional managers saw peasant land occupations as a natural extension of agrarian reform. Some, like Pablo, were attracted to the northern Caucan community of Corinto, where a radical priest named Pedro León Rodríguez and political figures like Gustavo Mejía, a leader of the left wing of the Liberal Party, the MRL or Revolutionary Liberal Movement, were beginning to organize land occupations among peasants and Afrocolombians. The National Association of Peasant Users (ANUC) was founded at this time (Zamosc 1986). Affiliated officially with the Colombian government in its early years, ANUC also brought into the region an influx of individuals associated with official agencies, not as promoters of government policy but, Pablo recalls, to "strengthen the revolution or, at least, to bring about social change through work with peasants." Pablo's contacts with Gustavo Mejía brought him into dialogue with local sharecroppers. Ultimately, he worked his way south into the mountains of Silvia, where Guambiano activists were intent on setting up cooperatives on land purchased by INCORA. This group of indigenous leaders and colaboradores was instrumental in the founding of CRIC in 1971.

Thus, colaboradores were present at the very moment of CRIC's inception and continue to be active in the organization today. They serve as staff in CRIC's programs—communications, education, health, and production—and have played a significant role in fortifying the development plans advanced by the member communities of AICO (Indigenous Authorities of Colombia), the Caucan organization to which the Guambianos belong (although, for reasons I discuss below, in AICO they are called *solidarios*). They served as *comandantes* in the Quintín Lame indigenous guerrilla movement in the 1980s and as staff members of the nongovernmental organization Fundación Sol y Tierra, which the demobilized guerrillas founded after negotiating with the Colombian state. Colaboradores working in association with the nongovernmental organization FUNCOP (Popular Communications Foundation) energized the discussions that nourished an indigenous think tank called the Escuela del Pensamiento Nasa (School of Nasa Thought) that was based in the politically independent community of Pitayó. In northern Cauca in particular, radical priests and nuns have stimulated regional development projects organized within cabildo associations. It is impossible to speak of the indigenous movement in Cauca without considering its nonnative supporters.

Nonindigenous activists' authenticity as members of an indigenous movement qualifies and is, in turn, qualified by the dilemmas of native activists. If Nasa intellectuals cannot lay claim to an authenticity necessary if they are to speak for other Nasa, then who is to blame? Is it the colaboradores' fault? Do colaboradores knowingly or unknowingly introduce an alien ideology into organizations, and are they less capable of entering into indigenous ways of interpreting reality than the already conflicted indigenous intellectuals? Are colaboradores full members of the movement, who can be counted on regardless of the risks involved? Or are they intruders from the dominant society, whose usefulness is limited to particular political junctures and organizational projects? Colaboradores cannot be viewed as entirely external to the organizations with which they are associated, but they are not altogether internal, either, because they are not indigenous. Perched on a frontier like their indigenous colleagues, colaboradores are figuratively joined at the hip to native intellectuals, but at the same time, they coexist in an uncomfortable rivalry with them. They contribute to the discourse through which the indigenous movement speaks for its constituents, but they cannot do so except in the company of native people. Not quite "inside" and not quite "outside," the intercultural quandaries of colaboradores mark the indigenous movement as an ambivalent space within which unequivocal public identities are constructed. The question of who speaks for indigenous people in Cauca is thus complicated by the very intercultural nature of the movement.

The Intercultural Nature of Indigenous Movements

Students of Latin American indigenous organizations frequently treat these groups as though they were homogeneous, with exclusively indigenous memberships and demands. Michel de Certeau (1986), for example, read early CRIC political manifestos as archetypes of the "indigenous voice," ignoring the fact that the vast majority of these statements were coauthored by colaboradores. Providing a critical perspective on the relationship between indigenous identity and Colombian citizenship, as well as technical capabilities that in the early years many of the unschooled indigenous leaders lacked, colaboradores were instrumental in aiding the movement in its insertion into the broader Colombian political arena and in finding its voice as a political alternative to leftist parties.[2] Their role in the creation of what has been termed "new social movements" is critical to understanding how popular organizing in Latin America has integrated class into a wider horizon of political rallying points, including ethnicity, gender, and modes of livelihood, among others (Alvarez et al., 1998; Edelman 2001; Escobar and Alvarez 1992).

Perhaps de Certeau cannot be taken to task, given that his reading of CRIC was based exclusively on textual analysis and not on any sustained experience with the organization. Yet scholars from a variety of disciplines who have come into direct and prolonged contact with indigenous movements across Latin America commit the same error of homogenizing the makeup of native organizations, with the unique exception of the attention paid to the charismatic mestizo spokesperson for the Zapatistas of Mexico, Subcomandante Marcos (Gilly 1995). Colaboradores are, similarly, absent from the work of analysts of the Colombian indigenous movement, who paint a polarized portrait of indigenous organizations in conflict with the state (Gros 2000); they are also missing in discussions of more recent ethnic organizing by Afrocolombians (Grueso, Rosero, and Escobar 1998; Restrepo 1997; Wade 1995). In fact, as I focused in on this chapter, I sought a theoretical literature that would provide me with avenues for interpreting colaboradores, but found only a handful of very recent undergraduate theses and doctoral dissertations that document their existence (Caviedes 2000; Laurent 2001) and the polemical writings of solidarios addressing the failings of movement politics (Bonilla 1995; Vasco Uribe 2002). Nevertheless, indigenous organizations are the product of a deep and sustained dialogue between native activists and their nonindigenous allies, something that is entirely apparent at any workshop, mobilization, or internal discussion where colaboradores take part freely in political debate and are charged with important political tasks, although they may not always take center stage before an external audience.

This is not to say that scholars have purposefully concealed the ethnic pluralism that marks these organizations. Monolithic descriptions of indigenous politics display forms of essentialization that have carried over from the strategies we once employed to describe indigenous communities. However, our erasure of the heterogeneity of the indigenous movement is as much the product of the dynamics of indigenous organizations themselves as it is the result of our external gaze. In periods of extreme repression, particularly in the early days of the movement, nonnative activists had to be protected from government surveillance because they were invariably accused of acting as movement ideologues. Thus, they were not always obvious to external observers, and when they were, sympathetic academics chose not to focus on them for fear of endangering the organization. Moreover, until recently, the identities of both colaboradores and individual indigenous activists was kept out of movement documents in the interests of conveying a unified political voice. Today, when such secrecy is not as necessary, when indigenous authorship is openly acknowledged, and when colaboradores have come out in public view, the multicultural nature of the militant base of these movements is still imperfectly understood by the public at large and by academics. Indigenous organizations are frequently criticized as being "manipulated" by "external advisors," a notion that perpetuates long-held stereotypes of indigenous inferiority by failing to recognize the political vision and organizational talents of native leaders, who are entirely capable of engaging in equal exchanges with colaboradores without being controlled by them. Finally, when penned by indigenous leaders (Avirama and Márquez 1995) or their allies (Findji 1992), the projection of a homogeneous movement is a strategic move underscoring the specific nature of organizational demands and the role played by the movement in the national political sphere, rather than as a reflection of everyday political practice.

By neglecting the crucial part played by colaboradores in indigenous organizing, we academics minimize the complex intercultural workings of the movement, despite the fact that we are increasingly attentive to heterogeneity in our studies of race and ethnicity. As a consequence of our inattention to such issues, our analyses come up short. We deny ourselves the conceptual space needed to interpret the multiculturalism internal to indigenous organizations and observe how they function as incubators for the generation of pluralist demands in the national arena. Instead, we have persisted in essentializing the movement as purely indigenous, producing an image of a package of separatist demands lodged in the nostalgic appeal to a primordial culture. This in no way reflects the intellectual dynamism and the intercultural depth of indigenous cultural politics, nor the protagonist role that these organizations are playing throughout the continent. By reducing the scope of these movements to their influence in the native sphere, we lose sight of the significance of the national projects they support beyond the indigenous arena.

CRIC and the Left

Most colaboradores are former leftists who sought out the indigenous movement as a prime site for constructing a new nation. Coming out of a heterogeneous Colombian left that for years had worked with sharecroppers as well as industrial workers, colaboradores moved into the sphere of indigenous organizing as an extention of their commitment to peasants. They quickly learned that the very struggles they were seeking to nourish had for years been deeply influenced by the same leftist discourses that guided their own collaboration with oppressed sectors. Peasant leagues inspired by the Colombian Communist Party were active in Nasa communities in the 1930s and 1940s, particularly among indigenous sharecroppers, and Caucan indigenous leaders were welcomed into the leadership of the Party (Rappaport 1998b, chap. 6). Riochiquito, one of the strongholds of Violencia-era Liberal guerrillas who ultimately moved to the left to found FARC, lies immediately to the east of the resguardos of Tierradentro. Toribío was an important corridor of movement for this irregular army, whose troops skirted the snowcapped Nevado del Huila to descend into the Cauca Valley. As a result of continual contact, the resguardos of northern Cauca have boasted a sizable contingent of both FARC supporters and Communist Party members. As other guerrilla movements and leftist parties emerged onto the Colombian political scene in the 1970s and 1980s, indigenous areas were sought as fertile ground for political organizing, translating in some instances into bitter, and even deadly, conflict between rival factions. As a result of this long-standing and deep process of leftist penetration into native communities, colaboradores encountered an indigenous leadership that spoke the same political language they did. This discourse was apparent in the demands and organizational structures of CRIC in its early years, marking an organization that at the time saw itself as an indigenous sector fighting alongside other oppressed groups, such as workers and peasants. Since then, the organization has adopted a politics of peoplehood and of the self-determination of the ethnic communities who make up its membership; however, indigenous self-determination is accompanied by the parallel and intersecting project of constructing pluralism on the national level.

It is not surprising that colaboradores share with indigenous activists a utopian dream that transcends the demands of the movement. Many of them would say that their most fundamental objective is to imagine a new kind of Colombian society. Graciela Bolaños, who has participated in CRIC since its foundation in 1971, and who is Pablo Tattay's wife, expresses it this way: "We are working for a project that is much larger than the indigenous movement itself. . . . From this perspective, the indigenous movement is for me . . . a space of action. It's not 'Indianness' itself [that is at stake]." Indigenous activists would concur with Graciela, as Nasa linguist Abelardo Ramos told me: "In the sense of a colaborador-indigenous relationship within an indigenous movement, I believe that what must be kept in mind is that, quite simply, we indigenous are Colombians belonging to different peoples and the indigenous sector also plays a role in the transformation of the country."

At the risk of simplifying their position, indigenous activists and colaboradores alike seek what Laclau and Mouffe (1985) call a radically pluralist democracy, characterized by an emphasis on social justice and a positive deployment of ethnic difference, to be achieved through the construction of alliances among politically equivalent popular sectors. This is precisely what occurred in 1999, when CRIC and AICO, following the lead of peasant organizations, joined a coalition to demand that the state make good on its promises to provide services to marginal populations. The result was a month-long blockage of the Panamerican Highway that disconnected Popayán from the rest of the country. The coalition ultimately gave rise to an electoral movement that put a Guambiano leader, Taita Floro Alberto Tunubalá, into the governor's office in the Caucan capital and created a viable alternative to the traditional political parties that have dominated Cauca since the nineteenth century. The participation of colaboradores in the indigenous movement marks the intention to construct just this sort of ethnically pluralist democracy, both within indigenous organizations and in the broader society. Many progressive sectors in Colombia see the indigenous movement as filling this particular need, despite the paradox that only 2 percent of the country's population is native. In other words, as in Ecuador and Mexico, the Colombian indigenous movement has come to represent other popular movements (Laclau 1996, chap. 3). By virtue of its capacity for mass mobilization, its decades-long organizing experience, and its ability to articulate discourses of citizenship in addition to its own ethnic demands, the indigenous movement sets the tone in broader political coalitions and provides the leadership necessary to coordinate broad political action.[3]

Colaboradores and the Crisis of Latin American Intellectuals

One of the obvious places to search out the origins of many colaboradores is in Colombia's left-leaning intelligentsia. Latin American intellectuals are in crisis, writes George Yúdice (1996, 159–160), because they are no longer able to articulate national imaginaries in a globalized world. Basing his observations on the work of Brazilian sociologist Renato Ortiz (1985) and Mexican political scientist Jorge Castañeda (1993), Yúdice argues that intellectuals have traditionally mediated between strong Latin American states and weak civil societies. In their role as importers of ideas from abroad—what Brazilian literary critic Roberto Schwarz (1992) has called "misplaced ideas"—intellectuals have simultaneously stood in for international thinkers and for local constituencies. As Castañeda so cogently observes, "A close look at the type of function intellectuals have frequently fulfilled in Latin America reveals they are nearly always substituting for someone or something. They write, speak, advocate, or do what is accomplished elsewhere by more specialized institutions or groups" (182). In so doing, argues Ortiz, they reinterpret local and international ideas, creating national philosophies: "If intellectuals can be defined as symbolic mediators, it is because they fabricate a link between the particular and the universal, the singular and the global" (139).[4]

Since the cold war, such globalizing factors as migration and the expansion of transnational markets and, at the grassroots, the rise of subordinated groups in rapidly decentralizing states have obviated the need for such "keepers of truth" (Sarlo 2001, 142), who, like their North American peers (Jacoby 1987), have migrated to universities, forsaking their public role, or have been transformed into "experts," sharing their specialized knowledge with the state (Sarlo 2001, 147–148); they have thus become a kind of "specific intellectual," to use Foucault's (1977) terminology. Such trends are evident in Colombia, where formerly Marxist intellectuals can now be found in government ministries or in the Banco de la República. Many Colombian intellectuals, however, can also be found in the United States, in France, and in Canada, not so much because they migrate in search of international funding, as Castañeda (1993, 181) would have it for the intellectuals of other Latin American countries, but in the wake of death threats from both the paramilitary and the guerrillas, which have substantially reduced the volume of liberal commentators in the country.

Colaboradores have not entered into the same crisis as have other intellectuals in Latin America.[5] Indeed, they have played a role in articulating new national imaginings in Colombia. But they have not served as mediators between the state and indigenous societies, a role that has been assumed, instead, by indigenous leaders themselves.[6] Colaboradores' efforts have been more closely focused on fostering the organizing capacity of the grassroots. Unlike national intellectuals, whose crisis preoccupies contemporary scholars, colaboradores might be more properly understood as team players, not as influential individuals. In this sense, colaboradores do not fit the mold of the intellectuals associated with leftist political parties, whose members inserted themselves into grassroots struggles under the assumption that they were a vanguard capable of leading the oppressed toward revolution. Instead, colaboradores have always seen the indigenous leadership itself as a kind of vanguard for alternative politics in Colombia and, for this reason, have chosen to work alongside them. Colaboradores do not speak *for* a subordinated sector, but are speaking *with* them, something that I understood only after several years of participating in meetings and collaborating on projects. They are not ventriloquists, as some Colombian critics would have it (and as I imagined when I began this project): they listen, and on the basis of their listening, they contribute to an intercultural dialogue at the heart of the indigenous movement.

A number of national researchers who rejected university-based investigation in favor of studies in collaboration with peasant and indigenous movements formulated a research strategy that incorporated the politically committed dialogue that marks colaborador practice into the very fabric of their work (Bonilla, Castillo, Fals Borda, and Libreros 1972); in turn, they provided activist intellectuals like Graciela and Pablo with new models for action. The approach, which I come back to in the next chapter, was called *investigación-acción participativa* (participatory-action research). Herinaldy Gómez, a former colaborador and now an anthropologist at the University of Cauca who works with the resguardo of Pitayó through FUNCOP, commented to me that in CRIC, the methodology used in workshops and meetings was not so much investigación-acción-participativa as an inversion of the terms: *participación-investigación-acción*, participation and mutual dialogue forming the heart of the collaborative relationship between indigenous leaders and nonnative activists.

Colaboradores or Advisors?

This does not mean, however, that colaborador-indigenous relations are entirely harmonious. In a movement dedicated to achieving indigenous self-determination, the presence of outsiders working at the heart of the organization rankles a certain sector of the membership. Within CRIC an undercurrent of distrust between some colaboradores and indigenous militants has led to an extended discussion over terminology: whether, originally, the nonindigenous founders and builders of the organization were colaboradores, or were instead "advisors"; what the difference between the two terms might be; and why the role of the colaborador has changed over time. In part, this distinction harks back to the camaraderie of the colaboradores who joined CRIC in its early years, some of whom are distinguished from their younger colleagues as being, in some intangible way, "closer" to indigenous militants. Early nonnative activists supported the nascent organizations with their unpaid labor and many suffered severe repression from the state alongside their indigenous counterparts; in a certain sense they "earned" their acceptance in CRIC. On various occasions, Graciela Bolaños, who had been with CRIC since its inception—and spent a year in prison during the antileft repression of the Turbay administration of the late 1970s for her loyalty to the organization—was identified to me by indigenous militants as being much more than a colaboradora; some people spoke of her as fulfilling a deeper, more maternal role in the organization.

But other colaboradores understand their own insertion into the organization as a pragmatic choice made by indigenous leaders. Álvaro Cabrera, who on various occasions has served as a colaborador in CRIC's bilingual education program, speculates that the term colaborador constitutes a kind of legal fiction that solved the need in the early years for expertise that was at the time lacking in the indigenous sector:

> I think that the category of colaborador in CRIC, particularly in the Education Program, was not seen from the perspective of interculturalism, but that it was a person who could contribute other elements to enrich the process. I think that the title of colaborador was seen more in contractual terms to preclude any difficulties that the organization would have in the sense of not being able to

respond to economic or salary expectations. Since there wasn't any possibility of paying a professional with all of those contractual guarantees, fringe benefits and all that, the figure of the colaborador was created, the professional—indigenous or not, because they didn't even think of the colaborador as being exclusively mestizo—who wanted to contribute to an organizing process, a political process, an educational process, who more or less shared affinities in terms of the work being done. That is my analysis of the concept.

In contrast, today's colaboradores not only make passable salaries, but find that adding CRIC to their résumés enables them to move on to highly paid or prestigious positions in the state or even international organizations. The perceived threat posed by the presence of colaboradores hinges on the loss of knowledge and expertise when nonnative sympathizers decide to abandon the organization, something that can be seen as an alarming dependence on outsiders.

Just as the image and role of the colaborador has been transformed over the history of the organization, the nature of indigenous participation in CRIC must also be conceptualized historically. One cannot be comprehended without the other. In CRIC's earliest years, being indigenous meant membership in an exploited sector, similar to other populations, such as peasants or workers, with the qualification that the nature of the exploitation of indigenous peoples was highly particular and that they had specific tools at their disposal to fight it, such as the laws stipulating the communal nature of resguardo lands and the semiautonomous institution of the cabildo. In other words, the structural relationship that indigenous populations shared with other exploited sectors, such as the peasants with whom CRIC has always entered into alliances, was more significant for the movement than was cultural difference, even though such identifying features as language and "customs" punctuated CRIC's publications and educational projects. It was only in the 1990s that "indigenous" came to imply cultural difference, as native rights movements matured and came to national and international prominence across Latin America. In CRIC, this transformation was accompanied by a corresponding emphasis on the particularity and specificity of indigenous identities, heightening the deployment of cultural difference within the organization. There was a move from the generic identity of *indígena* to the affirmation of peoplehood—Nasa, Guambiano, Ambaloeño, Coconuco, Quizgueño, Totoró, Yanacona—accompanied by the project of revitalization (*recuperación*) of the knowledge bases of these peoples.[7] As indigenous intellectuals began to appreciate the epistemological possibilities of their subject positions, the category of *asesor* began to replace that of *colaborador* for some militants, suggesting a contractual relationship instead of a political connection and hinting that the contribution to the movement by nonindigenous activists could never achieve the same depth as that of natives because the colaborador would never have a distinct epistemological basis from which to frame their political strategies.[8]

Solidarios

The long-standing but problematic relationship between CRIC's colaboradores and indigenous militants influenced the founders of AICO, the other major indigenous organization in Cauca, to accuse CRIC's nonnative supporters of setting the political line of the organization (Vasco 2002). AICO has no formal colaborador status; nonnative supporters of the Indigenous Authorities created a parallel organization in solidarity with AICO, calling themselves solidarios to distinguish themselves from the colaboradores of CRIC. While the solidarios criticized colaboradores for their hegemonic control of CRIC, they also perpetuated the fiction that solidarios played no role in decision making—despite their significant (and necessary) role in both organizations (Caviedes 2000). At the root of these conflicting terminologies is an interorganizational rivalry between CRIC and AICO that hinges in part on the ethnic differences between the two organizations—CRIC is largely Nasa and Kokonuko, whereas AICO concentrates Guambiano militancy—and in part on differences in strategy that have been largely superseded.[9] Caviedes (2000) and Laurent (2001) document the CRIC-AICO rivalry through interviews with colaboradores and solidarios. What emerges from their work is the conclusion that solidarios were in several meaningful ways quite different from colaboradores.[10]

Solidarios, like colaboradores, came largely from the left, from peasant organizations, and from the university, running the gamut in terms of class position, profession, and schooling. However, in contrast to colaboradores, solidarios were never an organic component of AICO. They constituted a separate organization with some three hundred members, which held its meetings in urban areas and which seems to have focused largely on coordinating research projects in support of the movement, a kind of extension of the participatory-action research that Víctor Daniel Bonilla, one of the solidarios' founders, had promoted in the late 1960s, along with politically committed academics. The activities of colaboradores, on the other hand, take place in the institutional context of CRIC and colaboradores never meet as a separate unit. Both solidarios and colaboradores see their goal as inserting indigenous demands within the larger context of popular movements seeking to transform Colombia, assisting in building bridges between the indigenous movement and progressive sectors of the dominant society. Both solidarios and colaboradores told Caviedes that their efforts were fundamentally different from those of members of leftist parties, although his solidario interlocutors accused the colaboradores of trying to insert CRIC in a centralized leftist framework. A quotation from an interview with Luis Guillermo Vasco by Mauricio Caviedes (2000, 67–68) suggests that the solidarios saw themselves as intermediaries or brokers working *between* the indigenous movement and other popular sectors, as opposed to operating as comilitants alongside indigenous activists: "The solidario movement was constituted as a 'two-way street,' that is, not only for the demands and the search for achievements of the indigenous movement, but at the same time, for the demands and the search for a political position for those who, not being indigenous, were in solidarity with them." Thus, according to Vasco, the solidario movement sought an institutional arrangement that would permit nonindigenous activists to "find themselves" politically without losing their particular identity in the movement. In other words, the solidarios quite firmly placed themselves on the other side of the frontier from indigenous militants, thus perhaps alleviating some of the awkward predicaments in which the frontier-straddling colaboradores frequently find themselves, but never resolving in practice the ambiguous nature of their political allegiances.

Mediating Spirituality in Localities

If colaboradores define themselves as an integral part of the movement and solidarios as a parallel organization whose activities intersect with those of the indigenous sector, a third group of outsiders plays a crucial role in establishing, promoting, and disseminating indigenous politics by inserting themselves in localities as opposed to regional organizations. Politically progressive priests, who are seen as "natural" members of the indigenous community, insofar as they play a formal and socially accepted leadership role at the grassroots, frequently straddle the same uncomfortable frontier as do colaboradores, solidarios, and indigenous public intellectuals. As Orta (1995, 1998, 2000, 2005) argues with reference to the work of the church in the Bolivian *altiplano*, locality is constructed through the interactions of local and transnational actors, the latter including Catholic missionaries working through local catechists to instill new appreciations of Christianity that are steeped in reworked indigenous cultural forms.

During the summer of 2002, FARC guerrillas threatened the municipalities of Cauca with violent reprisals if their elected officials did not immediately resign their posts, an attempt at destroying the Colombian state from its very foundations (*El Tiempo*, Bogotá, 15 July 2002, pp. 1.1–1.5).[11] Particularly threatened were those municipalities whose mayors were members of the Indigenous Social Alliance (ASI), an alternative indigenous political party, because their constituents had successfully demanded that they not resign and vowed to defend them in the face of FARC aggression (*El Liberal*, Popayán, 4 July 2002; *El Tiempo*, 11 July 2002, p. 1.5). Toribío was one such defiant municipality. Attacked on the evening of 11 July and the early morning of 12 July, the population, led by one of its priests, demanded that FARC free the fourteen policemen whom the guerrillas had taken prisoner. The cleric who assumed this leadership role was Ezio Roattino, a Consolata Father born in Italy. Ezio is multilingual; apart from his native Italian, he speaks Spanish, Nasa Yuwe, and some Croatian. He has forged alliances with thê' walas (shamans) and catechists working from the inside with whom he carries out hybrid rituals that mix Catholicism with shamanic practice. On one occasion, after inviting me to give a workshop to catechists on Juan Tama, the historical Nasa *cacique*, Ezio celebrated mass in Nasa Yuwe, drawing a connection in his homily between Moses (the subject of the reading from the Old Testament), Jesus Christ, and Tama.[12] The following morning, he took all the catechists to a sacred lake for a cleansing ceremony under the supervision of three shamans, followed by another mass said at lakeside and participated in by the thê' walas.

Ezio's pastoral practice presents deep contradictions with the burgeoning Nasa religiosity of many frontier intellectuals and some colaboradores, who have rejected Christianity in favor of Nasa ritual practice. One thê' wala, who is himself a return migrant from the urban center of Cali, devised a Nasa baptismal ceremony to take place at a sacred lake, aimed at replacing the Catholic rite that the Nasa have observed for the past four centuries. This ceremony, which provoked fierce debate among priests, intellectuals, and local Nasa Catholics, developed out of extensive bibliographic research, coupled with the use of shamanic investigative strategies of dialogue with the supernatural world. CRIC has also organized numerous cosmovision workshops in which communities are cautioned to develop their own Nasa religiosity before embracing Christianity, a topic I take up later in this book.

While Nasa intellectuals attempt to define their precarious identity through the introduction of new rituals, Ezio establishes his own frontier standing by merging Christianity and shamanism—something that is acceptable to many rural Nasa, most of whom are devout, albeit syncretic, Christians. Ezio is a proponent of inculturation, a postliberation theology pastoral practice that makes use of "religiosity to maintain, re-elaborate, and re-create the utopic hopes of the poor" (López Hernández 1992, 9) through the appropriation of indigenous mythic and symbolic language. For proponents of inculturation, Christian theological positions are not contradictory to indigenous theologies, which are seen as more authentically Christian than more orthodox practices (Jolicoeur 1994; López Hernández 1992; Orta 1995, 2000). This stands in marked contrast to earlier Catholic pastoral practice, including the Christian base communities associated with the theology of liberation, which advocated a return to orthodoxy and attempted, unsuccessfully, to introduce a modernizing and homogenizing theological discourse in indigenous communities (Orta 1995). Ezio describes inculturation in the following terms: "Inculturation is the incarnation of the word, of a message of salvation within the cultural space of a people. There is no word of God, according to our reading, that is not inculturated. When Jesus of Nazareth speaks, it is a Hebrew who is speaking. . . . And within this cultural context, we must decode a message that we hold to be universal and recode it within a different space. Evidently, this should occur with close attention to the cultural protagonists; to do it in accord with them, in communion with them. It is a liberatory proposal."[13]

Ezio, who arrived in Cauca after the assassination of Father Ulcué in 1984, takes the precepts of inculturation very seriously. His charge is to build on what he believes was the mission of the fallen Nasa priest. In fact, he and his colleagues have virtually sanctified Ulcué as an emblem of their movement. Ezio has reflected on the Christianity of his precursor and, supported by the hybrid faith that he felt characterized Ulcué, has opted to install himself on the frontier between Nasa and European, using inculturation as a means to bridge inside and outside. Ezio calls this act a "double belonging" (*una doble pertenencia*) and an accompaniment of the "Nasa people on the Christian path," something he feels that his parishioners desire. This option for inculturation led Ezio to introduce a symbiosis between priest and thê' wala:

> We would meet each month, with shamans, midwives, pulse-takers [*pulse-adores*], always someone new comes from the side of the Word [from the ranks of Catholic religious specialists]. There were forty, fifty people and we did one- or two-day workshops. Principally, it was about medicinal herbs. . . . It was also

to share myths and to do rituals. We also hoped to return to how it used to be, what had been lost, but evidently, without moonshine liquor [which is used by most thê' walas and reviled by the priests]. The rum used was made from other plants and was fermented underground for a month. We reintroduced all this a little. And there was also the Eucharist as part of this, the Eucharist where we used our voices, where the symbols were the bread and wine and also the presence of the *chonta*-wood [staff of office, a symbol of indigenous authority], the *jigra* [woven bag for carrying coca], medicinal plants, and they also requested the blessing. It was a process of socialization, we listened to what was done in olden days, we recovered some practices that had been lost. What was the marriage ceremony like before? How was the shamanic ritual? Finally, we hoped to accomplish this recovery, but not in writing: in reality. To anticipate sensory signs, to listen to the people. And to once again give the shamans a sense of ethics. So that they would not be drunkards.

Nevertheless, during my conversations with Father Ezio, I questioned whether, in reality, the result of the process of inculturation was a deepening of Christianity among the Nasa or whether, in contrast, it was the reverse: a deepening of Nasa culture among religious agents, something that Orta (1995, 101) notes in his discussion of how this approach to evangelization is "mutually transformative" for both missionizers and the missionized.

In fact, Ezio recognizes that inculturation has led him to a cultural frontier that he feels he has permeated, although not completely:

I believe that there is always some doubt. You are marked by it, you are reborn, you believe you can be reborn and that I am no longer as I was in Turin some ten years ago. But when I go to Turin I don't think as they think in Turin, because of what entered me, that part of me that they gave me. So, I am sure that you cannot inculturate the Gospel . . . but that you yourself, in some form, become enmeshed . . . through no fault of your own. I will never be Nasa. But if in some way I hear them saying in a mass, "The Father is Nasa," it's because in that context it would be accepted here. In a way, I am led by a particular path. . . . Doubtless, I am changed by it. I speak with my own [people] and I am no longer he who was born, grew, and was brought up over there. The Nasa have modified my faith and my personality. But inculturation is unitary: being Nasa now, I feel this interpretive line in life and in theology as unitary, as change and exchange. I am an evangelizer and they evangelize me. Well, news that I did not know, although I had read the Bible. . . . In my church I did not find what I have found here.

Ezio's metamorphosis as he enters into dialogue with the Nasa is, obviously, expressed in more spiritual terms than in the narratives of secular colaboradores. Moreover, Ezio's reminiscences are considerably more intimate, homing in on the emotional transformations he has experienced over time. His relationship with the Nasa is, furthermore, of a different nature, given that he is supported by a powerful institution and because not only the community but the state and other armed sectors (such as FARC) recognize his authority. Thus, the frontier on which he is balanced is perhaps more solid than that of the secular colaborador. Yet, it is, nevertheless, a frontier that always separates Ezio, to some degree, from the Nasa (Orta 1998). It is also a frontier that has, over the years, become increasingly contentious, as indigenous leaders enter into rivalry with the progressive church, attempting to break the historically naturalized bond that the missionaries have forged with their flock, an issue I take up later in this book.

CRIC, Colaboradores, and Guerrillas

At the end of the 1970s and during the 1980s an organic relationship developed between CRIC and an armed self-defense organization that had arisen in the indigenous communities, the Quintín Lame Armed Movement (MAQL); I will also call them the "Quintín," as they are referred to by activists. Unlike the other guerrilla groups operating on the Caucan stage at the time, such as FARC and the M-19 (19th of April Movement), the Quintín did not advocate the overthrow of the Colombian government. Their central objective was the defense of indigenous peoples against predators, including the police, the Colombian army, hired assassins organized by large landowners, and even sometimes other guerrilla groups, particularly FARC. Unlike CRIC, which included nonnative activists but represented indigenous communities, the MAQL was established as a multiethnic organization in which indigenous fighters, peasants, urban militias, and mestizo intellectuals were all seen as equal members, a clear indication of the importance of pluralism in the early years of the indigenous movement.

It is worth dwelling momentarily on the MAQL's pluralist goals with an eye to comprehending the broader insertion of colaboradores into the movement. Pablo Tattay, colaborador and MAQL leader, recounts:

> An important consideration was to never differentiate completely between indigenous people and the rest of the needy sectors of the country. That's to say,

in the face of political change, in the face of social change, indigenous people were a sector, but not a sector that was totally different and with characteristics so distant from those of other sectors, especially peasants. And I think this was reflected in the orientation of the Quintín Lame Movement. It was an indigenous guerrilla group, but in reality, the Quintín was never a totally indigenous movement. Why? Man, its very composition and its relationships with other activist sectors—with peasants, it worked with urban sectors, and compañero Monroy [an Afrocolombian] was the first comandante—and it worked with indigenous people. But not from a closed anthropological perspective with the indigenous people here, and the rest over there, but of the indigenous people in the service of social change that interested all of the Colombian people.

Nevertheless, the MAQL's membership was nourished by an indigenous collectivity, the cabildos, who regularly sent recruits to be trained in military tactics and, especially, to receive political education on indigenous legislation. Unlike other guerrilla groups, these recruits regularly cycled in and out of the Quintín, parallel to their rotation in and out of the cabildos, making for a highly irregular fighting force. In fact, former M-19 members, who fought alongside the Quintín in an international guerrilla unit called the Batallón América, bemusedly recounted to me their reading of the Quintín's attitude toward guerrilla struggle as a temporary calling, highlighting their unmilitary propensity to abandon their posts in midcampaign and return home.

This indigenous self-defense force was named for Manuel Quintín Lame, a Nasa sharecropper who mobilized the indigenous communities of Cauca, Huila, and Tolima during the first half of the twentieth century (Castillo-Cárdenas 1987; Castrillón Arboleda 1973; Rappaport 1998b; Vega Cantor 2002). Lame himself was a frontier person of sorts. Monolingual in Spanish, he was brought up on an hacienda, not a resguardo. He spent a great deal of time conducting research in libraries and archives, finally dictating a treatise to his secretary that outlined his philosophy (Lame 2004 [1939]), which has served as a foundational text in the political schools of the Quintín Lame Armed Movement. The voice of Lame, which is exceedingly mystic, enigmatic, and sometimes quite opaque, was reedited by a group of Quintín guerrillas who, during periods of rest, reorganized the treatise into what they felt was a more coherent exposition (Mejía Dindicué 1989; Rappaport 1998a). As new fighters joined the ranks of the Quintín, each recruit adopted a nom de guerre taken from a fallen comrade. The three editors of the Quintín version of Lame's treatise, one of them Nasa and the other two mestizos, signed their edition with the names of

Quintines who had been killed in action, confecting a signature that suggests a single author: Luis Angel Mejía Dindicué. "Luis Ángel" was taken from Luis Ángel Monroy, an Afrodescendant and the first commander of the Quintín; "Mejía" was chosen in remembrance of Gustavo Mejía, the early mestizo colaborador; "Dindicué" was a reminder of Benjamín Dindicué, a Nasa from Tierradentro and vice president of CRIC in the late 1970s. All three of these leaders fell at the hands of hired assassins or the army. By merging the names of these three heroes, the text positions colaboradores inside, accentuating the pluralist character of the movement.

Although in the early years of the MAQL the Turbay administration was bent on imprisoning potential subversives, including various indigenous and nonnative members of CRIC, and the civilian organization distanced itself publicly from its armed wing, a relationship continued between the political strategists of CRIC and the indigenous combatants of the MAQL. The armed organization grew out of the need to protect certain critical zones, such as northern Cauca, where indigenous leaders from throughout the region had congregated to occupy an hacienda, López Adentro, a move that played a critical role in reincorporating the then defunct resguardo of Corinto (Espinosa 1996; Peñaranda 1998; Tróchez, Tróchez, Maya, and Avila, 1997). López Adentro was politically significant because it abutted the fertile Cauca Valley, where large commercial sugar mills and elite cattle ranches occupied lands usurped from the resguardos at the beginning of the twentieth century. An organic relationship between guerrillas and civilian militants was, therefore, at a premium. Likewise, it was necessary for the guerrilla fighters, many of whom had no previous experience in the indigenous movement, to be trained in indigenous political philosophy if they were to truly represent a native constituency. This need was filled by the indigenous leaders in CRIC's executive committee and by several key colaboradores, some of whom joined the MAQL, although most never learned to fire a gun.

Political training in the MAQL took place in the context of military instruction. That is, guerrillas were concentrated in a safe location for one or two months at a stretch where they studied military strategy and attended political lectures, sessions to which members of surrounding indigenous communities were sometimes also invited. Alfonso Peña, a Nasa member of the MAQL's military leadership, describes these sessions:

> The activities had defined themes. They'd say, "Today we'll talk about problems of the indigenous communities." "Today we'll touch upon the peasant prob-

lem." "Today we'll touch upon the crisis in our country, the political juncture, the situation." . . . Sometimes with videos, all that. And sometimes about tactics, about military tactics in theory. They'd talk about everything we would do the next day, how to organize the ambush, how you make a bomb, what is a *clima*, which was a homemade bomb. All of that in theory, and the next day we applied it in practice. . . . When there was a political issue, then they were combined.

Henry Caballero is a former Quintín who later served under Taita Floro Alberto Tunubalá as secretary of government for the Department of Cauca and, most recently, as his peace commissioner. Henry began his career as a militant in the Regional Indigenous Council of Tolima (CRIT), a sister organization to CRIC. His first introduction to the Quintín was a visit to a guerrilla school, to which he was invited as a member of CRIT's multiethnic political leadership (Laurent 2001, 356–357). His account of the school is indicative of the ways colaboradores of all stripes, indigenous leaders, and even members of other guerrilla groups were incorporated into the armed movement as mediators between the MAQL guerrillas and the civilian organization: "It was a joint school. Both political and military personnel participated, and those who came to teach politics participated, too. Yes, everyone had to participate, and those who came to teach military [tactics] had to participate in political training, and the military trainer was from the ELN [National Liberation Army] and in politics, there were some compañeros at the time. Daniel [Piñacué] was there, who was in charge of political education, and Pablo [Tattay], always telling the story of CRIC and of La Gaitana."[14] The relationship of the political trainers with the MAQL was, then, as a kind of symbolic mediator, much as Renato Ortiz cast the role of Latin American intellectuals in general. But in the case of the Quintín, the mediation was internal in character, between the leadership and the grassroots, and those called on for collaboration were expected to participate alongside the rank and file in all activities.

As Daniel Piñacué (Susana's brother and a former Quintín) describes it, the collaborative relationship was not considered deep enough. The compañeros whose duties were essentially political (the *políticos*) were not well enough integrated into the guerrilla forces. They stood, like the frontier Nasa, balanced on a precarious frontier:

I consider the Quintín to have been well trained militarily, but ideologically or politically, as usually happens, they had little to show. And the compañeros who knew more, those in the political organization, were the leaders, who were at the front of the military organization, but weren't permanently mobilized with the others, and this was also one of the problems that came out in evaluations or meetings of the general command. They evaluated all of this, they argued that the políticos were outside of the military structure and therefore, the políticos should be within that military structure so that all of the combatants and commanders would have the possibility of fluid analysis, of comprehension of things, and be able to debate with anyone, should the necessity come up . . . in the political workshops, especially about a basic level of indigenous legislation, what it meant to tell history, and who are the indigenous people, where we come from, and why we are struggling and why we are fighting for land. In short, all of these very basic things.

Daniel highlights the need for both indigenous and nonnative colaboradores with the MAQL—that is, people working within the political structure of CRIC and coming into collaboration with the Quintín—to understand the organization from the inside:

> In the workshops they had in CRIC, there were many compañeros colaboradores who were well-versed technically, specialized in a field, like the lawyers, or the anthropologists and the sociologists, or the journalists, who all moved within their specialties. But within the organizational structure this was questioned. The journalist compañero shouldn't only work on journalism . . . but should know about the juridical problems within the organization, the anthropological problems, the Caucan indigenous organization's line regarding the problem of land tenancy. All of the white colaboradores should be able to use that discourse, and all of the indigenous colaboradores as well should be able to use that discourse. All of them needed the necessary information in order to interact with the compañeros to inform them, to share with the grassroots, with the cabildos. There was a very good methodology for working with the communities, and in the Quintín there weren't these human resources, you could call them technical. There was only the possibility of sharing with all of the political compañeros, which happened at the moment of developing the political schools, the military schools.

In other words, the MAQL looked toward CRIC to replicate its collaborative model, one in which no colaborador was treated as an expert or a specialist, but was expected to be familiar with the work of the entire organization, to become a kind of general militant. In this sense, CRIC's colaboradores were very deeply inserted into the workings of the organization itself and cannot be thought of in the sense of external advisors. From this vantage point, the colaborador was a kind of insider.

Note that Daniel, whose charge was to coordinate between the political trainers and the guerrillas, thinks of *all* of the political specialists who worked as educators in the MAQL as colaboradores, that is, as civilians—regardless of their ethnic identity—who shared their expertise with a multiethnic guerrilla base. The indigenous leadership of CRIC, as much as the nonindigenous political trainers, were colaboradores with respect to the Quintín. Conversely, any member of the MAQL, whether Nasa or mestizo, was an insider. Once again, the question of a monolithic ethnic or cultural frontier is rendered more complex by the members of the movement itself, who expressly situate indigenous militants, as well as colaboradores, somewhere between inside and outside.

An Uneasy Collaboration

Notwithstanding the fact that indigenous activists and colaboradores share a common set of objectives, when nonnative supporters first joined indigenous organizations they discovered that native leaders were striving to create a new type of movement that was attentive to its Nasa, Guambiano, and Kokonuko base. As Graciela recounts, the colaboradores affiliated with INCORA were integrated into the nascent indigenous organization, placed under the tutelage of native leaders:

> We were part of INCORA, but under very special conditions. When we joined INCORA, there was a team of *políticos* [politically minded people], if you could call them that, who co-opted those they thought were useful. In other words, from there on in, we were ideologically closer to CRIC than to INCORA, and our role centered around CRIC. INCORA itself was just a . . . way of earning a salary. It was the team that defined the work. This was very important, [because] there were many people, not only those of us in CRIC itself, [but] other people who were working with peasants on alternative projects. There was [University of Cauca education professor] William [García] and there was a large team that had arrived with the clear intention of orienting a process of change here, and who came together with those who were from here, internal [to the process], like [Guambiano leader] Trino [Morales], who had been working for a long time. When CRIC was founded, Trino and [Guambiano leader] Javier [Calambás] told me, "Come on, compañera, let's go through all these documents."

They set me to work going over all of the documents of the cooperative [of Las Delicias], and from all those documents we made the central placards [of demands] that later formed the basis for CRIC's program.

As Graciela emphasizes, the relationship that grew between the colaboradores and the indigenous leaders was not paternalistic; the colaboradores did not orient the leaders or inculcate an external discourse. Instead, colaboradores listened to indigenous activists and activists to colaboradores, each bringing to bear their own knowledge, experience, and opinions in workshops dedicated to the analysis of issues of land ownership, the study of indigenous legislation, and the recounting of oral tradition and the history of indigenous resistance.

Graciela remembers that her own leftist projects never reached fruition in the midst of intense discussion with indigenous leaders. Instead, political strategy grew out of a process of grassroots historical remembering, not through the development of proposals presented full-blown by colaboradores to the team, a clear departure from standard leftist practice:

> The people spent entire evenings telling their history. A central element was history, the history of the people's resistance, for example. I considered history to be a unifying thread that articulated the different understandings of the people. Initially, we had a project. I personally wrote up a project on historical materialism, in order to develop it, but it was impossible [because] the dynamics were different. So we worked without losing our political north, continuing to internalize the concrete process that provided experience, because initially we believed that the parameters of the internationalist revolution could not be brought to the rural sector, because the workers were those who would begin a process of change.

The colaboradores' relationship with their indigenous allies was, from the start, a dialogue between equals in which each contributed his or her skills and knowledge. This was possible because the indigenous leadership in both northern Cauca and Guambía demonstrated such a long political experience—in many cases, longer than that of the colaboradores—and had reinscribed their leftist political practice in the values and procedures of local cabildos. The dynamic of the indigenous-colaborador dialogue led both parties to shed their leftist objectives, particularly their early goals of creating peasant unions, and moved them toward a project of strengthening cabildo autonomy, which since then has been the backbone of the programs of all the indigenous organizations in Colombia.

But leftist discourses are still not entirely absent from the indigenous-colaborador relationship. As a member of an expressly interethnic organization, Henry Caballero, the nonindigenous Quintín ideologue, considers himself to have been a full member of the MAQL, something that colaboradores in CRIC have not achieved, no matter how well they have been integrated in the organization. Henry feels that the distance between colaborador and indigenous militant is largely of the colaborador's making:

> Sometimes . . . there are well-substantiated criticisms [of colaboradores]. . . . Most of us come from the left, with rigid positions in the sense that we feel we hold the truth and want to lead the people toward it, and in the last instance, all this happens through a political style in which all actions are justified if they lead to the goal. So, many colaboradores, thinking that they hold the truth, operate by ignoring others or passing over them. They say that we are logical, that the indigenous members can also acquire this rigid style, but it also helps that they want to lead the indigenous movement.

The style of the colaborador, well-honed in leftist traditions of debate and confrontation, contrasts radically with the indigenous movement's emphasis on consensus.

Luis Guillermo Vasco (2002), an anthropologist and solidario who worked for years with AICO, was initially confused by the procedures of indigenous assemblies, in which breakout groups (*comisiones*) appeared to mull, interminably, over discussion points without reaching firm conclusions, a process that was then repeated in plenary sessions. Ultimately, he concluded that what appeared as aimless discussion was, in reality, a process of arriving at group consensus through collective reflection:

> The work in breakout groups organized by indigenous people in their meetings was, in reality, a research meeting, in which knowledge of a problem was intensified through discussion, in which they confronted the knowledge of every participant with that of the rest in order to finally arrive at group knowledge. . . . My idea that there were no conclusions at the meetings was wrong; there were conclusions, but they did not take the same form as those with which I was familiar, nor were they written. Later, it became clear to me that after the breakout groups and the multiple discussions that ensued in them, in the mind of every participant lay certain conclusions: a broader knowledge of the problem than what there had been before the meeting, now that it was no longer personal knowledge, but knowledge held by the entire group. (461)

Somewhat like the discussion style of U.S. women's groups, the focus here was on collective process, on arriving at implicit conclusions without forcing them or making them explicit. Indeed, this style of collective decision making would mark a difficult transition for a leftist from the dominant culture.

Outsiders frequently fail to perceive the intimate connections between organizing and research methods, on the one hand, and political priorities, on the other. Javier Serrano, a specialist in popular education affiliated with the Jesuit research institute CINEP (Center for Popular Education and Research), worked with CRIC in its early years in the creation of an innovative culturally based pedagogy. His association with the organization was short-lived, however, because, much as Henry suggests for colaboradores in general, Serrano brought an unbending attitude to his work, assuming that his expertise precluded the need for sensitivity toward indigenous ways of operating. In particular, Graciela stated to me that Serrano placed too much emphasis on pedagogical considerations, ignoring the political objectives that were paramount in the organization; he did not listen enough.

However, the gulf between Serrano and his indigenous colleagues went further than just this. Some colaboradores told me that although they are fully committed to the organization, they feel they are always perceived as external agents with alien philosophies. This kind of accusation is frequently referred to as being *cuadriculado,* or boxed into an ideology or a set of procedures. Serrano concedes that only two decades after his aborted collaboration with CRIC did he recognize that the political space in which he was operating belonged more to indigenous activists than to him: "I think that there was something there that I didn't understand. . . . 'Look, I can help you,' for example, in this case, in educational and pedagogical things, 'but the rest has to come from you.' And I wasn't very clear on that and I think I only understood it later. I couldn't represent the culture. I could help in what I was invited for, but there were things in the work of the Nasa organization that had a different logic from what we have in national society, in the conventional educational system." This is the crux of the problem. The colaborador is always conscious of the frontier on which he or she stands and the fact that it is only imperfectly bridged. Notwithstanding Henry Caballero's excellent relations with the indigenous movement and his conscious effort to set aside the rigid political customs that characterized his leftist past, he confessed, "So, then, there has always been a closeness, but in spite of everything, you always felt that in one way or another you were a stranger."

Mauricio Parada, who recently left CRIC after years of collaboration, confided to me that he thought the sentiments of exclusion he felt in the organization arose out of the impossibility of creating a team characterized by equality; he spoke in terms of the lack of "horizontality" in the organization. Although the coordination of CRIC's programs rotates among the indigenous militants, Mauricio felt that there was always someone giving orders, a kind of individualism, as he called it, that he also saw in communities, where cabildos gave orders to their members. In this context, according to Mauricio, it was impossible for a colaborador to contravene the leadership. Thus, from Mauricio's perspective, the quote I reproduce above of Luis Guillermo Vasco's is, in large part, utopian, at least with respect to the relationship between colaboradores and indigenous activists.

It always surprised me that almost none of the colaboradores in CRIC or their counterparts in other indigenous organizations—with the exception of linguist Tulio Rojas, who was a member of our collaborative research team, and Father Ezio Roattino of Toribío—made any effort at all to learn an indigenous language (whether or not they would actually master that language is another issue). Given that much of CRIC's research into cosmology is linguistically based and given the priority CRIC places on bilingual education, a sensitivity toward indigenous languages should be at a premium in the organization. Language, however, is also an emblem; competence marks a person as belonging to a particular social category. In effect, language is one of the ways indigenous activists distance themselves from their colaborador counterparts. Serrano suggests that knowledge of Nasa Yuwe may be used as a means of isolating colaboradores from the base of the organization:

> One time I said to Abelardo, "Listen, brother, I can't continue working on a project like this if I don't learn [Nasa Yuwe].... You should require and help me to learn. . . ." And Abelardo pulled my leg and told me, "I'm going to tell you something. The organization will never help you to learn." And I asked him, "Why not?" "Because then you could speak directly with the grassroots." I remember that I went ballistic and I told him, "But this is an error on your part. You can't have someone in charge. . . . Not in charge, but consulting, on such an important project." That's what I felt, and probably Abelardo as well and for you [Graciela], if not for the rest. "[You can't have] a person in whom you don't trust enough to allow to talk directly with the community. You should think of some other person."

Similarly, Inocencio Ramos complained to me that he felt that colaboradores were isolated from indigenous activists, who neglected to teach them

Nasa Yuwe: "It's simply because the discourse is fossilized, it's about toler-ance and the sharing of knowledge [*diálogo de saberes*], about intercultu-ralism. The problem right now, I think, is one of attitude, because after so many years the colaborador should be speaking Nasa Yuwe, but you don't see it. We should be pointing this out, we should question it, because the co-laboradores themselves taught us that discourse. True, they aren't applying it, but neither are we." In effect, the lack of pedagogical grammars, which have been made a lower priority than materials for Nasa speakers, combined with deep-seated attitudes preclude the widespread acquisition of Nasa Yuwe among colaboradores.

This distancing is exacerbated by the fundamentally monolingual ethos in which colaboradores, as members of Colombian society, were raised. These mores are sometimes justified by colaboradores through recourse to political considerations. Graciela, for example, feared that her influence would become too overbearing and that she would lose her grip on her own identity if she mastered the Nasa language: "But look, for example. I would learn with the children, but the time came when it was all so complicated and I, a mono-lingual Spanish speaker, felt totally lost, without knowing if I was thinking in Spanish or if I was thinking in Nasa Yuwe, and I finally said, 'But what am I doing here? This is going to be impossible. I'm going to wait until there are better tools and I'll wait to see what I can do.' Also, I began to think about a lot of things that are very delicate for the culture and I said, 'No. What if I do more damage by learning the language?' "

While language functions as an emblem for separating indigenous activists from colaboradores, varying degrees of linguistic competence among Nasa activists themselves preclude any simple polarization equating Nasas with bilingualism and colaboradores with monolingualism. Language is a partic-ularly troublesome symbol given that at least half the Nasa population is monolingual in Spanish and many indigenous activists, particularly those from northern Cauca, lack access to this highly significant icon of alterity. I participated in one CRIC workshop in which Nasa speakers lobbied for their own breakout group in which they could speak in Nasa Yuwe. Their very lively and highly philosophical discussion drew heavily on Nasa cosmology, as op-posed to the culturally unmarked political reflections of the other discussion groups. When the Nasa-speaking group shared its very profound conclusions in the plenary session, they were rejected by monolinguals—both Nasa and nonindigenous—as too simplistic, marking the incommensurability between political discourse in the two languages and emphasizing the pitfalls of polarizing the relationship between indigenous activists and colaboradores. The frontier lies not only between Nasa militants and colaboradores, but also within the Nasa sector itself. Language is not a simple marker between Nasa and non-Nasa, but an emblem that cuts at the heart of what it means to be Nasa in modern Cauca and hence, how identity should be generated and mobilized in an indigenous organization.[15]

Colaboradores on a Frontier

If Nasa public intellectuals and rural communities inhabit a common conceptual space that they do not always recognize as mutual, where might we situate colaboradores? This sector moves in social circles similar to those of indigenous intellectuals. Colaboradores frequently appropriate Nasa customs, such as consultation with shamans, in their everyday lives. Just as the organization becomes the center of indigenous activists' lives, so, too, it structures the affective relations, discourses, and daily schedules of colaboradores, who spend most of their workday and the bulk of their free time with native activists. In the first years of the movement, colaboradores played a critical role in training indigenous leaders and in the consolidation of their political platform, but as the movement matured and began to play a decisive political role at the regional and national levels, a new layer of schooled indigenous leaders displaced many nonindigenous activists, despite the lip service paid to the intercultural nature of the movement.

The colaborador—whether religious or secular, inserted directly into CRIC or working in solidarity with AICO—like the indigenous intellectual, senses that a frontier that is only partially bridgeable looms between him or her and the organization. Like the indigenous activist, the colaborador moves within a contact zone, replete with deep contradictions. The ambivalences that the indigenous intellectual feels upon return to the home community or when engaged in dialogue with representatives of the dominant society are, however, different from those felt by the colaborador. Whereas the native intellectual finds a true place of enunciation within the indigenous organization, the colaborador has no clear point from which to exercise a voice, leading many to abandon the movement for university positions, bureaucratic posts, or other organizations. The colaborador is a particular sort of "outsider-within" who will never gain complete entry into the indigenous political world. Nevertheless, despite these differences, the ambivalences felt by indigenous intellectual and colaborador are forged in a common space. Historically, the indigenous intelligentsia would not have survived in the absence of dialogue with colaboradores, and the nonindigenous activist loses a piece of herself when she breaks relations with indigenous intellectuals. In other words, it is impossible to interpret the role of one sector without appealing to the other.

CHAPTER 3

Risking Dialogue

Anthropological Collaborations with Nasa Intellectuals

Thus far, I have confined my ethnographic gaze to Nasa public intellectuals and their nonindigenous supporters, mentioning only in passing the anthropologists whose research is appropriated by the movement and, correspondingly, the place of external researchers in an intercultural dialogue. I count myself among these scholars, as I have worked in Cauca since 1973, since 1978 among the Nasa, and my publications have circulated in Caucan intellectual circles, both indigenous and academic. It has been my practice to alternate between historical work and ethnography. When I begin to feel discomfort with the voyeuristic nature of ethnographic field research, I move to the documentary record; when I sense that my work is too removed from everyday life, too comfortably sheltered in the archives, I return to the field. This alternating strategy has allowed me to draw connections between archival and field research, given that I have always been concerned with the relationship of native peoples to the documentary record. But it also expresses my fundamental uneasiness with ethnographic fieldwork as an extractive, and not a dialogic, practice. The research on which this book is based represents a compromise, a way out of my quandary. Instead of working *on* the Nasa, I have chosen to work *with* them, a strategy that allows me to view Nasa activists as intellectuals with whom I can engage in a mutually beneficial exegetic conversation, as opposed to treating them as ethnographic objects.

I discovered early on that such a step involved much more than simply engaging a new research question that positioned the Nasa in a different light. It also meant entering into a different kind of dialogue with them, a more equal exchange marked by a mutual desire to engage in joint interpretation. I hoped I would accomplish this through direct cooperation with CRIC's bilingual education program, where I taught history workshops to indigenous university students and in Nasa communities, as well as collaborating on an oral history of the education program itself. My goal was to enter into circles of discussion where all of the participants sought to harness the knowledge and critical perspectives of all the others, not a one-way conversation where an ethnographer devoured the knowledge of informants. I was able to accomplish this because I had published in Spanish, my work had been read by several activists and presented in summary form to the grassroots at workshops, and I had something useful to bring to the table. I was in a position to remake myself as an *antropóloga* (anthropologist), not an *antropófaga* (cannibal).[1]

In the mid-1990s I participated in a collaborative research team with Colombian academic scholars based in the Colombian Institute of Anthropology in Bogotá. Our focus, the politics of ethnicity in postconstitution Cauca, was a prime site for engaging in dialogue with indigenous intellectuals, and indeed, that was my own objective within the project. I discovered, however, that the structure of the team was not conducive to the integration of indigenous scholars in its ranks. Together with Popayán anthropologist Myriam Amparo Espinosa and U.S. anthropologist David Gow (my husband), both of whom had participated with me in the Institute's project, I began to think about establishing a collaborative research team that would include Nasa scholars as well as academic researchers. This chapter explores the methodological and epistemological implications of that option.

Ethnographers and other scholars studying popular culture and subordinated minorities in Latin America have begun to confront the fact that the people we have traditionally studied are increasingly engaged in their own research projects, sometimes through customary academic channels but more commonly through grassroots activism or nongovernmental organizations. These organic intellectuals attached to new social movements are aware of our research and are increasingly anxious to engage us in dialogue and debate. They are, however, highly critical of academic approaches that constitute them as exotic objects. They point to the gaps in our research and the misinterpretations that characterize our work. They chafe at the imposition of imported theoretical models that clash with their own epistemologies. They are particularly disturbed by the refusal of academic scholars to recognize the intellectual contributions of grassroots scholars and our tendency to judge them by academic standards. Critics of area studies have focused on the implications of northern scholarly projects that treat Latin America as a place to conduct research, but not as a space from which intellectual projects can be articulated (Mignolo 2000). This predicament is only intensified when we confront the kind of organic intellectuals to whom I am referring.

The intercultural dialogue sought by such researchers, particularly in the case of the indigenous public intellectuals with whose activities I have been concerned over the past few years, presupposes that different forms of knowledge and different methodologies will be recognized as equally valid, if not entirely commensurate with Western academic orientations. I use incommensurate here to indicate that these approaches diverge from accepted models of research and analysis, not to imply that they are incomprehensible to us. Furthermore, I am not attempting here to trace a polar opposition between discrete and opposing bodies of "indigenous" and "Western" thought. After almost five centuries of European domination and Spanish alphabetic literacy, the influence of anthropological writing, a long-term engagement with the Colombian left, the growing incursion of indigenous students into universities, and the indigenous movement's espousal of an intercultural philosophy, such essentialist notions are unsustainable. Instead, my contrast underlines the different positionings of the two groups of intellectuals, with the most salient divergences being their relationship to institutions and their discourses, such as the academy and the ethnic movement.

An orientation toward a constructive dialogue between academic researchers and native peoples involves more than fostering tolerance in the face of intellectual diversity. It goes beyond an academic multiculturalism that incorporates professionals from different ethnic backgrounds into a common academic dialogue (Turner 1993). In contrast, it requires a conscious and active commitment on the part of academics to situate indigenous interpretations on an equal footing with academic analysis, to accept that both hold significant—but different—truths (Field in press a; Vasco 2002). This move calls, moreover, for an abandonment of the traditional ethnographic procedure of accepting local knowledge as data to be framed by Western social and cultural theory. Instead, it requires that indigenous knowledge be embraced as a truth capable of generating a deeper mutual dialogue. In the long run, if this dialogue is to escape the trap of being framed by academic ethnographic discourse and theory, such a project must necessarily coincide with the movement's own objective of pursuing the internal study of indigenous epistemologies. This step would lead to the development of an expressly native theoretical discourse to be employed by indigenous public intellectuals.

Participatory-Action Research in Colombia

A small number of Colombian scholars—one of the most well-known being sociologist Orlando Fals Borda, but also including journalist Víctor Daniel Bonilla, anthropologist Luis Guillermo Vasco, and archaeologist Marta Urdaneta—have explored the possibilities of institutionalizing such a dialogue through the creation of research teams in which academics and nonacademics participate on an equal footing in the collection and analysis of ethnographic and historical data. Fals Borda (1979a) initially coined the term *investigación-acción participativa* (participatory-action research) to conceptualize how academic research could be harnessed in popular struggles, eventually establishing an organization, La Rosca de Investigación y Acción Social (Circle of Research and Social Action), to promote this politically committed approach (Bonilla et al. 1972).[2] The best published example of La Rosca's methodology is a four-volume history of the Colombian Atlantic coast (Fals Borda 1979b, 1981, 1984, 1986), a series of two-channelled books in which the fruits of collaborative research and theoretical discussions of its implications are displayed on alternating pages. But the fruits of La Rosca's labors impacted outside of the academy as well. Pamphlets destined for movement readers on Nasa history, written by Bonilla (1977), historical picture-maps (*mapas parlantes*) for use in communities (Bonilla 1982), and Gonzalo Castillo's edition of early twentieth-century Nasa leader Manuel Quintín Lame's (1971 [1939]) writings distilled the group's research into organizational tools used to train leaders and to promote political reflection in localities.

Ethnographer Luis Guillermo Vasco, an associate of Bonilla's and a solidario, provides an insightful critique of La Rosca's methods with the hindsight that came from his own collaborative experience in Guambía in the 1980s. He argues that the politically committed scholars of the 1970s made the positivist error of separating theory, a rational process conducted in the university, from practice, sensorial knowledge acquired in the field. These two facets of ethnographic and historical investigation are commonly separated by space and time in academic research, as they were by La Rosca (Vasco 2002, 454–457). Vasco argues that La Rosca members' attempt to "return" their research to the communities with whom they had collected the data was, ultimately, unsuccessful, because they erroneously assumed that their research techniques were politically neutral and did not reproduce existing power relations or constitute the groups they studied as objects when, in practice, they did just this (457–458). Most important, La Rosca used its own academic basis for evaluating the materials it had collected jointly with local people, which is why, as Vasco reminds us, Fals Borda's books are two-channeled, one academic and the other community-based. La Rosca did not attempt—nor was it even a conceptual possibility at the time—to analyze its data using theoretical perspectives generated from the community itself (459). In short, La Rosca's political commitment did not preclude its adherence to traditional ethnographic procedures, and as a result, its writings were never fully assimilated by the communities in question.

More recent work has attempted to resolve some of these dilemmas. In the indigenous community of Guambía, Luis Guillermo Vasco (2002) and Martha Urdaneta (1988) worked with teams of Guambiano researchers intent on rewriting the history of their ethnic group to press territorial claims. The results of this research were written by the national scholars in Spanish after lengthy exchanges with their Guambiano interlocutors (Dagua et al. 1998; C. Tróchez, Camayo, and Urdaneta 1992). Vasco and Urdaneta were inserted in internal research teams concentrating, respectively, on oral history and archaeology, whose composition and topics of study were dictated by the Guambiano cabildo. Their methods were collaborative, not only in the collection of materials, but also in their analysis. Urdaneta, for example, worked with her Guambiano colleagues to develop classifications of historical time and topographical space, which were then employed as guides for the establishment of a chronology of archaeological sites and, ultimately, for the interpretation of Guambiano prehistory (C. Tróchez et al. 1992). Vasco and his Guambiano coresearchers developed what he called *cosas-conceptos* (concept-things), theorizations of the shape of time extracted from Guambiano material culture, as a basis for theory (Vasco 2002, 466–473). Unlike standard anthropological research, or even La Rosca's approach, the work in Guambía was intimately collaborative and, in some sense, subordinated the professional ethnographer's methods and epistemology to those of the collectivity (Vasco 2002, 449).[3]

While collaboration between native peoples and external researchers bears obvious political and intellectual consequences for the social movements in which it is based—which is what the writings of its proponents accentuate—it also generates deep intellectual implications for academics, altering our methodologies, our research agendas, and our appeals to theory. As various Latin American scholars have argued, when we question the relationship between researcher and subject we must pay greater attention to our field practice, in contrast to the postmodern turn in anthropology and its focus on the writing of ethnography (Riaño-Alcalá 1999; Vasco 2002). The ethnographer's task has always been characterized by dialogue in the field, the conversations that take place during the interview process revealing forms of local knowledge, which are subsequently converted into a unilateral written exposition by the ethnographer (Tedlock and Mannheim 1995). However, in an interethnic collaborative research venture, this one-way exchange is transformed into a mutual process of exegesis in which internal and external ways of knowing enter into dialogue. In other words, with this stance, ethnography moves from its focus on "taming" forms of knowledge seen as exotic to a far-ranging conversation between different subject positions, their epistemologies, and the ways this knowledge is transmitted.

In my previous experience in Tierradentro (Rappaport 1998b) and in the Pasto community of Cumbal on the Colombia-Ecuador border (Rappaport 1994), I took ethnographic dialogue to consist of formal interviews and informal conversations, which were precisely the tools I first used to set about learning about indigenous intellectuals in millennial Cauca. But when I entered into dialogue with CRIC activists, I was swiftly drawn by them into a broader array of conversational venues. During the first research season, I sought out Jesús Enrique (Chucho) Piñacué, Susana's brother and at the time president of CRIC (he is now a national senator). Chucho informed me that if I was to conduct research in CRIC, I would be expected to collaborate in community projects; he was referring particularly to my expertise in historical research, which would be of use in a number of localities. When I first became involved with CRIC's bilingual education program and, to a lesser extent, with a history project in northern Cauca, I swiftly learned that dialogue with activists did not occur only on a one-on-one basis, nor could I confine my fieldwork to traditional forms of participant-observation, where "participant" meant accompanying the activities I was observing and not intervening in them. The collaboration that the activists sought involved expanding my venues of dialogue to include workshops, in which I not only participated but occasionally acted as a facilitator, work on joint research projects with CRIC personnel, engagement in exegetical meetings with the research team and with CRIC's bilingual education program, and the exchange of commentary on written work. In other words, I was enjoined to become an actor in the process I was studying, albeit temporarily and only in specific projects. It is not enough, however, to simply list these sites of dialogue. The conversations in which I have participated during the past eight years differed profoundly from those of my earlier fieldwork.[4]

My dialogues in Cauca were an exercise in interculturalism, in which we all recognized that conversation was more than a process of turn taking among culturally distinct equals; the notion of dialogue as turn taking is implicit in Tedlock and Mannheim's (1995) critique of ethnographic writing that I cite above. Instead, it was a process of appropriation and reappropriation on all sides, which recognized that although we might cast our interpretations in terms of the inside/outside opposition, we all stand on the frontier. When we described our relationship explicitly at meetings and assemblies, we depicted ourselves as socialized in distinct regimes of "truth." However, we all knew implicitly that these "truths" were not so much opposed as commingled long before our conversations began. This is why it is difficult to draw a contrast between us as Western and indigenous actors, given that such categories neglect the more subtle positionings of frontier denizens like indigenous intellectuals, colaboradores, and politically committed anthropologists. Perhaps for this reason inside and outside became an apt metaphor for our relationship, because what constitutes the two sides of this opposition is entirely contextual. Nasa-speaker versus Spanish-speaker, local versus regional, indigenous versus colaborador, activist versus academic, and CRIC versus those beyond its fluid boundaries: all constitute parameters whose occupants and roles are in continual negotiation in the Caucan indigenous movement.

A brief example will suffice. Over time, I came to realize that Nasa-speaking activists in CRIC, particularly those with academic training in linguistics, employ translation as a fundamental tool for exercising interculturalism. As I explain later in this chapter, they appropriate concepts from the dominant society by translating them into Nasa Yuwe; in the process, they transform their meanings. Such a methodology provides the necessary tools permitting them to resignify such important ideas as "nation" and "culture" and, ultimately, confront the state about the nature of ethnic pluralism. Obviously, translation is not the product of a Nasa "regime of truth," but arose out of the appropriation of the academic discipline of linguistics harnessed to Nasa semantics, thus creating a unique theoretical instrument.

The translation methodology is not one that I had encountered in the past, nor is it entirely akin to the exegetical process that we anthropologists use to analyze native terms, as I consider later in this chapter. It is, moreover, a method that can be used effectively only by those for whom Nasa Yuwe is a mother tongue, because it requires such profound knowledge of the language that even an individual who is proficient in Nasa Yuwe as a second language cannot bring a sufficient level of sophistication to the exercise—not to mention my highly rudimentary knowledge of the grammar and lexicon of Nasa Yuwe. Nevertheless, in the course of my conversations with Nasa speakers and in the course of workshops I attended or facilitated, I came to appreciate how compelling this methodology is and began to employ it, secondhand, as an interpretive tool. That is, I came to recognize their resignified concepts as theoretical tools that could illuminate my own analyses. I discovered, however, that many Nasas who did not speak Nasa Yuwe and many colaboradores, positioned on the organizational inside in relation to me as an outsider, saw translation simply as a tool useful for converting texts composed in one language into another. They could not comprehend why this strategy was so essential to cultural experimentation, nor why it was so innovative. The dialogues I describe in this book are, indeed, messy conversations in which unlikely actors claim as their own the tools and discourses of their counterparts.

The spaces of collective discussion in which indigenous activists seek to generate dialogue also diverge from the individualistic methodologies in which most academic anthropologists are trained. Like the translation methodology, they are appropriations of dialogic forms from the dominant society, particularly from the culture of nongovernmental organizations. In particular, I see workshops as a critical scenario, where issues are reflected on by groups, generating not only data but interpretation, as well as making possible the assimilation of research results by diverse publics. Such a research strategy is not new among Latin American ethnographers (García Canclini, Castellanos, and Rosas Mantecón 1996; Riaño-Alcalá 1999; C. Zambrano 1989), who have long been involved in harnessing academic research to social commitment (Caldeira 2000; Jimeno 1999, 2000; Krotz 1997; Alcida Ramos 1990). Nor is collective interpretation alien to the methodologies of politically committed minority anthropologists in the United States, as the work of John Langston Gwaltney (1981, 1993) in African American communities in the late 1960s so eloquently attests.

Workshops and seminars have become ubiquitous in rural Colombia, organized not only by NGOs and researchers, but also by government institutions, a process that Carlos Vladimir Zambrano (1989) sees as going hand-in-hand with the de-academization of Colombian anthropology and its repositioning within the state bureaucracy. In this sense, the workshop strategy has been co-opted by the state. Notwithstanding the influence of the state in promoting such strategies, they have also been internalized by the indigenous movement, to some extent substituting for traditional modes of consensus building; Susana Piñacué (2005) decries this development because it has led to the diminished participation of women in public political events at the local level. In some of the communities of northern Cauca, indigenous militants spend at least half their time attending such events. Workshops generally consist of a list of questions prepared by the organizers that is discussed in breakout groups and then summarized in plenary sessions. The extent to which the workshop format determines the nature of the results is an important question before the movement and politically committed researchers. In the course of my research, which included attendance at many such events, I grew to question whether the format impeded the grassroots from taking control of interpretation.

Notwithstanding the shortcomings of the workshop strategy, its incorporation into the research process brings to light significant epistemological questions.[5] Just how such collective methodologies force us to reconceptualize our ethnographic predilection toward inscribing radical alterity when we work with indigenous peoples is not widely analyzed, with the notable exceptions of Vasco's writings and the recent work of Les Field (1999). The shift to ethnography as politically motivated dialogue brings forth several central questions: (1) How compatible are the intellectual agendas and interpretive methodologies of indigenous researchers with those of academics? (2) What are the necessary changes in research strategy, particularly in terms of the nature of the insertion of researchers in the social reality they study and participation in new spaces for exchange, that must accompany the creation of an interethnic dialogue between peers? (3) How is academic research enriched through an exchange with indigenous organic intellectuals, and how is indigenous research made richer through dialogue with us? (4) What does it mean for an academic to assume the consequences of his or her research, a commitment that the internal researcher has always had to undertake?

Pluralist Research in Indigenous Cauca

This chapter reflects on such concerns based on my own experiences in Cauca. Since 1999, in association with Myriam Amparo Espinosa and Tulio Rojas (Colombian social scientists), David Gow (a U.S. anthropologist), and Adonías Perdomo and Susana Piñacué (Nasa intellectuals), I have participated in a collaborative project focusing on transformations in ethnic politics during the past thirty years of indigenous militancy. Our objective has centered on the construction of a dialogue sensitive to the three subject positions we occupy and the diverse intellectual agendas that they imply, while recognizing that each of these subject positions is heterogeneous and mediated by myriad factors, including institutional affiliation, gender, age, and access to resources. Our team has striven to develop a complex dialogue among its members, each of whom has undertaken a distinct research project that resonates with the objectives of the others. We explore various facets of the intercultural space of indigenous politics, ranging from issues of gender in the indigenous movement (Piñacué), to the nature of grassroots development (Gow) and cultural planning (Rappaport), language policy (Rojas), the creation of institutions promoting interethnic dialogue (Espinosa), and the problems inherent in the development of indigenous structures of justice in Colombia's process of judicial decentralization (Perdomo). Our first attempt at bringing together preliminary results of our collaboration has recently been published in Colombia (Rappaport 2005). However, our central objective was not so much to write together as to engage in dialogue, the writing serving only as a point of departure for our discussions and a means of making public our collaboration.

Our extended conversation has developed since 1999, taking place at periodic meetings in which we exchange analyses of key moments in contemporary ethnic politics and comment on one another's written work, the latter serving as a pretext for discussion, not as a final objective. We also presented our research at movement events, where we received the commentary of activists, and in Colombian academic venues, where professional anthropologists reflected on our work. We have chosen to develop separate but related research projects to achieve a more equal working relationship. If we had instead chosen to work together on a single research project, hierarchies based on levels of education, professional experience, familiarity with research skills, and unequal access to bibliographic resources might have disrupted the process of forging a deeper peer relationship. In contrast, through the vehicle of what we have called "methodological *mingas*," we have striven to arrive at common lines of analysis that crosscut our heterogeneous projects.

Manuel Quintín Lame, a Nasa leader of the early twentieth century, spread his indigenista message through "teaching mingas" (*mingas adoctrinadoras*), meetings at which his political demands for indigenous territorial rights and self-government were aired (Castrillón Arboleda 1973, 91–92). These gatherings adapted the traditional notion of the minga, an Andean institution coordinating the reciprocal exchange of labor that unites members of a community within a network of mutual obligations (Alberti and Mayer 1974), to the highly charged political context of Lame's movement. Since Quintín Lame's time, the minga has become a key metaphor for conceptualizing the intellectual exchange that nourishes the political and cultural discourse of the indigenous movement in Cauca. As I argued in the previous chapter, this movement cannot be understood as purely indigenous. Although its leaders most certainly hail from native communities, it is decidedly multiethnic in character, bringing together indigenous actors with intellectuals from the dominant society who have identified the indigenous movement as a prime site in which agendas highlighting social justice and articulating political utopias can be forged. These mingas are intercultural conversations, which take place in public assemblies, in local workshops, and in community schools, where ideas are shared by diverse social actors.

Perhaps the best example of this is the translation of the 1991 constitution into Nasa Yuwe (Abelardo Ramos and Cabildo Indígena de Mosoco 1993). The Spanish original of this document (Colombia 1991) was drawn up in a nationally elected Constituent Assembly that included three indigenous delegates, one of them Nasa (Alfonso Peña of the Quintín Lame Armed Movement). Accomplished by an intercultural team that included Nasa elders, bilingual teachers, indigenous linguists, and academics and lawyers from Bogotá, the mingas that gave rise to the translation project were aimed at distilling a distinctly Nasa methodology for appropriating Western concepts and making sense of Nasa neologisms, not strictly the production of a definitive translation of the national charter (Rojas Curieux 2000). In other words, minga is seen here as a space in which pluralism is generated in the interests of creating intercultural tools for ethnic representation and revitalization, as Nasa linguist Abelardo Ramos recounts:

> In Nasa Yuwe we have the everyday practice . . . of the minga—in Spanish, or maybe, I suppose, it is a Quechua word, while in Nasa Yuwe we say "house of the minga" *pi'kx yat.* . . . In this sense, our collective work is interesting, in that the relationship between the lawyer and the teachers was a minga: we all contributed, we all learned, we were all enriched, we all benefited, and the final result was meant for the Nasa. And also, as we felt that it was also for intellectuals interested in ethnic issues, we were also engaged in a task that in the long run would have a dual purpose, and we were content, we were happy in our work, because as indigenous people we always value living side by side with mestizos, with Colombian citizens, [enjoying] fraternal relations.

In the case of the translation team, the dialogue had a dual purpose. On the one hand, they intended to translate selected articles of the constitution into Nasa Yuwe in such a way as to reflect both Nasa political priorities and cultural meanings; on the other hand, they planned to capture in their translation the sense conveyed by the original Spanish text (Rojas Curieux 1997). In the process, intercultural dialogue was harnessed to create distinctly Nasa definitions of key concepts such as "nation," "state," and "rule of law," a novel attempt at reconceptualizing the nature of the state from its margins, which I take up in detail in the last chapter. Such an approach to translation involved transcending the original constitutional text by bringing it into line with Nasa ideals. In other words, as Abelardo recounted to me, the goal was to allow the indigenous language to draw "its own preferences and priorities in order to foreground the contents of interest to the culture" ("La lengua indígena hace sus preferencias y prioriza, para poner en relieve ese contenido lo que a la cultura le interesa").[6]

Translation Strategies in Native Anthropology

Let me return now to the indigenous public intellectuals with whom I have been working, whose agendas and methodologies have arisen within this dynamic context. For them, research involves more than the collection and analysis of information; it is a process of intercultural dialogue and of appropriation of conceptual tools from the dominant society, characterized by a methodology centered on translation and the creation of linguistically based classificatory models for analyzing sociological reality. Film critic Rey Chow suggests that translation is more than a unidirectional movement from an original language to a less authentic one, but is instead a process through which linguistic priorities become confused. Although the original text is in one language, the translation is written in the *native* language of the translator. In this sense, " 'The native' is the 'original' point of reference" (Chow 1995, 189). In other words, in Chow's mind, translation might be better understood as a bidirectional movement *between* or *across* languages (183; see Liu 1995). Following Walter Benjamin (1968, in Chow 1995, 186), Chow proposes that translation involves the act of supplementing an "original," thus "liberating" it from its original limitations.

This is precisely the strategy the Nasa translators of the constitution sought, and which informs subsequent indigenous research methodologies. My first encounter with this approach came in a workshop I facilitated with forty-odd bilingual teachers studying in a university program in community pedagogy organized by CRIC. In the seminar, theoretical concepts that I presented to the students were interpreted and reconceptualized through their translation into Nasa Yuwe, thus altering their meaning; my description in the first chapter of a Nasa exegesis of double consciousness came out of that event. Similarly, at a meeting of cultural planners to discuss CRIC's university curriculum, various Western concepts, such as "interdisciplinarity" (*integralidad*), "life project" (*proyecto de vida*), "interculturalism," and "cosmovision," were translated into and reinterpreted from the vantage point of Nasa Yuwe. Translation is an integral component of the methodology of CRIC's bilingual education team.

A brief example is in order to show how this strategy affords a vehicle for appropriating and transforming external ideas. In the Nasa translation of the constitution, neologisms are back-translated into Spanish in a glossary. The back-translation of "culture" is "[la] forma de comportamiento que resulta de la permanencia en relación armónica con la naturaleza," or "the form of behavior resulting in a permanently harmonic relationship with nature" (Abelardo Ramos and Cabildo Indígena de Mosoco 1993, 116). The Nasa term is *wêtx ûskiwe'nxi*. *Wêtx* signifies "harmony"; *ûs* translates as "permanence"; *kiwe* is "territory"; the suffix *nxi* links these terms into a cause-effect relationship. Harmony is understood here as the interpenetration of past, present, and future, which activists identify as an essential feature of Nasa cosmic thought as well as a goal toward which political and spiritual authorities aspire, carefully regulated through shamanic ritual and corporal punishment. Nasa leader Jesús Enrique Piñacué (1997, 32–33) speaks of it as a distinct system of causation, within which events do not "cause" other events to occur, but coexist within a constellation of experiences that cannot be ordered chronologically because they are distributed in space, not in time, so that only shamans can determine their logic.

This reading of "culture" through Nasa Yuwe draws on anthropological discourse, inasmuch as it describes Nasa culture as a coherent and discrete whole. Nevertheless, the way it is employed by activists is by no means static or bounded, as are anthropological realist notions of culture. Nasa intellectuals' concept of harmony draws on models of space and time formulated by indigenous linguists who argue that in Nasa Yuwe, the past is located in front of the speaker, making it infinitely malleable (Yule 1995). Much like Luis Guillermo Vasco's insistence on the importance of concept-things in Guambiano thought, the Nasa reinterpretation of culture is grounded in the material world, particularly in the experience of territory. Territory is made "permanent" by political action, which realigns peoples' historic relationship to the land by returning sovereignty to them, thus restoring harmony where it had ceased to exist. In contrast to realist anthropology, this is a very dynamic notion of culture, underlining the agency of culture bearers and their capacity to transform the conditions under which they live.

Almost two decades ago, Talal Asad laid out a case for understanding ethnography as a kind of translation "addressed to a very specific audience, which is waiting to read *about* another mode of life and to manipulate the text it reads according to established rules, not to learn to live a new mode of life" (1986, 159). Thus, ethnography is "governed by institutionally defined power relations between the languages/modes of life concerned" (157). Translation is also crucial to the indigenous project. However, when the Nasa engage in cultural translation, they do so to "learn to live a new mode of life," appropriating external concepts into their own linguistic and political matrix. In other words, their brand of translation is concerned with harnessing cultural potentialities, as opposed to textualizing cultural difference.[7]

Nasa translation strategies also involve the generation of typologies that reappropriate Western classifications of knowledge through translation into Nasa Yuwe. After the 1994 avalanche that destroyed numerous communities in Tierradentro, the Nasa heartland in northeastern Cauca, a group of leaders from the indigenous community of Pitayó organized the Escuela del Pensamiento Nasa (1997; School of Nasa Thought), a discussion group that hoped to harness knowledge articulated in the Nasa language in order to forge the unity needed to present a strong Nasa response to the disaster. The school was organized by, among others, Adonías Perdomo, a member of our team, who served on several occasions as a cabildo member in Pitayó and who recently graduated from the Universidad del Cauca with an ethnoeducation degree. The school's founders conceptualized their plan as a vehicle for Pitayó's participation in regional cultural projects, despite the resguardo's nonaligned stance toward the various indigenous organizations operating in the region. Although Pitayó has always maintained some distance from CRIC, its goal of revitalizing traditional Nasa thought by imbuing it with insights gained from contemporary identity politics is certainly in keeping with the discourse of the regional organization. The school's activities comprise collective discussions concerning basic problems of Nasa politics, such as forms of government and community authority, socioeconomic development, and the challenges of indigenous higher education (19).

To gain insight into contemporary problems, the members of the school constructed classifications of knowledge that build on an appreciation of the Nasa language, grouping areas of knowledge within three broad classes: *kwe'sx fi'zenxi* (our daily life), which includes history, language, education, diversity, science, and cosmovision; *kwe'sx peku'jni* (our surroundings), including territory, politics, and economics; and *kwe'sx ûus dxi'j* (our breath), concerning epistemology, sociocultural relations, religiosity, and sentiment (Escuela del Pensamiento Nasa 1996, 6–7; Rappaport 1998a). This profoundly spiritual approach to the construction of Nasa philosophy represents an attempt at engaging endogenous knowledge in dialogue with exogenous thought, given that the classification is based on a regrouping of areas of academic research in overarching and overlapping Nasa metaphors, thus defamiliarizing their original referents and opening their meanings to holistic internal spheres of reflection. At the same time, the school's categories delineate groups of political priorities that are generally articulated in Spanish and are common across the various ethnic groups that make up the indigenous movement in Cauca. Kwe'sx fi'zenxi, then, would correspond to the activities of education committees that study indigenous culture and create new ways of reflecting on it in educational settings; kwe'sx peku'jni, the construction of political and territorial autonomy, is generally the province of the political leadership; and kwe'sx ûus dxi'j refers to the search for epistemological vehicles, most appropriately accomplished in collaboration with shamans. This suggests that we would do well to expand our understanding of how Nasa intellectuals theorize so that we focus not only on specifically Nasa cultural forms, but on the diversity of intellectuals involved in this project and on their political practice as well.

Such epistemological exercises, executed through the process of translation, are central to the research strategies of the Nasa members of our team, whose written work articulates linguistically inspired classifications that harness the political sentiments of native activists at the same time that they foster an intercultural exchange of knowledge. For example, Adonías (Perdomo Dizú 1999) analyzes Nasa terms deriving from customary law to argue that the Nasa legal system founded on the restoration of harmony to the community and the cosmos, is incommensurable with the Colombian legal system, which is based on punishment and retribution in a secular world, an issue I return to in the final chapter. Such research is highly introspective, in the sense that Adonías spends a great deal of his time reflecting on what such classifications mean to him as a speaker of Nasa Yuwe. Let me turn to how introspection and the creation of linguistically based analytical frameworks lead indigenous intellectuals to validate their knowledge and to disseminate it in vastly different ways than we do.

Working with the Outside

Instead of citing academics in their work, which they do quite sparingly, my Nasa colleagues prefer to cite traditional authorities, shamans, or elders, thus validating their knowledge and entering into dialogue with them, as Adonías suggests:

> How can we validate internal knowledge? The problem of validating knowledge from inside is [that it is] always done by those outside. I joined this team in order to blaze a trail for others and to show that an insider can value the knowledge that is found inside, but thanks to the support of others, who are not necessarily insiders, because it is outsiders who have been the most involved in studying the "inside." A confrontation arises between the way someone from the inside views the inside, accompanied by someone accustomed to studying it from the outside, and in the process, a credible document can be produced. That was and continues to be my obsession: How can an insider reflect and transform that reflection into a product that can help us to continue to survive?[8]

Adonías routinely presents his papers to Pitayó's cabildo before circulating them; in fact, the cabildo provides him with his research questions. Susana has sought criticisms of her analyses from elderly Nasa women and from CRIC's bilingual education program.

But this is more than simply a method of citing sources and evaluating analytical rigor. Adonías emphasizes that endogenous knowledge is grasped with difficulty by external researchers, not because we cannot comprehend it, but because we do not recognize the locus of its legitimacy in the legacy of the elders. It is not that we find it conceptually incommensurable; we do not evaluate its veracity in the same way, and hence, we appropriate it differently. He asks of this internal knowledge base: "How can we appropriate it? Can we grasp it as objective? Or is it simply a type of knowledge? Or do we judge it to be subjective?" In other words, far from accepting ethnographic knowledge as a dialogical process in which local knowledge is ultimately enveloped by academic discourse, which is what external ethnographers do, Adonías problematizes the very hierarchy on which ethnography is based, questioning whether it is indeed possible to privilege exogenous over endogenous interpretive forms.

This does not mean, however, that external analysts are excluded from the research process. As Adonías observes: "I believe that that . . . thing that is the word 'agenda' is clearly marked by the global context [we] live in [our] territory. . . . On the other hand, when one speaks of this whole task, and what differences there are between Nasas and non-Nasas, one confronts an unyielding internal struggle. Even if you say, 'I'm writing from [the vantage point of] Nasa thought,' which in great part is true, you never lose your connection to— many times you're influenced by—models from outside." Clearly, we enter into dialogue with internal scholars on the basis of the fact that our social scientific models and our writings provide some of the foundations on which they work, affording them conceptual handles for interpreting the reality in which they live.

But more important, Nasa critical appraisals of the work of external scholars serve as the ground on which their own intellectual projects can be conceived, something that Rey Chow (1995) emphasizes is a fundamental characteristic of autoethnography. She calls it "being-looked-at-ness," the recognition that the autoethnographer is simultaneously the subject and the object of his or her research:

> In the vision of the formerly ethnographized, the subjective origins of ethnography are displayed in amplified form but at the same time significantly redefined: what are "subjective" origins now include a memory of past objecthood—the experience of being looked at—which lives on in the subjective act of ethnographizing like an other, an optical unconscious. If ethnography is indeed autoethnography—ethnography of the self and the subject—then the perspective of the formerly ethnographized supplements it irrevocably with the understanding that being-looked-at-ness, rather than the act of looking, constitutes the primary event in cross-cultural representation. (180)

The best example I know in anthropology of the harnessing of "being-looked-at-ness" to the ethnographic project is African American anthropologist John Langston Gwaltney's (1993) *Drylongso*, which attempts to get at the root of what is meant by the notion of "core black culture" through a series of workshops in the black community, in which everyday folk reflect on how the academic world has perceived and described them, in the process building their own appreciation of who they are.

In the work of the Nasa team members, the external ethnographic gaze is corrected through the creation of typologies that foreground categories in Nasa Yuwe, while they implicitly critique Western categories of knowledge, as I described above. But "being-looked-at-ness" also incorporates the self-reflexive gaze of the native scholar as a critical member of his or her own society. This process is, necessarily, inspired by the values inherent in identity politics, such as notions of autonomy and interculturalism, but at the same time it provides a vehicle for criticizing how these values are operationalized in political action, something I return to later.

It is not, however, quite as simple as Chow's autoethnographic viewpoint would suggest. Nasa ethnographers, like their Colombian academic colleagues and us, are simultaneously engaged in a *philosophical* and an *analytical* project. They expressly state that their objectives are *scientific*, that their work must be evaluated as *comparable* with that of external scholars, and that their intuitive faculties are being harnessed for the construction of a *theoretical framework*, not as a substitute for rigorous scholarship. What is different about Nasa autoethnographers is the fact that they engage different translinguistic horizons than we do. That is, their merging of an incipient Nasa theoretical framework with external theories and methods engages with different interlocutors than does our external project, notwithstanding our desire for intercultural intellectual dialogue.[9] Nasa autoethnographers seek dialogue with sectors of their own society with whom we are not in conversation. They do this because their priorities are different from ours and their interpretive vehicles are, correspondingly, distinct, as the following example suggests.

In her analysis of the heterogeneity of women's roles in CRIC, Susana (Piñacué 2005) classifies Nasa women according to three categories: (1) activists in the regional organization who live in a non-Nasa world and employ a cultural discourse, striving to achieve a Nasa cosmogonic idiom; (2) community activists who move between the inside and the outside, gazing nostalgically at those whom they see as authentic carriers of Nasa culture; and (3) women on the inside, those who most openly evidence Nasa behavioral and cultural forms, particularly those who are elderly and monolingual in Nasa Yuwe. Susana's classification is driven by the Nasa titles she gives to her categories:

1. Regional activists are *nasa u'y nasan'aw u'jusa*, or "Nasa women who move about as Nasa." The suffix -*n'aw* that is attached to the second appearance of *nasa* in this phrase modifies it so that it signifies "as Nasa," while the suffix -*sa* at the end of the phrase defines as an attribute the word *u'jusa*, which means "to walk" or "to live." The literal translation of the phrase is "a Nasa woman who lives or walks as a Nasa." Susana argues that what she means to convey here is a woman who projects Nasa culture to others.

2. Women working as activists in the community are *nasa u'y nasana' wçxa*

yaatxisa, or "Nasa women who think as Nasa." The suffix -*çxa* modifies a word also used in the previous category, so that here it no longer signifies "as Nasa," but "as Nasa in a reduced sense." *Yaatxisa* means someone whose attribute is to think. According to Susana, this category of women is profoundly preoccupied with Nasa cultural roots, but is in danger of losing them through intermarriage. There is a certain political urgency in this category, which translates literally as "the Nasa woman who thinks as a Nasa, but in a restricted sense."

3. Women on the inside are *nasa u'y dxihk fxi'zesa*, or "Nasa women who live actively." Here, the act of living is not defined by the root *u'ju*, as in the first category. Instead, Susana makes a different lexical choice, opting for *fxi'ze*, a term that she also employs as a gloss for *vivencia*, or a practice of everyday life. "Life" becomes "culture" in her usage, suggesting that women on the inside are carriers of Nasa culture. Thus, this category translates literally as "the Nasa woman who lives her culture with agility."

What is interesting about this classification is how Susana distinguishes the relative distance of each category from what she takes to be authentic Nasa lifeways—that is, Nasa culture as a *vivencia*, an everyday experience, a term that appears only in the third category (*fxi'zesa*). Elderly women in communities actively live their identity, but community activists only think it; regional leaders project the vivencias encapsulated in the third category to others. What Susana has created is a relational classification, not a taxonomy. Each of the three types of women is related to the two others, with the inside woman as the foundation.[10]

Susana's classification, which hinges on the possession and transmission of cultural knowledge, indicates that, far from being an essentialist, she problematizes gender categories in significant ways that differ from our own insistence on class, "race," and ethnicity. This is because she orients her analysis to a very different purpose. The contrasts Susana draws point to the profound urgency of her research, in contrast to the less pressing tone of the writings of those of us working from the outside.[11] Susana describes the older women as having been "silenced." Her anxieties in the face of this state of affairs reflect the intensely political intent of her work, which is doubly urgent for her, given that she writes from a subject position on the Nasa frontier. She identifies with the movement of the first category, questioning their—and her—authencity and their efficacy as leaders, criticizing their silencing of older women and their wearing of Nasa culture as an emblem, not a lifeway. Susana recognizes where she stands in this classification and conceptually embraces her own positioning on the frontier in order to define what it means for her to write as a Nasa. In fact, in many of our meetings Susana expressed her desire to interpret her participation in the group as a voyage of self-discovery. Simultaneously, however, she finds it impossible to write as a Nasa insider, both because the conventions of Western-style writing effectively inhibit her self-expression and because she is unsure as to whether she is, really, an insider at all. Susana continually expresses her concerns over the gulf between Nasa intellectuals and rural community members, highlighting the incommensurability between *these* discourses, and not just between the discourses of exogenous and endogenous researchers. In this sense, she feels that it is only through repeated returns to communities that she can attain a sense of coevalness, as Johannes Fabian (1983) urged anthropologists to do.

Methodological and Conceptual Transformations

How did the self-discovery project of our Nasa colleagues impact the methodology of the non-Nasa members of our research team? Clearly, though self-discovery has always been among the aims of external ethnographers (Clifford 1986; Shostak 2000 [1981], 5), it has never taken on the same urgency in our work as it does among Nasa intellectuals. It is precisely our team's rethinking of the intellectual consequences of this difference that led us to revisit earlier anthropological debates and view them in a new light. I believe that the ways the Nasa scholars problematize cultural categories to refocus the process of overlapping identity formation in the Nasa community forced the rest of us to rethink our ethnographic toolkit. In the current intellectual climate, in which anthropologists have rejected the notion of "culture" as an essentialist construction, and hence, of "cultural group" as a delimited entity, the team's discussion of the significance of what could be termed a fluid, but still very real "cultural inside" forced us to set aside some of our own theoretical frameworks and to recognize the tangible experience by Nasa activists of an internal sphere of social exchange (Gilroy 1993). In this sense, our group discussions forced me to go beyond the usual apology made by students of indigenous activism—that such a position is an example of "strategic essentialism." The inside, our group discussion highlighted, is not a bounded social group but a utopian project for creating necessarily hybrid cultural forms that can fortify the political aspirations of the indigenous constituency.

At the same time, the notion of a culturally authentic inside is a projection of the concerns of organic intellectuals such as Adonías and Susana, who note a growing gulf between the native leadership and the community rank and file, and who seek to bridge it by steeping themselves in Nasa culture, by becoming *nasnasa* (very Nasa); the repetition provides emphasis and, I suspect, authenticity. Their apprehensions are frequently expressed in a discourse that simultaneously invokes the authenticity of common folk in contrast to the leadership and prescribes culturalist solutions to counteract the centrifugal pressures that the dominant Colombian society imposes on localities. Thus, their notions of authenticity are quite different from our own. In the world of art collecting and ethnographic classification, James Clifford warns us that "authenticity is produced by removing objects and customs from their current historical situation—a present-becoming-future" (1988, 228). For indigenous activists, in contrast, authenticity resides in the creation of political projects, a reinsertion (as opposed to a removal) of objects and customs into everyday life. Such concerns are fundamental to the work of Susana and Adonías. In my own case, they have led me to explore the metaphors and meanings that arise at the interstices of the inside and the outside, problematizing my notion of inside by persuading me to study the role of nonnative collaborators as interlocutors in CRIC's ethnic project and forcing me to question my initial identification of the indigenous culturalist discourse as essentialist, analyzing it instead as a pluralist political project. David Gow (2003), who comes from an intellectual tradition similar to my own, was similarly led to reconsider his constructivist critique of development to comprehend what alternative development means when it originates in the inside of an intercultural and globalized relationship, such as is always the case in development planning.

The group discussions also obliged me to transform my ethnographic practice by reorienting my research priorities at the urging of the Nasa members of the team, who felt that by focusing on the problematics of inside and outside I would help to open a space of intervention for them in which they could reflect on the dilemma of the positioning of internal intellectuals. In part, this transformation included my own reorientation to the field situation as a space in which I could collaborate as a researcher. As I adopted this role, I found myself obliged to reflect on the risks I would have to begin to assume, risks with which internal intellectuals have always had to contend.

Taking Risks

The autoethnographic project interjects a critique of the autoethnographer's own society (Chow 1995, 180), as Susana demonstrates in her endeavor to disclose the gendered tensions that cut through the movement to inhibit the full participation of indigenous women in the construction of a truly pluralist project. The Nasas in our group perceive their participation on the team as a platform from which they can intervene critically in local communities, something they accomplish through workshops, assemblies, and presentations of their work to traditional authorities and women's organizations. CRIC activists value critical thinking as a hallmark of their approach to cultural planning, calling it by the somewhat awkward Spanish neologism *criticidad* ("criticalness"). Adonías's (Perdomo 1999, 2003) essays delve into the crisis of authority of Nasa communities, where the appearance of a new schooled generation of leadership has facilitated communication with the dominant society and the erection of a semiautonomous local administration within the limitations set by the state, but only at the cost of distancing these leaders from traditional forms of exercising authority and from those elders who led the communities in the early days of the movement. Consequently, the autonomy of Nasa political practice, particularly as regards the use of customary law and the introduction of a justice system based on notions of harmony instead of punishment, becomes, in Adonías's eyes, impossible. This is a direct criticism of the current political leadership.

Such statements demand that the internal researcher risk profound criticism on the part of his or her community or organization. Given the neocolonial environment in which we live, Nasa scholars are exposed to greater internal critique than are external researchers. Moreover, as the internal researcher gains external recognition, his or her position in the community becomes even more problematic: "It's that, in [our] culture there is something you need to take into account, and it's the form by which we address ourselves. For example, one who knows something does not say, 'I know,' but waits for others to say you know it. That's how you must deal with it. I cannot come as 'the intellectual,' but if the community . . . shows that I am an intellectual, then I am one." Here, Adonías underlines the problematic position of the indigenous intellectual, who must gain community recognition in order to intervene in local affairs. However, it is through taking the risk of intervention that the political work of the indigenous movement is accomplished. Both Adonías and Susana emphasize that one cannot reflect on one's own culture without taking risks, given that it is out of such uncertainties that a dialogue on the inside is founded. In the words of Susana: "The urgency I see . . . is an urgency to learn to articulate myself, in order to take more and more professional risks. My urgency is to live and learn to live and learn to approach people on cultural issues, especially identity, directly within the community." However, such risks place internal researchers in danger of being ostracized by their communities of origin or by their organizations, leaving them unmoored in an alien world.[12] At the same time, native ethnographers who engage in scientific analysis, as Adonías and Susana do, risk being marginalized by external scholars, particularly in the provincial settings in which they move, given that many local academics are profoundly threatened by the indigenous scholarly project and, when they cannot exclude autoethnographers on the basis of a lack of rigor, will do so through an appeal to their lack of "authenticity."

The stakes are clearly not as high for those of us on the team who are not Nasa, given that our links to native communities are not constitutive of our most intimate identities; unlike Adonías or Susana, if David or I were rejected by CRIC or by some of the Nasa communities with whom we have worked, we would be wounded, angry, nostalgic, but not cut off from that which most clearly defines us as a social actor.[13] It is more problematic for national scholars, whose relationships with the indigenous movement are not buffered by distance but are, in contrast, fortified by continuous collaboration (Alcida Ramos 1990). Nevertheless, they, too, can survive as social and cultural actors outside of the indigenous community. Neither national scholars nor foreign researchers are forced to live the daily consequences of their research in quite the same way as do insiders (Smith 1999, 137). We have, moreover, a more secure perch from which to engage in critical analysis. While our choice of conducting collaborative research might be looked on as eccentric, inconsequential, or marginal to theoretical debates, the nature of academic intellectual dialogue grants us a certain license to engage in such pursuits without incurring the consequences that Nasa intellectuals experience in their own spheres of interaction. Ironically, moreover, the intellectual risks that we take do not necessarily compromise our relations with the indigenous movement, as do the projects of indigenous intellectuals. I have found that by achieving a certain degree of transparency in my analyses, some of my assertions may be debated by Nasa activists, but they will not resort to the ad hominem critiques that internal researchers invariably suffer (at least, not in my presence). Moreover, public criticism of our work (particularly that of foreign researchers) is muted, not only in the broader movement but at times on the research team itself, where critiques of external members have taken place only in indirect exchanges. This suggests that we still have a ways to go in forging entirely horizontal relations between Nasa and external researchers.

Notwithstanding the differences between the risks taken by Nasa and non-

Nasa scholars, as team member Tulio Rojas expressed, "We are being observed by the Nasa people." That is, we share with autoethnographers a sensation of being-looked-at-ness that goes beyond the academic world to encompass the research space, impacting profoundly on our intellectual practice in the sense that we not only are subject to Nasa scrutiny, but become increasingly obliged to engage with the analytical forms shared by indigenous activists and colaboradores. In the context of traditional ethnographic research, Jean-Paul Dumont (1992) underscores the fertile nature of the intersubjective relationship between the researcher and those she or he studies. For Dumont, ethnography is more than a simple process of collecting data; it is a progressive engagement between the subjectivities of the researcher and the subject, opening a space in which it becomes possible to learn about the culture of the other. But in a collaborative enterprise of the sort in which we are engaged, the role of intersubjectivity is considerably more central than in traditional research, because it impinges on exegetical discussion as well as everyday conversation. I will provide an example.

In 2000 we decided to share our work with community leaders, bilingual teachers, indigenous activists, and nonnative collaborators. I presented an analysis of the dilemmas of Nasa intellectuals, who, like Janus, look simultaneously toward the inside and the outside in an attempt to engage concepts I had encountered in organizational venues.[14] Conversations after my intervention indicated that various activists did not accept being labeled as "intellectuals" because of the elitist connotations that the marker carried for them. Once I opened this space through my analysis, I was forced to enter into a dialogue in which I, like my interlocutors, was obliged to bare my feelings and listen more closely. I had to explain my own political goal of seeking recognition of internal knowledge, not only of shamans—who, for my utopian and nostalgic interlocutors, were the only true Nasa intellectuals—but also for other "pathbreakers" (to employ a term used by Adonías) in indigenous communities, such as traditional political authorities, bilingual teachers, and CRIC activists, among others. Those who had criticized my analysis recognized the importance of the issue but also conveyed to me the sense that I had touched a sensitive nerve, insofar as I had identified one of their most painful weaknesses. I cannot say that we have come to an agreement on the designation to be applied to internal thinkers, although the initial encounter opened a space for a more long-term dialogue characterized by the Nasa discursive form of joking, which has permitted us to deepen our relationship in a less precautionary mode. On the other hand, these same interlocutors were very much engaged by my analysis of inside and outside, leading to countless discussions that ranged from debates about the impact of missionaries in Nasa communities, to interpretations of the meaning of essentialism. Clearly, by appropriating their own analytical terminology and making it my own, I had opened a critical space for further dialogue.

Nasas and Academics, Colombians and Gringos

It is a truism that knowledge is constructed in relation to a specific institutional or ideological context. Nevertheless, in the team's research process the recognition of the multiple trajectories and connections on which our dialogue rests has been a constant thread in our conversation. Indeed, ethnic identity is produced across time in relation to the dominant society (Nelson 1999; Warren 1998a) and its dialogue with international ethnic organizations (Brysk 2000); similarly, the construction of majority identity also develops in relation to minority identities (Chandler 2000). Our interethnic research team provided an arena in which we could reflect on the heterogeneity of our own identities. More specifically, the complex nature of the indigenous movement, with its multiple factions, organizational divides, and alliances, impinged repeatedly on our discussions of the location of indigenous researchers as internal or external actors and their relationship to the equally ambiguous character of colaboradores. Over time, the indigenous movement has developed a pluralist political project out of both pragmatic necessity and the intersection of their utopias with those of other activists. In recognition of the plural nature of the movement, the team was drawn to reflect on the identity of colaboradores in relation to the process of indigenous identity formation, thus problematizing once again the categories of insider and outsider, on the one hand, and of national and foreign, on the other.

Although we initially created the research team to open a dialogue across international, national, and indigenous subject positions, we came to learn that within the team, lines were drawn in the course of our research practice. Ultimately, a deep polarization emerged between two conceptually distinct camps: anthropologists versus Nasa. Here, one of the two opposing poles is characterized by its institutional affiliation and its disciplinary discourse; the other is marked by its ethnicity, suggesting that we are not dealing with polar opposites, but with radically different forms of affiliation that have been historically intertwined in a hierarchical relationship. In Bolivia and in Guatemala, class differentiation in the indigenous population, coupled with a growing professionalization among urban native sectors, has produced a layer of indigenous intellectuals attached to universities and government institutions, their legitimacy ensured by postgraduate study (Grandin 2000; Ticona 2000; Warren 1998a). In Cauca, in contrast, the professional training of indigenous people is relatively recent, and university-educated community members normally affiliate themselves with projects based in indigenous organizations and not in external institutions, leading them to identify themselves politically and ethnically instead of professionally.

Furthermore, many indigenous intellectuals feel excluded from Colombian institutions of higher education; it is more probable that they will be invited to a professional panel in the United States or Europe than in Colombia. Long-standing rivalries between the cultural planning teams of indigenous organizations and the Universidad del Cauca have led to the distancing of most local academics from indigenous organizations. Some of the discord owes to the fundamentally elitist function of a provincial university operating in a conflictive multiethnic milieu, an issue that is only now being resolved with the incorporation of CRIC's community pedagogy program within the university's ethnoeducation concentration. Tensions between provincial academia and indigenous organizations have also led to a difficult process of integration of indigenous students into university programs. However, problems between university faculty and the movement are not entirely related to such issues. Many of Popayán's social scientists were at one time affiliated with CRIC and, like many other colaboradores, came into conflict with its indigenous leadership; some of these individuals have sought to continue working with indigenous communities through nongovernmental organizations instead of the regional indigenous groups. As a result of these different processes, the Nasa members of the research team continually took refuge in the collaborative team as a space that was different from that of the university, where they felt excluded and infantilized and where they saw little possibility of an opening to culturally hybrid modes of thinking.

The distinction between academics and Nasas could have played a destructive role in the team, if not for the deep affective relations and mutual respect that had developed over the first year of research. Perhaps most important, the Nasa members of our team cast academic ways of thinking in disciplinary cubbyholes as antithetical to the broader activist project of indigenous intellectuals. Nevertheless, they emphasized that many of the shortcomings of academics are equally at issue in the indigenous movement, particularly in the relationship between indigenous activists and colaboradores, who come to indigenous organizations with a more disciplinary or bureaucratic perspective. Thus, although Adonías and Susana did draw a distinction within the team between insiders and outsiders, they stressed that such tensions and ambiguities were as internal to the movement as they are in other circles. In the last instance, however, we consistently returned in our conversations to the distinction between academics, whose identity is disciplinary, and Nasa, whose belonging is ethnic. This led to the creation of a Nasa subgroup, where Adonías and Susana exchanged their ideas and writings in more familiar surroundings before presenting them to the team as a whole, thus creating a distinction between the "we" of the team and the "internal we" of the Nasa team members.

But there was also a distinction drawn between a we and an internal we among the academics, given that, on the one hand, the two international members were a married couple, and on the other, the Colombian academics frequently felt at odds with what they perceived as an alliance between the Nasas and the "gringos," who generally agreed on most matters and enjoyed close personal friendships. The category of "academic" was, therefore, by no means monolithic, but continually negotiated. The conflicts between nationals and foreigners that developed on the team owed in part to the fact that one of the Colombian academics, Myriam Amparo Espinosa, whose activist experience is as long as her curriculum vitae, perceived her own identity on the team as ambiguous. As a result, she attempted to define her position by drawing a contrast between the foreigners and herself, particularly when it came to defining the risks each of us took. As a former colaboradora, she was uncomfortable with being classed with the foreign professionals as opposed to being accepted as a member of the movement; even on the team she experienced the eternal predicament of the colaborador. Tulio Rojas, on the other hand, does not see himself as a colaborador, although he has worked for years with the movement; perhaps this owes to his solidario past, but he also chooses to think of his role in the movement as that of an academic specialist in Nasa Yuwe, making him, as he told me, an "interlocutor" as opposed to a full-time colaborador engaged in a broad range of activities in the organization. However, because Tulio defined himself from an exclusively academic subject position, he also was at odds with Nasa assertions of their privileged position as interpreters of Nasa culture, something I return to below.

In short, major transformations in Colombian anthropology became an arena of contention on our team. The increasing professionalization of anthropologists in Colombia has led to a disciplinary abandonment of activism in favor of applied work as "experts" or theoretical work in the university, and from the point of view of indigenous activists, they have become increasingly distanced from anthropologists, who are no longer viewed as compañeros but, cynically, as *doctores*. This presented a critical juncture for Myriam Amparo, who was ensconced in the university but yearned for the camaraderie she felt in the movement. However, the Nasa team members, who were full-time activists and saw all of the academics through that lens, had come to the team as researchers, on a par intellectually with the professionals, not as compañeros.

Tulio, on the other hand, came out of the much younger field of ethnolinguistics.[15] Ethnolinguistics appeared in Colombia in the 1980s in the guise of an innovative M.A. program at the Universidad de los Andes in Bogotá with the stated objective of training Colombian linguists to replace the missionary linguists of the Summer Institute of Linguistics. The program drew on international support to provide scholarships to indigenous students, among them, Abelardo Ramos, Marcos Yule, and Luis Carlos Ulcué, thus creating a layer of native professionals and, ultimately, spawning regionally based ethnolinguistics programs, such as the one Susana attended at the Universidad del Cauca. It seems to me that Tulio's experience at Los Andes, where indigenous students were viewed as colleagues who regularly participated in vigorous scholarly debate with their nonnative peers, led him to engage the Nasa members of our team in the same way. This, however, wounded their sensibilities as activists.

The predicaments encountered by Myriam Amparo and Tulio were not the product of a refusal on their part to engage Nasa researchers. Like David and me, they were highly enthusiastic about the project and committed to it. What made them different from us was the proximity of their activist and their academic worlds, which intermingled in a way that our Nasa colleagues would not accept. The distance we enjoyed as foreigners, who could come and go without living the consequences of our research arrangements in our daily lives, was what simplified our relationships with Adonías and Susana. Furthermore, while both the foreigners and the Nasas operated from a firm conceptual positioning marked by our appeals to distinct bodies of theory, I think that the Colombian academics could not as easily position themselves along a similar continuum because their anthropological practice had always involved the appropriation of multiple bodies of theory, both academic and practical, domestic and foreign. The construction of a Nasa internal we on the team propelled us to reflect on the nature of what a "Nasacentric" ethnography might look like. The dynamics of the national-international debate never resulted in a similar kind of discussion, notwithstanding the fact that the issue was brought up repeatedly at team meetings. I have no explanation for this, beyond the speculation that it is only recently that Colombian anthropologists have begun to reflect on what makes their anthropology Colombian as they enter into dialogue with other Latin American colleagues (Jimeno 2000; Tocancipá 2000; M. Zambrano 1996), making the issue still too incipient to be aired in a context such as our team. Perhaps, moreover, the very hybridity of Colombian anthropology, which draws as much on an international corpus of theory as it has been nourished by a close activist relationship with communities, made it difficult for Myriam Amparo and Tulio to define their relationships within the team.

Doing Research from a Nasa Subject Position, Speaking as "Bi"

One of the major bones of contention in team discussions was whether or not Nasas could lay claim to a privileged vision of Nasa culture—a direct attack on anthropologists, but a necessary stance for nonprofessional native scholars. To do research as an academic, suggests Adonías, is to engage in a project of discovery, whereas to conduct research as a Nasa is to embark on a more intuitive project of self-discovery. Adonías feels that the task of the internal researcher demands a series of sentiments and experiences that the mimesis of external ethnographers can never achieve, notwithstanding the arguments of some anthropologists (Stoller 1997) or the rigor and usefulness of our research. The possibility of conducting deeply intuitive interpretation, which is precisely what the Nasa translation methodology achieves, allows the Nasa researcher to move back and forth between inside and outside, in the sense that he or she can couple emotional experience and linguistic sentiment with the analysis of empirical data and with an awareness of how indigenous experience has been represented in the past by outsiders.

Adonías outlined for us the risks implicit in this endeavor, emphasizing that the authority that stems from autoethnography not only involves the potential for producing a more authentic account, but that its very veracity makes it more gripping, more persuasive, and, hence, infinitely more hazardous because, in his words, "That certainty can mean life or death for the process." What Adonías is suggesting is not that external researchers are incapable of studying the Nasa, but that the insertion of native researchers into social movements endows their work with a force that our more distanced reflections could never achieve. Moreover, only the Nasa can theorize from a Nasa subject position, producing interpretations that, while they complement the work of non-Nasas, also hold the possibility of transcending our observations; although we can appropriate such theories, we cannot produce them. Such a theoretical stance is still incipient, however, and will develop as Nasa scholars succeed in studying their own epistemology, based largely on linguistic research (Nieves and Ramos 1992; Yule 1995) and co-investigations with shamans (Sisco n.d.). Such an enterprise necessitates, moreover, a sustained exegetic dialogue between internal and external observers. From this standpoint, the role of the external researcher is to listen to that which the academic world has refused to accept as comparable to our own intellectual production. Of course, the basis for such a role lies in the experience and knowledge that we would potentially bring to such a dialogue and the common ground that we can both stand on if we are engaged in a collaborative project.

But to what extent are we capable of heeding the exhortations of our Nasa colleagues? According to the African American sociologist W. E. B. Du Bois (1989 [1903]), African Americans, like other peoples of color, experience a sensation of twoness. Although they feel themselves to be simultaneously African Americans and North Americans, the second identity is denied them by racism. As a result, they hold the possibility of acquiring a "second sight" that, under certain conditions, would permit a privileged view of reality. Such an insight is very much in keeping with Chow's being-looked-at-ness, given that it constitutes a highly relational form of knowing. Keeping in mind that in Colombia, race is not bipolar in character and that Nasa intellectuals prefer to substitute notions of culture for Du Bois's insistence on race and racial discrimination, the metaphor of doubling that is articulated by Nasa activists is cultural in nature. For Adonías, indigenous researchers enjoy a kind of second sight based on the cultural experience that he calls "sentiment," something I come back to later in this book. To Susana's mind, Nasa intellectuals exhibit not only a double consciousness in the sense of a double sense of belonging, but a kind of diglossia (Bakhtin 1981 [1975]) that leads them to accept that they can communicate with us from only one of the two worldviews they inhabit, that of the dominant society:

> It's "bi" which is . . . the construct that is closest, without violating the essence: bilingualism, biculturalism. Because finally it seems [the anthropologists] have understood that this is how we, the native people, function, in a "bi" mode. And that term, bilingualism, or biculturalism, wasn't gratuitous: it was a chal-

lenging task for the students of humanity, until they finally understood that, "Listen, those pricks are bi." And that's what they show themselves to be: they live "bi" and they wake up "bi," they sleep "bi" and they build or invent this meaning to capture a sense of what's out there. That's what makes it so difficult for us to converse with you, to share what we think. Because it's obvious: you have a code for research, you have a code for exposition, you have a code for reflection, you have a code for situating your analysis, you have a precise code for evaluation, and so do we. Only, we cannot . . . converse on this issue. Our only alternative, conducted with your permission, is that you accept us as "bi." From the vantage point of "bi" we can converse [with you].

The uncomfortable doubling that Susana sees as characterizing our inter-cultural exchange is more than a linguistic issue involving competence in Nasa Yuwe. It is a position deployed to assert authenticity and to distance indigenous intellectuals from academics and colaboradores, with the aim of strengthening the indigenous discourse. It is, furthermore, an epistemological barrier that arises not exclusively from cultural difference, but also from the power that academic disciplines have traditionally wielded over the Nasa and the control over what constitutes acceptable research that the university continues to enjoy. In other words, by highlighting the "bi" mode, Susana is emphasizing that academic methods, forms of analysis, and epistemologies have tradi-tionally taken precedence over Nasa forms in intercultural dialogue.

Gayatri Spivak's (1988) assertion that the subaltern cannot speak as a sub-altern but only in the dominant discourse is pertinent here. As a frontier Nasa, an intellectual who straddles both worlds, Susana and her colleagues can speak only in the dominant idiom. As they move between the Nasa sphere of influ-ence and Colombian social space, people like Susana are ambivalent about their identities. A Nasa who projects but does not live her Nasaness, what Susana is after is precisely a solid ground on which to stand, where she can develop her own identity as an urban activist, an indigenous woman, and a Nasa intellectual. Part of what this task involves is precisely achieving a theo-retical discourse in which Nasa intellectuals can engage their own code for research, for exposition, for reflection, for situating their analysis, and for evaluation (to build on Susana's own words). It is through theorizing that they will be capable of moving beyond the "bi" mode to assert their analytical capabilities on their own terms as Nasa intellectuals. For now, however, such a theoretical discourse is only nascent, and they can speak to us only in our idiom. But notwithstanding Susana's crushing intervention, some degree of exchange does take place, even if challenges exist to more productive forms of intercultural communication. In fact, the possibility of dialogue lies at the heart of the intercultural philosophy that CRIC and its activists espouse. As I illustrate in the following chapters, the nature of this dialogue is conditioned by the scenarios in which it takes place, the kinds of discourses through which it is expressed, and the character of the interlocutors.

Susana's statement forces me to reflect on the initial objective of our team, back when we began to conceptualize our project in 1998. At that time, we thought that our goal would be the fusion of our agendas and our methodologies. This result was impossible, due to the different discourses we employed and the weight of our various subject positions. But we also have come to realize that such a fusion would have spelled an end to our exchange, forcing us back into the straitjacket of the academics speaking for the ethnographic subject. What we have learned is that our conversation does not require an abandonment of our individual objectives and methodologies, but their subordination to an equal exchange. Note that unlike Luis Guillermo Vasco, I do not think that this dialogue requires our subordination to Nasa thinkers, but our acceptance of them as serious interlocutors. Such a conversation presupposes that all of us, not just the Nasa team members, experience the state of being-looked-at-ness, exposing all of us to the scrutiny of our counterparts and turning all of us, to some degree, into autoethnographers. That is, as the Nasa team members, other Nasa activists, and community members react to and evaluate our research, we cannot but conduct a self-conscious ethnography that takes a critical view toward the constructs produced about the Nasa in both the external academic world and within indigenous organizations.

CHAPTER 4

Interculturalism and *Lo Propio*

CRIC's Teachers as Local Intellectuals

Frontier Nasa like Susana Piñacué and Adonías Perdomo, colaboradores like Graciela Bolaños and Henry Caballero, and even academic interlocutors like Tulio Rojas and myself are intertwined agents who contribute to differing degrees, in varying capacities, and from distinct positionings to the construction of Nasa cultural discourse. We are not, however, the only participants in the broad-ranging process out of which a Nasa intelligentsia has emerged. Our exchanges unfold largely at the regional level, running parallel to and in dialogue with the work of locally based activists. Susana, in her research on Nasa women, has called these community-based cultural workers "Nasas who think as Nasa," to be distinguished from regional activists like herself, who "move about as Nasa," and from the communities they serve, whom she refers to as "Nasas who live actively [as Nasa]." Susana was concerned with an array of local players, including female cabildo authorities, teachers, and members of the women's committees that have sprung up in the past fifteen years across indigenous Cauca. However, by far the majority of local intellectuals are educators affiliated with community schools. Many of them received training in CRIC programs. Their salaries are paid through agreements negotiated by indigenous organizations with the Colombian state in the wake of the mass mobilizations over the past five years that demanded the government provide basic social services to native communities.

Local activists are positioned quite differently from the frontier Nasa of the regional office. For one, their daily lives unfold within the indigenous community, meaning that if they are bilingual, their everyday conversations are largely in Nasa Yuwe; if they are monolingual Spanish speakers, they interact largely with people who have negligible contact with literate communication. Many of them are only somewhat familiar with the technical discourses employed by regional activists and, therefore, tend to privilege political over pedagogical ways of framing their objectives, leading to distinct emphases in practice. Second, they work under the direct supervision of cabildos and thê' walas and so are more subject to local priorities than are activists from the regional office. I frequently heard regional cultural workers make this distinction between themselves and community activists, saying of themselves, "We don't have the endorsement of a cabildo" ("No tenemos el aval de un cabildo"). Regional activists come into contact with local authorities at assemblies and regional meetings, but their lack of formal attachment to resguardos leads them to follow regional, as opposed to local, directives. Teachers, in contrast, follow the lead of their cabildos, whose priorities may diverge not only from regional agendas, but frequently also from those of neighboring resguardos. Third, the interactions of local intellectuals with the regional office and with intellectuals from the dominant society are only sporadic and are frequently organized around the agendas and schedules of the outsiders, creating a hierarchical relationship between regional office and the grassroots. Finally, community-based educators are closer to what people like Susana call the "inside," and they consciously deploy this identity in opposition to regional cultural workers.

As a result of their positioning, many of the policies, methodologies, and conceptual approaches that issue from the regional level are analyzed and recontextualized by local intellectuals. The tensions generated between regional priorities and local instrumentalizations of them do not, however, mean that the two operate in a polarized relationship, nor that the Popayán office has failed to impose its worldview on localities. To the contrary, regional priorities are built on the basis of consultation with localities in assemblies, congresses, and other meetings, and local practices based on these policies are devised by community activists in intimate contact with the regional level, whether through positions on CRIC's executive committee, previous experience in regional programs, or training provided by regional activists. In other words, these tensions are fruitful. The differences between regional and local visions of cultural policy that I explore in this chapter center on the tensions between intercultural approaches to education espoused by regional intellectuals and a local focus on Nasa cultural agency. Although they diverge in several significant respects, they are best understood as differences in em-

phasis, as parallel but interlocking conceptualizations of a communally created agenda.

Local Intellectuals

My first prolonged contact with CRIC's bilingual teachers was in the bilingual
education program's community pedagogy project, a university course of
study created and administered by the organization, which combines long-
distance learning and local research projects with biannual classroom seminars in which students come together to reflect on readings they have done at
home and to weave together technical skills and theoretical approaches with
their studies of the local realities that surround them. Ensconced in the mountains of Caldono, where the program was holding a month of workshops, I
met a diverse range of local intellectuals. Benilda Tróchez, a bilingual teacher
in the militant community that grew up out of the repossession of the hacienda López Adentro in northern Cauca in the early 1980s, came to Caldono
in search of a university education that would enhance her articulation of Nasa
culture with her teaching in a locality that is urgently trying to revive Nasa
Yuwe. Benilda is from Jambaló and moved to López Adentro at the invitation
of the community to serve as a bilingual teacher. Although she was not born in
López Adentro, neither were its other residents, whose community was born
out of a land occupation, making her as much a community member as they
are. Benilda is fluent in Nasa Yuwe, whereas most people in López Adentro are
not; therefore, her appointment filled a perceived gulf in the community's self-
identification as Nasa and they hoped she would help to coalesce this collection of newcomers to the region into a Nasa community.

Benilda received her previous education in CRIC's high school proficiency
program (*profesionalización*) after completing primary school and spending
years as a rural teacher in CRIC-sponsored schools. Like others who graduated
from this and similar programs, she is a sophisticated political analyst whose
academic skills, in a conventional sense, at least, do not always measure up to
her interpretive talents, a difficulty that Universidad del Cauca ethnoeducator
Cristina Simmonds told me is common to profesionalización graduates in
comparison to graduates of high schools, normal schools, or secondary-level
Catholic seminaries.[1] In other words, Benilda is unschooled in conventional
academic discourse and her language diverges from that of regional indigenous intellectuals like Susana Piñacué or Inocencio Ramos, who are either
university students or graduates. While she clearly engages the complex politi-

cal and cultural issues that are aired at the regional level, Benilda tends to reflect on them using narrative forms and vocabulary common to rural people, not the political or pedagogical jargon that sometimes characterizes the speech of regional leaders. As I discovered in other workshops where local curricular projects were aired, Benilda and her colleagues in López Adentro are inserting innovative educational ideas in their own analysis of Nasa history and epistemology.

Local teachers like Benilda are considerably more rooted in rural Nasa communities than are their regional colleagues and never voiced to me any preoccupations over whether their Nasa identity was authentic, or whether they felt they truly belonged to their communities, Susana's classification to the contrary. Benilda does not perceive herself as an outsider balanced on a frontier, although like many of the teachers associated with the indigenous movement, she is in search of an identity different from that of traditional schoolteachers, who frequently replicate hegemonic discourses (Houghton 1998, 62).

Fernando Peña, a schoolteacher in Pueblo Nuevo, has a profile in some respects comparable to Benilda's. Fernando also completed profesionalización and eloquently deploys CRIC's political discourse. A handsome man in his late twenties, he generally showed up for class in stylish clothing, a propensity he developed during his years as a laborer in Cali. But Fernando is also a thê' wala, a shaman, as were his father, his grandfather, and his great-grandfather, in a line that goes back seven generations. As a shaman, the source of Fernando's authority lies not in the act of harnessing exogenous human or social knowledge for endogenous ends or in mediating the assimilation of national discourses at the local level, but in articulating internal knowledge for a Nasa audience through the intimately sensorial process of divination. He mediates between an inside and outside distinct from that of most CRIC intellectuals, in the sense that as a *sabedor* he moves between the human world and other realms of nature that are not entirely accessible to most humans. However, Fernando is also an organic intellectual in the same sense as Benilda, because as a teacher who has passed through profesionalización, he is a researcher. Fernando has brought to bear historical and anthropological readings to create new shamanic rituals that sustain the desire of local teachers and regional planners to abandon Christianity in favor of a renewed Nasa spirituality. Thus, Fernando's activities move across multiple, intersecting, and opposing insides and outsides, as they are defined by contemporary Nasa activists.

A final group of students initially confounded me because they did not fit the mold of university students I am used to. A gray-haired veteran of the organization's early years, Roberto Chepe teaches in the CRIC school in the resguardo of La Laguna. He assumed his post with only a few years of primary school under his belt, having been selected as a teacher by his community on the basis of his leadership in local land struggles. In other words, his appointment was made according to criteria that were more activist than academic. This affords Roberto a more organic connection with his neighbors than that enjoyed by most educators. He carries a personal memory of CRIC's attempt to create alternative schools as pivots around which local organizing activities could rotate, a constant reminder of the political intentions with which these schools were founded. Thirty years of experience and CRIC's profesionalización course have not erased the discrepancy between Roberto's volubility in Nasa Yuwe and his difficulties in expressing himself in fluid Spanish. Yet, his interpretations of the realities in which he lives contain sharp and highly original insights. His written work in my seminar routinely overflowed the bounds of the questions to which he was asked to respond, incorporating personal reminiscence, visual representation, and the new ideas to which he had been introduced into far-ranging, painstakingly researched, and unusually eloquent treatises. Roberto is a fiercely dedicated investigator on a host of topics related to Nasa history, cosmology, and material culture. The results of his research, written in Nasa Yuwe, are immediately channeled back into his teaching. When I asked the students to reflect on a Bolivian Aymara community history written in comic-book form (Mamani Quispe 1988), Roberto did not respond to my essay questions, but went out into La Laguna to conduct interviews that led to an eighty-page pictorial history of his and neighboring resguardos. While Roberto is certainly an intellectual, the source of his legitimacy is, like Fernando's, not rooted in academic exigencies, and his work diverges more than does that of other teachers from the kind of intellectual production recognized by the dominant Colombian society.

Henry Giroux (1988, xxxiv), a radical pedagogical theorist, considers schoolteachers to be "transformative intellectuals" who "combine reflection and action in the interest of empowering students with the skills and knowledge needed to address injustices and to be critical actors committed to developing a world free of oppression and exploitation" through the use of innovative and participatory pedagogical techniques. Giroux's vision transcends the four walls of the schoolhouse, merging politics with teaching in a bidirectional movement, because "central to the category of transformative intellectual is the necessity of making the pedagogical more political and the political more pedagogical" (127). In this sense, he echoes Brazilian educator-activist Paulo Freire's (1993) goal of harnessing pedagogical techniques promoting reflection by members of subordinated sectors on their own oppression to the process of political organizing.[2]

The people I met in Caldono are grassroots intellectuals in the same sense, although they labor in more rudimentary conditions and are far less schooled than the teachers about whom Giroux writes; they are more like the marginal sectors with whom Freire collaborated. The distance between frontier Nasa and these local teachers is something that Susana Piñacué is obsessed with transcending. It is the articulation—or the utopian strivings toward such a relationship—between cultural planners in the Popayán office and teachers in the field, between people like Susana, on the one hand, and Roberto, Fernando, or Benilda, on the other, that underlies the central mission of CRIC's bilingual education program (PEB), whose goals have been the establishment of alternative schools in localities. The connection between the leadership and the grassroots is not premised strictly, however, on the sort of educational objectives voiced by Giroux: the conversion of the school into a space in which the consciousness of *students* should be raised. Instead, the CRIC subject shifts its orientation to the communities in which such schools are located, focusing on the school as an axis around which community militancy coalesces rather than a site for training children. This point is key to an understanding of the principles underlying PEB and the goals that drive many indigenous intellectuals in Cauca.

PEB as a Contact Zone

The notion of the contact zone provides a useful point of departure for understanding how PEB operates. An idea initially arising out of Mary Louise Pratt's (1991, 1992) attempt to make sense of the hybrid writing of colonial indigenous authors such as Felipe Guaman Poma de Ayala, the contact zone refers to "social spaces where cultures meet, clash, and grapple with each other, often in contexts of highly asymmetrical relations of power" (1991, 34). The writings produced in this zone are not "authentic" or "autochthonous," but transcultural in nature, engaging indigenous symbols with Western modes of representation to create a consciously hybrid form that Pratt calls "autoethnography." The notion of the contact zone is at once highly suggestive and uncomfortably illusive, for it dangles before us a conceptual tool that might assist us in comprehending how culture travels across boundaries, but provides distressingly little direction as to how we are to engage it to analyze concrete sociopolitical situations.

Claudio Lomnitz (2001, chap. 6) goes some ways toward operationalizing Pratt's tantalizing proposition. For Lomnitz, the contact zone comprises the set of contexts in which national identity is produced and from which particular "dynamics of nation building and transnational interactions . . . can be isolated on the analytic plane (129)." Lomnitz hopes to analytically separate the flows between nation and locality, and between nation and the global sphere, where narratives of nationality are produced (130). He lists four fields into which the contact zone can be differentiated and out of which such narratives are generated: "(1) The material culture of capitalism; (2) the ideological tension between tradition and modernity that is necessary to the founding of nation-states; (3) the entropy of modernization, which is intrinsic to the development process; and (4) the international field of ideas and models of civilization, science, and development that forms part of what could be called the civilizing horizon of nation-states" (130). Lomnitz's own analytical concerns lead him to orient his discussion from the vantage point of the nation-state. We can appropriate his insight as a tool for understanding how alternatives to the nation-state are constructed from below, as occurs in indigenous Latin America, where, in an appeal to remake the state in a pluralist guise, native peoples have attempted to redefine what it means to be a citizen. In indigenous pluralist discourse, citizenship does not imply the erasure of cultural difference but the incorporation of difference into political process; in Ecuadorian sociologist Jorge León's (1994) words, native citizens become *ciudadanos diferentes*, or citizens marked by cultural difference. Marcia Stephenson (2002), building on the work of Nancy Fraser (1977), has coined the term "indigenous counterpublic sphere" to identify the spaces that indigenous intellectuals in Bolivia have carved out in the course of historical research and social activism.

By merging these notions with the conceptual tools provided by Lomnitz, we can begin to comprehend such projects as that of PEB. CRIC's educational project is more than a setting in which educational policy is constructed. Instead, it is a social laboratory controlled by indigenous people, in which intercultural relations are redefined from a native vantage point and framed by processes of cultural revitalization and identity production. The interculturalism that characterizes PEB is generated through the day-to-day interactions that take place among the political leadership, indigenous intellectuals, and their colaborador allies. Moreover, PEB is a site for the appropriation of external ideas, a place where notions culled from outside contacts can be reinterpreted in light of indigenous political and cultural objectives. Finally, PEB constitutes a space of theoretical reflection out of which an indigenous pluralist alternative to current homogenizing constructions of citizenship and contemporary neoliberal policies can be projected into the national sphere. In this sense, PEB does indeed pose the project of constructing a different kind of contact zone along the lines of Lomnitz's four fields: (1) the culture of capitalism is confronted by indigenous alternatives to neoliberalism; (2) reconstructions of native traditions provide a context for building an alternative modernity; (3) modernization sheds the exclusively economic trappings it has come to acquire in development discourse; and (4) international flows of ideas come to bear in a localized construction of citizenship.

The Community Foundations of PEB

Although PEB's project is educational in nature, including curricular development, linguistic and historical research, the generation of theory, and teacher training, its most central objectives revolve around creating schools that are firmly inserted into community activities (Ulcué et al. 1994, 15). Teachers serve as political mediators between the regional leadership and the grassroots, as PEB's documents argue: "Teachers are key representatives of CRIC in the community and for this reason are charged with a series of obligations that in other political contexts would be tasks falling to other social actors" (48). William García, a professor of education at the Universidad del Cauca and a long-time colaborador, emphasizes the "strategic role of the school as a sociopolitical objective" (1996, 3), characterizing CRIC's teachers as "political agents of change" (1998, 59). In this sense, PEB contrasts with many other indigenous educational projects in Latin America (López 1991; López and Jung 1988; Luykx 1999), whose point of origin is the state or large international nongovernmental organizations and whose goals are more narrowly pedagogical. PEB activists characterize their own project as contestatory in nature, nourished by a critical appropriation and politicization of pedagogical methods. Correspondingly, PEB has rejected the strings attached to most external funding, preferring to work with small leftist NGOs from Europe, like Terre des Hommes' member organization in Germany or Mugarik Gabe in the Basque Country of Spain (Bolaños and Strack 2001; CRIC 1996; Sodemann 2001).[3]

CRIC and PEB grew out of a series of workshops in various rural communities sponsored in the late 1960s and early 1970s by the Colombian Institute of Agrarian Reform (INCORA) and aimed at revitalizing the roots of resistance that it perceived there. This was a time in which many leftists entered into government service, hoping—against all odds—to contribute to an effective agrarian reform. Although INCORA set its sights on organizing mestizo and Afrocolombian peasants, dynamic work by indigenous leaders led the workshop facilitators to expand their purview to native communities, where local militants had been engaged in land claims. This ultimately led to the foundation of CRIC in 1971, at a massive assembly held in Toribío, in which a series of demands aimed at strengthening the political autonomy of cabildos, ensuring the territorial autonomy of resguardos, and protecting indigenous culture were voiced. By the late 1970s, as the organization began to consolidate itself across Cauca, CRIC's interest in education was embraced by its Nasa vice president, Benjamín Dindicué (Penagos 2000). This was a period of intense repression exerted by the national government against popular organizations. Dindicué was murdered in the late 1970s by assassins hired by large landholders, just one of a string of assassinations of indigenous leaders, indicating that political violence is not at all new to indigenous Cauca. Various members of CRIC's executive committee and some colaboradores were imprisoned for associations with guerrilla groups like the populist M-19 (19th of April Movement) and indigenous self-defense organizations like the Quintín Lame Armed Movement, accusations that they denied at the time, although CRIC was, in fact, enmeshed in these groups. As several PEB activists told me, it was hoped that the creation of an education program would demonstrate that CRIC was a law-abiding organization engaged in cultural projects.

Unlike most popular education programs in Latin America, PEB did not spring from an educational movement but from a political organization. Schools were established in communities that had demonstrated the greatest capacity for political organizing and struggle: La Laguna, a multiethnic territory where Nasa sharecroppers had reclaimed lands and formed a cabildo; Las Delicias, whose land claims activities began several decades before CRIC's 1971 founding; El Cabuyo, whose leadership had struggled for years against the hegemony of the Apostolic Vicariate of Tierradentro and its stranglehold on cabildos and schools. Choosing such locations for CRIC schools ensured that they would be supervised by militant communities and consequently would quickly become pivots of political organizing, their priorities aligned to those of the cabildos. Parents and cabildo members organized the schools, oriented their activities, and evaluated their progress, developing their ideas in work-shops and community assemblies.

In those communities that founded CRIC schools, it was activists and not schooled educational professionals, such as normal school graduates, who were chosen as teachers. Given that CRIC and the founding communities saw the Colombian educational establishment as fostering the development of teachers dedicated to instilling in children dominant nationalist political values, they looked instead to politically active individuals in their search for teachers, regardless of their level of training. Some of these people, colabo-rador William García told me, were reluctant to participate but were forced by their communities to become teachers:

> I collected testimonies of how teachers were selected. [For example], from Henry Corpus, from the Nápoles school in Caloto. He told me that he didn't want to be a teacher, that he wanted to be a farmer and I argued, "But a farmer, that's working the land all day . . ." And he: "No," that he wanted to be a farmer because since childhood he had liked plants. . . . "But, then, why did you become a teacher?" "Because the community selected me and ordered me to teach." And he: "I couldn't read nor write." And I said to him, "And why didn't you tell them to send you to study in a normal school?" "Yes, I told them, but they said 'No,' they said that I had to be a teacher," and that his father had been a worker. What's it called? A slave. He was a sharecropper on an hacienda they had reclaimed and he had stayed on that hacienda and for that reason, now he would be a teacher. I finally insisted that why hadn't he studied, why hadn't he done something else. And he told me, "But the community knows, and the community has me here because the community says that I am useful." That's what he said.

These activists-cum-educators were sent to training seminars that concen-trated more on a critique of the traditional school than on the development of literacy skills or teaching methodology that characterized official in-service workshops of the period; they also introduced participants to indigenous legislation, Nasa history, and methodologies for cultural revitalization, facili-tated by radical pedagogues from the Universidad del Cauca and from popular education programs in other parts of the country. When the newly appointed educators returned to their schools, they understood themselves as participat-ing in a laboratory for social and political change, and not in a school per se.

Leaders like Benjamín Dindicué were strong supporters of the development of an educational program on the regional level, and their sentiments were echoed in the resguardos, particularly in places like Tierradentro, where activists had long opposed the hegemony of the Catholic Church in indigenous education; religious control was legitimized by a concordat between the Colombian government and Rome that, among other things, ceded responsibility for education in some indigenous territories to the Church (D. González n.d.; Rappaport 1998b; Sevilla Casas 1986). Ángel María Yoinó, a cabildo member in Vitoncó and an important thê' wala, recounts why he and his compatriots sought to wrest control of education from the Vincentian Fathers, who ruled the region with an iron fist:

> Since my grandmother was so furious, she used to say, "What are you learning?" She would say, "Aren't you learning to be exaggerated and brutal with the people?" She would say, "That is not our way of life," and she would ask this until she broke out in tears. She would say, "We don't want those attitudes, we don't want it." She would rage over the fact that after so long in school, our word [thought] was still not taught, and she urged us on. And we thought, "What is she talking to us about?" That old woman, what she demanded was that we teach what is ours. She yearned for them to teach our lifeways. This should be like this: When Christopher Columbus came to these lands, back in the olden days . . . from that moment on he confronted our authorities and among the things he said, he told us he had come to educate us. Having done that, he pillaged and deceived us so. But he didn't achieve it all for the following reason: for us, the so-called Indians, it is a duty to be crafty [*malicioso*]. But to say *idxu* [*indio*] is also a Spanish expression. We, the Nasa, think as fluidly as water. We take care of ourselves. And if we move with caution, that is the only way to walk.
>
> This is good, uhuh? This is how: we converse, we communicate with the elders of the upper world [the Thunder], with the *ksxa'w* [guardian spirits], we talk to the *duende* [trickster spirit], we talk to the rainbow when it appears. Well, we talk with everything before us. That is why we are told, "This is how it is." We are not of a single form.

Ángel María's approach to knowledge embodies structures of shamanic thought that are not always verbalized, but are instead sensorial. This is conveyed in his distinction between how he, as a thê' wala, thinks, and how priests learn: "[Priests] learn only through questions. But we guide ourselves without questions. So that we can identify a thief without interrogating him." This is the sort of knowledge that PEB sought to internalize in its educational project.

In one of our conversations, William García characterized this first phase of

1. *Cartilla de Aprestamiento:*
Coca bag. Courtesy of CRIC.

the history of PEB as having a distinctly ideological or political emphasis. There was no clear articulation of the notion of culture beyond a vague appreciation of the importance of language, handicrafts, music, and history (Archivo de la Casa Cural de Toribío, ACCT n.d.) and the key spiritual role played by thê' walas in the struggle. This can be seen in the picture-textbooks, or *cartillas de aprestamiento* (CRIC n.d.a, n.d.b, n.d.d), that were used for oral reflection in the classroom, using Nasa Yuwe (figures 1–3). In fact, during PEB's first years, culture was a political icon, not a self-conscious object of reflection. Within PEB itself, which was at the time a small collective of indigenous militants and colaboradores whose time was spent largely in communities, working without benefit of a salary, indigenous activists assumed the primary political responsibilities in the program. They engaged with nonindigenous supporters in the course of their work but did not interpret this relationship in terms of intercultural relations. Instead, collaboration was understood in its strictly political dimension. In this early period, the regional office—at the time, a mere garage in a residential sector of Popayán—was more or less isomorphic with the militant communities that had founded the organization a few years before, just as the nascent PEB blended imperceptibly into the community schools whose development it stimulated. Under such conditions, there was little conceptual distance between the incipient educational program and the small number of militant resguardos it served. PEB's activists and colaboradores were learning and creating, side by side, with local teachers like Roberto Chepe, sharing not only an ideology but strategic emphases in that ideology.

During the first years of the program, PEB emphasized local research proj-

2. *Cartilla de Aprestamiento:* Thê' wala. Courtesy of CRIC.

ects focusing on the revitalization of cultural forms such as those alluded to by Ángel María Yoinó, although they did not necessarily embrace academic research methodologies. In the schools, much of this work was accomplished through the Freirian methodology of collective exegesis on key words written in Spanish and in Nasa Yuwe on posterboard. This approach was introduced by CINEP (Center for Popular Education and Research), a radical Jesuit think tank based in Bogotá, as a means of achieving a methodology appropriate for the community-appointed CRIC teachers, who demonstrated very low levels of schooling at the same time that they exhibited very high levels of ideological commitment to the indigenous movement (García 1998, 53–54, 60–63; Moreno 1998; Pabón 1986). The project lasted some two years, concluding when the organization came into conflict with the objectives of CINEP researcher Javier Serrano. Whereas Serrano's goal was to construct an educational movement—PEB activists talked about it in terms of his goal *hacer escuela*, literally, "to form a school"—CRIC was much more concerned with building a political movement.

But, as I will illustrate, despite the political goals that have always oriented PEB's activities, the day-to-day practice of the program grew to involve the

3. *Cartilla de Aprestamiento:* Agriculture. Courtesy of CRIC.

operationalization of pedagogical approaches that subtly shifted teachers' attention toward the school as an educational institution that trains children. Regionally based activists have felt this pull, particularly in their collaborative work with outsider experts, for whom education, and not political organizing, is the fundamental objective. Tensions between political objectives and pedagogical strategies have also marked the character of their articulation with Nasa intellectuals working at the local level. The distancing of the grassroots from the regional office came about as PEB gained increasing public notoriety as an innovative program.

Out of Clandestinity: Official Recognition of PEB

The 1980s marked a period of change in Cauca. Coinciding with the creation of zonal organizational processes, the fall of the Berlin Wall brought about a sea change in the Colombian political landscape, heralding the ascendancy of new social movements over class-based organizations, such as leftist parties (Alvarez et al. 1998; Escobar and Alvarez 1992) and propelling already existing ethnic organizations, such as CRIC, onto the national stage (Edelman 2001). The intense repression of the late 1970s had abated (although it never entirely disappeared), and CRIC grew as a regional organization, organizing cooperatives and reclaiming lands at the local level. According to some critics, such as its rival, AICO, the executive committee of CRIC and its burgeoning programs swiftly became bureaucracies.

PEB's greatest expansion came in the mid-1980s, after the national legislature passed a series of laws in support of ethnoeducation, defined by the Ministry of Education in a language that at once echoes indigenous demands and confines them to a bureaucratic straitjacket: "A permanent social process, immersed in the local culture, that permits, according to the needs, interests, and aspirations of a people, training for the exercise of cultural control (a maximal relation between decisions and resources) by ethnic groups and their interrelationship with the hegemonic society in terms of mutual respect" (Bodnar 1989, 76). In other words, the Colombian state began to appropriate the demands and organizational guidelines of the indigenous movement, whose schools were now in competition with state-sponsored ethnoeducation, and to mold them into official policy (77–78). Such shifts in government policy away from assimilationist models of indigenous education were accompanied by new official curricula that fostered local research and the expansion of schools beyond the classroom (Parra Sandoval 1996). Enhanced training was required for teachers, who, in rural areas, were still largely unschooled beyond the primary level. To fill this need, profesionalización programs were introduced: normal school proficiency courses that "converted individuals into professional subjects" (García 1996, 5), injecting them with academic discourses and methodologies. As in the Bolivian normal school studied by Aurolyn Luykx (1999), profesionalización was meant to convert teachers into *national* subjects. By now, CRIC had consolidated more than a dozen community schools with culturally inspired curricula whose contents diverged from that of the national curriculum, although they retained the traditional subject areas that characterized most primary schooling in Colombia (CRIC 1990a).

PEB established its own profesionalización program in 1998, but though it received the financial support of the Ministry of Education, its goal was not to convert teachers into professionals but to create community leaders (CRIC 2000, 112). From 1988 to 1999, CRIC trained several hundred teachers, most of them indigenous, in a multiyear cycle of courses scheduled in various resguardos during school vacations (10). Although participation in profesionalización legitimized PEB in the eyes of the state and played an important role in converting the population of teachers in Cauca into normal school graduates,

CRIC's engagement in the process must be understood as an arena for working with greater rigor through objectives and methodologies that were already in place in community schools. Concurrently with the development of profesionalización, regional education activists became acquainted with the concept of interculturalism, which came to provide a basic operating notion for teacher training and, eventually, for the development of local curricula.

Interculturalism

The intellectual foundations of the PEB project have been circulating for the past three decades throughout indigenous Latin America, embodied in the notion of *interculturalidad,* or interculturalism. Interculturalism developed in Latin America alongside the popular struggles of the 1970s and 1980s that posed alternatives to traditional notions of representative democracy, as the countries of the continent began to shed their dictatorships and to explore options for constitutional reform (López 1995).[4] In the Colombian case, where the 1991 constitution establishes the legal potential for a truly plural nation, interculturalism poses a radical alternative to the multiculturalism that might dampen the political potential inherent in this significant moment. Unlike multiculturalism, it does not envision pluralism as the simple fostering of tolerance for minorities, permitting them to participate in a representative democracy that dilutes their impact on the nation. Instead, it seeks new ways to forge conditions of equality and consensus while enhancing minority voices (Heise, Tubino, and Ardito 1994).[5] Interculturalism goes beyond multiculturalism insofar as it implies more than an "encounter" framed by hegemonic relations. Instead, it seeks to create new horizontal relationships (Gottret 1999) in the paradigm of a pluralist state (López 1999). What is more, interculturalism injects cultural difference into leftist calls for radical political pluralism (Laclau and Mouffe 1985; Mouffe 1995).

Clearly, interculturalism is an emergent project, not an existing social reality, a political objective fostered by radical pedagogues who have built local bilingual education programs based on this concept (Caiza 1989; León and Quintero 1989; López 1991) and are training indigenous educators at the university level (Luykx n.d.).[6] The incorporation of interculturalism into bilingual education presupposes a direct link between education and social change. Promoters of the concept argue that the school is a critical locus for the construction of democracy, where cultural self-esteem and the creation of nonhierarchical ethnic relationships lay the groundwork for building democracy beyond the schoolhouse (Heise et al. 1994; Gottret 1999; López 1996, 1999). In fact, this current of bilingual education grows out of educational efforts intimately linked to popular political struggle in indigenous areas (López 1991; López and Jung 1988). Intercultural education makes cultural difference explicit with an eye to facilitating the incorporation of new ideas into an emergent constellation of cultural forms (Mengoa 1999). In the process, the notion of cultural revitalization is reconfigured as a process oriented toward the future, instead of the recovery of customs from the past (Heise et al. 1994). It becomes a project in which external ideas and cultural forms are absorbed and reworked in a local cultural matrix. This is a very different conception from that of bilingual-bicultural education used in the United States, because interculturalism fosters a broad field of intercultural exchange characterized by nonhierarchical relations—an indigenous contact zone—as opposed to the encapsulation of cultural difference within a dominant cultural matrix with an eye toward assimilation (López 1999, 54–55).[7]

CRIC (1990a, 4) publications define interculturalism using familiar precepts: "To start from a knowledge of one's own culture in order to integrate other forms of knowledge" and "Relations that are generated and experienced as a result of the valuation and respect for the Other in a search for conditions of equality within a system of differences" (CRIC 2000, 2). As the educators who coined the notion of interculturalism intended, CRIC's operationalization of interculturalism involves its projection in a broader political project, something that became apparent to me in a curricular planning workshop for the community pedagogy program. In this case, we were some twenty participants, including regional Nasa activists, colaboradores, a facilitator who had been flown in from Mexico in an advisory capacity, and myself, brought together for an intense weekend in a rustic holiday cabin in Cajibío, some two hours from Popayán.

The workshop began with small group discussion of key concepts, some of which were translated into Nasa Yuwe by participants and others reflected on exclusively in Spanish. One of the latter was interculturalism, which was defined by the participants as "a reciprocal process of the construction of a life project by peoples, in which culture should be transferrable and should allow for the reaffirmation of identity in relation with others." Note that they used the term "peoples," incorporating a political discourse that has marked a turn since the 1990s toward constructing the movement as a coalition of cultural groups, as opposed to using "indigenous" to denote a category of oppressed people characterized by a particular type of discrimination or exploitation based on their ethnicity, which is how CRIC defined its mission during its early years. In a marked appeal to Nasa cosmology, the participants saw interculturalism as encompassing not only human beings, but the spiritual world as well, fostering a "reaffirmation by an indigenous people of its territory, its cosmovision, and social relation[s], permitting harmonic coexistence." Simultaneously, interculturalism is directed toward the outside, through the act of "knowing about the diversity of the cultures of all peoples and respecting them, always recognizing the values, needs, and aspirations of each people, allowing for feedback from the Other's culture."

For PEB activists, interculturalism is accompanied by a dynamic concept of culture, what Martha Pabón (1986, 105), a Colombian ethnolinguist and former colaboradora, has called "counteracculturation," a process in which culture is *generated* through research in the interests of survival, not unearthed in search of a return to the past (CRIC 1990a, 47). Many activists would argue that the culture that emerges out of this process must obey certain key criteria. In particular, cultural forms should function to restore equilibrium in the universe, what activists call "harmony." Remember that this is a central element of the Nasa translation of "culture," or "the form of behavior resulting in a permanently harmonic relationship with nature." In a sense, then, the role of the researcher is very much like that of a shaman, who restores harmony to the universe, only the thê' wala accomplishes this through divination and ritual, whereas the researcher does it by reintroducing carefully researched indigenous cultural forms back into the community. When this process is harnessed to the goal of interculturalism, it is understood that the appropriation of external forms of knowledge must occur in such a way as to not break that harmony (CRIC 1990a, 13–15).

The only way to ensure the maintenance of harmony in the exercise of interculturalism is to assume a critical perspective, not only toward the hegemonic culture, but toward indigenous cultures as well (1990a, 14; Chow 1995, 180), because this is what allows activists to identify how indigenous cultural forms should be supplemented, and ultimately transformed, in dialogue with imported ones (Luykx 2000, 153–154). The following quotation from a CRIC report alludes to the conflicts inherent in self-critique, although it does not explore the dilemmas that arise out of a cultural project that emphasizes native culture at the same time that it critically examines aspects of it (Luykx 2000): "The fact of departing from the home culture and, little by little, integrating knowledge from other cultures has meant much conflict and [many] problems, but also advantages. You begin to reflect upon what types of knowledge we have and what we need to appropriate for education, for development, [thus] establishing a degree of control over the dominant culture" (CRIC 1990a, 8). In its interpretation of interculturalism, CRIC prefers to foreground the benefits of *lo propio*, the most salient aspects of local culture, emphasizing in particular the centrality of harmony in the Nasa cosmos. For the authors of this report, harmony arises out of a conscious process of appropriation, in which the dominant culture is not permitted to encompass the indigenous culture. In fact, it is the opposite that should occur. The indigenous culture should surround elements of Western knowledge, incorporating them according to its own criteria, transforming itself in the process—very similar to how activists envisioned the process of constitutional translation. According to PEB theorist Manuel Sisco, appropriation implies a "philosophy of diversity, of complementarity," that is mediated by the exercise of autonomy (CRIC 2000, 114–115).

Such philosophy that couples diversity with autonomy is implicit in discussions of even the most technical of proposals, although it is not always apparent in the written summaries that issue from meetings. For example, at the curricular meeting I described above, participants were asked to draw up teaching modules using a model that broke each element down into its objectives, its justification, and the competencies, abilities, and values it would stimulate. Such discursive forms are standard procedure in Latin American pedagogical circles, even politically progressive ones. However, this discourse does not convey in written form the intense political discussions that underlay the creation of the curriculum, a problem inherent in PEB's sometimes uncritical appropriation of pedagogical methods, which I come back to later in this chapter. In effect, although it is not always obvious, intercultural dialogue and the appropriation of pedagogical discourses on the regional plane interact intimately with micro-level local political experience. However, at this meeting, political issues were reduced to a standard Latin American curricular exposition, which left its radical intent invisible to all but the workshop participants.

Profesionalización and the Operationalization of Interculturalism

CRIC's profesionalización program organized countless grassroots workshops with rural teachers to develop their guiding concepts: *educación propia*, interculturalism, interdisciplinarity, and community control, notions that I touch on in the remainder of this chapter. These were accompanied by a strong linguistic component coordinated by a cadre of Nasa linguists trained in graduate programs in Colombian universities. The turn to linguistics, which William García suggested to me characterized the third stage of PEB's history, lent rigor to a native-language literacy orientation that heretofore had been embraced only in theory, for lack of technical expertise. But despite—or perhaps better put, *because of*—its insistence on the primacy of indigenous languages, the use of linguistics in profesionalización presents a key instance of the operationalization of intercultural ideals.

During PEB's first years, the organization relied on an orthography for Nasa Yuwe developed by the Summer Institute of Linguistics, a U.S.-based missionary organization whose affiliates were given a limited amount of linguistic training. Although more recently, the Institute has sought graduate training for its missionaries, their representatives in Tierradentro had only rudimentary training, reflected in the Nasa orthography they developed (Slocum 1972), which did not capture the phonological complexities of the language. Once a small core of Nasa activists had completed graduate work in ethnolinguistics in the mid-1980s, they began to devise a new alphabet whose relationship to the structure of Nasa Yuwe was more coherent than the Institute's version had been. By the late 1980s, a new orthography crystallized in the publication of a proposal for a Nasa alphabet (CRIC n.d.c), which formed the centerpiece of linguistic training in profesionalización.[8]

Not only the teachers registered in the profesionalización program but also community leaders were introduced to the new alphabet, whose use was encouraged in rudimentary form in communities and cabildos, for example, in official seals, in school names, and later, in the name of zonal cabildo associations.[9] The adoption of the new orthography facilitated the creation of didactic materials with Nasa contents (figure 4) that stimulated research by students and teachers, thus drawing them out of the classroom and into the community (CRIC 1991). Standardization of Nasa orthography also facilitated a process of creating neologisms in Nasa Yuwe, so that the appropriation of external ideas could be facilitated through their grounding in the native language. Nasa linguists gave workshops in which the neologisms they had created were written out and explained to the profesionalización students. Although most never made it into common usage, the methodology employed for their creation became an important tool for reconceptualizing ideas appropriated from the dominant society, something that I touched on in previous chapters. That is, when terms such as "development," "culture," and "nation" were cast in Nasa Yuwe, they were not simply translated, but their meanings were transformed in accord with a Nasa conceptual framework.

4. *Sa't ûus:* a culturally focused primary school textbook in Nasa Yuwe (cover of CRIC 1991). Courtesy of CRIC.

The extent to which CRIC was successful in its introduction of interculturalism in profesionalización varied considerably. Those profesionalización students who were affiliated with the regional office—many regional activists took advantage of the opportunity to obtain training and a *normalista* degree—and the teachers in PEB's experimental schools (CECIBs, or Intercultural Bilingual Community Educational Centers) were drawn into an intense dialogue concerning theory and method. They learned to draw on interculturalism as a tool for cultural revitalization. Educators like Benilda, with whom I opened the chapter, devised innovative curricula for their local primary schools that focused on the indigenous community and on Nasa Yuwe as a point of departure in the early grades and progressively incorporated broader interethnic, national, and global visions, as well as proficiency in Spanish, as students moved on to the upper grades (Bolaños et al. 1998; CRIC 1996, 1997, 2000; López Adentro 1999; Abelardo Ramos et al. 1996, 2000). Likewise, CECIB teachers, almost all of whom were bilingual, learned to read the CRIC alphabet and employed it with ease, if not with complete accuracy, in their classrooms.

Profesionalización graduates whose relationship to PEB was not as constant or as intense, however, did not take away such perspectives from their training. Many teachers, I have been told by PEB activists, found the CRIC alphabet, which used apostrophes to denote both glottalizations and palatalizations, too difficult to decipher in the absence of the close supervision that CECIBS received from the regional office. Working outside of the CECIB structure, they were not given the support needed to create intercultural curricula, nor were the official schools in which they worked scenarios in which innovation was encouraged. In fact, as in rural schools across Latin America, these teachers were working in conditions of extreme poverty with few resources at their disposal to facilitate the application of new methodologies (Montoya 2001). In the late 1990s the Ministry of Education required that all schools produce Institutional Educational Plans. CRIC, in turn, pressured the state to require indigenous schools to present plans drawn up in consultation with community authorities (Community Education Plans), as opposed to the standard teacher-prepared documents requested by the Ministry. The most successful of the Community Education Plans were, predictably, from the CECIBS, and the least successful were from unaffiliated schools, where community participation was sparse, teachers continued to adhere to traditional curricula, and conditions impeded the creation of plans of the sort envisioned by the indigenous organization. Thus, although PEB has had a significant impact on the national level, state recognition forced it to extend its services to a population too vast and insufficiently politicized to internalize its objectives. As PEB grew, its very complexity tended to distance it from its local base, whose roots lie in the indigenous organization, orienting its attention toward indigenous education professionals schooled in university ethnoeducation programs (García Bravo 1998, 53–54).

After Profesionalización

PEB has been distanced in recent years from its constituency by the centrality it began to attribute to pedagogy, which developed alongside its national acceptance as a training institution. William García identified this to me as the most recent phase of the history of the program; in his writings, he suggests that profesionalización fostered an overly academic emphasis on pedagogical discourse (1996, 6). The consolidation of community schools and the articulation of the program with state projects, such as profesionalización, led PEB to seek out pedagogical specialists who could assist them in expanding and deepening their offerings. The pedagogical emphasis became increasingly pronounced in profesionalización and, later, in the community pedagogy university program, where teaching methodology was a fundamental element of the curriculum. Indigenous intellectuals and colaboradores became increasingly cognizant of a variety of educational theories, including the philosophy of interculturalism, but ranging also to contributions from Europe and North America. Significantly, these theoretical appropriations, such as the work of Célestin Freinet (Clandfield and Sivell 1990; Lee and Sivell 2000), focused more squarely on education per se rather than channelling education toward broader political concerns.

Although this discursive transformation has made possible the elaboration of detailed and innovative teaching plans, some of the Nasa members of PEB, particularly those who speak Nasa Yuwe and are most intensely immersed in the project of revitalizing Nasa spirituality, feel that the pedagogical emphasis has been uncritical and schematic, blindly appropriating Western discourses to the detriment of indigenous frameworks:

> The equilibrium I was speaking of and true cultural dialogue, there's much to deal with there, because I think that we are still carrying the baggage of 500 years. It's not easy to abandon it. Many times, we're using Nasa Yuwe, but with Western contents. So it's necessary to generate a serious process in relation to teaching, but that teaching continues to operate in opposition to what is indigenous, crosscutting the issue of identity. When I say we need to work on our pedagogy, it can't be thought of as strictly technical. We can't look at it like that. You can't separate things. You have to look at them from a holistic perspective. (CRIC 2000, 107)

Here, Inocencio Ramos calls for a radicalization of how PEB approaches pedagogy so that it can be appropriated within a Nasa framework, instead of the inverse. In this case, even within PEB, interculturalism is a goal that has not yet been attained, given that discursive hierarchies that privilege Western academic approaches continue to exert considerable influence in the indigenous organization. Correspondingly, the discourse of some advisors, brought to Cauca at great expense from other Latin American countries, tends to carry greater weight than that of indigenous activists. This exacerbates the growing gulf between indigenous and nonindigenous members of PEB, on the one hand, and between indigenous activists who have internalized the pedagogical discourse less critically—for the most part, monolingual Spanish-speaking Nasa—and the Nasa speakers, who reproduce it but at the same time are conscious of its deficiencies.

This was brought home to me at the planning meeting that I attended in Cajibío that developed a portion of the curriculum of the community pedagogy program. It was at this meeting that a modular planning scheme popular in pedagogical circles superseded the highly politicized contents of small group discussion. As Linda McNeil (1986, 13) argues, such schemes fragment cultural knowledge, reinserting it in pieces into a curricular sequence that reflects bureaucratic priorities. CRIC's (1997) community pedagogy curriculum does this by fragmenting skills and knowledge bases, which are interdisciplinary and merge academic learning with local knowledge, into discrete modules comprising readings and seminars in pedagogy, linguistics, and history that run parallel to a research component meant to immerse students in social and cultural issues proposed by their communities. The idea of students conducting research from their very first day in the program is innovative in comparison to most university courses of study in Colombia, but individual and group projects were never fully incorporated into the modules and thus never shaped curricular content, as one might expect in an educational project in which community priorities determine practice in the classroom. To the contrary, I discovered that student research tends to conform rigidly to pedagogical needs, to the extent that many projects have no meaning outside of the curricula of the schools in which these educators taught.

The pervasiveness of the pedagogical discourse was also apparent in the visual images presented at the meeting. A Mexican educator brought to Cauca in an advisory capacity to chair the curricular workshop dominated the plenary sessions of the meeting, setting a tone and a discourse for the proceedings. Working in tandem with a colaboradora who was a relative newcomer to PEB, he presented a highly schematized diagram of the PEB project (figure 5), in which key concepts of interculturalism, interdisciplinarity, community participation, and territoriality were represented by circles that intersected in a central circle representing cosmovision. An axis symbolizing social, political, and economic organization crosscuts the intersecting circles. At the central point of cosmovision, where all of the circles intersect, lie what are called "life projects," community projections of their social, cultural, economic, and political future. This is a schematization that can potentially mold the discourse of activists in predictable ways that are obscured by the apparent naturalness of its visual layout (Fabian 1983).

It is indeed the case that PEB aspires to establishing cosmovision as the ground on which educational processes unfold and that this constellation of objectives can be generated only through political organizing. It is also true

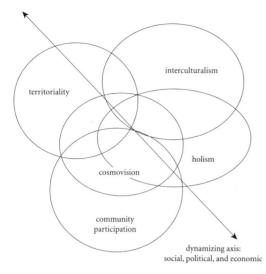

territoriality

interculturalism

cosmovision

holism

community
participation

dynamizing axis:
social, political, and economic

5. A schematic
representation of
the PEB project.

that in any locality the culmination of the process would be a community life
project, a long-range plan that takes myriad issues into consideration, in
addition to economic priorities, which is what distinguishes the life project
from the more usual development plans that cabildos draw up in consultation
with specialists (Gow 1997, 2005). However, it is not at all clear to me that the
diagram adequately conveys the relationships among these components as
they are understood by Nasa intellectuals working at a regional level or by local
teachers, nor that different participants would even concur as to how their
ideas should be represented.

The Nasa speakers I know best would undoubtedly prefer to represent the
project in a spiral form, which, as I illustrate later, has become a central trope
in cultural planning. The spiral emphasizes the simultaneity and the equal
importance of the circles representing cosmovision and territoriality, which
would be at the center. Moreover, they are accompanied by a circle representing autonomy, thus completing the three fundamental goals of CRIC as
represented in its slogan "Territory, autonomy, and culture." I intuit this
model on the basis of my experience with a discussion group at one of the
seminars organized in Caldono for students in the community pedagogy program. After reading some examples of Guambiano and Aymara historical
writing, we were reflecting on possible conceptual models that could guide
Nasa authors of historical texts. One of the participants drew a spiral with
territory at its center, progressively inserting language and history into the
unwinding spiral (figure 6). On the outer edges of the spiral, the temporal

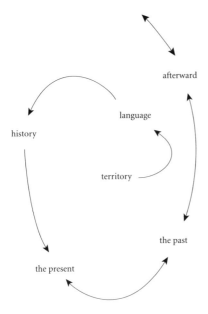

afterward

language

history

territory

the past

the present

6. A spiral model of history.

point of "the present" is connected with bidirectional arrows to "the past" and "afterward," suggesting a fluid movement between past and present. This very different scheme, however, was supplanted in significant ways in the diagram presented by the Mexican facilitator, as it traced a discrete and linear relationship among components and established a clear hierarchy among them, resulting in an epistemological arrangement and a set of political priorities that differ from PEB's. Nonetheless, no one at the workshop addressed the flaws in the diagram. Although Inocencio and his allies in PEB continually criticize such schema, calling them *cuadriculado* (organized in rigid squares), they are hard-pressed to move beyond their "naturalness," which is, of course, learned. For this reason, Inocencio's concerns over how pedagogical emphasis causes PEB to become so schematic are dead serious and extremely difficult to resolve.

The kind of schematic diagram presented at Cajibío envelops and transforms PEB's culturalist discourse. But if we remain at the regional level and focus exclusively on the written products of internal discussions, as opposed to those discussions themselves, we lose sight of the processes that have developed in a parallel course locally in conversation with regional activists. Here, the pedagogical schemas concocted at the regional level are deconstructed through the transformation of their cultural components into vivencias, lived experience. This is what has occurred with local appropriations of the notion of interculturalism.

Interculturalism: The View from Below

Whereas regional activists can move between a global vision of interculturalism and a local view of political practice, in the local context their interpenetration takes a different form. The notion of interculturalism is articulated by only some cultural activists working in localities, namely, those teachers who are intimately associated with CRIC's experimental schools. The following report from López Adentro illustrates community teachers' command of the concept: "We have worked on the concept of interculturalism to build relationships to the inside and the outside, [so that] we can express ourselves easily from within each culture and ensure that others respect that thought, and with the union of knowledge interculturalism and diversity can be strengthened, as much inside and outside. But at the moment we need to learn more about the knowledge . . . of the whites because they still have us dominated" (B. Tróchez and Secue 2001, 1). Notwithstanding the sophistication of the local teachers affiliated with CRIC's experimental schools (the CECIBS), the concept of interculturalism does not always make its way into most communities. Pabón (1986, 140), who worked with PEB in its first decade, asserts that the kind of intercultural dialogue that takes place at the regional level between indigenous intellectuals and colaboradores is not widely replicated at the local level (with the exception of the CECIBS). Teachers in schools whose curricular development is not directly supervised by CRIC are frequently unfamiliar with the complex ramifications of the concept, even if they are aware of its existence.

At the local level, activists prefer to emphasize a complex bundle of ideas that they call *lo propio*, a term that defies any simple gloss in English. *Propio* translates literally as "one's own," and the article *lo* transforms the adjective *propio* into a noun. *Lo propio* refers to how culture is experienced (*vivenciado*) on the ground. Vivencias, however, are experiences that are fluid and heterogeneous in nature. They incorporate both habitual and unself-conscious practices (such as the nonverbal exercises of the shaman, verbal forms of address in Nasa Yuwe, and the planting of crosses along the peak of thatched roofs) and intentional appropriations (the revival, for instance, of woven woolen vests and the introduction of the story of Quintín Lame into the oral tradition). Lo propio is a more self-conscious construct than the broader category of vivencias, in the sense that it abstracts out of the latter a constellation of practices generated through research and reflection. These practices are foregrounded as emblematic of "Nasa culture," constituting a bundle of cultural attributes worthy of use as political symbols or as vehicles for cultural revitalization: Nasa Yuwe, shamanic ritual, and the house garden, or *tul*, which I describe at the end of this chapter. The philosophy of interculturalism as it is embraced by regional activists views lo propio as the ground on which external elements—theories, methods, and technologies originating in the dominant society—can be evaluated, transformed, and appropriated.

Local Nasa intellectuals emphasize the centrality of lo propio from a different angle. Far from suggesting a dynamic dialogue with the dominant society, interculturalism is operationalized by resguardo-based cultural workers as a horizontal cross-cultural dialogue between different indigenous groups, in which the appropriation of ideas from the dominant national society goes entirely unremarked. From their perspective, interculturalism means the sharing of lo propio with neighboring native peoples. The difference in emphasis may owe to the fact that local activists are not as cosmopolitan as are regionally based cultural workers. They have traveled less, read less, engaged in fewer intellectual conversations with outsiders, and speak Spanish with less fluency. Moreover, resguardo activists live in localities in which indigenous people frequently are the majority (or the plurality), thus redirecting the meaning of "inter" in "intercultural" to center on the native population, its ethnic neighbors, and perhaps the Afrocolombians and peasants who share their territory, as opposed to the more abstract dominant culture of the state, of the regional educational system, and of the educated elite. As a result, local activists are more attuned to the cross-cultural relationships that are most proximate to them.

Furthermore, the very process of inculcating these new philosophies at the local level fosters this distinct perspective on interculturalism. Local teachers acquire concepts like interculturalism and lo propio through training workshops, frequently given by native activists from the regional office, which frame their experience of such ideas within a dialogue between *indigenous* speakers, not as an intercultural conversation. Sometimes, these dialogues are indeed intercultural, such as when a Nasa regional activist facilitates a workshop in Guambía or in Totoró. But once again, this is an indigenous-indigenous dialogue. When colaboradores coordinate in-service training, the dialogue is no longer internal to an indigenous circle, but it is still nevertheless internal to the indigenous movement.

The intellectual worlds of local teachers are simultaneously expanded by ideas they receive from the outside and circumscribed by their ethnic contacts. Institutional transformations within indigenous organizations have broadened the contours of the indigenous world, while maintaining its autonomy by privileging the authority of local cabildos. In the late 1990s, CETIC (Education Committee for the Indigenous Territories of Cauca) was established to provide a cabildo-based forum for educational policymaking that went beyond the communities whose schools were already under PEB supervision. CETIC activities include regional workshops in which members of various ethnic groups share their similarities and differences, as Luis Yonda, a member of the Tierradentro-based CETIC team, describes:

> Yes, we found a great difference, because the Nasas said, "We think and feel with our hearts, the Guambianos with their livers." So, this was a large difference. The other was that we were confused when we tried to reflect: "But what is the center of education?" And there was confusion about the sense of education in those spaces in which it is transmitted, or disseminated, or taught about. We coincided on the point that the center was the territory, those spaces that one or the other [culture] emphasized—for example, for us, the hearth was important as long as we had firewood and as long as there were hearths, but when we moved on to the electric stove or to the gas stove, the hearth lost importance or lost prominence. So these were the types of reflections.

Here, we do not encounter a group of educators consciously engaged in the appropriation of concepts from the dominant society, although they are clearly employing ideas that emanate from the contact zone generated by the indigenous movement—notions such as "education" and "territory"—without discursively highlighting their externality.

As Héctor Muñoz Cruz (1996) suggests, regional indigenous organizations have come to be understood as deterritorialized projections of local communities. In Cauca, this fact was legitimized by the Colombian state when, after a series of mass mobilizations that came to a head in 1999, it was forced to recognize CRIC's executive committee as a "traditional authority," comparable to a local cabildo. Hence, the concepts that emanate from the regional office are seen as moving within an internal sphere of discussion. As teachers come of age in the midst of a mature ethnic movement and as the space occupied by the movement expands, concepts that were once understood by local activists to be external have been internalized. In contrast, regional activists in PEB *do* perceive the externality of concepts such as "educational system" and go to great pains to reconceptualize them within an indigenous framework that draws on interculturalism (CRIC 2002). This intercultural framework is incomplete at the local level. In Luis's narration, we see teachers and community leaders from different ethnic groups who are searching for a basis for comparison with other indigenous cultures and are encountering insurmountable barriers. The fact that the Nasa think with their hearts and the Guambianos with their livers was clearly of interest to them, but it did not lead to any point of convergence from which a fruitful conversation or a set of critical appropriations could issue. More useful was their evaluation of the common experience of lodging education in the concept of territory and the ways consumption habits and environmental deterioration have led to the appropriation of alienating technologies that dilute a sense of place in rural communities. These discussions explicitly rejected influences external to the indigenous movement. They were not oriented to engage in the politically inspired critical appropriation of external ideas. For these local activists, cross-cultural appropriation does not revolve around a distinction between indigenous and majority cultures. Instead, it arises out of a combination of minority cultures within the inclusive locus of the indigenous movement. In this sense, then, ideas originating in the external sphere, like "territory" and "education," are repositioned as internal and thus go unremarked.

Whereas CRIC is an interethnic organization, unifying Guambianos, Nasas, Totoróes, Yanaconas, and other cultural groups under common political demands, PEB has largely focused on the Nasa, in part because this is the largest constituency of the organization, the most militant indigenous population with a deep historical consciousness and a long tradition of struggle, and because it is a group that retains its own language and is thus an appropriate venue for bilingual education. AICO, the other major organization in Cauca, has a large Guambiano membership with its own very active education committee, making the CRIC-affiliated Guambianos a distinct minority within the organization. Other ethnic groups affiliated with CRIC—Totoróes, Ambaloeños, and Quizgueños—all descend from populations that once spoke variants of Guambiano, although long-standing rivalries with Guambía that antedate the indigenous movement and the isomorphism of CRIC with the Nasa and AICO with Guambía have led some of them to identify more closely with the Nasa. These populations look to the larger groups, whose cultural discourse is more fully constituted in the political sphere, as sources of referents for their own process of cultural revitalization.

Hermes Angucho is from Totoró, a community that only recently instituted a program of linguistic revival. In the following quotation, he looks to the Nasa and Guambiano for cosmological referents from which a self-conscious

Totoró cultural discourse can be forged, evaluating them in terms of their incorporation into educational schemes:

> There are stages in Nasa culture. We arrived at the conclusion that the center might be the father and the mother. But there I didn't understand clearly if the mother was the moon and the father was the sun—that's where it all started. The Guambianos said that for them there were many referents, like the hearth, the family, but they also have a Guambiano origin myth which I don't remember right now, but culture itself revolves around some central points which aren't the same ones you work on in mainstream education, where the center is the student and what has to be perfected is the student, while the teacher collaborates, and everything is done around this, forgetting the rest. In Nasa cultures, that's not how it is. You work with the student, but what is being fortified is the culture, the language, customs, identity.

Although Totoró culture as it is being reconstituted is neither Guambiano nor Nasa, there is a clear consciousness of the need to analyze these neighboring groups and to appropriate cultural elements from them.

In this vein, some Nasa schoolteachers see interculturalism as an opportunity to share alternative pedagogies with their less organized neighbors. Roberto Chepe, whom I introduced at the beginning of this chapter, works in a resguardo that was recently established after a protracted land struggle with hacienda owners. The majority in La Laguna is Nasa, but there are also numerous Guambiano settlers and mestizo peasants. For Roberto, interculturalism means the sharing of Nasa models with other subaltern groups:

> Education is not in keeping with the needs of the peoples, not only indigenous peoples, but all the peoples. So we said to ourselves, an education that is in accord, that projects itself, for life, not only for the teachers but also for youth, that projects something, that is analyzed, this project that we analyze in order to continue living: it's not only for Nasas but for everyone. And many times they say that bilingual education only means speaking your language, but it means consolidating what is ours and appropriating what is alien, but strengthening what is ours. An education that is in accord with and for all the peoples. Not only for indigenous peoples, but something that will be useful for peasants, for blacks, and so on.[10]

In other words, for local teachers and cultural workers, interculturalism operates from the inside out and involves extending the indigenous model to nonindigenous subordinated peoples, a conceptual model that subtly redirects to the grassroots CRIC's hopes of introducing its model of pluralism to the Colombian nation.

Luis Yonda, Hermes Angucho, and Roberto Chepe are all conversant with the discourse of PEB but invert it so that interculturalism in the local arena is reconstituted through a focus on indigenous culture and on sharing it with other subordinated groups, including not only other native Colombian cultures but also nonindigenous peasants. While these three men are associated with PEB's regional office, their daily work transpires in localities and the decisions they make are shaped by local priorities to a greater extent than are those of Popayán-based activists, hence altering the ways they appropriate the notion of interculturalism. However, local leaders whose ties to the regional office are more tenuous than those of Luis, Hermes, and Roberto exhibit even greater discrepancies with PEB's discourse. CRIC's (2000) evaluation of its profesionalización program indicates that despite its efforts, local appreciations of the notion of interculturalism do not always coincide with PEB's regional priorities. Sometimes interculturalism is misinterpreted as multiculturalism at the local level. For example, in a list of responses to questions formulated by CRIC regarding the history of education in Jambaló, the Nasa municipal education administrator answered as follows: "We are working on interculturalism without bias as to race. We share with mestizos, with Guambianos, and since the majority here is indigenous, we do not privilege any of the races, giving opportunities, respecting the beliefs of all" (Pabón 2001, 1). In other words, his take on interculturalism was more akin to the liberal notion of multiculturalism than the radical concept articulated by PEB, a misinterpretation found in schools throughout the Andes (Luykx and Bustamante 2000).

The interface between the indigenous community and the dominant society is not, moreover, the primary concern of local teachers. Former profesionalización students who participated in evaluation workshops were much more inward-looking than are regional activists, emphasizing such concepts as educación propia—an approximate gloss might be "community-generated education"—over interculturalism. This, despite the fact that CRIC's own definition of educación propia is itself intercultural in nature: "Educación propia refers to the capacity of people to [interpret] experience and to intervene, as much inside the communities themselves as in broader social spaces, [while] conserving their identity. The fact that it is propia does not only mean that it begins with autochthonous elements, but that consciousness and analysis of elements from society and their origins are part of the education that each community requires and needs. This implies reflection, selection, and appropriation" (2000, 8). Nevertheless, profesionalización graduates dwelled almost exclusively on the Nasa character of educación propia, emphasizing its collective nature and its contribution to building identity, not its intercultural dimension (139–142).

Meanings of key concepts clearly shift as one moves from a regional to a local context, as homegrown political priorities and social networks gain ground over theoretical propositions originating in the national and international arenas. In rural areas, interculturalism takes the form of an interindigenous dialogue aimed at protecting the native community from the ravages of the dominant society, while Western concepts like "education," "curriculum," and "interculturalism" itself go unmarked as appropriations from the dominant society. For local activists, even if you build a struggle with your master's tools, this is not acknowledged; it is more important to recognize the utility of your *neighbor's* tools, even when you are not in a position to appropriate them effectively. Thus, political unity is fostered at the expense of conceptual borrowings.

Cosmovision and Lo Propio: The Tul

If numerous local teachers who passed through profesionalización failed to absorb interculturalism in the form that PEB facilitators presented to them, they enthusiastically embraced the prospect of a community-generated education focusing on the native culture. Within CRIC, as well as in other indigenous organizations, cosmology, or cosmovision, as they call it, affords a primary vehicle for articulating the concept of culture in specific native conceptual frameworks. Cosmovision is understood by Nasa activists as an approach to everyday experience that inserts human beings into a broader spiritual universe and stimulates them to engage in ritual aimed at ensuring cosmic harmony. Implicit in this conception is the notion that human beings share the cosmos with other beings who, though they inhabit a different plane from humans, animals, and plants, are not isolated from the rest of the universe as supernaturals but are seen as integral components of nature. While thê' walas have always understood the need to restore a cosmic harmony that is continually being lost in the course of human activity, the articulation of such values into a coherent and verbalized political ideology came only as CRIC embarked on a conscious program of cultural research, a project I look at in later chapters. Susana Piñacué (2003) translates cosmovision into Nasa Yuwe as *fi'zenxi*, or "lived culture"—what they call *vivencia*, which is also translated as *fi'zenxi*—thus linking the concept of unconscious lived experience to the conscious search by organic intellectuals for a Nasa theory of the cosmos.

The *tul*, or house garden, furnishes one such vivencia. The garden is explicitly described as a cosmic microcosm in a CRIC video (Borque and CRIC 1996). The film opens with childbirth and the ritual burial of the newborn's placenta under the three stones of the hearth. The house is like a human being, recalls the video's narrator, with ribs, eyes, ears, a heart, and a stomach, just as the earth has bodily parts and is a living, sentient being. The tul surrounds the household, just as a woman's skirt surrounds and protects the human body; note the common root in *a'ts tul*, the word for the skirt. The spirits similarly protect the house-body from harm. In the house garden are a variety of medicinal herbs, condiments, and edible plants, situated in relation to one another according to their implicit properties, such as whether they are spicy or bland, whether they are "hot" or "cold"—this latter pair denoting essential characteristics of foods, not their degree of heat. Domestic animals, birds, and insects live in symbiosis with the plant world in the tul, as do the humans whose house lies at its heart. All of these beings—people, animals, and plants— are called *Nasa*, thus implicitly identifying humans as just one more component of the cosmos.

The tul as a project represents a conscious deployment of Nasa cultural forms within politicized spheres of interaction. Alcida Ramos (1998) distinguishes between the ways concepts like "nation" and "citizenship" are naturalized by the Brazilian state and how the indigenous movement redeploys them in its move to define its own membership in the nation. Ramos speaks of this act by referring to indigenous "instrumentalizations" of notions that lie at the heart of the national imaginary. That is, Brazilian indigenous organizations make conscious choices as to which cultural forms are to be generated to such political ends. Likewise, we can comprehend the centrality of cosmovision in terms of how particular elements of it are instrumentalized through negotiations that, in CRIC, take place primarily in the educational arena. The tul provides an excellent example of this process, given that it is ubiquitous in the curricula of CRIC's community schools, functioning as a microcosm in which cosmovision can be researched, defined, and generated by local teachers and students.

When local teachers talk about their research, they are generally referring to small hands-on projects that they have undertaken in their class plans, which they supplement with information they have gathered in the community or with knowledge acquired through the classroom participation of such community members as thê' walas and cabildo authorities. Such projects include the creation of organic fertilizer, the revitalization of weaving skills, the collection of toponyms in the vernacular; the tul is one such pedagogical project. By introducing a tul into the school's landscape, teachers turn the educational experience of cosmovision into a vivencia, a natural part of the school day, marked by a form of agricultural labor that also punctuates the home lives of the students. The school garden serves as a kind of laboratory in which children can learn about the energy flows that constitute their world. Maintaining the balance of the tul requires, moreover, a concerted effort on the part of its human inhabitants, who must perpetuate its diversity by continually replenishing the plants and animals that inhabit it and who ensure its harmony through ritual. The tul thus stands, in all its diversity, as a coherent alternative to the monoagriculture of the commercial farms that are steadily encroaching on Nasa subsistence agriculture. Furthermore, the need to engage in ritual to ensure the harmony of the tul provides a concrete antidote to Christianity. In this sense, the tul is not just a microcosm of the natural world, but a projection of CRIC's political world as well.

The tul exists in a harmonious relationship to the community as a whole, linking the garden into broader spheres of interaction that also operate according to cosmic guidelines. This point was driven home at a curricular meeting in which Mincho Ramos, Inocencio and Abelardo's brother, drew a spiral that moved in ever-expanding circles from right to left—just as, he explained, the thê' wala's arm movements begin on the right side of the body and move to the left. He referred to a petroglyph depicting a spiral, located on a sacred stone in Tierradentro, as evidence of the enduring significance of this symbol among the Nasa. Then he described the relationships of various levels of social integration that make up the community, which are reproduced in the curricula of the community schools. He drew a spiral whose center was a hearth, with its three stones, where the family interacts and where Nasa newborns' placentas are buried. The circle enclosing the hearth is the tul, which protects the house. Surrounding the house garden are the agricultural fields that encircle it, forming the community. In turn, the community is enveloped by the resguardo, the municipality, and the department (or province). In other words, all of these levels, whether they are distinctly Nasa, the product of the history of indigenous-European relations, or instances of the Colombian administrative geography, are inextricably linked into a cosmos that must be balanced, just as the tul is by its owners and by shamans, a very Nasa image of interculturalism.

Western Discourses versus Nasa Models

In the best of all intercultural worlds, the tul constitutes a space in which Western and Nasa environmental science can coexist, where issues of ecology and conservation can be wedded to notions of cosmic harmony. However, this is not always the case, for both local teachers and PEB activists attempt to sidestep the incorporation of Western concepts by instead emphazising cosmovision as an overarching philosophy. That is, instead of embracing interculturalism as a fruitful dialogue between cultural worlds, they frequently view the outside as a force impinging on lo propio, breaking its coherence. I observed this at a meeting called to evaluate CRIC's secondary school curriculum in the area of community and nature, a curricular area that folds science, cosmovision, agriculture, and development into a single interdisciplinary unit. Workshop participants included members of PEB's regional team, teachers from the three active CECIBS—Juan Tama, Las Delicias-Buenos Aires, and López Adentro—and some members of the local community in which the meeting was held, in this case, resettled Nasa earthquake victims from Mosoco, Tierradentro, now living in the municipality of Morales near Popayán (who were silent observers at the meeting).

Western concepts of agroecology and hydrography, which are central to the curriculum as it was presented, were identified by most of the participants as too narrow to serve as successful vehicles for integrating the broad range of ideas that fall under cosmovision. Significantly, the negotiations that took place around this point illustrated the breach between the regional office and local teachers. Regionally based colaboradores focused on narrowly pedagogical issues, including the specific language and categories of the curriculum, thus diminishing the impact of the broader ideas that its authors sought to convey. For example, they argued over whether "themes" and "indicators" were sufficiently connected and whether general objectives should correspond more closely to "themes." Local teachers, on the other hand, were more interested in confronting Nasa ideas like tul with Western academic concepts, such as agroecology, by asking how such concepts were situated within indigenous systems of knowledge. This spurred a fascinating discussion of whether, by defining indigenous constructs in opposition to Western ones, they were implicitly circumscribing the autonomous nature of cosmovision and privileging

Western forms of knowledge. This took place in a series of exchanges in which colaboradores employed a discourse deriving from social science—much like my gloss of the discussion—while CECIB teachers spoke of the need to relate Western terminologies to their everyday practice in the classroom. Significantly, this exchange once again brought to the fore the tensions between interculturalism and lo propio, insofar as it forced colaboradores to unveil in public discussion the ambivalences they felt as external interpreters of Nasa culture who could only imperfectly comprehend cosmovision. As one colaborador confided to me during a break in the deliberations, the extent to which lo propio is created through a constant movement between inside and outside remained a point of dispute between the teachers located on the inside and the regional activists and colaboradores who were always, to some degree, outside.

CHAPTER 5

Second Sight

Nasa and Guambiano Theory

Over three decades ago, Delmos Jones proposed that "native anthropology" would become feasible only when it developed "a set of theories based on non-Western precepts and assumptions in the same sense that modern anthropology is based on and has supported Western beliefs and values" (1970, 251). Jones was thinking, of course, of minority scholars in the United States who, armed with the double consciousness afforded by their position straddling the boundary between the dominant society and their own subordinated groups, could potentially develop what W. E. B. Du Bois (1989 [1903], 2–3) called "second-sight," a privileged minority vantage point from which to analyze social life. But theorizing is also the province of grassroots social movements such as CRIC and other Caucan indigenous organizations who generate novel conceptual tools not only to make academic sense of the realities they experience but to act on them politically. It is to the generation of theory in concrete social struggles that I turn in this chapter, exploring how native intellectuals in Cauca have created theoretical vehicles suited to the construction of an indigenous second sight that fosters the new ideologies, discourses, and practices necessary if indigenous peoples are to develop their own proposals of citizenship in a pluricultural nation. Many of their sources come from the study of aboriginal languages by native linguists, coupled with the archaeological search for pre-Columbian symbols that both represent their cosmovision—their unique view of their place in the cosmos—and provide models for disseminating this cosmologically oriented work to the community at large. This visual and philological framework can be grasped in their writings, most particularly in the work of the Guambiano history committee, whose creation of a spiral narrative structure to organize Guambiano historical experience I analyze here.

Various native peoples in Cauca have appropriated the spiral motif as a conceptual tool, despite the fact that its significance as a cultural form was not explicit in the past. Spiral motifs crop up in local material culture, particularly in petroglyphs and clothing, but traditionally were not set off as remarkable in comparison to the broader constellation of visual elements in which they were lodged; nor did earlier ethnographers point to their import. The significance of the spiral was a discovery made by contemporary indigenous intellectuals, a self-conscious appropriation originating in empirical research projects. The spiral emerged as a meaningful motif out of observations of how the Nasa shaman's hand moves during rituals, in the course of the archaeological mapping of ancient stone carvings in Tierradentro, a reflection on the significance of the shape of the traditional Guambiano hat, through the analysis of the structure of the Guambiano language. The spiral is a particularly illustrative case in point, which, as I demonstrate in the coming pages, permits Guambiano historians to conceptualize oral narratives in a nonlinear fashion that is grounded in the topography of their resguardo.

Elsa Barkley Brown (1989) argues that an African American theoretical framework is implicit in black material culture. She points, in particular, to quilts as affording an organizing trope for an alternative black epistemology. The patterns we observe in these quilts are not built through symmetry, she writes (923–924), but are founded on the blending of diverse elements (924–925). Brown asserts that quilt patterning is grounded in a nonlinear philosophy of knowledge, which she sees as the opposite of white Euro-American historical reasoning (926). A similar search for alternative patterns has emerged in Latin America. Kay Warren (1998a, chaps. 5–6) and Víctor Montejo (2002) suggest that organizing tropes for contemporary Guatemalan Mayan research (Montejo 1987; Montejo and Akab' 1992; Sam Colop 1991) grow out of the revival of ancient narrative forms, such as cyclical notions of history and prophetic strategies that shed new light on the meanings of the violence that native Central Americans have lived through in the past few decades.

This is the kind of epistemological exercise that Maori educator Russell Bishop (1994) celebrates for providing critical tools to indigenous researchers. Bishop warns that a reliance on Western theory—even that of radical authors like Paulo Freire, whose writings influenced PEB in its early years—suppresses the development of a symmetrical dialogue between Maoris and Pahekas (Westerners). Recourse to such theories, Bishop argues, determines the types of materials that researchers can collect and, correspondingly, limits the nature of argumentation to Western logical and explanatory systems (179–180). Many Western theorists, he adds, reduce their arguments to binary oppositions, in contrast to Maori forms of argumentation, which, like the African American quilts indicated by Brown, rely on more complex networks of relationships (180). Thus, Bishop concludes, it is necessary to construct indigenous research tools.[1]

Such arguments tend to insert indigenous or minority logics into a bipolar opposition that contrasts them as monolithic wholes against an equally homogeneous category of "Western logic." This approach neglects the heterogeneous character of both poles and the fact that their positioning in opposition to one another is entirely contextual and a product of historical relationships. Whether or not African American, Maya, or Maori cultural forms are, in fact, as radically divorced from Western ways of knowing as these authors maintain remains a crucial question.[2]

Paul Gilroy, echoing Du Bois, indicates that African American cultural forms are "western and modern, but this is not all they are. . . . Their special power derives from a doubleness, their unsteady location simultaneously inside and outside the conventions, assumptions, and aesthetic rules which distinguish and periodise modernity" (1993, 73). Black epistemologies are hybrid. They are built on the experience of a discriminatory social system that only partially incorporates African Americans. The minority forms on which they are based are also historically constituted, not pristine. For this reason, they integrate both dominant forms and *reimagined* minority forms, creating what Gilroy calls a "dynamic antiphony." The essence of this hybrid system is modern, responding to the long history of resistance to discrimination. In Gilroy's words, it is, more specifically, "anti-modern":

> The anti-modernity of these forms, like their anteriority, appears in the (dis)guise of a premodernity that is both actively reimagined in the present and transmitted intermittently in eloquent pulses from the past. It seeks not simply to change the relationship of these cultural forms to newly autonomous philosophy and science but to refuse the categories on which the relative evaluation of these separate domains is based and thereby to transform the relationship between the production and use of art, the everyday world, and the project of racial emancipation. (1993, 74)

What Gilroy grasps here is essential. Minority theorizing is, by necessity, confrontational. It appropriates conceptual moves and research methodologies

from dominant paradigms and reconfigures them within a minority conceptual space, seizing indigenous forms and reimagining them in a modern context. This makes these strategies intensely modern, but in a contestatory mode.
They critique modernity by juxtaposing to it a revitalized and politicized
tradition that exposes modern forms for what they are: constructs that are no
more natural than are minority representations. Consequently, the use of
antimodern theories opens the way to cultural revitalization.

The Caucan critique of Western theoretical constructs is a reflection on the
relationship between inside and outside. As I have explained in previous chapters, Colombian indigenous intellectuals are engaged in comprehending what
it means to construct cultural difference in an enveloping national social
system and culture. They are bent on defining, through research and political
action, how their ethnic groups cohere into a palpable cultural inside distinct
from the dominant society, a positioning that lends meaning and direction to
their struggle for recognition. This inside is not an unchanging cultural essence of the sort that realist anthropologists once described, although, like our
academic precursors, indigenous intellectuals build on constellations of values
and structures of behavior that cluster within their cultural world, deploying
them in contrast to those of the dominant society. However, such cultural
forms and symbolic representations do not stand for a discrete and bounded
cultural reality that is observable "out there." Caucan indigenous intellectuals
are well aware that four centuries of colonial domination and boundary cross-
ings have spawned a heterogeneous and syncretic cultural topography. For
them, the inside is not that terrain, but the utopia they hope to build, for
which their reflections on indigenous culture provide a template.

Cultural interpretation cannot remain confined to the printed page, one of
the errors frequently made by scholars in cultural studies, who limit their
observations to the written products of such epistemological exercises. In fact,
the vast majority of Colombian indigenous theorizing does not culminate in
academic writing but in a political practice that, while it engages writing, does
so in the form of pamphlets, primary school texts, and internal reports, all of
which are secondary to social action. Moreover, the content of this theory is
not necessarily spelled out, but is more commonly implicit in the research
questions indigenous activists ask, in the methodologies they use, in the vehicles through which the work is disseminated, and in their choice of audience.
Turner (2002) has underlined this in his perceptive interpretation of how
traditional Kayapó structures of oratory and political hierarchy are engaged in
the intercultural arena of meetings with the Brazilian bureaucracy. At these

events, theorizing is condensed into a symbolically laden performance that reinterprets traditional structures of interaction in a novel context, as feuding Kayapó chiefs position themselves in hierarchies in relation to the visiting officials. These reimagined social principles are, in turn, retransmitted through the editing of the Kayapó filmmaker, who reiterates these social moves by careful montage. Theory is never made explicit. Nasa intellectuals are more openly theoretical, but they are more apt to interject theory into political meetings than to write it as academics would do. "Writing culture" is only a small part of these endeavors.

It is imperative, then, that we ground indigenous theorizing firmly within the political practice of the organizations to which these researchers belong, and not confine it to their texts. To begin with, we can look at the social organization of indigenous research. Guambiano and Nasa theorists do not work, as do most academic ethnographers, on individual research projects that elucidate concerns discussed in the literature. Instead, their research is conducted in teams originating in programs focusing on education, health, legal reform, human rights, and other areas of pressing concern to indigenous organizations and communities. In other words, they are not just researchers, they are also activists, who simultaneously study and act on social realities. They do not compile their data through individual interviewing techniques but in the course of exegetical workshops attended by their indigenous peers, where breakout groups analyze issues, thus incorporating communities into the research process and disseminating research results while fieldwork is in process. As a result, the research experience constitutes a theater for political organizing and a venue in which researchers and nonresearchers collaborate in generating social analysis. This is not unique to Cauca. Collective exegetic forms have been embraced for decades by African American academics as a tool for inserting scholarly research into ongoing social processes (Gwaltney 1981, 1993) and deriving new epistemologies that are nourished through dialogue between academics and nonacademics (Collins 1991). What is novel about the Caucan enterprise are the fact that such sophisticated ethnographic research and theorizing are occurring with such marginal participation by the academy.

But if we stop here, at the assertion that representational forms grounded in specific cultures are the major building blocks of indigenous theory, we run the risk of ignoring the fact that discourses arising from a multiplicity of sources inform such theorizations. Notwithstanding the centrality of cosmovision as a tool for redrawing cultural analysis, native peoples have also latched onto "universal" political ideals like "autonomy" and "territory" as the pivots of their historical and sociological interpretations (Chadwick Allen 2002; Smith 1999). These notions form the building blocks of what could be called the "culture" of indigenous organizations. In the space of dialogue that unfolds between indigenous militants and colaboradores, between leaders and communities, and between the organization and representatives of the Colombian state, universal ideals that fall under a rubric of "sovereignty" are reimagined and adjusted to local and organizational needs. This space is no more hybrid than that of the Guambiano historians who, after exposure to anthropological writings, reimagine the spiral. And it is no more distant from the everyday lives of indigenous villagers, who are equally concerned with modern meanings of territory or autonomy as they are with spiral motifs. In fact, there is undoubtedly more debate around changing definitions of sovereignty in communities that constantly suffer the encroachment of a host of armed actors than there is around the spirals interpreted for them by indigenous intellectuals. In keeping with this assertion, in this chapter I examine how a discourse of sovereignty supplies indigenous activists with an alternative basis for constructing theory, looking in particular at the ideals that went into the preparation of a history of CRIC's Bilingual Education Program, particularly the notions of interculturalism, community control, and cosmovision. All three are concepts that circulate throughout Latin America; nevertheless, they acquire a particular significance when they are generated as theoretical tools by specific ethnic groups and social movements, such as the Nasa and CRIC.

Theorizing Guambiano History

Intellectuals belonging to the Caucan elite—aristocratic scholars affiliated with the provincial Academy of History and other patrician institutions—traditionally identified the Guambianos as originating in Peru, interlopers in the mountainous territory they inhabit adjacent to Popayán. Since 1981, when the cabildo of Guambía embarked on a project of repossessing usurped lands lying within their resguardo boundaries, the leadership has felt it imperative that they debunk such theories once and for all. Beginning in 1983, the Guambiano history committee, composed of young schooled intellectuals as well as elders knowledgeable in the oral tradition, initiated collaborative research with cultural anthropologist Luis Guillermo Vasco of the National University of Colombia and Bogotá archaeologist Martha Urdaneta. Their aim: to historically ground the territorial claims that the community was making through land occupations by proving their primordial connections to the land.

The publications of the history committee engage in dialogue with metropolitan readers and the Guambiano community by adopting a new language for interpreting the past. On the part of the Colombian anthropologists concerned, this has meant privileging Guambiano debates and theories over the agendas of their own academic community. For the Guambianos, it has involved embracing a new narrative language, Spanish, and introducing imported written genres for encoding their findings. What emerges is a unique generic form, not strictly metropolitan academic discourse, but certainly not "typical" Guambiano orality either (Urdaneta Franco 1988, 56). The history committee does not simply reproduce oral tradition in written form—a genre that is ubiquitous across Latin America, both in the academic world and in native rights organizations—but weaves oral narrative into an account that is simultaneously retrospective and forward-looking.

The thrust of Guambiano research is in its juxtaposition of plural senses of the past, the multiple ways Guambianos (and other Colombians) read the historical record, organize it into a coherent narrative, and validate it through reference to sources. Guambiano notions of history are grounded in the topography in which they reside, providing constant experiential validation of the oral narratives whose contents play out on the land. The past, as it is remembered in stories and as it is lived in the terrain of Guambía, is also read against the backdrop of elements of material culture, including archaeological sites and articles of clothing. It is simultaneously projected into the future, where political action, principally land claims, corrects the errors made by historical actors. None of these various local historicities is privileged over the others in Guambiano writing. Instead, they are arranged so as to permit the reader to experience their diversity, much as might a knowledgeable Guambiano elder. The various historicities are embedded in a palimpsest of time frames and historical and mythic actors, which come to the fore at particular topographic locations. This multiplicity of ways of reading the past is counterposed to Guambiano history as it is interpreted by the elite of Popayán and as this dominant ideology is reconstituted in ethnohistorical writings. In the writings of the history committee, Guambiano historical reasoning is unambiguously favored over the narratives of the dominant society, which are exposed as politically inspired fabrications. But forms of ethnographic description that owe much to Colombian anthropology are incorporated as elements into the committee's constellation of narratives and experiences, particularly those that make sense of elements of material culture. This demonstrates that in certain contexts, academic discourses can enter into nonconfrontational dialogue with Guambiano logic.

Guambiano strategies for endowing historical narrative with a characteristic texture diverge markedly from those of other authors. Although it is true that academic ethnographers and historians are also concerned with validating the histories that we write and with confronting multiple narratives to construct a story of the past, as I argued in chapter 3, we commonly frame indigenous sources with our own theoretical constructs and we back them up with written evidence or materials collected through accepted ethnographic methodologies. We usually do not juxtapose different forms of evidence as distinct but equally valid, and we generally refrain from employing native procedures for validating sources, with only a few notable exceptions (Price 1990). Finally, we tend to organize our findings into narratives that lead readers to conceptualize history as beginning in the past and ending in the present. This is equally true of writings that disrupt linear chronology through the introduction of textual strategies such as flashbacks and retrospective analysis. Linear thinking also underlies the texts we organize according to analytical categories and even guides our interpretations when we recognize that historical narrative is constructed in the present.

Native Bolivian theorists, like the Guambianos, enjoin us to experiment with how the past and the present are interrelated. Aymara anthropologist Marcelo Fernández Osco (2000, 2002) has coined the term *qhip nayra*, the viewing of the past through multiple eyes, as a theoretical vehicle that not only expands the purview of what constitutes evidence but encourages us to take epistemological risks on the very basis of the multiplicity of modes of remembering the past. Fernández (2002) cites a local Aymara historian, Alejandro Mamani Quispe (1988), whose history of the town of Cohana, located on the shores of Lake Titicaca, juxtaposes a range of historical accounts acquired through interviewing (conveyed in a handwritten channel), through direct experience (recounted in comic strip–like pictures), and through writing (via photocopies of typescripts of legal documents). In Mamani's account, which, to Fernández's mind, epitomizes the notion of qhip nayra, distinct registers of knowledge are not subsumed into a unitary account. Instead, the reader is forced to move between channels without privileging one over the other, such as, for example, written narrative over illustrations. The very diversity of ways of imagining history provides a significant angle for comprehending Cohana's past (Rappaport 2000). Mamani's book echoes in graphic form the grammar of Andean languages, which, through the use of referential suffixes, distinguishes between types of knowledge that have been acquired through direct experience and secondhand narrative or that refer to a distant and mythical past in distinction to more immediate historical experience (Hardman 1988; Howard-Malverde 1990).

This sort of epistemological experimentation is implicit in the archaeological and historical publications of the Guambiano history committee, especially in a long article, "On the Second Day the Great People (Numisak) Sowed Authority and the Plants and, with Its Juice, Drank Their Meaning," in which the theoretical underpinnings of a dialogue between Guambiano historians and metropolitan anthropologists are depicted in the very act of narration (Vasco et al. 1993).[3] The article contains stories of the origin of Guambiano settlement, of colonial *caciques* (hereditary chiefs), of the loss and reclaiming of lands, and of the forces that have operated against Guambiano autonomy: the Church, the introduction of commercial fertilizers, and opium poppy cultivation, among others. These stories are interspersed with interpretive segments on the nature of Guambiano culture, some of which evince the hand of Luis Guillermo Vasco, the anthropologist, some the pen of young Guambiano analysts, and others the voice of Taita Abelino Dagua, the elder who was the driving force behind the committee. Although almost none of these fragments is identified by author, it is not difficult to distinguish the voices of the various committee members, because the language they use differs considerably. Some segments are highly reminiscent of the interpretive flavor of ethnographic discourse; others report historical events in the more immediate language of personal reminiscence; a third group of passages assumes a moralizing tone characteristic of elders. The narrative moves from one voice to another in a spiral that rolls and unrolls, a trope that provides the central organizing model of the article. The structure of the narrative arises not from an exclusively Guambiano subject position, but from an intercultural environment in which Guambiano intellectuals engage and reinterpret the theories and methodologies of metropolitan social scientists working in collaboration with them.

One of the most elegant segments of this history interprets the past as a spiral structure, embodied in various examples of material culture:

> Time is like a wheel which turns; it is like a *pøtø*, a ring, which returns to the original time; this is the path of the sun above the earth, this is the form in which the *køsrømpøtø*, the rainbow, walks, when it makes a circle upon turning

around. But it is also like the snail or like the rainbow, which has a *tøm*, an articulation through which everything is related, marking the epoch or the period. Time goes and returns, passes and returns, passes and returns. . . .

To speak of history implies a progression that is not linear, but is not circular, either. It is like a spiral in three dimensions, whose center is on high; the Guambianos say that it is a *srurrapu*, a snail. Many rocks in various localities of the resguardo are engraved with petroglyphs; among them there is a dominant motif: the spiral. Simple, double, inscribed in concentric circles, its presence is obvious and repetitive.

The traditional hat of men and women, the *kuarimpøtø*, composed of a long woven band with various threads, sewn into a spiral around a center, repeats the motif of the snail shell. The elders can read history in it, just as [they see] their vision of society as a whole and the ways in which things are interconnected. In it, the origins of time and space are marked. At its center everything begins and returns. (Vasco et al. 1993, 10–11)

This notion of spiral space was first developed by Guambiano linguists who, through an analysis of linguistic categories and temporal terminologies, describe time as something that rolls and unrolls in multiple temporal bands.

Linguistics provides a fertile ground out of which a great deal of Caucan indigenous theorizing springs. In part, this is due to the fact that the most comprehensive university courses that native activists have studied are in linguistics. In contrast to the vast majority of indigenous students, who have done long-distance university coursework without benefit of close readings, faculty supervision, or classroom discussions, study of ethnolinguistics (generally supported by scholarships at the Universidad de los Andes in Bogotá, the Universidad del Valle in Cali, or the Universidad del Cauca in Popayán) involves full-time coursework, providing indigenous intellectuals with viable conceptual tools that are not as easily attainable through the long-distance format. Moreover, linguistics is seen as immediately applicable in bilingual education and has therefore been a favored field of study. Finally, the approach to structural linguistics taught at these institutions affords students the means to make conceptual linkages between the structure of their languages and symbolic structures inherent in other cultural forms, leading them to study the linguistic construction of space and time (Muelas Hurtado 1995; Nieves Oviedo and Ramos Pacho 1992; Yule 1995).

Guambiana linguist Bárbara Muelas Hurtado argues that the rolling and unrolling of geographic and social space governs the relationships that Guambiano families establish with their surroundings: "When one or more people who live in a house are invited to leave for other sites, they are invited with the expression *pichip mentøkun*, which literally means 'let us unroll.' The opposite situation, when they are invited to return home, is *kitrøp mentøkun*, which means 'let us roll up' or 'let us collect ourselves'" (1995, 32). Similarly, this action of rolling and unrolling defines the Guambiano relationship with time:

> As the years unfold, in lived time, in the voyage of life and through the world, the ancestors have marked a path, they have opened a trail on which those who come behind, their descendants from today, must advance to make history. The past goes in front and the future comes behind. It is as though our ancestors had returned to look for their descendants or as though those who have already left (died) had returned to "judge" what their descendants have accomplished in their absence. It is as though a turn were made in the vast circular space, a new meeting with the ancestor, [of] past and future, an illusion, a hope, in Guambiano thought. The space before us and lived time (conserved in tradition) orient human life. They go ahead [of us] in life, and [continue] after life. The space that is left behind and time not yet lived are a space and a time that must still unroll. (35–36)

The entire publication of the history committee, comprising semi-independent fragments with distinct authors whose relationships roll and unroll, can itself be seen as a spiral, a *pøtø*, that continuously returns to or "sights upon" recurrent themes, such as the *pishimisak*, the people of the cold, who are the ancestors of the Guambiano, or the nature of time in the Guambiano worldview. The history committee's text rolls and unrolls, moving back and forth from the present into the distant past of the ancestors, the more recent past of the abuses of the hacienda, and the decisive moment of the recovery of cabildo authority and the repossession of usurped lands. This is not a linear chronological narrative, but a constant return to key moments in Guambiano history, which come up, again and again, as significant teachings.

The narrative begins with a far-ranging spiral that originates in the distant past and jumps ahead in time to the present. The story opens with the appearance of Mama Manuela Caramaya, the foundational chieftainess, or *cacica*, of Guambía, who was born in a river and defended Guambiano lands from indigenous and European invaders. Mama Manuela's story is followed by an inward turn of the spiral that moves backward in time to an earlier event, the creation of the world. Here, we learn of the earliest people, the pishimisak, who combined masculine and feminine attributes and whose lives were intimately connected with the circulation of water from the ancestral lands located in the high peaks of the Andes (the *páramo*) to the lower reaches, where the Guambiano now live. In a juxtaposition of past and present, the pishimisak are called the "fathers and mothers of the cabildo," linking the colonial and modern institution to a primordial point of origin. Time is then compressed with a leap to the 1980s, when Guambianos clashed with the leadership of CRIC after having played a seminal role in building the organization. The authors paint the Guambiano as a peaceful people, like their pishimisak ancestors, implying their difference from the warlike Nasa of CRIC. As they recount, Guambiano peacefulness was reoriented toward the occupation of the hacienda Las Mercedes and its reincorporation into the resguardo, leading to a politicization of the cabildo and, ultimately, to the founding of AICO. This first spiral establishes the foundations of Guambiano autonomy: the pishimisak, Mama Manuela, the roots of the cabildo, and modern organizing strategies, culminating in the repossession of Las Mercedes. It establishes its veracity through evidence that all Guambianos can experience in the topography, in their material culture, and in cabildo practice.

A second spiral retraces the contours of the first, this time focusing on the expanse of sacred territory that comprises Guambía and some of the moments at which the Guambianos have violated its sacrality. Unlike the first spiral, which more or less moves outward in time, unrolling from primordial events toward the present, the second loop moves back and forth in the more recent past, rolling and unrolling in an attempt to fill in the gaps left in the first account. In particular, the second spiral narrates how Guambiano autonomy was lost. The authors highlight contemporary problems that have arisen as Guambiano increasingly cultivate opium poppies that, for a time, completely blanketed the landscape, particularly in the higher reaches of the resguardo, hidden in valleys behind high mountain peaks.[4] The story of the expansion of poppy cultivation is followed by an abrupt shift to the distant past, with a story of how the Guambiano settled the Cordillera by moving from the hot Cauca Valley to the highlands, an ascent that mirrors the movement of poppies up the mountain slopes. Then follows a history of how Guambiano lands were lost to large landowners in the nineteenth century. Suddenly, however, a full circle is made, with a return to the pishimisak and the founding cacica. The need to reclaim Las Mercedes is explained in terms of the sacred importance of place, as the hacienda is located at the confluence of the two major rivers, male and female, the very spot where the cacica Mama Manuela was born.

A series of other stories flesh out the second spiral, or perhaps they form a third loop, documenting the modes of insertion of colonial institutions and habits into Guambía. Some of these, such as the collusion of earlier Guambiano governors with the landlords (undated) and how municipal authorities forced the Guambianos to assign individual plots to resguardo members (1920s), illustrate the process of land loss. Others focus on the influence of Christianity on the Guambianos, including visions of the Virgin Mary (undated), the entrance of the Missionary Sisters of Mother Laura into Guambía and how they taught the Guambianos to wear shoes (first half of the twentieth century), and the coming to Guambía of the Protestant missionary organization the Summer Institute of Linguistics (1955). What is significant about these fragmentary accounts, some of which are undated and hence take on an emblematic aspect, is that they do not blame domination entirely on the colonizers, but take Guambianos to task for collaborating with the landlords, for buying into Christianity, for embracing the teachings of the Catholic nuns and the Protestant missionaries. Their juxtaposition to the discussion of the significance of Las Mercedes in the sacred topography of Guambía indicates that the process of land loss went hand in hand with the colonization of the Guambiano mind, which erased such memories. Documentation of colonial domination is followed by an account of the 1980 occupation of Las Mercedes, then by an exegesis of the Guambiano terms for community and reciprocity, and finally, by a segment that reads very much like a sermon, which emphasizes the need to revitalize Guambiano culture. In this segment, the authors explain that history is susceptible to correction through ideological decolonization and militant political action. The building blocks of history are thus grist not only for the historian's mill but for the militant's as well.

Clearly, this is not a chronological narrative, but a history consciously made to roll and unroll, a series of spirals whose contours are dictated by the topographic features in which foundational beings live and by the political exigencies of the Guambiano struggle. The spiral organizing model is explicitly stated in those segments that engage in cultural exegesis; these passages appear to have been composed by anthropologist Vasco. The conscious adoption of a spiral structure was reaffirmed for me in discussions with Guambiano intellectuals.

However, a second format simultaneously structures the narrative. At the end of the article, there is a lengthy discourse by Abelino Dagua, the elder who was the motor behind the history project. Taita Abelino, as he is respectfully called by Guambianos, reiterates the history of Guambía and the need for cultural and territorial revitalization, framing the entire narrative as a political speech, much as he might do in a public assembly. This is reminiscent of the strategies of Bolivian filmmakers working in collaboration with local indige-nous actors, who found that their work was more clearly comprehended by native communities when sandwiched between oral recountings by respected storytellers of the events depicted in the film (Sanjinés and Grupo Ukamau 1979). Taita Abelino's overwhelming influence on the project can be appreci-ated when we consider that most of the early history being recounted was unknown to most Guambianos before the committee was founded, but was revived and reconstructed under his guidance. Taita Abelino's voice provides an organizing thread, teaching and advising Guambiano readers and listeners, much as he accompanies the cabildo.

The Limits of Guambiano Theorizing

Guambiano historical writing represents an attempt to restructure the very form of historical narration, to focus on Guambiano agency, and to recognize explicitly the close relationship between primordial mythic agents, like Mama Manuela, and the Guambianos of the present. But although it appears to succeed in "provincializing Europe" (to appropriate Dipesh Chakrabarty's [2000] notion), Guambiano history cannot effectively appeal to the multiple audiences that it seeks to reach; it fails in spanning the divide between Guam-biano and educated external readers (Vasco 2002, 318–319). While the commit-tee aims to revitalize Guambiano memory, it also seeks to engage in dialogue with non-Guambianos, particularly academics, and to transform the epis-temologies and methods of Colombian anthropologists and historians. It is for this reason that the committee has submitted its work for consideration in academic competitions and has published in academic venues. In short, they see their work as a tool for stimulating intellectual pluralism in Colombian society at the same time that it constitutes a revisionist account meant for Guambiano consumption.

But the literary nature of the narrative, which is what makes it a powerful tool for intercultural communication, inhibits its reception by the Guam-bianos themselves. It is coauthored by a Colombian anthropologist who does not speak Guambiano, forcing the history committee to write in Spanish. The committee is clearly a productive exercise in intercultural exchange, but its Spanish-language publications must be retranslated orally into Guambiano for use in bilingual schools, robbing them of their unique narrative structure when their contents are transmitted as a list of facts. Moreover, the project is framed by its articulation with the educational institutions in which it is employed, run by Guambiano intellectuals but still very much part of an official school system conforming to national curricular objectives. Let me briefly consider the implications of these issues.

History as written by the Guambianos is based almost exclusively on oral narrative, despite the fact that the committee conducted extensive (and as yet unanalyzed) archival research. While their reticence to incorporate documentary sources may have something to do with the fact that the committee members are not trained in paleography or in the interpretation of archival materials, it probably has a great deal more to do with the politicized nature of the contemporary Guambiano historical imagination. Anthropology has traditionally painted native Andean cultures as oral in nature, neglecting the very significant ways native peoples have participated in literate society since the Spanish invasion. In particular, the drafting of legal documents was ubiquitous since the sixteenth century, incorporating native peoples into a Spanish "lettered city" in which power was exercised through specific generic forms of the written word (González Echevarría 1990; Rama 1996). The lettered nature of Colombian indigenous society lost its potency, however, in the nineteenth century, when state policies of homogenization no longer recognized "indigenous" as a viable legal category capable of exercising its own administrative voice (Findji and Rojas 1985; Rappaport 1998b). As a result, past literacies have been erased from contemporary historical memory.[5] Following an anthropological model, Guambiano intellectuals characterize themselves as oral, but with a twist: Guambiano orality stands in opposition to the literacy of the dominant society in a conceptual model that conflates orality with the inside of indigenous culture and literacy with outside Europeanness. This vision differs from traditional anthropological discourse insofar as the oral Guambiano inside is not classified as "primitive" in comparison to the literate, modern, and European dominant society. Instead, the two are juxtaposed as *different* along a scale based on relative authenticity, with Guambianos located on the scale's most positive pole. However, this judgment enters into conflict with the intent of the history project itself, which is intercultural and literate, not exclusively Guambiano and oral.

The Guambiano strategy stands in contrast to approaches taken by indigenous intellectuals in other Latin American countries. Aymara historical theorizing appropriates alphabetic literacy as part of an Andean store of ancestral knowledge. The copyright page of all of the publications of the Aymara-led Andean Oral History Workshop (THOA) explains the derivation of Aruwiyiri

("He who sets fire with his voice"), the name of their publishing house, taken from an early twentieth-century indigenous bulletin by foregrounding the incorporation of "the written word into the genealogy of ancestral knowledge of our communities." Literacy is, thus, a hallmark of their methodology. THOA's strategy has been to collect both oral narratives and written documentation, as well as to focus on twentieth-century political movements in which native communities reappropriated their colonial titles, reconstituted their chiefdoms, and educated their populations in clandestine schools (Choque et al. n.d.; Condori Chura and Ticona Alejo 1992; Rivera Cusicanqui 1986). The embracing of literacy is part of the Aymara historical patrimony, but so it is, too, among the indigenous peoples of Colombia. The rigorous university training in historical methodology that THOA's founders received at the Universidad Mayor de San Andrés in the 1970s and 1980s probably has a great deal more to do with the Aymara insistence on literacy; young university-educated Guambiano historians are currently embarking on a project of extensive archival research, which may lead to a reconsideration of the existing conceptual pairing of indigenous/oral and nonindigenous/literate.

The othering of Guambiano history by the Guambianos breeds further dilemmas. "On the Second Day . . ." is indeed innovative in its effort to persuade the academic community of the feasibility of indigenous theorizing, but it does not depart substantially from academic genres of writing, however experimental its form, making it inaccessible to the Guambiano public. It is published in Spanish, typeset in a recognizable visual format that contains footnotes and bibliographies, and was incorporated into an academic anthology that invites a metropolitan intellectual audience, not a Guambiano readership. Thus, it remains inextricably connected to the "lettered city," in which Guambiano writers communicate with the outside and not with their own people.[6] "On the Second Day . . ." is not widely read in Guambía itself, where its contents are transmitted orally in the schools, following the standard Colombian educational practices of memorization and repetition that still characterize most indigenous education. This has ensured that an entire generation of Guambiano youth knows its history but has not internalized the innovative theory through which this history can be interpreted from a modern Guambiano perspective.[7] The writings of the history committee that do circulate in the resguardo are shorter pamphlets and a monograph (Dagua Hurtado et al. 1998), which do not attempt to reconfigure the histories the group has collected within a distinct narrative framework; many of my twenty-something Guambiano friends have proudly displayed to me their personal copies of these publications, which are sold in the cabildo office. Although they provide new narratives for a future cabildo leadership, they do not project the epistemological terms on which the history project is premised.

Paraguayan writer Bartomeu Melià (1997, 96) reminds us, however, that in a society with more writers than readers, we might do best to focus on the effects of writing on the *authors* and not their audience: "One can almost speak more of a society of Guaraní writers, than of readers of Guaraní. This affirmation must be understood, not in the sense of there being more actual writers than potential readers, but in the sense that the identity and activities of the former are more defined and constant than those of the latter." In this sense, we might do better to understand the workings of the history committee as essentially similar to those of any workshop, where the participants are exposed to new issues at the same time that they engage in analysis. Although this reading of the effectiveness of the history committee reduces its impact to a considerably smaller group of people, the committee provides a crucial arena for training potential leaders who will have a broader political impact on the Guambiano community.

Beyond Writing

There exist attempts at breaking the kind of impasse that I have detailed. Literacy can be bypassed entirely through a focused insistence on the primacy of oral narrative, accompanied by the collectivization of historical interpretation, replicating, in effect, what transpires in workshops. I am unfamiliar with the details of such efforts among the Guambiano, where I have not conducted extensive research, but I have been told about the construction of a building called the House of the Cacique Payán, which is meant to provide an interactive site for engaging Guambianos in historical remembering in their own language and without direct appeal to literate conventions of expression.[8] The first floor of the building portrays Guambiano history through murals that replicate the geography of the resguardo, and the second floor will expose Guambiano viewers to the genealogies of caciques.

Nasa attempts, with which I am more familiar, at subverting the hegemony of the lettered city suggest that it is indeed possible to "provincialize Europe" for internal interlocutors, although at the expense of furthering a dialogue with those on the outside, given that such enterprises do not result in extensive written publications. The School of Nasa Thought, the Nasa think tank founded by Adonías Perdomo in the resguardo of Pitayó, is a case in point. It meets several times a year at different rural locations in Cauca, providing a venue in which Nasa thinkers reformulate the terms of historical and cultural research, engage in dialogue with external scholars, and explore their own past. The members of the Escuela—some fifty to one hundred come to their meetings—arrive at their decisions collectively, conversing in Nasa Yuwe, effectively disseminating their results without the necessity of employing Western literary conventions or the Spanish language. In northern Cauca, CRIC-affiliated resguardos have just completed a broad-ranging oral history project for which scores of young people have sought out informants in the community, recorded their personal reminiscences of key moments in the history of indigenous struggles in the region, and are sharing this material with other community members through public assemblies. I return to this project, the Cátedra Nasa-UNESCO, in the next chapter, but wish to point out here that for these youthful researchers, it is the research experience, and not the published final project, that provides a venue for rethinking history on local terms.[9]

Such efforts do not reconfigure the terms of the lettered city. Instead, they bypass it entirely, thus ensuring a more effective communication within the indigenous community, although not necessarily with external interlocutors, both of which are priorities for the movement. Dissemination within the indigenous community and communication with a pluralist external reality engage different communicative strategies, one of them oral and the other literate, one unarticulated with the lettered city and the other attempting to redraw its contours. Perhaps the most effective vehicles for disseminating indigenous theorizations will not engage the terms of the traditional lettered city but transcend them to take up the challenges of electronic forms of communication that are more accessible to a community of nonreaders (Ong 1982), particularly when they are grounded in culturally appropriate conceptual frameworks. I am thinking, in particular, of video, which is becoming increasingly popular in the Colombian countryside.

Yu'up'hku/Han parido las aguas (The waters have given birth) is a video made by the Fundación Sol y Tierra (Osorio et al. 1994), the nongovernmental organization created by the Quintín Lame Armed Movement after they abandoned their clandestine way of life. The narrative revolves around the supernatural birth of caciques told from a Nasa perspective. Mythic and historical referents are superimposed with contemporary experience through the juxtaposition of visuals and taped narratives that depict a variety of time frames, just as do the Guambiano authors of "On the Second Day . . ." *Yu'up'hku* opens with the 1994 earthquake and landslide that devastated Tierradentro, moving to an evocation of the birth of a cacique, set in mythic time against a visual backdrop of a shamanic seance. Myth is juxtaposed to contemporary experience, implying a connection between the rituals that facilitated the incorporation of mythic caciques into Nasa society and the practice of thê' walas today. The history of the domination of the Nasa by Spanish soldiers, the Catholic Church, guerrilla organizations, and drug traffickers follows in a visual montage of photos of Tierradentro churches and Bibles, conquistador portraits, and clips of the opium harvest, counterposed to a narration by Manuel Sisco, a PEB activist, of the story of the birth of the cacique. Significantly, all of these historical images are very much of the present, insofar as they depict buildings that still stand in Tierradentro, portraits that are printed in school textbooks, and ritual activities with which indigenous viewers are intimately familiar. That is, they represent the past without being of it. A montage of shots of violent attacks on the Nasa and cabildo rituals also punctuates Sisco's narrative, violence being a fundamental referent of contemporary Nasa life, and the legitimization of indigenous authority its antidote. Note that unlike in standard documentary form, Sisco does not explain or validate the visual material. In contrast, his words run against the grain of the visual history of exploitation, providing a liberatory counternarrative.

The video then turns to dream time. Two important Vitoncó shamans, Ángel María Yoinó and Roberto Andela, recount the visions that alerted them to the impending 1994 disaster. Their faces and mannerisms display the sentiment that accompanies Nasa historical reflection and which various indigenous intellectuals told me is generally absent from the work of academic authors. This is followed by an explanation by Nasa linguist Marcos Yule of the fallacies of the interpretations of those who link the Tierradentro floods to mythical chiefly births, something I come back to in the next chapter. Several of these narratives are in Nasa Yuwe with Spanish subtitles. Manuel Sisco then returns to lecture viewers on the salient points of Nasa cosmovision that they must learn, interspersed with visuals of people wounded in the 1994 disaster and the parallel ravages of the land; Sisco's intervention is similar to the moralizing monologue of Taita Abelino Dagua in the Guambiano historical treatise. Finally, the circle is closed with shots of the arrival of the victims of the 1994 disaster in their new village, appropriately called Juan Tama, after the mythical founder of Vitoncó.

In *Yu'up'hku* a novel format for recounting history that is reminiscent of Marcelo Fernández's notion of qhip nayra is incorporated into a medium that is more accessible to community members than is writing, facilitating the dissemination of both its contents *and* its form. The audience's attention moves from mythic narratives to historical artifacts, from striking visual images that recall the 1994 disaster and accounts of personal experience to exegesis by public intellectuals without privileging one over the other and without providing explicit explanation of the montage's logic. It is left to the viewers, whether Nasa or nonindigenous, to make sense of the account.[10]

Theorizing in the Contact Zone

Chadwick Allen (2002, 18–20), reflecting on the work of Native American and Maori authors, argues that postcolonial theory misses the mark when it comes to Fourth World peoples because their relationship to colonialism is different from that of postcolonial subjects in countries whose indigenous majorities have won independence. Fourth World peoples—Allen focuses on indigenous minorities in developed countries like the United States and New Zealand, but his arguments are pertinent for Latin America as well—live in a perpetual state of colonialism, in which the independence achieved by European settlers has not been accompanied by the attainment of indigenous autonomy. The meaning of "native" is blurred and complicated in these societies, so that resistance must take unique forms. Dipesh Chakrabarty (2000) urges Third World scholars to move beyond the "metanarrative of the nation-state" in their writing of history; however, indigenous writers and activists in New Zealand and North America cannot reject colonial concepts such as "treaty," "nation," or "sovereignty." Instead, in Allen's view, they *rerecognize* them (20). In other words, they must use these concepts as "silent second texts" against which to write, in an effort to pinpoint the silences and broken promises inherent in them. I take Allen's notion of rerecognition to be similar to Alcida Ramos's (1998) use of "instrumentalization," the selective appropriation and transformation of key symbols in a political context. Rerecognized or instrumentalized constructs become central organizing tropes in indigenous thought, offering new and radical modes of reimagining (Allen 2002, chaps. 3–4).

Colombian native peoples' relationship to the settler societies in which they live is different from that of Native Americans or Maori. Latin American countries exist in a relationship of dependency to First World governments and a globalized economy. Unlike the settler societies of the United States or New Zealand, the Colombian settler population, including its intellectuals, see themselves as subaltern in relation to the United States. This perhaps accounts in part for the uncomfortable (but productive) relationships that have developed between academic and indigenous intellectuals in Colombia. In the Colombian situation in particular, dependency has translated into a U.S.-sponsored counterinsurgency war that has scourged the countryside, violating indigenous territorial autonomy in ways that Native Americans and Maori have not experienced for generations. Globalization has particular local manifestations in Cauca. Drug trafficking has fueled the violence, supporting the paramilitary and the guerrillas, who are capable of financing themselves without outside assistance (Kirk 2003). The drug economy penetrated indigenous communities in the 1990s, breaking the delicate balance that traditionally permitted native people to simultaneously cultivate for their own subsistence and engage in wage labor to acquire much-needed cash (Gómez and Ruiz 1997); today, poppies and coca have replaced other cultigens and people must buy their food in urban centers, resulting in malnutrition and an increased dependence on the market.

Furthermore, the brutal discrimination and marginalization that native peoples have historically experienced in a less developed country like Colombia mean that they lack a layer of indigenous professionals similar to the Native American and Maori researchers and writers described by Chadwick Allen (2002) and Linda Tuhiwai Smith (1999). This has led to a dependence on, but also a fruitful dialogue with, colaboradores, spurring them to seek intercultural relations. Moreover, there are no treaties that establish Colombian indigenous people as autonomous nationalities, even if only as a legal fiction, as occurs in New Zealand and the United States. Colombian resguardo titles are royal bequests, legitimized in postcolonial legislation, which grant only a limited autonomy to indigenous communities. Consequently, native rights movements seek equality within the broader Colombian society at the same time that they strive to build autonomous imaginaries.

Finally, the official policy of *mestizaje* that guided many Latin American governments in the nineteenth and twentieth centuries (Gould 1998) advocated the liquidation of indigenous communal institutions and the fading of indigenous identities. As a result, a vast mestizo sector makes up the majority of the population. Throughout the continent the state has appropriated indigenous heritage as a national patrimony, blurring the distinction between mestizo settlers and native peoples in ways that the indigenous movement has struggled for the past three decades to surmount. For all these reasons, indigenous organizations look to radical pluralism, the recognition of their equal place in society as citizens who are culturally different. To participate in the national arena, they must "rerecognize" core national values that, in the past, advocated cultural homogenization as a route to nation-building. Additionally, they must redefine anthropological concepts that relegated them to a subordinate place in the nation since independence in the early nineteenth century. In the following section, I look at how such highly charged external values are instrumentalized by CRIC.

Guidelines for a History of PEB

In 2001 I joined a collaborative research team, composed of Nasa linguist Abelardo Ramos and colaboradora Graciela Bolaños, charged with writing a history of CRIC's bilingual education program, a project funded by the German chapter of the European nongovernmental organization Terre des Hommes. My own take on the history of PEB is presented in the previous chapter. I return here to focus on the research process itself, paying special attention to how its organizing motifs were generated and the dynamics of the workshops in which collective decisions were made regarding research priorities. PEB hoped to produce a document for dissemination in Cauca, in the Colombian indigenous movement and educational establishment, and among its international contacts, including both European funding organizations and bilingual education programs in other Latin American countries. However, their more immediate objective was to incorporate the project into PEB's ongoing activities as a learning experience, particularly into its university-level program, where the most committed bilingual teachers study. To this end, a series of workshops and meetings were held in 2000 and 2001, in which PEB activists on the regional and local levels drew up a list of fifty-one questions meant to orient the research and to provide PEB affiliates with the wherewithal to gather relevant information in their localities. These questions afford a glimpse at the intellectual priorities of PEB and the guiding concepts inherent in the project.

The workshops that I attended were underscored by an ambivalence over the terms of the project. Participants argued over whether what they wanted was a *sistematización*, a synthetic document that would lay out PEB's major concerns in the present and compile information from its key components, or an *historia*, a retrospective narrative, resulting from research. To me, sistematización remained an unknown, even after it was explained at the workshop. It was unclear if it was a report of current priorities, a forward-looking analysis setting new directions for the organization, or a weakly retrospective compilation of raw data. Many of the eternal fault lines between indigenous activists and colaboradores, between Nasa speakers and monolingual Spanish speakers, and between those who had internalized a pedagogical discourse and those who remained critical of it, all of which I have documented in earlier chapters, were reopened in the course of this debate. The Nasa speakers and their colaborador allies preferred the *historia* approach, perhaps because they were keen to acquire new research methodologies. The monolingual Spanish speakers among the Nasa and their friends in the ranks of the colaboradores, who were more pedagogically oriented and more heavily involved in administrative duties and report writing, pushed for a sistematización.

The debate took place at a meeting in Paniquitá, a resguardo that is less than an hour's drive from Popayán. An initial plenary debated the organization of the workshop, whether the small number of participants in its first hours—there were no more than ten of us at first—merited the standard structure of plenary and breakout groups, and whether this structure was indeed Nasa. Ironically, the latter point was brought up by a Basque observer from Mugarik Gabe, a Basque NGO that funds PEB and which had sent a representative to visit its local projects, and not by the Nasa participants, who have thoroughly internalized the standard workshop format. We divided into breakout groups and were asked to consider various details concerning the impact of PEB on localities. Because I was assigned to a discussion group made up primarily of people from Paniquitá, where PEB had never been active, we could not answer the questions we were charged to consider. A second plenary followed the small group discussion. The central issue of debate here was over whether the research team would prepare a sistematización or an historia. Tension was palpable as the different sides attempted unfruitfully to convey their intentions. Proponents of sistematización were asked repeatedly what their approach consisted of. They responded with incomplete answers that emphasized the analytical dimension of the sistematización without ever explaining what such a document might contain. The structure and content of a sistematización was never fully explicated. Moreover, the most recent sistematización completed by CRIC, which collected a decade of information on PEB's profesionalización program (CRIC 2000), provided a negative example of what a sistematización might be. A compendium of interview transcripts, summaries of workshops, and curricular guidelines, the document was a rich but disorganized mine of information, ultimately unsatisfying to many PEB members because it belied the systematicity and synthesis they thought were inherent in the sistematización format.

This series of unfruitful exchanges unfolded parallel to a second line of argumentation introduced by the Nasa speakers, producing an uncomfortable double monologue in which colaboradores and monolingual Spanish-speaking Nasas advocated the sistematización format, while Nasa speakers took a completely different tack. They addressed the participants in Nasa Yuwe, cursorily summarizing their arguments afterward in Spanish. The very linguistic distance they imposed on the group underlined the tremendous conceptual distance that, they argued, lay between Nasa and pedagogical ways of thought. Through their interventions, which were alternately angry and mystical, they accused the organizers of ideological hegemony and a lack of sensitivity toward the Nasa. These two lines of communication continued to evolve, parallel to one another, throughout the plenary, without the two sides ever coming to an understanding. It was undoubtedly the doggedness of the Nasa speakers, who were in the majority, and their refusal to engage the discourse of the others that led the group to choose historia over sistematización.

In part, the struggle was about whether or not PEB would be guided by a pedagogical discourse, characterized by such methodologies as sistematización. But whereas what was ultimately decided was to produce an historia, the list of questions that was to guide this enterprise was more in keeping with a sistematización than with an historia, insofar as it dwelled more on guiding principles in the present than in their development over time. Most of the questions highlight the "whys" of organizational priorities in the present, as opposed to the "hows" of the historical development of PEB's objectives. I was not present at the initial workshops at which the list was generated and therefore cannot describe the dynamics of its compilation. However, on the basis of the many other workshops I have attended, I would suspect that many of these questions were worded by the Spanish speakers who preferred the sistematización option and who generally assume the role of note takers at such meetings.

The Guiding Questions

Most of the questions compiled in these workshops are highly presentist in orientation, focusing largely on the objectives that have characterized PEB work in the past decade. Interculturalism, educación propia, and cosmovision are notions that come up repeatedly in the research guide, although they had no currency before 1990. Many of the questions elicit validations of current PEB policies, as opposed to promoting retrospective thinking, because the group that generated the list was fundamentally concerned with consolidating its root metaphors through communal reflection rather than with mining its past experience. Unlike Guambiano history writing and Nasa video, which juxtapose events from the past to dilemmas in the present, using myth, ritual, and sacred topography as a kind of umbilical cord connecting the two, most of the PEB members who generated the list knew little of the program's past and to some extent resisted an interpretive form like history that would trace how the meanings of their guiding concepts had changed over time. Morever, they did not appeal to root metaphors originating in Nasa Yuwe but to universal notions with high currency throughout Latin America. Let me explore how some of these were generated.

PEB has always thought of itself as more than an educational program: it is an organizing tool charged with building CRIC at the local level. In this sense, it is a "movement," but not strictly an educational one. This principle, which is widely held at both the regional and local levels, constitutes the thrust of some of the research questions that emerged out of the workshops:

> Why has a political movement developed in Cauca, which has education as one of its strategies?
>
> Why does education become a movement in Cauca? In what sense?
>
> What conditions across time with respect to lands, history, autonomy, economy, and spirituality have impacted the educational process, and what has been the impact of the educational process on these conditions?
>
> What tools have been created by the educational process that permit its internalization and articulation to the general organization of the community?

As these questions demonstrate, education is a political vehicle for inducing communities to develop a particular cosmic and historical relationship with their lands and to construct vehicles for political autonomy, economic reconstruction, and community development. In this sense, this group of questions supplies a general baseline for the history project, laying the groundwork for an understanding of how community control of education constitutes a broader political strategy that ranges far beyond the schoolhouse. However, activists were not seeking to move back beyond the 1990s to answer these questions. Instead, they hoped to respond on the basis of their personal experience, which, for the most part, did not exceed a decade or so of activism. In a sense, their very questions supply the answers that they seek, instead of leading them to range more freely through the past. The questions elicit current discourses rather than historical explanation—which is precisely what the sistematización format affords.

PEB's objectives are also directed toward the movement as a whole, because it perceives itself as a vanguard capable of making the indigenous movement more "indigenous." Joaquín Viluche (2001, 1, 3), a Nasa member of PEB's regional team, responded to the guiding questionnaire in writing with a personal reflection on the pressing need to revive Nasa spirituality to ensure that CRIC's leaders do not speak through a "borrowed discourse" and so that the organization has mechanisms to minimize the "mental contamination of the Other." By lessening such "contamination," he argues, the movement will be able to confront the violent abuses that communities currently suffer at the hands of external actors. This issue was also brought up in the questionnaire in relation to the *escuela propia*, or schooling grounded in the primacy of the native culture: "What values are generated by the escuela propia in this situation of violence?" What is significant about this question is that it firmly links PEB's preoccupation with cosmovision to the experiences of indigenous people inhabiting a battlefield.[11] Although the question emphasizes unique aspects of Nasa culture, it does so through an appeal to pedagogical proposals that have been circulating for decades in Latin America. This emphasis on cultural reconstruction does not preclude the building of relationships with external agents through what PEB activists and educational innovators in Latin America have termed "interculturalism." In keeping with CRIC's objective of forging radical pluralism in Colombia, the framers of the questionnaire also sought guidance in the building of cultural alliances with other popular sectors: "Is it possible to construct educational proposals in conjunction with the social movements of Cauca?"

In the political context in which PEB finds itself, a critical issue is CRIC's positioning with respect to official education, which functions for the activists as a metonym for the state as a whole because schools have functioned for decades as a kind of state presence in indigenous communities. PEB-affiliated schools are located in the most militant communities. But what of the resguardos that are members of CRIC but are not as active as Las Delicias, Juan Tama, or Corinto? How does official education collude with traditional political parties and conservative religious leaders to dampen militancy in these communities? How can PEB address these problems without replicating the stifling atmosphere of the schoolhouse? The following questions dwell on these fundamental quandaries:

What are the characteristics of PEB's educational process, and how does it differ from other educational processes?

Various documents speak of the harm that the school has caused to cultures. Why do we continue working with the school? Why have we worked with the school structure and how has it been resignified?

In what sociocultural contexts has the proposal for educación propia developed and how have they experienced the concepts of diversity and interculturalism?

How have educational proposals developed in the different zones [of indigenous Cauca], and how have they related to PEB?

These questions underscore a crucial feature of PEB's appropriation of concepts originating in alternative sectors of the dominant society. What is implicit is the fact that PEB resignifies the concepts it borrows so that radical pedagogy and interculturalism are no longer exercises in education but tools for political mobilization.

Finally, language is placed center stage as a fundamental goal of indigenous educators, as the following question addresses: "To what extent is bilingualism a political position?" The linguistically minded questions contained in the list are key to how PEB understands cultural difference to work. For CRIC, bilingualism is a political position that underscores the distinctiveness of indigenous communities, permeating their worldviews and their ways of relating to the dominant society—a combination of a Whorfian perspective with keen political savvy. Language provides, in turn, a tool for constructing cosmovision, which, as I argue in the next chapter, consolidates diffuse sentiments of cultural difference into a coherent foundational narrative. In a circular way, then, language thus affords a conceptualization of how indigenous people think differently.

But bilingualism is only a political position when it is situated within the complex of approaches that ensure that attention to the native language will not be a transitory stage subordinated to an ultimate goal of proficiency in Spanish. Instead, vernacular literacy is conceived as a building block toward achieving horizontal relations between the indigenous culture and the cultural forms of the dominant society. For such a project to succeed, it is not only necessary for the school to develop innovative approaches to education, but it must also impact the broader community, which is where the political work of promoting pluralism must occur. This implies a deep understanding of education principles and their political significance on the part of community authorities, which can be achieved by opening lines of communication between schools and resguardos, by dismantling the schoolhouse walls through what they call *educación desescolarizada* ("deschooled" education):

> How has an education that is propia, community-generated, bilingual, intercultural, and desescolarizada been constructed and experienced?
>
> How can we explain the validity of community-generated, intercultural, and bilingual training to the communities?
>
> Why does the process of bilingual education begin in experimental schools?
>
> How have communities, PEB, and other institutions handled the politics of the writing of indigenous languages?

Bilingual education, PEB argues, must begin in experimental schools where such approaches are at the core of the educational project and where communities are sufficiently mature politically so that they can embrace the importance of writing in indigenous languages, the validity of interculturalism, and the centrality of their own role in the process. In other words, bilingualism must be resignified as a political tool in those communities that are best able to take advantage of it.

Once this is achieved, we come to a key question that distinguishes the PEB bilingual project from other efforts at bilingual education: "What has been the role of Spanish in the educational process?" In this view, the choice is not between Spanish and native languages, which are equally important for the development of culturally different Colombian citizens, although in distinct ways. On the one hand, bilingual teachers must strive to develop reading skills in Nasa Yuwe, in Guambiano, or in Totoró because it is in the mother tongue that literacy is most easily acquired. However, PEB activists believe that indigenous vernaculars cannot serve simply as bridges to Spanish-language literacy. Instead, their development must be nourished throughout the educational cycle, so that they flourish as vehicles of cultural expression and analysis, enhancing an appreciation of cultural difference among their users. On the other hand, indigenous people are also Colombian citizens, whose goal is to participate in national society by assisting in the construction of a pluralist alternative. Spanish is crucial to this objective. The question then becomes: In a country in which the national language has traditionally cannibalized and suppressed indigenous vernaculars, how can bilingualism promote a dialogue between equals instead of serving as a tool of cultural oppression?

Clearly, the basic principles of PEB are implicit in this list of questions, providing a guide to how a sistematización or an historia might be organized. They indicate the principal preoccupations of PEB activists: how to instill in members a comprehension of the educational and political principles guiding their activities, how to convey these standards to community authorities to ensure and deepen their participation, how to expand the purview of the program to regions that heretofore have been only marginally associated with the project. Such worries were formulated not in a proposal aimed at retrospective reflection, but in a plan for future action. Ultimately, however, they were instrumental in determining the conceptual configuration of the history project and in forcing the research team to instrumentalize internationally circulating ideas as theory.

Comunitariedad, *Interculturalism, and Cosmovision: Key Moments in the History of* PEB

Workshop participants were sent home with the list of fifty-one questions organized into four overlapping thematic areas: historical and sociocultural contexts, organizing concepts, investigation and methodology, and education and autonomy. They were asked to identify key narrators and to organize workshops in which collective interviewing would take place; various participants responded with transcribed interviews or with reports (B. Tróchez and Secue 2001; Viluche 2001), all of which were cursory in nature, reflecting the limited literacy and research skills of local teachers. Ultimately, the bulk of the interviews were conducted collectively by the three-person team, mostly with groups of narrators in a workshop-like format. Simultaneously, Abelardo, Graciela, and I developed a master chronology that identified significant events and the political processes surrounding them in an effort to ensure that the interviews did not dwell exclusively on the constellation of organizing concepts in the present, but contemplated their evolution over time; this was done at my suggestion, although the events and issues were chosen by Graciela and Abelardo. The series of pivotal events focused as much on developments within the organization in general as on the establishment of important programs within PEB itself.

The timeline provided us with much-needed historical referents, but the history we wrote was not chronological, nor did it focus exclusively on the key events we had outlined. In preparation for the work, I participated in numerous PEB meetings, including curricular planning sessions, program evaluations, and policy meetings. In the course of this fieldwork/collaboration, I observed that certain symbols were repeatedly engaged by local schoolteachers. One of these was the spiral. At a curricular workshop teachers from

7. *Sxabwes/El
Ombligo:* a spiral
board game pub-
lished in *Çxayu'çe,*
the magazine of PEB.
Courtesy of CRIC.

Juan Tama present their pedagogical research projects—community history,
organic farming, the tul, Nasa-language literacy techniques, and the like—in
a chart somewhat mechanically organized into a spiral. PEB's magazine,
Çxayu'çe, published a children's board game meant to stimulate the use of
Nasa Yuwe ("Sxabwes/El ombligo" 2000) in which players moved their pieces
around a spiral (figure 7). I enthusiastically suggested to the PEB team that we
consider engaging the spiral as an organizing motif.

The response of the Nasa speakers appeared to be positive, albeit noncom-
mittal. Nevertheless, it quickly became apparent to me that PEB hoped to
produce a more synthetic document that contextualized the program in a
broader political space. They wanted a sort of a hybrid between an historia and
a sistematización that would be accessible beyond the Nasa world. There was a
sentiment, moreover, that the history must be intercultural, incorporating the
experiences of non-Nasa communities like Guambía and Totoró, despite the
fact that the vast majority of PEB's advances had taken place in Nasa contexts. All of this precluded a focus on the spiral motif. What I discovered was
that my understanding of indigenous theorizing as grounded exclusively in
native cultural forms was naïve, at best. The regional contact zone of indigenous politics, where concepts originating in national and international debates were instrumentalized from local subject positions, was for CRIC a more

likely venue for finding the interpretive constructs useful for this particular project.

In my three decades of ethnographic research experience in Colombia, I had never followed an itinerary like this one: a research agenda whose objectives were more political than academic and a research plan that aimed at interpreting history through such presentist questions. Furthermore, all of my collaborative experience in the past was in teams composed of academics, and our conceptual frameworks had always resonated with those issues under discussion in academic circles. In other words, our conceptual framework always arose out of the team itself; although we routinely incorporated themes at the suggestion of the populations we were studying, they never dictated the direction that the research would take. Now, however, I was confronted with a radically different scenario. PEB provided the research team with our investigative agenda. Although we had decided in a workshop that we would produce an historia and not a sistematización, their guidelines pointed us toward the latter. I learned that research undertaken by a social movement does not follow academic methods, but instead, uses research projects as organizing tools to project toward the future (see Vasco 2002).

This does not mean that activist research lacks rigor. In the course of collecting oral histories with an array of PEB activists, I was struck by how extensive their knowledge base was and how carefully and continually it had been subjected to collective analysis over the years. CRIC's objectives differed from my own, nevertheless, because of the organization's political priorities. The history that we ultimately wrote was organized, at the insistence of Abelardo and Graciela, around three fundamental conceptual pivots: community-based education (*comunitariedad*), the fostering of cross-cultural dialogue framed by indigenous values (interculturalism), and a concern for maintaining cosmic balance (cosmovision). Notwithstanding their international currency, these ideas were instrumentalized in the PEB history through an emphasis on the specific set of contexts in which they were rerecognized.[12] Comunitariedad provided the framework for a chapter on how and why education was political for Caucan indigenous communities, focusing on schools as community-organizing tools. Interculturalism included a retrospective appreciation of indigenous-colaborador relations and an evaluation of the success of key moments in PEB programming. Cosmovision provided the hinge for creating an alternative historical chronology informed by a growing appreciation of the meaning of culture and language; the pivot of this chronology was the 1994 Tierradentro landslide, which many Nasa interpret as a spiritual emergency and which I turn to in the next chapter. Ultimately, Graciela added a final chapter focusing on pedagogical concerns (Bolaños, Ramos, Rappaport, and Miñana 2004).

This was not an easy process. Although Abelardo was one of the most vociferous supporters of the historia approach, he balked at the idea of moving back in history to a time in which cosmovision and interculturalism were only incipient concepts and not the full-blown strategies that they are today. Cosmovision was a particularly problematic point of contention. As it is articulated today, cosmovision is the product of intensive research by shamans and other cultural activists, which began in the mid-1990s. Its contents, in the unified and detailed form in which cosmovision is represented nowadays, were unknown in earlier years. Instead, there were only fragmentary narratives, secretive knowledge that was scattered among the thê' walas of Tierradentro. The question became, then: How were we to explain the emergence of this concept without portraying it as a fabrication? How could we convey the sense that cosmovision drew on a living knowledge base among the Nasa? The political contradictions implicit in the narrative choices that lay before us forced us to reflect on significant moral and intellectual dilemmas. In particular, they moved us to spend a great deal of time thinking about the meaning of essentialism and its role in PEB's cultural formulations.

On the other hand, comunitariedad was a viable concept in PEB's early years, before the program took on a bureaucratic function that dispersed its energies across many indigenous schools in Cauca. In the past decade, however, the scope of the program and the insistence on pedagogical discourse have distanced experimental schools from communities. At the same time, the impact of PEB's ideas in rural areas has been spotty, at best, which was evident when we compared the success of the Community Education Plan in the experimental schools with its mechanical application in most communities. Graciela was uncomfortable with this analysis, after having dedicated thirty years of her life to CRIC. Here I was confronted with a dilemma that Marc Edelman (1999) writes influenced him to reject an invitation to coauthor a history of a Costa Rican peasant movement. I, however, was not in a position to reject this collaborative venture, given that the very basis of my entree into CRIC was premised on my cooperation with its programs.

Our research team constituted a kind of a microcosm of interculturalism: a Nasa researcher, a colaboradora, and a foreign academic. We learned that each of us approaches the material from a different epistemological position. Graciela, who is monolingual in Spanish thus never fully grasped the potentialities of PEB's translation strategy, could not understand why Abelardo and I were so insistent on detailing the development of this methodology in the history we wrote. I, in turn, consistently felt that I was a step behind Abelardo and Graciela when it came to grasping the political intentions that they felt were so implicit in the work; after several years of collaboration, I could never fully accommodate my own image of a research agenda to that of the fifty-one-question guide provided to us by PEB militants. Ultimately, however, we wrote a history that satisfied all three of us, although each had to make significant compromises along the way. In the process, it became evident that our subject positions as Nasa linguist, nonindigenous colaboradora, and foreign anthropologist infused our writing in unforeseen ways, stimulating an intercultural dialogue in which culturalist, political, and academic forms of analysis intermingled under the rubric of a shared analytical backdrop that consisted of rerecognized or instrumentalized concepts.

Culture and Sovereignty

In this chapter, I have chosen the analytical move of contrasting two approaches to indigenous theorizing: the appropriation of native symbols as conceptual guides, which is what the Guambiano history committee accomplishes, and the rerecognition of universal ideas in specific political contexts, which is what we did in our history of PEB. However, the two approaches are not polar opposites. As Bruce Albert (1995, 4) so cogently argues in his interpretation of the discourse of Davi Kopenawa, a Brazilian Yanomami leader, the only way that the indigenous movement can hold its own in an ethnically heterogeneous political field is if it looks simultaneously to political universals and cultural specifics: "If the indigenous political discourse were limited to the mere reproduction of white categories, it would be reduced to empty rhetoric; if, on the other hand, it remained in the exclusive sphere of cosmology, it would not escape from cultural solipsism. In any case, the lack of articulation between these two registers leads to political failure."

As I hope to have illustrated here, the Janus-like character of the indigenous intellectual project, premised as it is on the construction of radical pluralism both within and beyond indigenous communities, demands such a two-pronged approach and forces indigenous theorists to penetrate into the interstices of the universal and the culturally specific in novel ways. Those of us who wish to collaborate with them in this project must become aware of this parallel set of requirements if we are to contribute successfully to the enterprise.

CHAPTER 6

The Battle for the Legacy of Father Ulcué

Spirituality in the Struggle between Region and Locality

On 4 June 1994, a massive earthquake and series of landslides tore through Tierradentro. Mountains crumbled, leaving what appeared to be gigantic claw marks carved into their slopes. Huge torrents of mud carrying trees, boulders, and other debris came raging down the Páez and Moras Rivers, completely burying the villages of Huila, Irlanda, and Tóez and destroying enough of Mosoco, San José, La Troja, El Cabuyo, Vitoncó, Tálaga, and Taravira to make them uninhabitable, at least in the short term. Approximately a thousand people disappeared in the disaster and thousands were left homeless.

Juan Tama, the Nasa mythic hero and the colonial-era hereditary chief, or cacique, of Vitoncó, is said to have been born in such a flood some three centuries before the 1994 catastrophe. The son of the waters and the star, the tiny cacique was, like Moses, carried in a nest of twigs down a stream, with the royal title to the resguardo of Vitoncó as his pillow. Tama was fished out of the river by shamans and raised to be the savior of the Nasa, founding multiple resguardos, protecting his people from invaders, and laying down laws for group survival. He disappeared into a highland lake, appropriately named Juan Tama Lake, which marks the site of the ritual installation of new cabildos and a major pilgrimage shrine for the Nasa and the indigenous movement in general.

The similarities between the conditions that gave rise to Tierradentro's mythic hero and the disaster that hit on 4 June led many to surmise that a cacique was born in 1994, but that the thê' walas, or shamans, of Tierradentro were unprepared for his coming and could not save him.[1] However, shamans dispute this interpretation. Various thê' walas dreamed of the impending disaster. They were visited by visions of rocks raining down from the hills or of houses collapsing on top of them, but they were incapable of interpreting their meaning at the time (Osorio et al. 1994). Even nonshamans reported having seen animals behaving oddly in the days before the avalanche, an indicator that something strange was afoot. But thê' walas Ángel María Yoinó and Roberto Andela, who are among the most renowned shamans in Tierradentro, do not believe that a cacique was born on that June day. Instead, they speak of the disaster as a wake-up call alerting the Nasa to their failings: their lack of attention to spiritual and ritual matters, their refusal to follow the laws that Juan Tama had set down for them, and, correspondingly, their loss of identity, their mistreatment of the land, and their surrender of Tierradentro to the cultivation of the opium poppy (Osorio et al. 1994).

The metaphor of a "sick earth" that emerged from shamanic interpretations of the tragedy was seized on by the various currents of Cauca's indigenous movement. A spate of videos issued by CRIC and the Fundación Sol y Tierra incorporated the metaphor into their visual narratives. Shots of refugees buffeted by winds and rain, of a swollen River Páez flowing through a devastated territory, of ravaged mountain slopes, and of houses folded in upon themselves are cut into films about a variety of topics, ranging from the disaster itself (Comunidad Indígena de Juan Tama 2000; Osorio et al. 1994) to poppy cultivation (Fernández and Osorio 1994) and the cosmic significance of the house garden (Borque and CRIC 1996). These visual reminders are used and reused in one film after another, their repetitiveness jogging viewers' memories, producing a unified discourse.

It was the shamans of Tierradentro who read the disaster as a signal for them to embark on an unprecedented project. They began to meet, first a handful of thê' walas, and later over a hundred ritual practitioners, to compile and interpret their knowledge of ritual practices, stories of origin, and the relationships among entities in the universe. Their aim was to use their newfound alliance to make explicit, unified, verbal, and public that which had previously been implicit, fragmented, sensory, and private, concealed in the minds of scattered shamans. In the process, they lay the basis for a coherent narrative of cosmovision as it is understood in Tierradentro, a meticulous account of the Nasa origin story and of the relationship between human society and the spirit world, a validation of the constellation of ritual practices that ensure the balance of the different spiritual forces operating in the cosmos. Twenty years ago, I might have called this an "invention of tradition" (Hobsbawm and Ranger 1983), for what the thê' walas compiled was unknown as a unified corpus to anyone before. But the hindsight afforded me by a relationship to activists in CRIC's bilingual education program and my own growing understanding of the extent to which grassroots research was galvanizing indigenous organizations and communities across Cauca led me toward a different interpretation of this daring project.

Shamans and Regional Intellectuals

I began to see the cosmovision project as a collaboration between regional intellectuals and sabedores, the appellation I have given to thê' walas to highlight their role as internal intellectuals. The results of shamanic research have been recast in usable form by Nasa organic intellectuals in narratives, reconstructions of rituals, elements of material culture. In effect, they are translating the shamans' discoveries into more accessible language for the multiple constituencies they serve. The narratives they produce are a form of ethnographic description, oriented toward local teachers, cabildo authorities, catechists, and health workers, disseminated through workshops and presentations. As I will demonstrate, the discourses that the interpreters of shamanic research have at their disposal are largely confined to models derived from Andeanist anthropology and the discursive strategies used by nongovernmental organizations worldwide, both of which frame shamanic knowledge within conceptual structures that compare and contrast the Nasa worldview to Western society, particularly to Christianity, subjecting it to an alien logic. On the one hand, these discourses essentialize indigenous thought by fitting it in realist anthropological categories; on the other hand, they schematize conceptual relationships, using highly standardized visual and verbal formats (Riles 2000, chap. 5) and polar oppositions between good/native and evil/global common to both NGO discourse and the language of the popular Catholic Church. Reinterpreted shamanic thought becomes a mirror through which activists critique the dominant society, neoliberal economic policies, and the spiritual vacuum of modernity. But at the same time, because it is refracted by a Western discursive lens, the internal coherence of shamanic logic, which is tightly bound up with ritual practice and local topography, is necessarily shattered. Hence, cosmovision can potentially appear to be "inauthentic" because it is conveyed according to external categories.

However, if we confine our comprehension to the explicitly analytical representations used in workshops and presentations, we blind ourselves to the deeper objectives of the cosmovision project. At a practical level, it is through the reappropriation of the knowledge of the thê' walas that cultural activists hope to derive a new indigenous political strategy that emulates the achievements of such forebears as Juan Tama, who is said to have reinvented Nasa society after the debacle of the Spanish invasion and to have protected indigenous lands from Spanish encroachment through the introduction of the resguardo. Shamanic learning functions as a source for historical models and conceptual structures capable of transforming the priorities and objectives of the indigenous politicians who run CRIC and other indigenous organizations, as well as local cabildo authorities. But there is another, more utopian facet of the project. The wealth of shamanic lore must ultimately be converted into re-authenticated indigenous lifeways—ritual made familiar by repetition, house gardens tilled by local hands, healing practices replacing Western medicine—so that local people begin to live their cultural difference in their everyday lives, making the personal political, to appropriate a slogan from the 1960s. For this reason, it is highly significant that CRIC linguist Susana Piñacué (2003) translates cosmovision into Nasa Yuwe as *fxi'zenxi*: vivencia, or everyday experience. This is where CRIC activists hope the cosmovision project will ultimately be rooted, in lifeways that slowly become habitual, unremarkable, unselfconscious, in short, authentic. This is why cosmovision is best comprehended as a utopian dream and not an essentializing discourse.[2]

Cosmovision is a strategy for the radical transformation of Nasa everyday life, in which shamans depend on organic intellectuals to convert their learning into synthetic interpretation and, ultimately, political practice. The two groups who have entered into this alliance, thê' walas and regional activists, are very different types of social actors. Unlike most activists, who elect their calling as intellectuals (even if they do not accept to be labeled as such), thê' walas are chosen, frequently against their own wishes. After a lengthy period of illness and persistent visions they come to the realization that they have powers that, if not harnessed through ritual, threaten to engulf them. Only those who are thus selected apprentice themselves to other shamans, learn the office of the thê' wala, receive a chonta-wood staff for ceremonial use, and engage in ritual activities to maintain the balance of the universe. It is uncommon for anyone to *want* to become a shaman, a calling that bestows an ambiguous status on its occupants, as they are capable of doing not only good, but also evil. Becoming a thê' wala also implies a significant loss of time and income from everyday agricultural activities. The suppression of shamanism over three centuries of Christian evangelization was surmounted only with the advent of the indigenous movement, which has imparted a renewed respect on thê' walas. Still, shamanism is certainly not an attractive career option. Organic intellectuals, in contrast, are drawn to the movement but can freely choose to participate or not. Their status affords them excitement, travel, educational opportunities, influence, community, and, sometimes, urban residence. This is a much more attractive option than shamanism.

There are also significant differences in the extent and nature of the knowledge bases of the two groups. Shamans are very much more attuned to oral tradition and sacred geography than are the frontier Nasa, and thus have a great deal more cultural material to bring to the table. Many organic intellectuals know little more about things spiritual than what they have read in movement publications, heard in workshops, or learned at shamanic seances. That is, their knowledge is secondhand. Both groups employ an intuitive methodology that combines culturally self-conscious reflection with the collection of empirical information, but the instincts of thê' walas are grounded in empirical knowledge they acquire through the interpretation of bodily signs—vibrations and pulses that they feel in their extremities—that nonshamans cannot fully comprehend and that no one can fully verbalize. With the advent of the cosmovision project, however, shamans also began to share narratives with one another, participating in the reconstruction of oral history. In a sense, then, the thê' walas of Tierradentro have successfully merged traditional shamanic research strategies with ethnographic methods of data collection and interpretation, producing an integrated corpus of knowledge that has transformed what was once a diffuse appreciation of culture into a symbolically dense militant intellectual project.[3]

Tierradentro and the North

Any examination of shamanic research must be rooted in the study of regional political struggles in Cauca, given that different wings of the indigenous movement and their nonindigenous allies all use shamanism as an organizing tool. Tierradentro, as I suggested early on in this book, has always been valued by CRIC as a repository of Nasa culture, a site of authenticity steeped in the spiritual power of the important shamans who reside there. At the same time, however, Tierradentro is a place where the intractable power of the dominant society is pervasive, particularly in the influence of the conservative wing of the Catholic Church and the clientelism of political bosses from mainstream parties. The Nasa heartland stands in marked contrast to northern Cauca, where a largely Spanish-speaking Nasa population that is highly integrated into the regional culture and market system has participated over the past half-century in numerous leftist movements and guerrilla organizations, furnishing most of CRIC's Nasa leadership.[4] Northern Cauca is home to the Consolata Fathers, an Italian order. They do not enjoy the luxury of the legal fiction of a "mission territory" facilitating their ministry over the indigenous population, as do the Vincentians of Tierradentro, who, thanks to a concordat with Rome, were officially recognized for a century as guardians of Nasa souls and minds.[5] Nevertheless, the Consolatas officiate with great dedication over a fiercely Catholic population. They came to northern Cauca after the 1984 murder of Father Álvaro Ulcué, a Nasa priest who had dedicated himself to the rediscovery of his Nasa values and was increasingly experiencing political persecution as a result of his support for the cabildos of northern Cauca and CRIC. Unlike the Vincentians, the Consolatas have actively participated in the indigenous movement. Simultaneously, they have energetically worked to introduce a radical brand of Catholicism called inculturation that merges Christianity with indigenous belief systems.

Tierradentro and the north have long been at odds, given their differing political orientations, their dissimilar insertions into regional society, their distinct relationships with Nasa culture and spirituality, and the antithetical natures of the religious institutions that serve them. At the height of the 1998 Colombian presidential campaign that pitted Horacio Serpa against Andrés Pastrana, Jesús Enrique Piñacué, former president of CRIC and a recently elected member of the Colombian Senate, appeared on national television in support of Serpa's candidacy. His speech provoked a torrent of criticism in northern Cauca, where both the Consolatas and indigenous political leaders had advocated abstention in the presidential run-off election. The leadership of Toribío proposed that Piñacué be lashed in public for disobeying the orders of the Indigenous Social Alliance (ASI), the alternative political party that he had represented in the elections. Whipping, which is confined to the legs and is accompanied by ritual, is considered to be a cleansing act, bringing to bear the power of lightning upon the culprit. However, given the pervasive influence of the Liberal Party in Tierradentro, its cabildos had themselves supported Serpa, and, accordingly, opposed such drastic punishment of Piñacué, who is a native son of Tierradentro. The thê' walas advocated a ritual bath in Juan Tama Lake instead of the whipping proposed by the northern authorities, ultimately succeeding in imposing the lighter sanction. This was a highly ambiguous act in the eyes of the north, as it was unclear whether a ritual bath could be considered a punishment at all—although, of course, shamans would also interpret whipping as an act of cleansing and not of punishment (Gow and Rappaport 2002).

Cosmovision has come to play a notable role in the rivalry between the north and CRIC, given the emphasis that both the regional organization and the northern church place on its potency, CRIC from a nativist position and the priests in conjunction with their philosophy of inculturation. CRIC activists, many of them from Tierradentro, have recast Nasa spirituality as an autonomous belief system, as opposed to a syncretic one, precluding the melding of native and Christian philosophies that characterizes inculturation. The marked rejection by CRIC cultural activists of the place of Christianity in Nasa everyday life thus threatens the legitimacy of the progressive church or, at the least, attempts to limit its insertion into indigenous politics. This stance is significant, given that the church plays a major role in the workings of ACIN (Association of Indigenous Cabildos of Northern Cauca), the zonal cabildo association that has effectively taken over many of the responsibilities that once accrued in the north to the regional organization. The Consolatas may be the indigenous organization's ally in struggles against common enemies like the paramilitary, the police, and the army, but the two groups are locked in a bitter fight for hegemony within the movement itself.

In an allegorical battle between leftist Italian priests and PEB's cultural purists, the martyred Nasa priest of Toribío, Father Álvaro Ulcué, has become a potent symbol for both sides. For the Consolatas, he stands as an emblem of the indigenous roots of the progressive church and a kind of a modern Juan Tama; for CRIC, his embracing of Nasa culture and indigenous organizing represents the potentialities of their political message and the irrelevance of Christianity for the Nasa. How Juan Tama and Álvaro Ulcué act as pivots for both culturalist and Christian cosmovision, and the ways that they play off each other, are the themes that I explore in this chapter.

Cosmovision as a Discourse

Cosmovision is a modern conceptual category that incorporates secular and spiritual behavior, mythic charters, and historical experience into a politically effective whole. It is defined in parallel ways across Latin America, as the similarities between the Nasa concept I have been using in this book and the following Maya definition indicate: "The harmonic relationship among all the elements of the universe, in which the human being is just one more element, the earth is the mother who gives life" (MENMAGUA 1999, 19).

The notion of cosmovision originates in anthropological studies of cosmology. In the Andes, such research interprets the structural similarities inherent in the organization of sacred space, myth, and social relations among the Incas and modern native peoples (Catherine Allen 2002; Lévi-Strauss 1963; Reichel-Dolmatoff 1971; Zuidema 1964), the relationship between categories of mythic thought and the structure of indigenous languages (Howard-Malverde 1990), the symbolism of gender (Harris 2000; Isbell 1978), which has been analyzed in terms of dual oppositions between male and female, and the intersection of this symbolic structure with astronomical observation (Urton 1981). Such approaches have also been attractive to indigenous academic researchers, particularly in Peru and Bolivia (Van den Berg and Schiffers 1992).

Cosmology provides a conceptual basis for the politicized discourse of cosmovision as it is used by nongovernmental organizations, Catholic missionaries, and indigenous movements worldwide. Particularly attractive for nonacademics is anthropologists' insistence on the structural analogies between myth and territorial organization, affording manifold possibilities for anchoring notions of cultural difference and for asserting rights to territory.[6] In contrast to academic treatments that take cosmology to be an abstract, self-enclosed, and unchanging set of structures of meaning, nonacademic proponents of cosmovision have reappropriated the concept in its concrete, dynamic, and intercultural dimensions. Accordingly, they couch cosmovision within an opposition between exogenous and endogenous knowledge bases, the former imposed by external institutions and the latter misunderstood or ignored by them. In this sense, on a general level, cosmovision presents a critique of modernity as lacking spirituality and as disregarding the balance of the universe. In Latin America in particular, cosmovision is an oppositional category that can be comprehended only within the institutional contexts of the antagonism between grassroots NGOs and large development agencies, on the one hand, and between national and minority cultures, on the other.

But notwithstanding their oppositional intentions, cosmovision's proponents are open to appropriating ideas from the outside, just as are interculturalist educators. In fact, their discourse is remarkably similar to that of the interculturalists, as the following quotation from an NGO bulletin illustrates: "However, far too often a gap remains between farmers and external agents and scientists. External agents are generally trained by formal education and employed by formal development organisations. The need to be '*de-schooled*' and retrained and the objectives of the development programmes need to be reformulated. To bridge the gap between farmers and outsiders (or between indigenous, cosmovision-related knowledge and conventional science), the outsider 'has to learn to walk in two worlds' " (COMPAS Partners 1996, 27; italics mine). Cosmovision is not a hermetically sealed belief system, but a fluid *habitus*, to appropriate Pierre Bourdieu's terminology, that is at once communal and individual, learned and appropriated, researched and consciously deployed, a central component of an indigenous countermodernity. Most important, cosmovision is a kind of "experiment with culture" (Fox 1989), something that is expressly stated by some of its proponents (Kieft 1999) and that sits well with CRIC's future-oriented notion of culture.

Such experiments are potentially highly charged politically. In Colombia, indigenous organizations have brought cosmovision to bear in a number of well-publicized disputes with the state, international corporations, and missionary organizations. In a 1998 case brought before the Constitutional Court concerning the presence of missionaries in the territory of the Ika (Arhuacos) of the Sierra Nevada de Santa Marta, it was decided that indigenous spiritual authorities (*mamos*) had the right to expel the United Pentecostal Church of Colombia on the grounds that fundamentalist Protestant evangelization threatened native uses and customs dedicated to the maintenance of cosmic harmony (Cifuentes Muñoz 1998). The discourse of cosmovision was also brought to bear in an internationally publicized dispute between the U'wa of northeastern Colombia and the Occidental Petroleum Company over oil exploitation in a region called the Bloque Samoré, which lies within U'wa traditional territory (Barrera Carbonell 1997). At issue was whether oil drilling in sacred territory would endanger the balance of the cosmos according to U'wa cosmovision. The court decided that the U'wa community's rights were violated (B. Sánchez 2001, 99–139); the case, however, continues to fester, because the Colombian national company recently discovered rich reserves in the region and plans to begin drilling there. In these two legal disputes, indigenous communities forced the Colombian state to recognize their collective claim to cosmovision as a basic constitutional right to be enjoyed by native peoples, a right that takes precedence over the individual rights of all Colombians. In the judicial context, cosmovision deploys ethnographic discourses of cosmic harmony and the interrelatedness of the sacred and the profane, but here, they are linked to juridical constructs that prioritize collective over individual rights under the rubric of the right of native peoples to maintain their cultural identity. That is, cosmovision has the potential to be harnessed to the broader national project of the construction of a new kind of plural society.

The Construction of Cosmovision

The Nasa origin story that issued from the shamanic workshops (Sisco n.d.) recounts the creation of a universe by two progenitors, or Nejwe (pl. *nej-wewe'sx*), Uma and Tay, a woman and a man, respectively. Their children are the sun, moon, and stars. The struggles that ensued among their progeny impelled the Nejwe to send the *ksxa'w*, or guardian spirit, as an intermediary to stand between material beings and themselves (7). The constant bickering of the living beings—*nasa*, which is a term given to all living beings, not just a particular human ethnic group—led the Nejwe to chastise them by forcing them to embrace into a single mass known as the Earth, or Kiwe, a feminine element (8). Sek Taki, the Sun, was brought into existence as her companion (9), engendering a multiplicity of children, all linked to Kiwe by their umbilical cords (10). Two components of the natural world, A' (Star) and Yu' (Waters), came together to produce a child, Yu' Luucx (Child of the Waters), from whence spring the human beings known as Nasa (19–22), who are associated with a series of mountains and are oriented by Êeka Thê' (Thunder, or Grandfather of Cosmic Space) (24). The remainder of the narrative recounts the exploits of the Thunder as he moves across a terrain that is identified by the toponyms of Tierradentro.

The process of constructing this primordial knowledge base began in the late 1980s in Vitoncó, Tierradentro, when Manuel Sisco, seven thê' walas, including Ángel María Yoinó, and, briefly, a Peruvian nun named Sister Bertha Salazar set about a collaboration to study the cultivation of medicinal plants. Their incipient project focused on thê' walas as curers, which was how they were understood at the time, not as the guardians of cosmic harmony, as they would come to be appreciated later. The committee's work ultimately led to the study of the story of Juan Tama, one of the yu' luucx, an exploration of the sacred geography of Tierradentro, and later, in the company of Nasa linguist Marcos Yule, a systematic investigation of the sacred geography of "Tierra-fuera," the western slopes of the Central Cordillera.

A brief description of these four key actors provides a glimpse at the heterogeneity of the cosmovision project. Ángel María, the towering intellectual figure in the group, is a Nasa-speaking farmer and one of the most respected thê' walas of Tierradentro. A wiry and grizzled man in his late sixties, Ángel María was once a Pentecostal pastor who returned to his Nasa roots. He is an active community historian and a skilled orator, capable of weaving novel interpretations of Nasa oral tradition together with readings of colonial-era resguardo titles. When Vitoncó was flattened in the 1994 disaster, Ángel María played a key role in facilitating the resettlement of refugees and in translating the topographic referents of the Juan Tama story to the new geography in which they would live, thus legitimizing the new settlement and providing essential spiritual coordinates for its inhabitants. He has also been an active member of CRIC since its inception, has assumed cabildo office on multiple occasions, was in the vanguard of CRIC's long-standing fight with the Apostolic Vicariate of Tierradentro over control of indigenous education, and was one of the leaders of the occupation of López Adentro in northern Cauca.

Manuel Sisco, in contrast, projects the urban face of the movement. A man in his mid-thirties, born in Pueblo Nuevo but affiliated by marriage with the resguardo of Santa Rosa in Tierradentro, Manuel is based in the Popayán headquarters of CRIC, a member of the team generating indigenous theory in the Bilingual Education Program. Although Manuel spent a few years in Bogotá working as a jeweler—his former life is reflected in the stylish clothing and jewelry he sports—he has some claim to shamanic knowledge. His grandfather was a thê' wala, and Manuel was once struck by lightning, marking his potential for a shamanic calling, although he has never received a chonta-wood staff. But his parents are active catechists in Pueblo Nuevo, fiercely Catholic, and Manuel's rigorous opposition to Christianity undoubtedly derives from the exigencies of his upbringing. An engaging and charismatic public speaker, Manuel has a keen intellect that is comparable to Ángel María's, although he does not have the authoritative stature of the thê' wala from Vitoncó. For the past half-decade, Manuel has been nourishing himself through shamanic research and as a long-distance anthropology student enrolled in the Salesian University in Quito, which runs a program expressly oriented toward indigenous students and imparts an anthropological vision grounded in Andeanist academic research.

Sister Bertha is a member of the Missionary Sisters of Mother Laura, a Colombian order that works largely in indigenous and Afrocolombian communities. She hails from Peru, the daughter of a bilingual teacher, and owing to her upbringing in a rural school is fluent in Quechua and conversant with southern Andean healing practices. She has lived and worked over the past three decades in a number of convents serving Nasas and Guambianos; I first encountered her in Guambía in the mid-1970s, and later, in Vitoncó in 1979. While Sister Bertha is a proponent of indigenous medicine, she is rabidly opposed to alcohol, a position that has led her to urge a transformation in shamanic practice, which generally involves the consumption of a great deal of cane liquor; she also encourages a syncretic combination of Nasa shamanism with Catholicism.

The final member of the team, Marcos Yule, hails from Toribío, where he was first attracted to indigenous politics by the Consolata Fathers, with whom he frequently spars but whom he also accepts as allies. Marcos is of the same generation as Manuel, but his life course diverged from that of many of his CRIC colleagues in the 1980s, when he studied as a full-time M.A. student in ethnolinguistics at the Universidad de los Andes in Bogotá. This experience marked him in many ways, particularly in his emphasis on academic rigor, which has led him to devote considerable time to research into linguistics (Yule 1995) and oral history (Yule 1996), as well as to coordinating educational activities in the north, where he lives. Nevertheless, it would be too simple to characterize Marcos as an academic, because he recently served two years as governor of the cabildo of Toribío, thus combining his scholarly proclivities with activist aspirations. A small man with a marked limp and broad smile, Marcos is a ubiquitous presence at assemblies in northern Cauca.

Manuel recounts how the team's work with healers soon morphed into a search for a mythic charter:

> So, there were two very important people in the other research I was involved in. [One] was my mother-in-law, the mother of Avelina [Pancha], a speaker [of Nasa Yuwe]. And I went there as a researcher; I went with a tape-recorder to ask her stories. Well, I noticed that she always spoke of Uma as a woman-being, but also, another time we were there, her counterpart in Taravira was Rosalba [Ramos, a shaman and the sister of Abelardo and Inocencio], who . . . began to speak of Tak. Well, Tak Ne' was the man, the first father; Uma was the mother, to whom the people made offerings, because the shamans, when I watched the shamans, the male shamans always make offerings to Uma and the women to Tay, so then I came to understand better, and this is very important, because Christianity always speaks only of the man, while for the Nasa, it's always the couple.

This startling breakthrough led Manuel to pursue an analysis of gender complementarity and to travel throughout the Nasa diaspora—to the Caquetá lowlands, where migrants from Tierradentro and Tierrafuera had settled in the 1950s and 1960s, to Florída, near Cali—where he discovered that similar cosmovisions were at play. He began to realize that the story of Uma and Tay had been covered up by shamans, who sensed a danger inherent in narrating the history of the primordial beings to communities that were in the process of deindianization. As a result, argues Manuel, thê' walas began to emphasize more immediate historical figures, such as Juan Tama, the father of the resguardo, leading to his centrality in oral tradition.[7] In other words, Manuel's story is a history of how shamans have been responsive over time to the political contexts in which they live. Simultaneously, research proceeded on material culture, because Manuel's mother-in-law recounted to him the symbolic structure of the motifs on the coca bag (see figure 1), with its seven rows of squares in a pyramidal pattern that, he learned, represent the seven levels of the cosmos.

Then came the 1994 disaster.

Galvanized by a sudden surge in visits by nervous Nasa to thê' walas and by the need to provide an adequate explanation of the catastrophe, a meeting of shamans was convoked in Tierradentro. Eighty of them attended, an unprecedented meeting whose scope has never been witnessed in modern times, although similar gatherings are recounted in the oral tradition. The shamans collectively interpreted their dreams and reflected on the disaster, concluding that it was a call to action in the face of gross transgressions by the Nasa of the cosmic order. The thê' walas undertook a visit to Juan Tama Lake, where they cleaned up the sacred precinct, which had been contaminated with the detritus of a decade of visits by activists, shamans, and tourists. Subsequently, they persuaded the Colombian authorities to take shamans on six helicopter trips across Tierradentro, where they performed cleansing rituals from the air.

The combination of shamanic workshops with high-tech ceremony was meant to urge people to return to a more pure state, what the movement calls *nasnasa*—the repetition conveys a sense of the essential attributes of a Nasa state of being, as Manuel explains: "This comes out of the concern that we have been derailed, that we are no longer nas nasa, but only half Nasa, or *nasa mekya'*—not Nasa. Well, [the Nasa] had gone astray, so that in order to be nas nasa, we had to take up that history and begin to act, and then once again they would be calling you 'nasnasa,' or 'You are behaving as a nasnasa.' It was a very important aspect, because being *nasa mea'* [un-Nasa] disappeared, was removed from society. So we all worked together to be nas nasa, but it was history that helped us out." The process snowballed, spawning shamanic workshops at both the regional and local levels—113 shamans met in Tierradentro alone—and meetings between thê' walas and the captains of cabildos, the only hereditary post that has survived in modern resguardo councils and which is seen as analogous to the position of the historical cacique. Workshops were conducted by PEB activists in the profesionalización program and in localities.[8] It is to these public activities that I now turn in an effort to understand how cosmovision is inculcated in nonspecialist circles, with particular attention to the subtext of such workshops, which urge the abandonment or, at the least, the containment of Christianity.

Teaching Cosmovision to Native Politicians

In the course of my research, I attended various events at which cosmovision was explicated, using distinct discourses and modes of presentation, depending on the audience. The differences among these expositions are quite telling, laying bare how cosmology has become a political tool for PEB in its efforts to become the indigenous conscience of CRIC. I focus on two of these here, the first, an exegesis of the nature of authority presented to CRIC's executive committee. At this meeting, PEB shared its moral vision with CRIC's leadership, whom the educators felt were in danger of becoming petty politicians. The second instance I consider is a cosmovision workshop for the inhabitants of northern Cauca held on a repossessed hacienda that serves as a communal meeting space. The discourse engaged at this workshop was aimed at weakening the hold of the Consolata Fathers on the resguardos of northern Cauca. Both events were facilitated by Manuel Sisco.

The first event involved a series of presentations in the summer of 2000 by PEB program coordinators to CRIC's executive committee, made up of regional-level indigenous politicians, most of them men from the Spanish-speaking resguardos of central Cauca or from the Nasa communities of the north; all of them have decades of experience in CRIC and have made forays into the electoral arena at the local, provincial, or national levels. The objective of the meeting was to render accounts of the program's activities and to convey to the political leadership the indispensability of the education program and its personnel. Manuel's presentation was one of the first, setting the tone.

He began with a rundown of the historical chronology he has devised for the Nasa, consisting of five ages. He began his history with what he called "the age of the women," led by mythicohistorical figures like La Gaitana, a cacica who resisted European domination during the Spanish invasion and who is well-known in the mythology of southwestern Colombia (Sisco 2000); although this age appears to allude to myths of matriarchy, I suspect that Manuel's interpretation more likely stems from the significance of La Gaitana in contemporary Nasa oral tradition (Rappaport 1998b, chap. 7). This was fol-

lowed by two periods of chiefly rule, "the age of the caciques," colonial founders of the resguardos, such as Juan Tama, and "the age of Quintín Lame," the
early twentieth-century Nasa organizer whose name was subsequently borrowed by the indigenous guerrilla group of the 1970s and 1980s. Then came
"the age of CRIC." His chronology culminated in the 1994 Tierradentro disaster. Manuel's chronology is driven by figures of Nasa resistance caught between
two cataclysms, the Spanish invasion and the 1994 disaster, the two major
turning points of Nasa history, in his view. Each of these ages, Manuel argued,
had its own "utopia"; he expressly employed this term, which can be understood as "agenda." He reprimanded his listeners, however, by arguing that
CRIC's utopia was sterile because unlike its forebears, the executive committee
had abandoned the thread of mythology that united the dreams of its predecessors. He cautioned that the current leadership had substituted what he
called "structural proposals" in place of myth. In other words, they had blindly
pursued marches and other mobilizations in a fruitless search for ideals. Consequently, he saw the leadership of the organization as trapped between the
opposing ideologies of the state and of indigenous culture. The demands of
the organization would remain ineffectual, Manuel warned, if they were not
suffused with indigenous cosmology.

Manuel then went on to describe what he called the seven foundations of
the Nasa world, which he equates with the seven rows of squares on the Nasa
coca bag. These levels are also marked, he noted, on the body of the shaman,
on his ankles and his wrists, his chest and his back, and on the top of his head,
a series that Manuel called the "utopia of the person." The seven foundations,
which he named in Nasa Yuwe, correspond to different levels of authority
across time and space, beginning with the Ne'jnas—an equivalent term for the
Nejwe, Uma and Tay—and concluding with the *ne'jwe'sxnas*, or cabildo authorities. He thus traced a direct line of descent from the primordial beings to
their modern earthly representatives, a relationship whose continuity, he argued, is maintained by the ritual exercise of the thê' walas and is preserved
through the use by modern authorities of the *palabra mayor*, the "greater
word," that springs from the primordial fount. I had not heard CRIC activists
use this term before this meeting, although it has great currency among the
Guambianos of AICO, who employ it to emphasize their cultural authenticity
and their ancient rights as the first Americans. Manuel argued that the palabra
mayor is only a reality insofar as it is grounded in this cosmic continuum of
types of authority, as he illustrated in a diagram (figure 8). In his rendition, the
cosmic and earthly planes are linked through the offices of the thê' wala,

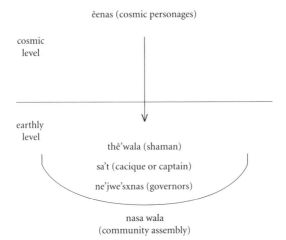

êenas (cosmic personages)

cosmic
level

earthly
level

thê'wala (shaman)

sa't (cacique or captain)

ne'jwe'sxnas (governors)

nasa wala
(community assembly)

8. The workings of Nasa
authority.

who establish connections through ritual to the *êenas* (cosmic personages) and traditional authorities in the human world, including the *sa't* (captain), *ne'jwe'sxnas* (governor), and *nasa wala* (community assembly).

This diagram, hastily jotted in marker on a large sheet of newsprint, provided Manuel with a critical prop. He was not the only presenter to illustrate his points with charts and diagrams; in fact, few indigenous speakers attempt to talk without them in such seminars. His illustration is schematic, dependent on alphabetic literacy, on a comprehension of graphic conventions, and on a familiarity with a range of pedagogical habits used by nongovernmental organizations, state representatives, and teachers. The scheme Manuel presented employs a dual structure that contrasts cosmic and earthly levels of existence, although he and other CRIC activists continually assert that there is no separation of the supernatural and natural realms in the Nasa worldview; from the perspective of cosmovision, the two realms should be superimposed on one another. This polarized scheme stems from ethnographic discourses on cosmology, but even more from the nature of the visual genre that Manuel employs, which is ubiquitous throughout Latin American popular organizations. But while the diagram operates according to dualistic principles that characterize popular education discourse and anthropological takes on the supernatural, its contents have a specifically Nasa political intent.

At the two poles are the cosmic personages and the community assembly, whose objectives are put into practice by three groups of Nasa authorities: shamans, captains, and governors. By equating cabildo officers, such as governors, with shamans, and by calling captains by the word sa't, which is a term generally used to refer to caciques such as Juan Tama, Manuel is asserting a new understanding of authority in the Nasa community, rehabilitating the status of shamans and captains, whose legitimacy had diminished over the course of the twentieth century. He is also urging political authorities to assume a new form of accountability that has cosmic implications. This is a direct appeal to CRIC to rethink its own political practice, which has been marked by the exercise of electoral politics and a dependence on wide-ranging political networks. The diagram thus represents a veiled critique by Manuel of the orientation of the executive committee, meant to assert the higher moral ground on which the Bilingual Education Program stands.

The audience responded positively to the presentation. At least, the PEB members did, as they were the only ones to do any talking, suggesting that Manuel's speech was neatly compartmentalized as irrelevant by the members of the executive committee. The commentaries of both indigenous intellectuals and colaboradores underlined the centrality of a culturally informed discourse that must replace the empty "Western" discourse they perceived among politicians. However, as occurred in the presentation of a schematic diagram of PEB's mission, no one criticized Manuel's diagram, whose structure has been naturalized in the indigenous political world of militant Cauca, imputing a series of key visual relationships to a Nasa worldview.

Cosmovision Workshops

The second event I attended was quite different, a workshop aimed at educating local activists. Workshops are a regular occurrence in indigenous Cauca. Some are sponsored by indigenous organizations and cabildos, others by NGOs or the Catholic Church, yet others by myriad government institutions. Participants generally include local notables, teachers, health workers, and other activists, who are sometimes paid to attend and who generally receive certificates of attendance at the end of the event; in the case of teachers, these documents, which resemble diplomas, are necessary to justify time spent away from the workplace and are accepted as evidence of in-service training in the determination of salaries. Hence, there are significant institutional incentives for attending workshops among the local indigenous intelligentsia. But these events also draw participants because they are entertaining and informative, providing materials that can be integrated into day-to-day activities, and because they permit local functionaries to interact with their peers. They are also highly political events, where people address one another in a stylized discourse of ethnic nationalism.

There is a culture of workshops in Cauca, particularly in northern Cauca, where the intensity of such events is unmatched elsewhere in the region, that only partially engages local cultural practices—or better put, has supplanted them—and mirrors similar events held throughout the world. This culture is stimulated by nongovernmental organizations, replete with the kind of diagrams and flowcharts I have already described. It is a culture with a particular organization and practice. Such events are always organized into plenaries, where keynote speakers from outside deliver addresses alongside the leaders of the organizations responsible for the workshop, and where participants are then given lists of questions to discuss in small groups. A secretary is always chosen for the breakout groups and is responsible for delivering a report at the final plenary session; needless to say, in a region in which most rural villagers have not completed primary school and do not write with ease, the minutes of these sessions are hardly comprehensive, but they are carefully archived with the proceedings of the event and are sometimes reproduced for further distribution. One of the highlights of the workshop is the lunch, not because it is tasty—it is usually a large communal soup pot containing starchy vegetables and scant seasoning—but because of the opportunity it affords for making new friends and meeting old ones, for playing soccer, and for a much-needed snooze; you have to bring your own spoon if you want to eat, and you are obliged to wash your bowl before returning it, generating long lines at the water hose.

What do participants bring home from such events? That is a difficult question to answer, but in the organizing frenzy of the past few decades, many key narratives of indigenous history, including the stories of Juan Tama and La Gaitana, and the objectives of the movement, as well as analyses of the dangers of neoliberalism and communal responses to violence, have become generalized across the Caucan landscape, suggesting that at the least, the basics of movement discourse enter into general usage through constant repetition at workshops and similar events.

At the cosmovision workshop I encountered a highly heterogeneous group of some fifty men and women from most of the northern resguardos, congregated in a huge open-air conference hall in Pílamo, near López Adentro. The audience included teachers, high school students, cabildo members, and farmers, some of them evangelical Protestants, others Catholic catechists, and yet others agnostic when it came to Christianity. Some came to argue with Manuel—the evangelicals, in particular, who, like many fundamentalists, tend to reject any cosmology other than their own. Others came to listen, some of them teachers hoping to replace a residual Christianity with a newfound Nasa spirituality; others, many of them catechists, aspired to a more informed syncretic religious practice. Hovering over the meeting was the specter of the Consolatas, who did not attend. The radical priests of northern Cauca have fought the Protestants tooth and nail, banning them from public protests. They are the organizers of the catechists, who blend Christian dogma with a discourse of indigenous rights, circulating it as a new form of the Christian Good News. They are the supervisors of the teachers, whose administrative structure and curricular planning are in the hands of local leaders affiliated with the Church. And they have been engaged in a long-standing debate with Manuel Sisco and other cultural activists who have repudiated Christianity in favor of a cosmovision inspired by the shamans of Tierradentro.

The absent-presence of the priests was remarked in Manuel's opening speech, which berated northerners for distinguishing between "traditional Nasa," "modern Nasa," and "new Nasa." Modern Nasa are those who reject their heritage, in distinction to the traditional Nasa, who hold on to it, but it was the third appellation with which Manuel was most concerned. New Nasa is a term in vogue among adherents to the northern brand of progressive Catholicism: "new" signifies "Christian," positing an evolutionary step in Nasa consciousness facilitated by the Church. It was particularly to this category, as well as to the absent participant, that Manuel directed himself.

The cosmovision workshop came on the heels of a series of presentations by schoolchildren from nearby López Adentro, who reenacted key events in the life of Juan Tama and sang songs in Nasa Yuwe; their teachers are among Manuel's most avid pupils. Members of the audience eagerly awaited the workshop but did not appear to have any idea of what would occur in it. Participants were divided into breakout groups to answer a series of questions concerning the place of religiosity in their lives: What is the origin of the world? What festivals do we celebrate in the course of our lives, and what are their meanings? What did our ancestors do to be true Nasa? How do we, as Christians, behave in society? Is Christ the only salvation? How do we become Christians? What is meant by sacred space? Why are the staffs of the shaman and of the cabildo sacred? What is religion? Is it true that the thê' wala consorts with the devil? How do thê' walas educate society? How should young people behave nowadays? What do we need to do to practice our religiosity?

Presentations by the breakout groups to the plenary indicated that the audience was only marginally acquainted with the orthodox Catholic doctrine, as is generally the case in the Caucan countryside, and knew even less about cosmovision. The small group conversations served, however, as a stratagem of Manuel's for convincing the participants that their worldview was contaminated by Christianity, which they needed to purge to become true Nasas. The remainder of the workshop was dedicated to persuading listeners that they must devote exclusive attention to Nasa cosmovision and ritual to ensure its autonomy from Christian narrative and ceremony. Only then might they consider appropriating useful elements from Christianity, once they had established a firm Nasa base. In other words, what was at stake for Manuel was the survival of Nasa sentiment, which could be ensured only in the absence of Christianity.

Manuel's lecture to the CRIC leadership was highly abstract and systematic, almost academic, oriented toward an audience of regional intellectuals well-versed in the discourse of the indigenous movement and familiar with heavily theorized political analysis. His aim was to draw a contrast between the "politics as usual" of the executive committee and a cosmologically oriented politics that, he felt, should be one of CRIC's utopias. In Pílamo, in contrast, Manuel made frequent jokes and spoke in colloquial Spanish, providing much of the same information but in a more accessible format and through a familiar set of oppositions. What was particularly striking was how, from the start, Christianity served as a hinge for explicating Nasa cosmology and ritual. The audience, Manuel asserted, had "its wires crossed," and had to begin to ask, "To what extent are we Nasa? To what extent are we Christians?" At the Pílamo workshop Manuel succeeded in harnessing the pervasive sentiments that flowed from these rhetorical questions to a series of concrete narratives that the participants could take home with them: about Uma, Tay, and other primordial beings, about the necessity of constantly enriching life with ritual, about the seven levels of authority and how the participants were inserted into the cosmic structure, about the symbolism of the material culture that they encountered in the course of their daily lives.

The cosmovision pamphlet from which I drew the Nasa origin story is a narrative that traces the history of the cosmos. Not so in the cosmovision workshop. Here, the origin story was reduced to its most essential protagonists, who were counterposed to the heroes of Christian cosmic history, thus correcting or supplanting the latter. Central to this exposition was the contrast Manuel drew between the asexual nature of Christian dogma and the gender complementarity of Nasa cosmovision. For Manuel, Nasa cosmovision is characterized by the parallel and equal development of male and female forces in the universe, beginning with the primordial couple, Tay and Uma. In the everyday lives of the Nasa, he argued, this translates into the complementarity of male and female activities—something that he did not dwell on in this presentation, but that he described in his exposition to the executive commit-tee—and the equality of men and women in Nasa society. This discourse derives from feminist ethnography, which dedicated many printed pages in the 1970s and 1980s to the study of gender dualism and to advancing the thesis that although patriarchy did exist in pre-Columbian society, it was under Spanish domination that Andean women's disempowerment was consolidated in the form we know today (Silverblatt 1987). Ironically, however, such argu-ments have fueled resistance to feminism among popular organizations in the Andes who argue that sexism is present only in the Spanish overlay that conceals the essential core of Andean culture, which they read as fundamen-tally egalitarian; this assertion owes, in part, to the primordialist sentiments of these organizations, but it also stems from the angry rivalries that have grown between popular organizations and middle-class feminists across the Andean nations. Manuel's exposition revealed similar sentiments, which are reflected in the opinions of many of the CRIC activists with whom I have spoken but are belied by the efforts of Nasa feminists, such as Susana Piñacué, to expose unequal gender relations in the organization and in Nasa communities.

The logic of Manuel's Nasa-Christian contrast follows in the footsteps of academic arguments concerning gender duality in the Andes. Like Silverblatt, who opposes pre-Columbian gender complementarity to colonial Spanish gender discrimination, in his talk Manuel used gender-based dualism as a hinge for making a distinction between indigenous and European cosmovi-sions. He began by explicating a diagram (figure 9) depicting two genealogical charts that bisect under the progenitor into parallel male and female lines, one representing the Christian cosmos and the other gender complementarity in Nasa thought. The diagram bears a striking resemblance to the models of Incaic cosmology, kinship, and political organization that have been offered by academic scholars (Zuidema 1990), which depict parallel descent according to pairs of oppositions between masculine and feminine entities. Manuel un-doubtedly encountered this representation in his anthropological coursework. It is an interesting appropriation because it operates according to a visual logic that contrasts with the other graphic representations I describe in this and other chapters, insofar as it takes kinship as its governing idiom instead of

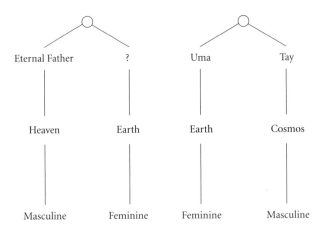

9. Gender complementarity in Nasa cosmovision.

following the conventions of the hierarchical flowchart. As I will illustrate, it is a problematic appropriation of an external discourse, but it also represents an attempt on Manuel's part to break out of the standard workshop discourse and seek new idioms to depict indigenous thoughtways.

How did Manuel use this appropriated visual discourse in his presentation? With the diagram serving as the ground from which he delivered his insights, Manuel contrasted Christian and Nasa thought through attention to the dimension of gender. He argued that Christians speak of God the Father (el Padre Eterno), but there is no equivalent God(dess) the Mother (la Madre Eterna), a space he marked by a question mark in his diagram. Furthermore, he added, many mestizos speak of the earth as a mother; thus, he surmised, for Christians, the sky must be masculine, an attribute he included in his chart. But in the Nasa view, Manuel reasoned, there is a man (Tay) and a woman (Uma) who have sexual relations, producing the Earth, which is a mother and therefore feminine; the cosmos was created as the Earth's sexual partner, hence, a second male-female pair in the Nasa diagram. In Nasa kitchens—at least in those without concrete hearths or commercial stoves—there are three hearthstones set in a circle that represent, Manuel explained, man, woman, and child (he drew a series of three circles interconnected by arrows), signifying procreation. This is not the Trinity, he advised, but a Nasa concept that signifies harmony, as both male and female have equal value. Once we accept Christianity, Manuel concluded, we must accept the existence of a supreme being who is masculine. Manuel argued that along with Christianity comes an acceptance of monogamy, which, he confided, was a difficult arrangement for Nasas to understand, for marriage is not all that common in many Nasa communities; he did not lay a clear basis for his conflation of common law relationships with polygamy, but I have heard women activists complain that Manuel's take on gender complementarity tends to justify, in part, his own proclivity for pursuing various amorous relationships at a time.[9] Clearly, he explained, the Nasas cannot fulfill the law of the Christian god.

Manuel's speech was highly reminiscent of the kind of schematic polarizations between modernity and native cultures that mark the discourses of grassroots NGOs and the popular church throughout the Andes, where cartoon-style pamphlets commonly oppose an idealized and generic indigenous culture to a corrupt capitalist reality, fashioning caricatures that simplify the realities of native peoples. The cosmovision workshop opposed a stereotyped Catholicism to Nasa beliefs in just this way. At the same time, it also ignored the fact that the Catholicism of northern Cauca, to which cosmovision was opposed in Manuel's presentation, presents the same, politically progressive, polarized vision of good and evil, capitalism and neoliberalism.

At a deeper level, however, Manuel does not view cosmovision as the polar opposite of Christianity, but as a replacement for it. To make such an argument, he draws contrasts between what he takes to be two structurally similar systems, Nasa and Christian. This is evident in his theological explanations, and he employs the same argument in his explication of ritual. Manuel lays a series of Catholic rituals on the table, beginning in the questions given to the breakout groups and continuing in his exposition, only to replace them with homologous Nasa practices. In some instances, the Nasa ceremonies are explained by direct reference to Christianity, as occurs when Manuel compares the burial of a newborn's placenta under the three stones of the hearth to Christian baptism. The sheer detail presented for the set of Nasa rituals associated with the life cycle suggests that the two systems are by no means homologous; however, the opposed sets of ritual practices are explained as though they were. It is as though the Nasa system were coherent only in relation to the Christian system, as though it filled the same needs as those satisfied by Christian ritual. In Manuel's exposition, then, Christianity provides the form, which is filled by indigenous content.[10] In fact, when I offered him my critique of his exposition, Manuel told me that he agreed with me, but he argued that the only way to persuade listeners of the importance of cosmovision was to link it to the Christian system of belief that most people in Cauca thought they understood. Ironically, the resulting presentation is much like that of in-culturationist priests, who reduce indigenous practices to Christian objectives, as I explain in the second half of this chapter. Such an analysis stands in marked contrast to how rural Nasa communities have appropriated cosmovision to a living syncretic tradition.

The Reception of Cosmovision

How does cosmovision as a construct play on the hearts and minds of every-day Nasa villagers who, unlike PEB activists, *do* attend Catholic mass or Protestant church services and *are* comfortable with syncretic ritual practice? The participants in the Pílamo workshop, particularly the teachers and the cate-chists, were very excited at the close of the session, effusive in their praise for Manuel, and equally anxious for him to return to teach them more. However, Manuel refused to return to Pílamo, indicating that a zonal cosmovision collective was studying local manifestations of Nasa cosmology, which, he insisted, would be more appropriate to a northern audience than is the Tierradentro-based worldview that he has been studying. Whether or not the participants went home bent on intensifying their ritual practice, as Manuel implored them to do, was unclear to me. The paucity of the practice of Nasa ritual in northern Cauca suggests that these people have a long way to go before they adopt the rigorous program advocated by him, which consists of the strict adherence to numerous ceremonies along the life cycle. When I conducted a cosmovision workshop in Corinto—Manuel was busy and, to my surprise, asked me to replace him—in which we collectively analyzed Juan Tama's colonial titles and compared them to the oral tradition, I discovered that only a handful of the forty or fifty participants knew anything at all about the culture hero, and some questioned why this sort of workshop was even necessary, revealing that Manuel's presentation tilted at northern windmills.

In chapter 4 I contrasted how regional activists and local teachers understand the concept of interculturalism. While their approaches are, indeed, distinct, they are not contradictory, but nourish one another. Similarly, there are vast differences between how cultural activists from CRIC's office reproduce the discourse of cosmovision and how local people absorb it. When we move to the grassroots, it becomes obvious that cosmology is not reduced to the polarized interpretation that Manuel conveyed in his workshop; local people do not seek to *replace* Christianity with cosmovision. As I will demonstrate, the discourse is internalized syncretically at the local level. This persuades me that although it is necessary to engage in a critique of the discourses that infuse regionally inspired accounts of cosmovision, if we do not consider how these accounts operate at the local level, we have not begun to understand the dynamics of culture discourses in the indigenous movement. Regional accounts of cosmovision are readjusted for local consumption, where they are conveyed in formats that resonate with the imaginations and experiences of villagers.

In June 2002, I participated in a community assembly of the resguardo of San José, at which Alcides Musse, a health worker who is himself a San Joseño, presented a report to the community. Alcides drew a schematic picture of a tree, an image that is comprehensible to villagers who, for centuries, have been exposed to naturalistic imagery (figure 10). The tree represented life, Alcides argued, speaking in Nasa Yuwe. From a Nasa standpoint, he explained, health is more than a constellation of curing practices; it is the basis of life and, as such, must be understood as part of all activities. Like a tree, life has ancestral roots, represented in the diagram by the hearth and the placenta that is planted at its base. The trunk of the tree represents the different rituals that sustain it, including the well-known ritual of refreshing cabildo staffs of office at sacred lakes, a ceremony that accompanies the dampening of the hearthfire, the Sakhelu celebration (a reconstituted ritual that I describe below), and offerings to fallen CRIC comrades that borrows from practices used in the November celebration of the Day of the Dead.[11] Note that unlike Manuel's exposition, Alcides's talk conveyed a *syncretic* explication of cosmovision, including not only reconstituted Nasa ceremony and rituals that have been maintained over generations, but also the Christian observance. I have been told that Alcides's exposition follows suggestions made by Manuel.

It is more likely that cosmovision would be embraced, albeit idiosyncratically, in Tierradentro than in northern Cauca. In comparison to the north, the impact of cosmovision is more visible in Tierradentro, where there are many active thê' walas and where rural villagers have participated for centuries in a syncretic ritual practice that has been abandoned in northern resguardos. But the receptiveness of Tierradentro villagers is also the result of decades of work by CRIC. When I conducted dissertation research in Tierradentro in the late 1970s, many of the cacique narratives that form a part of Manuel's origin story were known only in the localities to which they referred. Today, however,

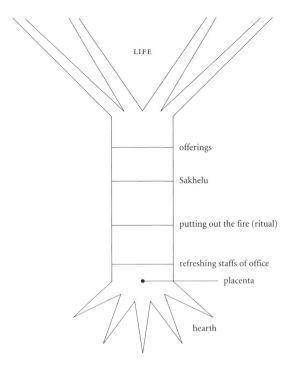

LIFE

offerings

Sakhelu

putting out the fire (ritual)

refreshing staffs of office

placenta

hearth

10. An explanation of cosmovision in San José.

cabildo associations and community institutions across the region are named for them. A bakery in Çxayu'çe, a new resguardo created by residents of San José displaced by the 1994 disaster, is named after La Gaitana, the heroine of the Conquest period. The association of cabildos of the municipality of Inzá is called Juan Tama (a somewhat anomalous appellation, given that he never ruled in that region, which was the home of the cacica Angelina Guyumús). This suggests that the cultural discourse of the regional office, complemented by the teachings of local thê' walas like Ángel María Yoinó, spurred the creation of generic narratives that recontextualize local knowledge in a regional political space. However, the reinscription of sacred topography in new territories has always been a component of Nasa history, as evidenced in the numerous sacred sites across Cauca that are said to be associated with Juan Tama, most recently including the resettled community of Vitonqueños in Santa Leticia, which has been named for him; its community center sports extensive murals depicting the life of the mythic hero (figure 11).

Thus, the long-standing acceptance of shamanism in Tierradentro has only been intensified by the work of CRIC. Shamans are now frequently called to conduct rituals for entire communities to ensure their well-being (Rappaport

11. Juan Tama mural at the village of Juan Tama, Santa Leticia.
Photo by author.

2003). This practice emerged on the heels of the 1994 disaster, when large numbers of the victims were resettled in new and dangerous environments outside of Tierradentro and sought all the means of protection that were at their disposal, including the offices of thê' walas. Çxayu'çe, the new town near Popayán that houses refugees from San José, offered a free plot of land to a shaman from any other Tierradentro community who was willing to relocate alongside them. Given the paucity of land in these new settlements, this indicates a strong conviction on the part of the San Joseños in favor of shamanic practice. Çxayu'çe is the name of a medicinal herb and in 2004, became the name of the resettled community that until then was called San José del Guayahal. The name change is a further indication of the pervasive influence of cosmovision discourse in Tierradentro. In addition to natural disasters, political violence has played a major part in the reintroduction of communal rituals. A few years ago, while visiting Çxayu'çe, I was invited to participate in a shamanic ritual aimed at protecting residents against a variety of armed actors operating in the vicinity. With their transfer from the largely Nasa environment of Tierradentro to Cajibío, a region long marked by peasant land struggles and violent conflicts, the people of San José were confronted by the simultaneous presence of two guerrilla organizations and paramilitary units, the latter responsible for a number of bloody massacres in the area. Faced with imminent danger, San Joseños, like other Nasa communities, felt the need to establish a buffer to protect themselves from the turbulence of their new home. Part of the ceremony included the blowing of coca on small stones while we repeated the list of Çxayu'çe's enemies, including the Colombian army and police, the guerrillas, the paramilitary, and the gringos. My recitation of the litany, particularly my mention of the gringos, who threatened to fumigate Tierradentro's poppy fields under the auspices of the Plan Colombia, was greeted with humor, although the ritual was dead serious and has been repeated in resguardos across Cauca.

Full-blown ceremonial recreations have also emerged. The rise of CRIC and of the Quintín Lame Armed Movement in the late 1970s brought a return of cabildos to Juan Tama Lake, where, after a hiatus of several decades, staffs of office were once again refreshed under shamanic supervision.[12] In August 2000, a highly ambitious revival of a fertility ceremony was conducted in Caldono (Camayo 2001). Based on the narratives of an elderly thê' wala who remembered his grandfather's stories about the ritual sharing of seeds and the adoration of the sun at a site called *Tä' Fxnu* (the Seat of the Sun), the cabildo association of Caldono sacrificed three sheep, hung their meat on a tall pole, and paid reverence to the sun and the moon. In the morning they shared the meat in a communal repast and the seeds of various cultivated plants were ceremonially presented to the congregation. Sakhelu was the name given to the ceremony by its modern creators. This was a highly self-conscious and didactic ritual revival, accompanied, predictably, by workshops and discussion groups in which the meanings of the symbols associated with the ritual were mulled over by the participants.[13]

Cosmovision workshops cannot be decontextualized from the broader array of localized activities experienced by Nasa villagers. It is true that they self-consciously reflect on their cosmovision differently from PEB activists, integrating cosmovision and Christian observance instead of rejecting the latter.

They also encounter the results of PEB's research program in their daily lives, in the enhanced respectability of thê' walas, the teachings of health personnel, participation in public rituals to protect themselves from guerrillas, and engagement in and exegesis of the Sakhelu. What is significant is that, for local villagers, cosmovision is *reinterpreted* from information disseminated by regional activists. Thus, it is not yet a vivencia, an unremarkable lifeway, for local people, but an object of conscious reflection and a strategy for physical and cultural survival. As we shall see in the following section, the Catholic Church contributes, in its own way, to the fortitude of this construct.

Inculturation

Inculturation came into vogue in the mid-1970s, when a reflection by Asian bishops on evangelization called for a church that was "indigenous and inculturated" (Damen 1989, 61); however, it was not until 1977 that an interpretation was offered of what this process might involve: "The incarnation of life and the Christian message in a concrete cultural area in such a way that this experience not only expresses the elements of the culture in question (which would be a mere superficial adaptation), but is converted into an inspirational, normative, and unifying principle that transforms and recreates this culture, giving origin to a '*new creation*'" (Arrupe 1978, 283 in Damen 1989, 61). According to this statement, the objective of inculturation is to transform the existing indigenous culture into a *new* culture, with the injection of Christ's good news. This process involves a search for an "evangelical legacy" buried within indigenous cultures, a hunt for "the face of Christ" in an unlikely place (Damen 1989, 71).

Inculturation demands that religious assume an active orientation toward indigenous cosmovisions. Myth supplies a critical site of connection between Christianity and indigenous belief systems, because it can be mined for its implicit Christian message: "One does not intend to christianize autochthonous myths, but to detect in them . . . the seeds of the Word as steps in a progressive revelation toward the plenitude of the revelation and the liberation in Christ Jesus." Such study can also reveal the sacramental nature of indigenous ritual (Manzanera 1989, 102–103).

In a sense, then, the goal of inculturation is to turn indigenous culture inside out, to discover what is implicitly Christian in it. As Andrew Orta, an anthropologist who has studied inculturationist missionaries in Bolivia, puts it, "The challenge of the new evangelization, some would maintain, is not to bring the Christian bible to the Aymara, but rather, building upon this base of (putatively commensurable) religious tradition, to empower and inspire the Aymara to live their own New Testament" (1995, 101). Accordingly, inculturation is the inverse of interculturalism, the educational philosophy espoused by CRIC. Whereas interculturalism seeks to appropriate external elements to strengthen an indigenous core culture, inculturation aims at revealing and fortifying those elements of that core that are identified as Christian to strengthen an external belief system. Proponents of interculturalism foster dialogue at the frontier between inside and outside as these constructs are understood by members of the indigenous organization; in contrast, supporters of inculturation accept Christianity as an essential component of the inside, prefigured in indigenous cosmology, thus erasing the inside/outside distinction as far as spirituality is concerned.[14] This does not mean, however, that inculturationists support the maintenance of traditional syncretic ritual practice (such as, for example, the civil-religious hierarchy of festival sponsorship that ethnographers have noted across Latin America). To the contrary, proponents of inculturation perceive traditional syncretism as a debasement of Christianity, an adherence to rituals without a full understanding of their transcendent meanings (Orta 1995). For inculturationists, both inside and outside have been corrupted, or perhaps better put, colonial Catholic practice maintains an unnecessary and disquieting barrier between the two worlds.

Inculturation articulates what Orta (1995, 111) calls a "center-periphery construction of pastoral geography," in the sense that the locus of true authenticity is identified as within indigenous cultures, as opposed to traditional Catholic missionary philosophies that brought the ideologies of metropolitan centers to the indigenous periphery. Inculturationists take a very different position from their predecessors, the proponents of liberation theology, who rejected local cultural elements in favor of a universal Christian culture (97). Inculturationists, in contrast, value the local as a site of the authentic, seeking out and validating the customs and cultural forms of the most isolated communities while rejecting their manifestations in urban areas; they are much like realist ethnographers. But they act on this authenticity by realigning its discourse toward a universal Christian conceptual grid in which local cultural forms become universal in the course of exposing and rectifying colonial contamination. As a result, inculturationist missionaries create an indigenous "metaculture" that homogenizes local practice in an appeal to a generic autochthonous tradition (Orta 1998, 172–173).

It might be argued that this is not so different from CRIC's drive to introduce cosmovision into Nasa communities. Despite the insistence of researchers like Manuel Sisco on the need to emphasize the diversity of local expressions of Nasa cosmovision, in practice it is a generic, erudite, Tierradentro-based form that is being taught by the organization, not the diverse local cosmovisions that are interpreted idiosyncratically by individual shamans. Manuel would probably not dispute this assertion but would point to continued efforts at studying cosmovision in areas beyond Tierradentro and among other ethnic groups in addition to the Nasa as an ongoing project of the organization.

The aspirations of inculturationists and interculturalists also converge on the political plane. Inculturationists are clearly concerned with the spiritual dimensions of their mission, but they assert that spirituality can be achieved only after reconstructing an autonomous social and cultural base through a political project. For this reason, the exercise of inculturation includes a number of secular tasks, which are not all that different from the objectives of CRIC: to defend the land, to value indigenous languages, to support political self-determination, to assist communities in negotiating contact with such dangerous external forces as capitalism, to promote the reinscription of indigenous memory, and to stimulate alliances with other oppressed sectors. But they incorporate these tasks into a spiritual agenda by reinterpreting them as "sacraments" (Suess 1993, 42–43), which is what divides them from the interculturalists.

Father Ulcué

A long list of martyrs furnishes a timeline for CRIC's history. Some of its earliest leaders and colaboradores were killed by assassins in the pay of large landholders and by military units; more recently, members of its executive committee were killed by rightist death squads or by leftist guerrillas. One of the most prominent martyrs is Father Álvaro Ulcué Chocué, the parish priest of Toribío, Tacueyó, and San Francisco from 1977 to 1984 and a native of Pueblo Nuevo. Posters bearing his likeness, labeled *nasa pal*, or Nasa priest, are tacked to walls throughout northern Cauca. For a time, CRIC's newspaper was named after him. In northern Cauca he is remembered through his impressive legacy, in particular, the Proyecto Nasa, a regional development corporation operated by the cabildos of Toribío, Tacueyó, and San Francisco, and by an indigenous-run high school that he is said to have dreamed of establishing on lands reclaimed from a nonindigenous landlord.

Ulcué returned to Cauca after seminary studies at the height of repression against the indigenous organization. From 1972 to 1979, the first decade of CRIC's existence, the Colombian Division of Indigenous Affairs reported 155 violations of the human rights of indigenous people in Cauca at the hands of the state and private armies funded by large landowners; the overwhelming majority of these abuses took place in Jambaló, Toribío, and Tierradentro, where the land struggles were most intense (Peñaranda 1998, 50–51). By 1984, conflicts with the elite intensified on the heels of a flawed, ineffective agrarian reform. Some 11,000 hectares were under dispute across the province, particularly in the north, where the indigenous movement had begun to occupy the rich cane-producing lands of the Cauca Valley (67–69). The largest and longest of these struggles was over López Adentro, 2,000 hectares of canefields that were repossessed by indigenous militants for much of 1984, in an ultimately successful bid to legitimize the then defunct cabildo of Corinto, which had lost its official status and its lands in the early part of the twentieth century (69–72). On 9 November 1984, the indigenous occupiers were ejected by the military. On 10 November, in what was seemingly a related move, Father Ulcué was shot by an off-duty policeman as he walked down a street in the nearby city of Santander de Quilichao. The coincidence of these two events propelled the incipient Quintín Lame Armed Movement to enter the public arena (75).

Biographers of Father Ulcué (Beltrán Peña and Mejía Salazar 1989; Roattino 1986) place a great deal of emphasis on the Nasa priest's last months, when he was uninterruptedly singled out by the military for questioning and his family was violently attacked. These repressive actions were instigated and legitimized by mestizo politicians from Toribío, who repeatedly denounced him as an ally of the guerrillas and who feared him as a threat to their stranglehold on the local political patronage system. Ulcué's biographies could almost be called hagiographies, given the picture they paint of the persecution of an intensely spiritual, politically committed, and courageous man whom their authors call a "prophet" and an "apostle," a Christlike figure. But Ulcué is also equated by these authors with Juan Tama as a savior of the Nasa, endowed with shamanistic abilities such as being able to foretell his own future. Father Ulcué's life can also be visualized in political terms, as many of the CRIC activists would prefer. He was a ubiquitous presence in northern Cauca, his activities ranging from early attempts at development planning and bilingual education, to some of the first studies of the Nasa language (ACCT n.d.; Ulcué Chocué 1981, 1983–84, 1984). He consistently attended CRIC congresses and cabildo meetings, and served as Toribío's cabildo secretary.

My purpose here, however, is not to add to the hagiographic literature, whether spiritual or secular, but to examine Álvaro Ulcué's role as a radical evangelizer in northern Cauca, an intellectual precursor to the inculturationist Consolatas. For although Father Ulcué was murdered before inculturation became a guiding philosophy of the radical church in Colombia, his merging of liberation theology with his appreciation of Nasa culture opened the way for such approaches. He saw the Nasa as a prime ground in which to discover Christ, demonstrating an incipient move toward inculturation in his thought, as several notes in his diary indicate: "What is Christology? It is the rediscovery of Christ in the Other," and "It is thus necessary to discover His authentic presence in the history of the continent" (Roattino 1986, 26–27).[15] Father Ezio Roattino showed me the following, very telling inscription that appears in Nasa Yuwe in Father Álvaro's Bible: "God is everywhere. He never sleeps. We [the Nasa] have always had God's word. Jesus Christ suffered for us, he died for us, he is again, alive. Popayán, February, 1983. Álvaro Ulcué Cho-cué, Nasa Priest." For Father Álvaro, Christianity and Nasa identity were inseparable.

One of the most illuminating pieces of evidence of how Father Ulcué merged evangelization with political activism is the record of two extended seminars held for cabildo members of Toribío, Tacueyó, and San Francisco in 1980 and 1981, supported by CENPRODES, the Center for Promotion of Development Projects, a Catholic nongovernmental organization (ACCT 1980–81; Gow 2005). Almost 150 community activists from the three resguardos came together for several intensive sessions to reflect on issues of pressing concern to them. These included strengthening community involvement in cabildo activity and land claims; support for bilingual education, health planning, agricultural development, and community cooperatives; strategies for the demilitarization of indigenous lands and an end to military repression; and the expulsion of Agape, a fundamentalist Protestant missionary organization. As in the hundreds of workshops that have been held in indigenous Cauca since the founding of CRIC, the participants in this series of seminars worked in breakout groups that reported to plenary sessions.

The two seminars were held to stimulate the creation of a school for "autochthonous leaders" (ACCT 1980–81, 2:1), what would later become the Escuela de Animadores Comunitarios (School of Community Animators), through which the Consolatas have created a layer of young Christian political leaders—the "new Nasas" upbraided in Manuel Sisco's cosmovision workshop. The project began with the collective analysis of indigenous legislation *and* biblical texts by the cabildo, followed by the workshops. The objective was, indeed, evangelist, but not in a standard sense:

> The characteristics for choosing these evangelizers is that they must be willing to serve the community. It is understood that their work will not only involve preaching, but animating and organizing the community around its own problems. Given that some compañeros do not understand the meaning of the gospel of liberation, it was clarified that it was a gospel analyzed from the standpoint of the unjust situation lived by an oppressed people and one that necessarily leads to a personal and communal commitment to struggle against exploitation [and] in favor of the creation of true communities of peace and justice. (2:2)

Thus, although the seminars were punctuated by biblical readings and prayers, the gospel was infused into the political discussion itself, which was understood to be an evangelizing task—or, as some of the inculturationist theorists have put it, a "sacrament."

The archival record of these seminars includes a series of drawings produced by the breakout groups and employed as keys for their presentations to the plenary session.[16] One of the drawings used in the 1980 workshop depicts a hand with five fingers growing out of a mountain (ACCT 1980–81, 1:47). The image brings to mind the popular icon of the Powerful Hand of God (La Mano Poderosa), a hand with a wound in its palm, above whose fingers stand St. Joseph, the Virgin Mary, St. Joachim, and St. Anne, and next to whose thumb is the Christ Child. The hand depicted in the Caucan diagram would later become a logo for the Proyecto Nasa. Its fingers point to a plot containing plants and animals, with people working nearby; a house; a heart with a couple inside it; a bedridden patient receiving a visitor; and a sunrise over a mountain, a book resting on its slopes and a cross and chalice above it. The images are generic, similar to those that might be drawn by peasants across the Colombian countryside, irrespective of their ethnic identity. The discussion group that produced the drawing explained the symbolism of its imagery to the plenary (1:48). The hand, they said, represented a unified community successfully exploiting its resources, "the hand that has broken the chains of slavery." The finger pointing to the animals indicated a community that respected its neighbors by fencing in its livestock. The house was meant to symbolize the need for good housing. The heart denoted a family union marked by harmony. The sickbed scene implored people to visit the sick, which is a Christian duty. The book on the mountain expressed the hope that there would be a Bible in each house.

Another commission presented its findings by focusing on the family, an ongoing concern even today in Catholic Toribío. For this group, harmony in the household springs from political consciousness, bilingualism, and evangelization, three goals that intertwine ethnic militancy, cultural revitalization, and Catholicism into a single, unified knot (ACCT 1980–81, 1:55). The same objectives are listed in a plenary summary (1:46) expressing a general desire for political unity, reciprocity among community members, strong families, and a conscious option for Catholicism promoted through evangelization. Such goals are realizable only through the more specific objectives the plenary outlined: schools and technical institutes, good nutrition, an end to party politics and to Agape, and a demilitarized community protected by a civic guard. Clearly, for the three resguardos working under the tutelage of Father Ulcué, politics was, of necessity, a moral and spiritual endeavor.

Making the "New Nasa"

The "new Nasa" whose appearance is fostered by the church emerge out of the intermixture of Catholic spirituality with ethnic political consciousness, a process begun under the tutelage of Father Ulcué and that has intensified under the Consolatas. A vast network of training programs that operate parallel to the cabildos, but with their support, contributes to the emergence of this new leadership in the north. Unlike PEB, which at present controls only three experimental schools and is influential in a dozen more, ACIN, the association of northern cabildos, supervises all of the schools in its jurisdiction, receiving expert assistance from FUCAI (Roads to Identity Foundation), a radical Catholic research institute. The north also maintains several indigenous high schools with innovative and culturally sensitive programs that cater to northern students. A number of university programs sponsored by the Missionary Institute of Anthropology and by the Universidad del Cauca, working in collaboration with the cabildos, operate in northern Cauca, providing degrees in anthropology, rural development, and ethnoeducation through courses of study that combine long-distance learning with month-long seminars held in Toribío.

Two programs are oriented directly toward the production of community leaders. The spiritual dimension of the northern political project is ensured by periodic workshops for community catechists (also called Delegates of the Word), who come together to discuss Nasa history and culture in addition to issues of theological interest and who engage in collective rituals under the guidance of thê' walas. These are local people, both young and old, male and female, who bring an inculturationist message that merges politics with spirituality to their neighborhoods. Delegates of the Word, however, do not transmit verbatim the ideas of the Consolatas, but, as in other Latin American settings (Orta 2005), reinterpret them according to their own needs and knowledge bases, informed by the priorities of their cabildos. They are comparable to the rural teachers who have been trained in CRIC's cosmovision workshops and countless other in-service seminars. Parallel to the organization of catechists is the leadership school, the School of Community Animators, which holds seminars for more than a hundred potential leaders from all of the northern communities on a variety of politically and culturally pertinent themes. In summary, the infrastructure of political leadership in northern Cauca is extensive and surpasses that of any other zone in the province. It is an intensely Catholic leadership, supported, as is CRIC, by a panoply of nongovernmental organizations, in this case, religious ones.

The Cátedra Nasa-UNESCO

The reach of the northern church is exceedingly long. Its earliest funding came from the U.S. Conference of Catholic Bishops, from whom Father Ulcué solicited U.S.$10,000 to build the Proyecto Nasa. A great deal of its current funding comes from the Italian sources with whom the Consolatas are connected. They have also achieved a great deal of support from the Colombian church and from progressive organizations and public figures in Colombia. It is this latter set of contacts that permitted the consolidation of a UNESCO-sponsored chair in Community Process, which in Toribío has been called the Cátedra Nasa-UNESCO.

Unlike most UNESCO chairs, which are established in universities and research institutes, the Cátedra Nasa-UNESCO was an unusual arrangement, in which an indigenous community itself researched its own history through work groups and seminars organized through the School of Animators and supervised by FUCAI. Parallel to this arrangement, UNESCO conferred the title of *maestro en sabiduría* (master of knowledge) on some forty Nasa political and cultural leaders named by the north and by CRIC, who were to take a leading intellectual role in the project.[17] Thus, some two hundred people became enmeshed in the Cátedra, which ran from 1998 to 2000. This was community research on a grand scale, combining intensive interviewing by the members of the School of Animators with massive public assemblies in which their work was analyzed by selected maestros en sabiduría, punctuated by addresses by such well-known figures as theologian and critical theorist Enrique Dussel.

The Cátedra was given a name in Nasa Yuwe: Nasa Ûus Kayatxisa, "to recover Nasa memory with sentiment." Such sentiment was, indeed, generated in the hundred-odd young people, many in their mid-teens, who set out to interview major players in the recent political history of the north. Many of the interviewers were monolingual in Spanish and more attuned to popular culture broadcast from nearby Cali than to Nasa lifeways; they embraced the Cátedra as a tool for rediscovering their roots. Whether or not they acquired extensive historical knowledge varied, of course. The active (and older) community leaders who participated in the Cátedra certainly learned a great deal during the interview process and by listening to regional and local political leaders at the public assemblies. Younger participants, I discovered, were frustrated by their lack of interviewing skills and tended to repeat simplified narrative that indicated that they had not digested the larger arguments brought to bear in the project.[18] Nevertheless, the Cátedra did succeed in organizing people, which was the central objective as stated at early meetings: "to think, opine, decide, and act," or, appropriating Father Ulcué's words, "to raise consciousness, to encourage participation, and to achieve liberation."

What interests me here is the participation of Father Antonio Bonanomi, the parish priest of Toribío and the mastermind of the Cátedra. A small and wiry man of some sixty-five years, a chain-smoker and an inveterate talker, Father Antonio came from Milan to Colombia to participate in social movements, first in peasant communities near Bogotá and later in Cauca. Although he has held posts of considerable authority, such as the directorship of the Consolata seminary in Bogotá, Father Antonio frequently stands at odds with the conservative leadership of his order and with the Colombian church hierarchy. He is a ubiquitous figure at workshops and assemblies, sharing his own, highly chronological interpretation of the history of the north, delivered in entertaining speeches whose contents are frequently organized in a series of oppositions between "before" and "after," punctuated by comic examples from everyday life, and illustrated by diagrams. Father Antonio's speeches reminded me of the way Manuel Sisco taught cosmovision.

But unlike Manuel, Father Antonio tends to isolate Nasa culture from

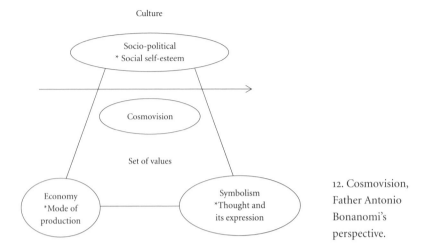

12. Cosmovision, Father Antonio Bonanomi's perspective.

northern politics and to subsume cosmovision under the heading of morality; in fact, Manuel's critique of Nasa politicians focuses on precisely the kind of approach taken by Father Antonio; hence the rivalry. For Father Antonio the story of Juan Tama is a reminder of the distant past, not a "utopia" running parallel to contemporary organizing, as Manuel presented in his cosmovision workshops. Nasa culture is reduced by Father Antonio to "customs," not expanded into an integrated system of thought capable of being harnessed politically. In fact, when I suggested in one of the workshops I was invited to teach to the School of Animators that it might be useful to consider Nasa modes of historical narration, the priest left no room for discussion but dismissed my observation as inconsequential. Father Antonio's view of cosmovision is summarized in a diagram that he explicated in one of the workshops (figure 12). Here, culture is defined as the intersection of political and social self-esteem, the mode of production, and symbolism, a very Marxist constellation, tinged by Christian psychology. In this view, culture evolves in a linear fashion. Cosmovision is reduced to a "set of values"—ostensibly, to allow for the infusion of Nasa and Christian thought, although in my time in Toribío I noted that Father Antonio frequently left the spiritual dimension to Father Ezio, who is more familiar with the inculturation literature and speaks Nasa Yuwe.

Like Manuel's expositions, Father Antonio's lectures and diagrams were "read" by the participants in ways that largely defied his master narrative. Cosmovision workshop participants listened to Manuel's purist message and then returned home to their syncretic observance; Father Antonio's listeners were also exposed to the much more personal and textured narratives of their interview subjects, many of whom were highly critical of the role of the Catholic Church in indigenous areas and who were capable of generating emotional responses from their interlocutors that Father Antonio went to great pains to counter during question-and-answer sessions. In a sense, then, events as highly orchestrated as the Cátedra Nasa-UNESCO gave way to more personalized relationships with history and cosmology. At the same time, however, the Cátedra served as a prime vehicle for organizing a politically autonomous north in opposition to CRIC.

Cosmovision versus Catholicism

It is not my intention to weigh the relative merits of CRIC's cosmovision project against the radical Christian orientation of the north. Both of these projects have been immensely successful in their own way. They demonstrate similar strengths and shortcomings. The two approaches are intercultural in nature, incorporating external ideas into a Nasa cultural base. Moreover, I have collaborated with both of them: with CRIC, in its history of PEB and in its cosmovision workshops; with the north, giving seminars on Juan Tama's titles to catechists and the School of Animators. Although I am personally partial to CRIC's approach, I respect the ideas and achievements of both groups. What interests me is to tease out of their approaches to spirituality a nuanced appreciation of the relationship between region and locality, paying particular attention to how these relations are filtered through research practices and within the networks connecting organic intellectuals, colaboradores, and sabedores.

In a perceptive reading of a national-level indigenous mobilization that took place in 1996, Jean Jackson (2002) inquires into the roots of the relationship between locally based organizations and the associations that connect them to broader movements. The scenario she interprets is a series of occupations of government and church offices by representatives of cabildos and by the National Indigenous Organization of Colombia (ONIC), which resulted in accords between the indigenous movement and the Colombian state. The dispute, originally between the Wayúu (formerly Guajiros) and the local office of the Division of Indigenous Affairs (DAI), began over funding at the local level but swiftly erupted into a national controversy when DAI's central office in Bogotá and the Episcopal Palace were occupied by indigenous demonstrators; a parallel regional mobilization in Cauca blocked the Panamerican Highway, forcing the government to its knees. The national organization offered a broad set of demands, ranging from land rights and the creation of indigenous territorial entities—territorially based administrative units provided for under the 1991 constitution but whose characteristics have never been legally defined—to control over development and public works funds and a call for government action to end human rights violations in indigenous territories (88).

Jackson's analysis hinges on the ways different actors in the dispute gauged the legitimacy of indigenous leaders. In a familiar but politically inexpedient move, DAI ignored ONIC's leadership on the pretext that cabildos were the only legitimate expression of traditional indigenous authority, not a set of national officers elected by regional organizations (2002, 92–95). ONIC, however, had a legitimate claim to represent a national indigenous constituency on the national stage in this dispute, which unfolded largely in Bogotá and in the media. Jackson notes that the kinds of discourses employed by national-level indigenous leaders and those used at the local level were quite different. Whereas ONIC uses a generic approach to its demands, focusing on what indigenous people have in common and using a universal language of sovereignty, cabildos are more culturally specific (95–97). What is at issue, Jackson explains, is how indigenous people are to be viewed by the national society, something that is intimately related to the two-pronged image that indigenous authorities conveyed to the public. On the one hand, they are *peoples*, employing culturally specific discourses; on the other, they are Colombian *citizens*, engaging a generic discourse of indigenous citizenship that is provided for in the 1991 constitution, which they helped to write (109). The former discourse is the province of cabildos as traditional local authorities, and the latter represents the space of activity of indigenous organizations, whose leadership is not directly elected by local community members.

During the ten-day blockage of the Panamerican Highway at La María in the summer of 1999, CRIC attempted to resolve this dilemma by including among their demands state recognition of the indigenous organization's status as a "traditional authority." This was a major point of contention in the negotiations between the Caucan indigenous movement and state representatives, one that was ultimately won by the organization. Today, CRIC's letterhead proclaims that it is a "traditional authority" and its elected leadership carries staffs of office as do cabildo members, investing in it a legitimacy that permits it to sidestep the sort of reaction that DAI had to ONIC in 1996. This does not mean, however, that the regional leadership operates as a cabildo, nor that indigenous communities or the state actually see it as one. In fact, Manuel Sisco's explication of cosmovision to the executive committee, which I described earlier as an underhanded critique of its generic politics, suggests that even within the regional office these issues are under constant dispute.

The clash between cosmovision and Catholic spirituality must be comprehended within the constellation of competing identities and discourses that Jackson analyzes for the indigenous movement at the national level, and not simply as an anti-Christian sentiment within CRIC or a defense of the legitimacy of inculturation by the church. PEB sees the Consolatas as attempting to speak for the indigenous communities of the north and succeeding in co-opting them, something that they voiced repeatedly at internal meetings I attended. The northern church and its affiliated communities see PEB as overstepping its mandate, as trespassing on local affairs that are not its province and that it does not understand. Particularly enlightening to me was a curricular meeting I attended in Caloto, one of the northern municipalities, in which PEB activists and leaders of northern Cauca disagreed over the place of Christianity in the movement. At one point in the meeting, Cristóbal Secue, a former president of CRIC and a leader of ACIN, called PEB to task for its misplaced priorities. The Consolatas, he stated, were not the Nasas' enemies, FARC was, and alliance with the church was a necessary arm in this struggle. Spirituality is a potent discourse fueling these rivalries.

But it is too simplistic to explain the fault lines between CRIC and the north as the product of a competition between region and locality. The north has supplied much of the Nasa leadership within CRIC's executive committee, thus blurring the boundaries between the two organizational levels. Leaders shift their priorities depending on the context in which they are operating. Furthermore, the northern leadership is divided between loyal adherents to the church in the mountains of Toribío and critics in the low-lying communities that abut the Cauca Valley. Moreover, if we are to adopt the argumentation so cogently presented by Jackson that distinguishes between discourses of cultural difference and of citizenship, their distribution in Cauca is inverted in contrast to what Jackson found at the national level. This suggests that it is crucial that we simultaneously study the indigenous movement in its national, regional, and local dimensions, instead of privileging one level over the others. In contradistinction to ONIC's position vis-à-vis the Wayúu, it is PEB, the regional apparatus, that deploys a culturalist discourse rooted in cosmovision, whereas the locally based northern leaders and the church speak in the generic cadences of new social movements and in a recognizably inculturationist key. This inversion of Jackson's case study has less to do with the distinction between region and locality, however, than it owes to rivalries of a local nature between the north and Tierradentro, where so many of PEB's culturalist activists are from. These rivalries are continually enacted in the regional organization itself. In other words, the play between national, regional, and local priorities is contextually specific.

Many of the activists I know from Tierradentro see the hegemony of the north in regional political affairs as a challenge to be assumed, specifically, by *nasnasa* from such inside places as Tierradentro (irrespective of the fact that there are militants on both sides of the fence in both regions). In a sense, this is what the shaman workshops were all about and this is the target at which Manuel Sisco aims in his cosmovision lectures. Because of the active role of the Consolatas in the north and the allegiances that many northerners give the priests—which is the opposite of the state of affairs in Tierradentro, where the movement struggles to free itself from a conservative church—and because PEB activists best express their position in culturalist terms that reject Christianity in favor of a pure version of cosmovision, this wider political rivalry is conceptually crystallized into the confrontation of Nasas and Christians. At the core of this rivalry is the battle for the legacy of Father Ulcué, who was both priest and Nasa until his final days. As we wrote the history of PEB, Abelardo Ramos continuously sought to instrumentalize Ulcué as a Nasa icon, not a Christian saint, and to link him symbolically with Benjamín Dindicué, also a martyr from CRIC's early days, a proponent of indigenous education, a towering—and secular—political leader, and most important, a native son of Tierradentro. In this symbolic confrontation, region and locality, colaborador and indigenous militant, culturalist intellectual and politician, Christian practitioners and shaman: all confront one another in a multiplicity of ways.

CHAPTER 7

Imagining a Pluralist Nation

Intellectuals and Indigenous Special Jurisdiction

Arquimedes Vitonás is a young activist whom I met several years ago in Toribío. When he was in his early teens, he took off for the coca fields of Colombia's eastern lowlands in search of a livelihood, as do many young Nasas. But Arquimedes was enticed back to Toribío by Father Antonio Bonanomi, his parish priest, who encouraged him to get involved in the political culture of the community. Arquimedes's commitment was exemplary, and ultimately, he was invited to join the Consolata missionary team, a group of lay and religious activists engaged in movement politics and evangelization, which they saw as one and the same thing. The spiritual intensity and discipline of the team did not sit well with Arquimedes but, nevertheless, he remained in Toribío, becoming a protégé of Father Antonio and, eventually, one of Toribío's prominent local leaders. For a time, he served as director of the Proyecto Nasa, a grassroots development corporation that grew out of a dream of Father Álvaro Ulcué's. The last time I saw him, some three years ago, he was serving as an advisor to Ezequiel Vitonás, the municipal mayor, or *alcalde*, of Toribío; in 2003 he was elected alcalde.[1]

This chapter looks at individuals like Arquimedes, young Nasa political leaders who have assumed positions of authority in communities across Cauca. These twenty-, thirty-, and forty-something men and women—in the past decade, indigenous women have stepped into positions of authority in cabildos and to a lesser extent in indigenous organizations—differ from the founders of political organizations like CRIC and AICO. The new breed of leaders has studied at least through high school and is more conversant with the discourses of the state and of nongovernmental organizations than were the militants who gave birth to the contemporary indigenous movement; the latter were generally unschooled agriculturalists bent on reclaiming lands usurped from native communities in the nineteenth century (Jimeno 1996). In the wake of the 1991 constitution, which devolves tasks of budgetary and development planning to municipalities and to resguardos, the capabilities of the younger generation are now at a premium in native communities, resulting in an almost complete turnover of leadership across indigenous Cauca.

The older leaders of the indigenous movement worked their way up the ranks of the cabildo and regional organizations. In contrast, many of the younger leaders received their political training outside of the cabildo, in the regional organizational culture with its numerous planning commissions, outreach committees, teacher training programs, and development projects. Activists like Arquimedes commonly enter the cabildo at its highest rungs, as governor or as lieutenant governor (*gobernador suplente*), or insert themselves into municipal government as high-level mayoral advisors or even alcaldes. The apex of local governing bodies is thus considerably younger than it used to be, occupied by activists in their twenties instead of seasoned militants in their fifties and sixties. The entry of young politicians onto the scene has heralded major transformations in the nature of indigenous organizations and cabildos. They have dynamized zonal cabildo associations like ACIN in northern Cauca and Nasa Çxhâ'çxhâ' in Tierradentro, and have moved CRIC toward a politics of peoplehood. On the local level, they have been instrumental in supporting social services in resguardos and in implementing long-term development planning (Gow 1997; Guambía 1994). In the minds of some, they have brought a much needed new orientation to regional organizations formerly dedicated to land claims in an era in which there are few lands left to repossess. For others, the new leadership has deviated from the grassroots contestatory politics of the indigenous movement, facilitating its integration into a network of nongovernmental organizations and government bureaucracies; in other words, some feel the new leadership has been co-opted.

While activists like Arquimedes are attuned to and draw on the contributions of the cultural workers to whom I have paid most attention in this book, the former are, at their core, politicians who make highly pragmatic decisions as they balance between their Nasa constituencies and the structures of the dominant society. As organic intellectuals, the discourse that they generate cannot always display the cultural purism of a Manuel Sisco, an Abelardo Ramos, or a Susana Piñacué. If, after Les Field (1999), we view indigenous politics as moving between culturalist discourses and the discourse of sovereignty, then Manuel, Abelardo, and Susana stand solidly in the first camp as the generators of cultural strategies that enhance ethnic difference, whereas people like Arquimedes are more concerned with harnessing difference to the construction of political proposals for indigenous autonomy within a pluralist society. Notwithstanding the divergence in their language and the locus of their activities, one cannot exist without the other because both discourses are not only essential to the survival of the indigenous movement, but nourish one another.

In this final chapter, I consider the impact of the work of culturalist intellectuals in the political arena, using two ethnographic scenarios to achieve this end. First, I look at how ideas of nation, state, and justice have been appropriated and redefined by the indigenous movement through an analysis of the translation of key constitutional terms into Nasa Yuwe. This process unfolded under the supervision of the cabildo of Mosoco, Tierradentro, with the collaboration of PEB. In the course of a dialogue between cabildo authorities and regional activists, culturalist constructs emanating from the cosmovision project were reformulated into cogent critiques of the Colombian state, laying the basis for what indigenous projections of ethnic and political pluralism might look like.

Cosmologically inspired critiques of the state also undergird the incipient systems of justice that are cropping up in native communities, where new political constructs are being operationalized in the wake of a constitutional mandate that devolves judiciary functions to cabildos in what has come to be known as "indigenous special jurisdiction." In this second scenario, I look at a constitutional lawsuit brought by a member of the resguardo of Jambaló, in which the legality of Nasa forms of judicial procedure and corporal punishment are under dispute. Such disputes emerge out of constitutional reform, which resulted in the recognition of indigenous uses and customs as legitimate forms of legality that must ultimately supplant Colombian legal usages in the resguardos. But the state's authorization of legal pluralism in the countryside does not preclude indigenous people's individual rights as Colombian citizens to due process and to fair and reasonable punishment should they commit an infraction, both of which frequently come into conflict with native uses and customs, which are not entirely commensurate with national forms.

At the interstices of national and local legal systems, where indigenous citizens dispute the relative merits of diverse forms of jurisdiction, it is local, zonal, and regional politicians who are the key actors. They are charged with reviving ancient memories of judicial autonomy in an effort to consolidate contemporary uses and customs. But they must also assert their hegemony over a territory that is contested by cabildos, regional indigenous organizations, the Colombian state and its military, guerrillas, and the paramilitary. In other words, customary law is being introduced in a modern and characteristically Colombian setting. It cannot be studied as an ancient lifeway that has persisted across time but, instead, must be seen as a kind of a "countermodernity" in which native peoples protect themselves both through assertions of cultural difference and through assuming state functions.

The battle over customary law is a privileged scenario for making sense of contemporary indigenous politics, because these are the contexts in which we can most clearly perceive the tensions inherent in the overlapping of discourses of sovereignty and culture. These are also spaces in which we can observe the tensions that arise among multiple social actors, including culturalist intellectuals, indigenous politicians committed to achieving sovereignty, representatives of regional, zonal, and local organizations, and the various state functionaries who intervene in various capacities in local disputes. In other words, indigenous special jurisdiction affords a window onto examining the heterogeneity of the movement and, consequently, the complex negotiations through which indigenous politics emerges.

My intention, however, is not to focus on the workings of Nasa customary law in and of itself. What I hope to achieve in this chapter is an evaluation of how the elegant cultural constructs of regional intellectuals are operationalized in the gritty world of local politics, where pragmatic leaders must balance their assertions of cultural difference against the complex realities of heterogeneous communities. Caucan localities are not only homes to shamans and advocates of culturalist discourses. They are also the theaters of operation of the "new Nasa," the radical Catholics whose fusion of Christianity with native culture has been encouraged by the popular church. Although they may coincide with CRIC's cultural workers in their recognition of the legitimacy of thê' walas and in the efficacy of ritual, they are actors enmeshed in a regional political struggle internal to the indigenous movement, of the sort that I described in the previous chapter, where localities dispute the hegemony of regional activists and where the regional organization seeks to purge localities of external influences, such as the church. Politics requires a balancing of these polarized positions.

But localities are inhabited by other important actors who, unlike the "new Nasa," oppose the movement's demands.[2] Fundamentalist Protestants, whose numbers are growing across indigenous Cauca, robustly reject cosmovision.

Nasa and mestizo members of the Liberal Party oppose CRIC because the autonomy defended by the movement threatens their power base created through political patronage. Finally, there are those Nasa who, against the recommendation of cabildos, support the various armies that operate in their midst. Thus, politicians contend not only with disputes internal to communities, but with the multiple circuits that connect localities with the state and the dominant society.

Despite frequent assertions about the absence of the state in rural Colombia, it is not an absent player in the indigenous communities of Cauca. State institutions and their proxies—the church, for instance, in a region where the administration of indigenous education was traditionally confined to the religious sector—have not always played a constructive role in rural life, nor have they provided the services that communities demand of them. However, state presence has been felt almost constantly in the past century through its emissaries (Gupta 1995): representatives of the national Agrarian Bank who provide loans to native farmers, the regional office of the Division of Indigenous Affairs that has supervised the activities of cabildos, local court officials who have judged offenders, and, above all, the army and police that have attacked communities while in pursuit of the guerrillas. It is, nevertheless, essential to remember that several state structures operate simultaneously in the Colombian countryside, each with its own rules of justice and its own guidelines for public behavior. FARC, the ELN, and AUC all have their own standing armies that police indigenous territory and come into conflict with local authorities, as well as with the Colombian army. The guerrillas also have their own systems of justice (Aguilera Peña 2001; Molano 2001) which, as I demonstrate in this chapter, intersect in complex ways with the Colombian and indigenous justice systems. Thus, while these armed organizations are not legitimate in the same sense as is the Colombian state, they do engage in activities that are experienced by local residents as state-like in those regions in which they exercise control. Moreover, pronouncements by Colombian indigenous organizations treat these armed groups as external agents similar to the state, particularly in regard to their encroachment on the exercise of autonomy by indigenous authorities (ONIC 2002, 12–17). From an international vantage point or from Bogotá, it appears as though the Colombian state were fighting off numerous insurgencies, yet from a local perspective, the various armed actors, both legitimate and illegitimate, effectively impose their own notion of the state on indigenous people. Nor are local people entirely powerless in the face of armed encroachment. Some actively oppose the hegemony of these various state structures through participation in cabildos, however, others encourage their continued presence. Particularly in the north, FARC and other guerrilla groups have a long-standing indigenous constituency; in addition, they forcibly recruit young people to their ranks.[3] Hence, despite official cabildo opposition to armed actors, resguardo councils are continually forced to negotiate with violent outsiders.

Under such circumstances, indigenous intellectuals face a quandary: constructed notions of cosmovision such as those being developed in the movement with an eye to creating a distinct cultural perspective cannot be mechanically imported into local disputes. Moreover, the introduction of these proposals for cultural reform must be reevaluated in light of the multiple internal and external conflicts in which communities are embroiled. For these reasons, cosmogonic referents appear only in muted form in the discourse of Nasa politicians. Nevertheless, cosmovision and the search for cultural essences reappear in amplified form in the language of the agents of the dominant society who intervene in indigenous areas. Magistrates on the Constitutional Court have, since the Court's inception, been especially concerned with defining indigenous cultures by virtue of their extreme otherness. Some judges have sought to limit the scope of indigenous special jurisdiction to only those communities who exhibit full-blown and coherent constellations of recognizable cultural traits (B. Sánchez 2001); others have teased cosmology out of precarious cultural referents in an effort to accredit cabildos with judicial autonomy. In an ironic twist, the state intervenes in the dialogue between indigenous cultural activists and politicians to endorse purist proposals as emblematic of indigenous legality, a significant move that shifts the stakes in the recognition of customary law.

Indigenous Special Jurisdiction

The complexities of the concrete functioning of the state in the resguardos has been compounded since the 1991 constitution, which provides for the replacements of national legal codes by customary law ("uses and customs") in resguardos, with the cabildo substituting for the judge in legal investigations and decisions (Colombia 1991, Art. 246; Van Cott 2000a). In essence, cabildos have been forced to assume the role of the state and have suddenly found themselves obliged to take control of a penal system whose exercise has been suppressed since the colonial period and replaced by state criminal statutes and enforcement. While cabildos have always controlled the distribution of communal lands and mediated disputes over land tenancy, as well as supervising public morals—such as adultery, parental obligations, and other aspects of family law—until 1991 they were at liberty to remand those accused of penal offences to the national courts, which they did in most murder cases and in some cases of theft. Over four centuries of European domination, local uses and customs in the penal sphere atrophied to such an extent that they would have to be adjusted, even reimagined, in light of the introduction of indigenous special jurisdiction. In short, the limited sphere of operation of the cabildo left communities at a severe disadvantage in the face of the complex conflicts over territory that have erupted over the past half-century.

Indigenous organizations responded to this quandary with the establishment of committees to explore the prospects of reintroducing uses and customs, making ample use of external legal advisors, including legal anthropologists; this process has been particularly advanced in northern Cauca, Tierradentro, and Guambía, but is happening only on a piecemeal basis in other Nasa communities. Indigenous politicians have also participated in numerous seminars in which native authorities and national jurists have exchanged their knowledge and experiences (Colombia 1997). Early on in the process of introducing indigenous special jurisdiction, the Colombian state funded the ethnographic study of a range of indigenous ethnic groups, including the Nasa (Perafán Simmonds 1995), in an effort to foster the written codification of uses and customs, as the British attempted to do in Africa (Moore 1992). That is, they presupposed that a coherent corpus of rules susceptible to written classification and commensurate with Western jurisprudence existed in native communities. Much of this research involved the ethnographic collection of descriptions of disputes and the identification of the penalties paid for particular crimes in a single resguardo. The local legal system—if it could, in fact, be called that at the dawn of the devolution of judicial authority to cabildos—was analyzed as emblematic of an imagined Nasa system. It was codified according to a framework that replicated the organization of national law into administrative, civil, and penal codes, despite the fact that such a typology was an artifact of Western, and not Nasa, jurisprudence (Perafán Simmonds 1995). Not surprisingly, the project met with criticism by Colombian jurists (B. Sánchez 2001) and by some indigenous authorities.

Many indigenous leaders vehemently reject any steps to codify native legal systems in writing on the grounds that these are inherently consensual, oral, and considerably more flexible than national legal codes (Morales 1997).[4] As activists have pointed out, the resolution of disputes is the province not only of native political authorities, but also of shamans, whose investigative methods are incommensurate with those of judges because they employ different notions of causation from Western jurisprudence (J. Piñacué 1997, 32–33). In other words, indigenous leaders assert that native legal procedures are framed by a distinct cosmovision and, therefore, operate according to a different logic from Colombia law.

But the assertion of cultural difference by recourse to cosmovision does not necessarily imply that the logic of a distinctly Nasa legal system is understood by, or even familiar to, many indigenous politicians. At the local level, the research of organic intellectuals concerning cabildo prosecutorial procedure (Perdomo 1999, 2002, 2005) and the work of nonnative academics on the cosmological basis of Nasa law (Gómez Valencia 2000) is only beginning to be appropriated by native authorities for the creation of autonomous legal procedures, which are not yet in place. For the most part, debates in Nasa communities have centered on the applicability of modes of corporal punishment, such as the stocks and public whippings, which are seen as restoring cosmic harmony, and not on methods of judging offenders.

Moreover, politicians must balance the incipient logic of cosmic harmony that is being constructed by researchers against the exigencies of the state, which has not entirely relinquished its control over indigenous areas. As the constitution states: "The authorities of indigenous communities will be able to exercise jurisdictional functions within their territory, according to their own norms and procedures, so long as these are not contrary to the Constitution and to the laws of the Republic" (Colombia 1991, Art. 246). The law of the state thus encompasses the systems of uses and customs currently under construction, because the constitutional article that recognizes ethnic pluralism is subordinate to a previous article that lays out the basic rights of all Colombian citizens. In the final instance, indigenous legal projections cannot contradict the fundamental precepts of the constitution. The autonomy that native organizations hoped to achieve through the constitutional project thus remains elusive because their legal projects are contested in the national arena.

This is precisely the problem that comes up repeatedly as members of indigenous communities bring constitutional lawsuits, or *tutelas*, against their traditional authorities, arguing that their (individual) rights as Colombian citizens have been violated by (communal) uses and customs (Gómez 1995, 1999; Ocampo 1997; Roldán Ortega 2000; B. Sánchez 2001; Sánchez Botero 1998). It is here that we can identify the fault lines that have emerged in the course of the implementation of indigenous special jurisdiction, because in these cases the competing and conflicting discourses used by indigenous complainants, native authorities, ethnic organizations, and the state's magistrates come to the fore. It is in this cauldron that notions of indigenous juridical control are being constructed—in grassroots legal committees, at cabildo meetings, and in the Constitutional Court. But before I tread this ground, let me turn briefly to a consideration of how some of the legal principles used in Nasa jurisprudence were generated, because this process sheds significant light on how culturalist intellectuals perceive their role in fostering legal pluralism.

Reconceptualizing the State through Translation

As I have suggested at various points in this book, translation provides an indispensable strategy used by Nasa activists to appropriate concepts from the dominant society and to reconfigure them into self-conscious indigenous categories. Following the work of Rey Chow (1995), I have tried to show how the translation into Nasa Yuwe of ideas originating in the national and international arenas supplements the original Spanish terminology, "improving" it by injecting it with Nasa significance. Chow's assertions are extremely useful for making sense of the way Nasa culturalist intellectuals have harnessed translation to their political imaginings. Their methodology developed out of the translation of selected articles of the 1991 constitution into several major aboriginal languages (Rojas Curieux 1997, 2000), two of which are spoken in Cauca: Nasa Yuwe (Abelardo Ramos and Cabildo Indígena de Mosoco 1993) and Guambiano (Muelas Hurtado et al. 1994). In the Nasa case, the translation emerged out of a series of workshops hosted by the cabildo of Mosoco, Tierradentro, and participated in by local bilingual teachers and shamans, advised by lawyers from Bogotá, and coordinated by Nasa linguist Abelardo Ramos, who is native to the resguardo of Tálaga, Tierradentro. The translation process afforded a space in which the translators could reconceptualize notions of justice and nationhood. That is, they did not *translate* the constitution in a strict sense, but *reimagined* its fundamental precepts from a Nasa subject position, constructing a Nasa critique of the Colombian state. In this sense, they were not seeking commensurability, but a means for arriving at their own political principles that could eventually enter into dialogue with those of the state. This is not translation as we know it, but a subaltern methodology for taking on the new political challenges facing the movement. The translation team's deliberations were grounded in a hierarchy of political values quite different from those of the original constitutional text, values that are, in part,

Nasa, in the sense of being culturally different, and in part, contestatory and shared by a broad range of critics of the Colombian political system. That is, the process of translation involved the articulation of culturalist positions within discourses of sovereignty. What is interesting is how the two were combined to create political values that would subsequently underlie the creation of uses and customs.

From a Nasa point of view, translation is an apt starting point for legal imaginings, as it involves the interpretation of speech (*yuwe*), a fundamental building block of Nasa uses and customs. Yuwe is the term used for the resolution of a dispute. It refers to the process of public confession through which both wrongdoers and the community at large come to recognize the root causes of the disharmony that caused the crime to be committed in the first place. That is, it is not only a rendering of accounts, but a collective form of analysis. As a result of this oral performance, which is sometimes followed by ritualized punishment such as whipping or the use of the stocks, the accused and his or her neighbors are rehabilitated and social harmony is restored (Perdomo 1999, 28–32; see Gómez Valencia 2000, 55–58).[5] Nasa law is, therefore, intimately tied to the public airing through performative speech of the causes of community rupture. Of course, Colombian law also relies on performance in legal cases, which generally transpire in the literate channel. But the Colombian courthouse is not a place of rehabilitation; that is the province of the prison. In the absence of prisons, which indigenous activists oppose as places in which criminals become hardened and isolated from their cultural milieu, the cabildo office functions simultaneously as a space of judgment and of rehabilitation.

The translation of speech, rather than of writing, was a fundamental component of the creation of the Nasa version of the 1991 constitution. Traditional authorities reconceptualized notions of justice and nationhood through dialogue. First, constitutional articles were glossed orally in Spanish by lawyers acting in an external advisory capacity; then they were discussed in Nasa Yuwe in a series of workshops whose participants ranged from cabildo members to local teachers and Nasa linguists. It was only in the final stages that yuwe as speech and performance gave way to the written inscription of the articles in Nasa Yuwe. Let us examine some of their conclusions.

The expression of sovereignty through cultural difference, which is the essence of CRIC's pluralist proposal, is particularly salient in the translators' use of notions of political rectitude and legitimate authority. They translated "constitution" as *eç ne'jwe'sx*, or "the principal or fundamental book" (Abelardo Ramos and Cabildo Indígena de Mosoco 1993, 116), drawing on the word *ne'jwe'sx*, which is used to denote cabildo and comes from the traditional usage in "Tierrafuera." The root of *ne'jwe'sx* is *nee*, which, according to Abelardo Ramos, is a term used in animal husbandry:

> Let's begin with /*ne'jwe'sx*/, the "leader." This name or lexeme was chosen to refer to indigenous authority and to differentiate it from nonindigenous authority. It appears that we can accept that it comes from the lexeme /*nee*/ which is what we call the "domestic animal, male or female, who is given preference," which is associated with (or for) the luck of the owner. Thus, these animals die of old age, of natural deaths. When you select [animals] with reproductive ends in mind, we also say /*nee*/. So, these animals end up knowing the territory and their habitat completely, which is why they are the leaders of the herd.[6]

The same root, *nee*, is present in the word for the primordial beings Tay and Uma, the Nejwe, who are described in the origin story that grew out of shamanic research into cosmovision. Both the Nejwe (the primordial beings) and the ne'jwe'sx (cabildo authorities) are thus marked as preferred leaders associated intimately with the territory; they can be either male or female.

Ne'jwe'sx, or "principal authority" (Abelardo Ramos and Cabildo Indígena de Mosoco 1993, 115), stands in contrast to *npiçthê'*, the term coined by the constitutional translators to designate elected officials; state authority is *çxab wala kiwete npiçthê'*, or "the authority of the territory of the greater people" (115).[7] As Abelardo pointed out to me, *npiçthê'* differentiates those officials who are merely elected from ne'jwe'sx, whose authority is grounded in their intrinsic merit. Abelardo explains this lexical choice:

> This refers to an animal or person who imposes himself upon others. This is why it is associated with power (of the state or of actions related to the use of the force of law), with someone who should be followed, not so much for reasons of fact, as for reasons of power, which is what in practice characterizes the leader (of the state). . . . The segment -*piç*- contains the idea of "masculinity." From before the time of the translation of the constitution the term already existed, but here we adopted it in the sense of the powerful male (*macho-potente*) and/or the overbearing (*prepotente*) male; it is also applicable to women who have the same attitudes.[8]

In other words, ne'jwe'sx are born leaders and are either male or female; the term npiçthê' appears to denote a swaggering macho who exerts power rather than leadership. To have chosen such a term to represent state authority is an

implicit—and searing—critique of Colombian politics. The translation de-
values the electoral process as the motor behind the state, a usage deriving from
the contestatory politics of the indigenous movement (and of other social
movements), which classifies most elected officials as petty politicians (*politi-
queros*); in this sense, the state is a collection of npiçthê'. But there is a deeper
Nasa critique implicit in the terminology. The lexical choices of the translators
express the values inherent in cosmovision, given that the constitution and
cabildos are equated with the primordial nejwe, with territory, and with gender
complementarity, while the state is equated with raw, masculine political
power. The opposition between npiçthê' and ne'jwe'sx also builds on a critique
of indigenous politicians who follow the model of the dominant society, instead of that provided by Uma and Tay, something that, as I described earlier,
was explicitly recognized by Manuel Sisco in his exposition before CRIC's
executive committee regarding the state of research into cosmovision.

The translation team went on to question the consequences of leaving
justice in the hands of npiçthê'. *Eena' eena' kafxi'ze'nxi*, their neologism for
"justice," means "to be permanently in the light" (Abelardo Ramos and Cabildo Indígena de Mosoco 1993, 118). As Abelardo explained to me:

> We interpreted that justice is to place someone, an individual, permanently in
> the light. With this we were thinking that we have a cultural value that is
> common to the family council [the nuclear family] and the cabildo council. . . .
> Because in the discourse of the captain or the governor, [in] the context of the
> cabildo, the council is what is communally expressing the category of authority
> in a more generic form, but it is more precise. So that authority is he who causes
> the people to live and remain in light. And we, as a cultural value, say that as a
> life project, as a cultural goal, an authentic Nasa, with all the force of Nasa
> identity, should be an *eena'* person. So, by virtue of culture, of cultural princi-
> ples, we are called to be transparent in our attitudes, in our conduct, in our
> spirit . . . to be honorable, because we are transparent. We express dignity in
> these categories of light, so that transparency for us, cannot be simply a slogan,
> a discourse, something ideological-political. Light is like an everyday experi-
> ence [*vivencial*] and should be lived.

This is a complex statement, which evinces the utopian political project that
has intimately concerned Nasa intellectuals, whose lives are dedicated to the
struggle for achieving a transparent authority oriented by what they project as
a primordial logic; Abelardo realizes, however, that the movement always trails
a step behind this objective.

At the heart of Abelardo's explanation is the relationship he draws between the clarity of justice in the family and in the cabildo. In the writings of Adonías Perdomo (1999, 2002, 2005), an unusual amount of space is dedicated to tracing the workings of authority in the family, among shamans, in the cabildo, and in other spaces of everyday life. Authority is thus more than a mode of exercising political power; it is a vivencia, a lifeway that permeates the everyday activities of everyone in a Nasa community, whether in a family setting, in the cabildo office, or at a regional assembly. The nature of authority, Adonías argues, is generated in the family, so that the political authority of the cabildo cannot be exercised in isolation from this most basic unit of Nasa society. As I demonstrate later in this chapter, it is precisely this connection that is being sought in contemporary Nasa law because, of course, legitimate authority is a utopian dream. The' walas are constantly being criticized for charging exorbitant fees to their patients, cabildos are accused of indulging in petty politicking, and families have become brittle entities in the face of labor migration, language loss, and rampant violence. The very demands of the current political, economic, and social situation in which indigenous people of Cauca find themselves have forced cabildos to participate in ever widening spheres of action in which the connections between the domestic sphere and the public sphere must be retraced. The local meanings of justice and the hopes for a legal system that will resolve the dilemmas of Nasa communities are intertwined at the heart of the creation of constitutionally derived neologisms for such terms. But the latter have yet to be worked out on the ground.

Metaphors of light and clarity are key to emerging concepts of Nasa justice; by examining them, we can begin to perceive how the constitutional translation process interacts with the construction of legal procedures in localities. One of the crucial concepts that has been the focus of exegesis by Nasa intellectuals is the notion of *tardecer*, literally, a Nasa pronunciation of *atardecer*, or "dusk." This is a term that appears in the Nasa neologism for "justice." The gloss for *eena' eena' kafxi'ze'nxi* is "to be permanently in the light." But the word-by-word back-translation that was published reads: "clarity/clarity/ *atardecer*," with *atardecer* translated as *fxi'ze* (Abelardo Ramos and Cabildo Indígena de Mosoco 1993, 118).[9] As a situation is clarified by the passing of the light of day, it is possible to trace connections that cannot always be corroborated with evidence or explained by recourse to causation. Tardecer permits cabildos to impute guilt to a party because his or her actions, however divorced from a direct impact on the crime that has been committed, ultimately led to that act (Gaviria Díaz 1997; Muñoz Alvear 1997; Passú and Fiscué 1997;

Van Cott 2000b, 219–220). This is a theory of justice that implicates the actions of everyone, forcing the entire community to be transparent at all times, because their deeds can, at any moment, be entangled into a web of consequences. Tardecer is a lucid expression of how criminal activity can be interpreted as a disruption of community harmony.

Nasa Uses and Customs

Legal scholars have argued that the Colombian constitution does not validate existing indigenous uses and customs so much as it gives native communities the right to "create laws and rights" (Santos 2001, 208). The constitution introduces the possibility of reimagining legal systems whose autonomy has been violated over the centuries (B. Sánchez 2001). I would be hard put to draw a synthetic map of a single, coherent system of Nasa uses and customs as it might have been extant at the time of the birth of the 1991 constitution, because such a unified constellation of practices did not exist. Thê' walas, who today are an authoritative pivot of reconstructed Nasa systems of justice—I purposely use the plural here to emphasize the decentralized character of Nasa juridical imaginings, which emerge out of multiple local variations—had only begun to come out of clandestinity in the two decades preceding the constitution. Their public and political roles were not, at the time, determined by a unified corpus of knowledge like the system of cosmovision that has emerged in the past decade to represent the public face of Nasa shamanism. While cabildos and community assemblies have always deliberated over issues of land tenancy and solved disputes within families, what in Western jurisprudence would be called penal law was not applied uniformly across Cauca and was certainly not used for resolving the kinds of violent interethnic conflict whose solution is at a premium today. In this sense, the logic and procedures of what activists and scholars call the Nasa legal system emerge out of a locally based set of practices that must be adapted to current needs and circumstances. A bird's-eye view of the multiplicity of approaches to justice across Nasa communities dispels any notion of the existence of a single basis for uses and customs.

In 2000, I was invited to coordinate a series of oral history workshops in the resguardo of Belalcázar, Tierradentro, a multiethnic community of Nasa, Afrocolombians, and mestizo peasants living on the outskirts of the municipal center. The resguardo had become a focal point of indigenous militancy with the return to the community of younger activists who had previously worked in CRIC's regional office. They immediately allied themselves with the captain of the cabildo, who was one of the founders of the regional organization. Together, they proposed to rebuild a strong leadership base to take the place of the weak cabildo that had lethargically governed in the wake of the political persecution of the Violencia of the 1950s. This new group of Belalcázar militants played an instrumental role in the creation of Nasa Çxhâ'çxhâ', the zonal cabildo federation for the municipality of Páez, where the resguardo is located. In 1999, in a major setback to this leadership project, the governor of the cabildo was murdered by two young resguardo members. The community was at pains to rediscover its customary procedures for judging and punishing murderers, which they had forgotten, given that in living memory they had always remanded criminals to the Colombian justice system. The results of the workshops were inconclusive as far as uses and customs were concerned. No one could remember any cabildo procedures for dealing with murderers. When the accused were ultimately tried in an open discussion the cabildo judged them to be guilty of the crime, but determined that they were too dangerous to be punished by the stocks or public whipping, the sanctions that have been adopted by neighboring cabildos. The two men in question, they decided, were beyond rehabilitation and would not profit from the cleansing action of confession and corporal punishment because they would probably take their vengeance at some later point. In an agreement with the Colombian penal system, the men were sent to a Colombian prison, locked away to keep them as far as possible from the community. In this way, the cabildo sidestepped the issue of the absence of any memory of an autonomous justice system.

San José, which is also in the municipality of Páez but would be classified as part of the Nasa cultural inside by my friends in PEB, is a very small, cohesive, and culturally homogeneous community that lies along the course of the Moras River, a day's journey by foot from Belalcázar. San Joseños remember their cabildo having judged and punished wrongdoers up to the mid-twentieth century. Lisandro Campo, the captain of San José, was particularly eager to share his memories with me. His recollections focus primarily on the use of the stocks, a roughly hewn apparatus some six feet high with multiple holes from which the accused are hanged by their feet for periods of two or three minutes to a half hour. This extremely painful procedure was described to me not as a punishment, but as a means of reconciliation between an individual and the community. Lisandro related how the community suffered along with the individual and how the cabildo sat with him for hours afterward, giving him advice and welcoming him back into the community; Nasas from other resguardos corroborated Lisandro's report by reminiscing about the shamanic ceremony that accompanied the event and the ritual washing by women of the offender's wounds. But despite Lisandro's nostalgic account, not all San Joseños approved of the practice; the cabildo buried its stocks in the 1960s, after much debate as to their appropriateness. Since then, the cabildo has remanded wrongdoers to the courthouse in Belalcázar.

I was unable to learn more about the destruction of San José's stocks. No one remembered—or cared to tell me—how and why the apparatus was buried. I suspect it probably owed to the influence of the Apostolic Vicariate of Tierradentro and may have been precipitated by the fact that San José's entire cabildo, accused of complicity with communist-inspired peasant leagues, was murdered during the civil war of the 1950s, thus weakening the institution. The first half of the twentieth century is marked by the abandonment of the stocks across Nasa territory, coinciding with a historical low point in political organizing, cabildo fragmentation, and church persecution of shamans. Most striking are the stories I heard in Corinto and Jambaló, where oral tradition recalls that the stocks were destroyed after a pregnant woman was hanged in them and died; in Corinto, this event was said to have led to the liquidation of the cabildo by the municipal judicial authorities. While the formulaic nature of these accounts suggests that they might be better understood as a contemporary analysis of the reasons for abandoning the practice rather than an account of what "really" happened, this gendered condemnation of the stocks establishes some of the limits beyond which indigenous forms of punishment cannot encroach. A recent incident in the resguardo of Tóez provides a modern context for these narratives. Here, a twelve-year-old girl was hanged in the stocks in retribution for having run away from her adoptive parents and taken up with "mafiosos." Given that her adoptive father was governor of the community, some saw her punishment as a case of family problems being aired in a communal setting; others were disturbed by the fact that such a young person would be subject to this drastic punishment. It is clearly significant that in Tóez, just as in Corinto and Jambaló, it is the punishment of a woman that pushes the envelope when it comes to the debate over the appropriateness of the stocks. Such limits, however, have been exploded by constitutional reform.

With the introduction of indigenous special jurisdiction, San José was abuzz with the possibility of reintroducing the stocks. Most of the older people, Don Lisandro very vocal among them, supported the proposal, as did the twenty- and thirty-something political leadership and the local teachers. All of them had become attuned to CRIC's teachings on cosmovision, which views the stocks as a remedy for restoring cosmic balance, and not as a punishment. San José's youth, however, argued that the stocks were a Spanish introduction and had no place among the Nasa. In the late 1990s a particularly violent man allied with FARC was disturbing his neighbors in the neighborhood of Bota-tierra. The cabildo could no longer appeal to the Colombian justice system to judge and punish this individual, given that by then such cases were rejected by the courts and returned to indigenous special jurisdiction. So the governor turned to FARC, an obvious choice given the individual's associations with the guerrillas but also telling evidence of the entanglement of the multiple systems of justice that operate in Tierradentro. FARC refused to apply its own judicial system in this local dispute, however, and the cabildo was forced to take matters into its own hands. A new set of stocks was erected, accompanied by proper shamanic ritual. The accused was hanged in those stocks, but harmony was never restored; after several years of continued conflict with the community, he was drawn into a dispute with FARC, which executed him.

In Pitayó, in contrast, criminal offenses have been tried by the cabildo for many years, extending back before the 1991 constitution. Adonías Perdomo (2002), who has served on Pitayó's cabildo in various capacities over the years, and external researcher Herinaldy Gómez (2000, 55–69), who is one of Ado-nías's academic interlocutors, describe local uses and customs in terms of the intersection of specific cabildo procedures with Nasa theories of justice. Herinaldy's analysis remains on the level of Nasa legal theory, echoing the discourse of culturalist leaders that grounds the legal system in cosmogonic needs to restore harmony (J. Piñacué 1997); Adonías's description ranges over a multitude of concrete cases he has observed and focuses on cabildo pro-cedure rather than on the mythic supports of the system. Both authors assert that offenses against the community are the result of a lack of harmony that must be remedied through ritual in a set of practices that engages thê' walas as well as secular authorities and is directed not only at the offender but at the community at large. As Herinaldy suggests, the culprit in a homicide not only victimizes others, but is a victim himself (Gómez 2000, 25).

However, there are also marked differences between Adonías's vision of Nasa uses and customs and that of other interpreters, whether indigenous or external. Adonías does not speak of harmony in cosmic terms in his written work, but refers more specifically to the social harmony of the community, something that he reiterated in discussions with me and that is the tack that cabildos have taken in particularly well-publicized cases. In addition, the aim of achieving social harmony through ritualized penalties does not preclude for

Adonías the notion of punishment as an integral part of Nasa justice. In fact, in a recent discussion with him I was informed that the stocks were used to force confessions. In his writing, Adonías constantly refers to punishment as a form of vengeance. In short, his analysis of the Pitayó system of justice is only partly in concordance with the idealized and cosmologically informed system described by ethnographers and promoted by indigenous activists. Such discrepancies underline the heterogeneity of Nasa uses and customs and suggest that we might do best to comprehend much of the current discourse concerning the homogeneity of the Nasa legal system as a political utopia, not a lived reality. But we also need to break out of an exclusively Nasa world to understand how indigenous special jurisdiction operates. For the process of defining legal jurisdiction is as much about the supplanting of national law with Nasa uses and customs as it is an attempt to establish a legitimate local authority in the face of the threat of guerrilla, paramilitary, and army hegemony in the absence of efforts on the part of the Colombian state to contain armed actors. That is, the construction of legal procedure is a concern that is important, but only within a broader project of building an autonomy that is at once territorial, political, and cultural. But before I get to this issue, I must turn briefly to a consideration of how customary law is negotiated in the Colombian court system, because this is where the limits of indigenous uses and customs are currently being determined.

The Constitutional Court as a Site for the Production of Legal Pluralism

Since 1991, the Constitutional Court has defined the boundaries within which indigenous legal systems can operate freely. The creation of law through judicial decision is a very piecemeal process, subject to the diverse philosophies of the various judges and the antagonistic political interests that are at play in each case. Moreover, the forging of indigenous special jurisdiction through judicial interpretation makes indigenous legal projects subservient to Western forms of jurisprudence, enveloping cosmovision within state law (B. Sánchez 2001; Sánchez Botero 1998; Van Cott 2000b). In essence, the court, working in concert with attorneys, legal anthropologists, other expert witnesses, and indigenous spokespersons, is being asked to provide a definition of legal pluralism. Sally Engle Merry defines legal pluralism in the following way:

> A legal system is pluralistic in the juristic sense when the sovereign commands different bodies of law for different groups of the population varying by eth-

nicity, religion, nationality, or geography, and when the parallel legal regimes are all dependent on the state legal system. This situation creates a range of complex legal problems, such as the need to decide when a subgroup's law applies to a particular transaction or conflict, to what group particular individuals belong, how a person can change which law is applicable to him or her . . . , choice of law rules for issues between people of different groups, and determinations of which subjects . . . and in which geographical areas subgroup law should be accepted. (1988, 871)

Merry notes that legal pluralism is considerably more diffuse and encompassing than this definition presupposes because it is difficult to pinpoint the boundaries between legal norms and cultural values. Furthermore, normative orders do not operate parallel to one another in a society but participate together in a single social field (873). In a brilliant explanation of how pluralism functions, Boaventura de Sousa Santos (1987) uses a cartographic metaphor to conceptualize the relationships among local, national, and international law, explaining that they operate, as in maps, according to different scales. Consequently, it is the productive dialogue across these scales, or the translation from one scale to another, that constitutes the plural legal process.

For many anthropologists this is a truism, but it is also an issue under debate today in the Constitutional Court. How should legal pluralism be reconstituted in relation to politically sophisticated and well-organized indigenous communities, whose legal systems are inherently hybrid, fragmentary, and in the process of reformation? Should these systems be accepted only when they are coherent and of long-standing tradition, or should the court take to heart the idea that what the constitution bestows on native peoples is a right to *create* their own laws? The court's responses have depended on the ideological positions of the magistrates responsible for each case.

In an early decision regarding whether or not indigenous urban migrants enjoy the same exemption from military service as do resguardo inhabitants (Martínez Caballero 1994), the court decided that the locus of indigenous culture must be confined to the rural ambit and that the complainant, an urban migrant, could not be considered indigenous for the purposes of exemption from military recruitment. That is, they imposed essentialist and stereotypical notions of who is indigenous on a complex modern Colombian reality and, correspondingly, divested urbanized native people of their indigenous identity and the rights that accompany it (B. Sánchez 2001, 36–38). In the past, urban migration meant the abandonment of indigenous identities and "indigenous" was associated exclusively with the communal space of the res-guardo; in other words, "indigenous" was a group, not an individual, identity. However, there are multiple ways to be indigenous in contemporary Colom-bia. Urban cabildos can be found in most major cities, highland indigenous people have colonized lowland areas and legally created resguardos there, and resguardo members move freely between city and country, between resguardo and other rural centers of wage labor, between one ethnic group and another. The space of the indigenous organization has succeeded in expanding the notion of resguardo beyond the rural sphere. For all these reasons, the court's definition of "indigenous" is hopelessly out of step with contemporary reality.

Traditional anthropological assumptions about the stability and discrete-ness of indigenous cultures have weighed heavily in the Constitutional Court. The court considered a case from Coyaima (Cifuentes Muñoz 1994), a Spanish-speaking native community in Tolima that has been closely integrated into the regional society and culture for the past century but that also has a strong indigenous movement and was one of the zones of operation of Manuel Quintín Lame in the first half of the twentieth century (Castillo-Cárdenas 1971; Tello Lozano 1982). In this dispute, a resguardo member and his family were expelled by the cabildo and appealed its decision to the Constitutional Court as a violation of their right as Colombian citizens to be exempt from punishments involving exile. The court overruled the cabildo's sentence, privileging univer-sal human rights over collective indigenous rights and permitting the man to remain in Coyaima.[10] The Coyaima decision is particularly telling because the court used it as a case in point to argue that the extent to which juridical autonomy accrues to indigenous communities is directly related to the degree to which they have maintained their uses and customs ("a mayor conservación de sus usos y costumbres, mayor autonomía"):

> Colombian reality shows that the numerous indigenous communities that exist within the national territory have suffered a greater or lesser destruction of their culture as an effect of their subjugation to the colonial order and their subsequent integration into "civilized life" (Law 89 of 1890), weakening the capacity for social coercion of the authorities of some indigenous peoples over their members. The need for an objective normative framework that guarantees juridical security and social stability within these collectivities makes it indis-pensable that we distinguish between the groups that conserve their uses and customs—which should be, in principle, respected—from those who do not conserve them and, consequently, should conform to a greater degree to the

laws of the Republic, given that the constitutional and legal order is contra-
dicted when a person can be banished to the periphery of the law as the
consequence of an imprecise or nonexistent delimitation of the normativity
summoned to regulate his rights and obligations. (Cifuentes Muñoz 1994, 7.1)

In other words, only those who are most recognizably "other" have the right to
exercise indigenous special jurisdiction (Sánchez Botero 1998, 222). This is a
critical issue, given that numerous indigenous groups, including many Nasa
communities, are as integrated into the dominant society as is Coyaima, and
most groups are in the process of reconstructing the contours of their uses and
customs. The existence of indigenous legal systems that are in some way
ancient or "primordial" is simply not a reality in Colombia. It was not until
1997, in a *tutela*, or constitutional lawsuit, brought by a member of the Nasa
resguardo of Jambaló (Gaviria Díaz 1997) that such issues would be resolved in
a manner sensitive to indigenous aspirations, a case to which I turn now.

The Trial and Sentencing of Francisco Gembuel

In 1997 Francisco Gembuel appealed to the Constitutional Court, alleging that
the cabildo of Jambaló had violated his fundamental rights as a Colombian
citizen. Gembuel is a Guambiano, and like many other Guambianos living in
the Nasa resguardos of Tierrafuera, he is a former sharecropper from the
hacienda of Ambaló (Ulcué 1997, 45). He has lived for decades in Jambaló and
in the course of his life became an active member of the resguardo, serving on
the cabildo and even assuming the presidency of CRIC. In 1996, he belonged to
a civic movement involved in the local mayoral electoral campaign. His group
opposed another wing of the movement, whose candidate, Marden Betancur,
ultimately won election to the *alcaldía* of Jambaló.

On 19 August 1996, in the midst of a municipal celebration, Betancur was
gunned down and murdered. The National Liberation Army (ELN) subsequently took responsibility for the killing, alleging that the mayor had allied
himself with the paramilitary; they called him a *pájaro*, a hired assassin. Francisco Gembuel and a number of his Nasa and Guambiano associates were
rounded up in short order and imprisoned, accused of being the intellectual
authors of the assassination. They were said to have been seen meeting with
the ELN, and in any event, during the mayoral campaign their political group
had accused Betancur of being a pájaro, which, in hindsight, placed them in
the discursive company of the guerrillas. The cabildo convoked an investiga-

tory commission that determined that Gembuel was guilty of tardecer, sentencing him to sixty lashes and exile from Jambaló and barring him from occupying elected office in Nasa territory. The punishment was to take place at a public assembly in Jambaló on 24 December 1996, but it was interrupted by Gembuel's daughter and by mestizos from the municipal seat who physically blocked the cabildo from touching the defendant after he had received eight lashes (*El Tiempo*, 10 January 1997).

Gembuel took his case to the Colombian courts, first, in early 1997, to the municipal penal court in the neighboring city of Santander de Quilichao, where he alleged that he had not been given due process in the cabildo deliberations because he was not allowed to cross-examine witnesses. He also argued that his fundamental human rights as a Colombian citizen had been violated by the corporal punishment to which the cabildo had sentenced him, which, in his eyes, constituted a form of torture (Muñoz Alvear 1997). The presiding judge, Leoxmar Muñoz, is a politically progressive man who is anxious to engage in dialogue with the indigenous movement but who also has a strong sense of what constitutes a universal definition of human rights—and corporal punishment does not fit into that equation. While he upheld the right of the cabildo to conduct an investigation of Gembuel's culpability in the murder, Muñoz also ruled that the defendants had not enjoyed due process and that whipping was, in fact, torture (Muñoz Alvear 1997), a conclusion with which Amnesty International concurred (*El Espectador*, 8 January 1997). As legal scholar Beatriz Sánchez (2001, 85) argues, the lower court was faced with a quandary. Gembuel could not have been charged in a Colombian court for a murder he did not, and did not even conspire to, commit. Yet, from the perspective of Nasa uses and customs he was guilty because his accusations against Marden Betancur had set the stage for the guerrillas' actions: he was guilty of tardecer. Clearly, the judge in Santander chose to decide the case using Colombian legal logic and a universal discourse of human rights, rejecting Nasa forms of jurisprudence as, Sánchez (76–82) argues, the Constitutional Court had done up until then.

The most dangerous of Gembuel's assertions was that there was no "tradition, nor use or custom, related to the investigation of homicides, which has always been conducted by the [Colombian] justice [system]" (Muñoz Alvear 1997, 2). He thus put indigenous special jurisdiction to the test, forcing the court to pronounce on a variety of issues. Most prominent, he called to question the existence of conditions for the official recognition of uses and customs. He challenged the ability of cabildos, former cabildo members, and shamans in the settlement of penal cases (4), and he disputed their authority to establish norms and procedures. Ultimately, he questioned the legal context in which indigenous jurisdiction was established. Muñoz upheld the right of the community to judge Gembuel according to Nasa uses and customs only to a limit, recognizing their right to try the case but not the procedures they used or the punishment they selected, which, he told me, he found unconscionable.

Ultimately, the case moved to the Constitutional Court, where significant aspects of the decision of the lower court were overturned by Carlos Gaviria Díaz, the presiding magistrate. Gaviria is a nationally prominent jurist who had served earlier as the vice rector of the University of Antioquia, one of Colombia's major public institutions of higher education. A year before he took up the Gembuel case, he occupied the position of president of the Constitutional Court. Since then, he has given up his seat on the court after being elected to the national Senate in 2002 on a platform that included extending equal treatment to ethnic minorities, homosexuals, and women. His written decision (Gaviria Díaz, 1997, 1–3) diverged from previous court decisions because he argued that not only must the Colombian state guarantee the coexistence of different worldviews, "formas de ver el mundo," regardless of their incommensurability, but that such concepts as human rights, due process, and torture can be defined only in culturally specific ways. He thus laid the groundwork for the broad acceptance of indigenous values and procedures by the Colombian state. Gaviria ruled that the procedures used by the cabildo of Jambaló constituted legitimate uses and customs that could not be overridden by standard legal notions of due process; he also decided that the use of the whip accorded with Nasa cosmovision and was, therefore, not an instrument of torture. In other words, he did not take it upon himself to decide if Gembuel was guilty or not, but left this determination to the indigenous legal system. His job as a jurist was to recognize that system's legitimacy.

What is interesting about Gaviria's decision is his bold move away from previous Constitutional Court practice that imposed on indigenous people a static realist definition of culture and employed Colombian forms of jurisprudence to analyze conflicts over native uses and customs. In the words of Beatriz Sánchez (2001, 86), Gaviria assumed a cultural relativist stance that broke with notions of acculturation that characterized the two 1994 decisions I described earlier. In other words, he "lowered the burden of proving 'cultural purity' that had been set by [earlier decisions]" (Van Cott 2000b, 221). Significantly, he framed his decision with a multiculturalist discourse very much in accord with the politics of such indigenous organizations as CRIC by arguing that the solution to the case can only proceed "from an intercultural dialogue capable of establishing minimal standards of tolerance that encompass different value systems" (Gaviria Díaz 1997, 1). Let me examine how Gaviria grounded his decision.

In the magistrate's view, tradition—uses and customs—is a dynamic process, not an unchanging set of procedures and values. This is stunningly evident in the following quotation, in which Gaviria Díaz (1997, 12) refers to the constitutional limits within which minority legal systems can be tolerated by the Colombian state: "It is obvious that this limit does not require that the practices and procedures must be carried out in the same way as the ancestors did, because the rights of indigenous communities, as in any juridical system, are dynamic. What is required is compliance with those actions that the accused can anticipate and that approach the traditional practices that ensure social cohesion." Authenticity, then, does not imply fidelity to ancient norms, but grows out of a consciousness of cultural specificity that, in the Nasa context, has led to a process of cultural revitalization (9). For Magistrate Gaviria, tradition and authenticity are ongoing political projects.

From this standpoint, Gaviria was empowered to outline the spirit, if not the letter, of Nasa legal tradition. Nasa justice, he argues, revolves around deliberations concerning "the actions that broke equilibrium, according to the word of its members" (1997, 10). Harmony is ensured by an attitude toward justice that seeks not vengeance, but balance: "In the first case [the Colombian justice system], punishment occurs because an offense has been committed, in the second [the Nasa justice system] punishment occurs in order to re-establish the order of Nature. . . . The first rejects corporal punishment as an attempt against human dignity, the second considers it a purifying element, necessary so that the accused subject feels liberated" (14). Although the practices used to ensure harmony, such as the whip, have been appropriated from Europeans, Gaviria argues that they acquire a particular significance in the course of their embedding within Nasa cosmovision. Whipping, "which consists in the flagellation of the body with a 'lash for herding cattle' that even though it is a practice inherited from the Spaniards, has a particular significance, that of the thunderbolt, which the . . . [Nasa] think of as a mediator between light and darkness, that is, as a purifying element" (14). This was, indeed, a welcome departure for the cabildo of Jambaló from the stance taken by earlier magistrates, one that ensured that the indigenous authorities would ultimately prevail. However, full punishment was never meted out. Before Gaviria's decision was published, Gembuel had already left Jambaló to reside in the mestizo peasant community of Piendamó, never having received the fifty-two lashes still due him (*El Espectador*, 22 February 1997).

Gaviria's decision leaves indigenous legal planners in the uncomfortable position of upholding a system of uses and customs whose precepts are acceptable only after having been legitimized by an external agent, not by themselves. The magistrate's recognition of Nasa legal autonomy is framed by Colombian legal procedure; culturalist discourse is acceptable because Gaviria has said so. Gaviria was able to legitimize Nasa law only by "othering" it through a pointed appeal to cosmovision. The alterity championed by Gaviria is, quite likely, the result of information given him by indigenous leaders and by anthropological expert witnesses, both of whom were anxious to validate Nasa uses and customs (Sánchez Botero 2001). Cosmovision constituted a persuasive tool for defining the nature of Nasa uses and customs, particularly given previous court decisions, which fostered definitions of indigenousness that foregrounded alterity but defined cultural identity through primordial sentiments and not contemporary political constructs. Gaviria, in contrast, tended toward the latter interpretation.

There is certainly a shamanic facet of the Nasa legal process, but this does not mean that the unified discourse of cosmovision has been absorbed or totally accepted by the indigenous population as a whole, nor that this aspect needs to be foregrounded in the public performance of law. As a result, cosmological referents are muted, almost absent, in the highly pragmatic utterances of Nasa politicians regarding this case. They focus more on strengthening indigenous authority in the face of armed interlopers than on maintaining an internal cosmic balance among the Nasa themselves.[11] Moreover, as far as relations with the dominant society are concerned, it is politically expedient to step back from a discourse grounded in cosmovision. Indigenous politicians are faced with a dilemma when they "other" themselves in the legal world. When they advocate cosmologically based legal procedures autonomous from those of the dominant society, they problematize the basis for indigenous sovereignty, which presupposes the participation of the Nasa in the political life of the Colombian nation in their capacity as ethnic citizens, and not as autonomous others. As Van Cott (2000b, 222) cogently argues, the Jambaló decision places indigenous organizations in a quandary over their relationship to the state and to the international community: "The . . . 'total autonomy' position puts indigenous organisations in the ambiguous position of rejecting the control of a constitution on which their own elected representatives left such an indelible mark, a constitution that recognises indigenous authorities as legitimate public authorities and, therefore, part of the Colombian state."

The court's decisions regarding the fate of Francisco Gembuel and the Nasa justice system, though illuminating, take us only so far in understanding the nuances of the construction of legal pluralism in Colombia. Judicial decisions do not provide us with an adequate picture of the kinds of arguments that indigenous litigants generate for the consideration of magistrates. Nor do they pay attention to the internal process of construction of indigenous uses and customs that nourishes the statements that indigenous representatives bring to court. To appropriate Boaventura de Sousa Santos's metaphor once again, the large-scale cartographic view we obtain from a study of judicial decisions is not sufficiently detailed to permit a more penetrating appreciation of the role of indigenous organic intellectuals in the creation of a newly recognized legal system. It is to this that I turn now in an effort to reconsider the Jambaló case from the perspective of its indigenous participants.

Nasa Intellectuals and Legal Imaginings

Immediately following the ruling in Santander de Quilichao, the governor of the cabildo of Jambaló, Alberto Passú, in company with Luis Alberto Fiscué, president of ACIN, penned a response to Justice Muñoz's decision (Passú and Fiscué 1997).[12] Parts of this lengthy document look as though they were prepared in collaboration with a legal advisor, perhaps Carlos César Perafán, the author of the government-sponsored codification of Nasa customary law and a long-standing colaborador. The response lays out the theory behind the cabildo's legal procedure and outlines the participation of the zonal organization in the local proceedings, which was made necessary both by Gembuel's stature as a well-known regional politician and by the fact that the case had erupted in the national media and was in the process of moving to the Constitutional Court.

Three organs were empowered to take control of the dispute, according to the cabildo's letter. An investigatory commission was named and had completed its work, with Cristóbal Secue of Toribío at its head; Secue, a former president of CRIC, was selected on the basis of his long experience in the indigenous movement and his familiarity with uses and customs in his native resguardo of Corinto. Judgment was pronounced by the cabildo of Jambaló with ACIN assistance on the basis of the investigatory commission's gathered evidence, and a sentence was arrived at by the general assembly of the members of the resguardo (Passú and Fiscué 1997, 2). As the authors of the letter emphasize, the organization of the proceedings differed from those of the Colombian justice system, with those aspects that we generally associate with due process—cross-examination of witnesses and representation by an attorney, among others—emerging only in the later stages of the case. In other words, investigation, sentencing, and punishment would come only after a period dedicated to preparing the accused for a public confession in what the authors called an "inverted pyramid" structure (15).

In a discourse reminiscent of anthropology, Passú and Fiscué write that Nasa justice grows out of webs of reciprocity based in kin networks extending out into the community and its cabildo (1997, 6–7). If conflicts cannot be resolved within such family settings, as they generally are, they must be brought into the public realm. The aim of the public hearing is to forestall the retributory violence that frequently erupts in such cases, an issue that went unnoticed by the Constitutional Court: "As you can see, our procedure is constructed as a strategy for preventing internal violence in our communities and protecting the lives of those affected" (16). Public confession, they argue, takes precedence over sanctions, focused as the system is on the future security of the community. Note how Passú and Fiscué use metaphors of light to explain the logic of public legal proceedings as an extension of the authority of the household: "Because the society now requires of the individual the *clarity* that was handled before in private. With it, the individual demonstrates his 'affiliation' with the community as a whole and allows for his punishment to be carried out as it would be in his own home" (8; italics mine). Confession is the fundamental goal of the process, not in the sense of forcibly extracting information from the offender, but with the objective "of the accused opening his heart to the community to commence on the path of [receiving] advice" (8).[13]

At the heart of the procedure was the notion of tardecer, the linking of events into a noncausal sequence. The hope of the Jambaló cabildo was to induce Gembuel's confession in order to halt a chain of events that might lead to further violent retribution, an aim that they express through recourse to tardecer:

> The two acts that [Gembuel] . . . is accused of, in and of themselves infractions, in our opinion, are part of the aforementioned tardecer. . . . His visit to the armed group, in one way or another, since we are dealing with a person of high status, is part of the process of the legitimization of the group in our territories. . . . The former does not constitute an additional accusation, but [is] evidence that they were implicated in the path of a process that could lead to

serious tardeceres. This is not in itself an accusation, because the procedure that it generates is principally aimed at impeding, or contributing to impeding, that the sequence of acts takes its course. It is the "halting" of the process of this sequence, so that tardecer does not happen. (Passú and Fiscué 1997, 11)

In this sense, they argue, confession is a "therapeutic process," a collaborative endeavor between the accused and the community (11), and one in which Gembuel refused to engage.

In the Gembuel case, however, public confession and punishment also filled a distinctly didactic function:

In the case of serious tardeceres, with broad social effects, the participation of the accused consists in "giving an example," converting himself into a "living testimony" of the events in the sequence, with the didactic objective of leading his compatriots to earnestly avoid acts or omissions that could result in a determined tardecer. In the case that occupies us, to take care to not spread rumors on the basis of which the guerrillas exert their own power, to abstain from the treatment and familiarity that legitimizes their presence, not to mention strictly observing the prohibition of requesting their services to settle conflicts. It involves, therefore, a didactic effort, making an example insofar as circumstantial actions, without apparent causal links, are recognized as errors, having the effect of "dusk" and abstention from which can become a viable strategy for impeding the tardecer of the sequence. In particular in this case, which can be understood as of importance for the ethnic survival of the [Nasa] people. (Passú and Fiscué 1997, 11)[14]

The indigenous leaders are at great pains here to explain a logic that, clearly, they have trouble expressing in the discourse of a legal brief. They are not inventing tardecer for this document, nor is it an innovation in the Gembuel case. However, in this dispute they have been forced to explain its relevance to the unusual circumstances in which they find themselves. They are obliged to engage in a delicate process of cultural translation, not in the productive direction from Spanish to Nasa Yuwe that the movement has used as a conceptual tool, but in the infinitely more perilous direction of Nasa Yuwe to Spanish. On the one hand, they must ethnographize themselves, highlighting their cultural alterity as opposed to their membership in the Colombian nation, despite the fact that their participation in the drafting of the constitution, in the tutela process, and in the construction of legal pluralism is intimately connected to new notions of indigenous citizenship. On the other hand, in a double process of translation, they must convert this ethnographically based alterity into legal regulation. To appropriate the language of cultural activists, they must translate a vivencia into a use and custom, transforming a dynamic and experientially based habitus into a codified practice.

The Gembuel imbroglio is a case that involves a great deal of intercultural and interlegal dialogue: between a Guambiano defendant and Nasa judges, between a local community and a regional organization, between an indigenous cabildo and a Colombian courthouse, between the native legal system and the guerrilla code of justice. In this sense, the issues involved in this case are considerably more complex than the simple equation of Nasa uses and customs versus national law. What is at stake is the legitimacy of indigenous authority in the face of the other systems that encroach upon it. This is the central problem of contemporary indigenous legal imaginings: the construction of a legitimate authority in a world in which the Colombian state and the state projects of the guerrillas and the paramilitary are under dispute, with indigenous territory as a battleground. Nasa politicians intent on forging uses and customs through the Gembuel case were forced to go beyond the discrete cultural categories of realist legal ethnography to take into account the consequences of patterns of indigenous migration within the Caucan highlands that brought the Guambianos to Jambaló, the rivalries between ACIN and CRIC that determined the insertion of leaders into the dispute, the ideological transformations that have swept over CRIC in the past two decades and inform discourses of cultural alterity and sovereignty, and the strategies by which Nasa communities have attempted to defend themselves against the depredations of armed actors who occupy their territories against their wishes.

This had to be accomplished within a discourse that privileges cultural autonomy, in a world in which autonomy is all too elusive. Indigenous politicians were forced to draw on a binary logic that contrasts indigenous legal systems with Colombian law in a situation in which it is unclear which of the *multiple* legal systems that impinge on local communities is hegemonic. The cabildo of Jambaló was not engaged in codifying a distinct legal logic that separates the Nasa world from the dominant society, but in bringing that logic to bear in an intense and violent intercultural conflict. This is why, at the end of the paragraph I cited, the authors emphasized that a successful resolution of the Gembuel affair was "of importance for the ethnic survival of the [Nasa] people." Applying the notion of tardecer to the global situation in which they found themselves, they rightly asserted that the stakes in this case were of life and death, both of individuals and of Nasa autonomy.

Public Debate

A month after the cabildo's letter a public assembly of several thousand was held in Jambaló, presided over by the local indigenous authorities and by the governor of the cabildo of neighboring Pitayó, who had been invited to serve as a mediator; representatives of all of the Nasa cabildos in Cauca were also present. This highly vituperative session belies the assurance with which Nasa forms of jurisprudence are explicated in the letter by Passú and Fiscué and, at the same time, underlines the deep stakes that the movement had in resolving the Gembuel dispute. A transcript of the meeting, at which I was not present, suggests that the assembled leaders were at great pains to construct a procedure that would at once intersect with the legal theories they had defended and be acceptable to the participants.[15] This was not an easy task, given that the cabildo had never before been obliged to judge a dispute that was simultaneously under consideration by the Colombian courts and observed by world public opinion. Furthermore, when the dispute reached the grassroots assembly, all resguardo members, regardless of their opinions, could participate. They were joined by representatives of other Nasa cabildos, who each had a distinct relationship with ACIN, the northern cabildo association that had played such a significant role in the process. Given such a scenario, the theoretical limits of Nasa jurisprudence would be severely strained. At play were intersecting and opposed loyalties to the local neighborhoods, called *veredas*, to the cabildo, and to the supralocal organizations ACIN and CRIC.

The public assembly was an event that combined oral performance with the reading of written documentation. Extending over an entire day, the meeting included presentations by local and regional leaders who had been involved in the investigation, as well as the cross-examination of witnesses and procedural discussion. At the heart of the matter was a report of the findings of the investigatory commission, which contained evidence that Gembuel and his associates had met with the guerrillas shortly before the death of Marden Betancur and that their specific role in his murder revolved around their allegations that Betancur was a pájaro, a hired assassin.

The committee empowered to direct the judicial process encountered considerable difficulty in retaining its membership, which was to include former governors of the resguardo of Jambaló and was later expanded to incorporate neighboring indigenous authorities. Various of those appointed declined to participate, citing their "lack of knowledge of legal norms and difficulty in understanding the process to that point." In other words, they had trouble reading the written testimony of witnesses and felt they had no experience judging a murder case. Their anxieties exposed the gulf between the young politicians and their predecessors. Julio Dagua, who served as Jambaló's governor in 1977, went so far as to state that he thought the cabildo was not experienced enough to judge a murder case: "The state has its public officials. For that, there are judges. This murder is in their domain, not the cabildo's, because we are not in a capacity [to take it on]." He emphasized the need for ACIN to be involved because "we don't know how to read correctly, we can't sign our names well." Dagua, who is from Zumbico, the same vereda as the accused, also worried that his neighbors would eventually hold his participation in the deliberations against him.

What was most problematic for the commission was the unusually wide net that had been cast in the investigation. Several individuals had been accused of complicity in the crime, only to have the charges against them dropped when no evidence had surfaced to convict them, and there was no consensus as to how their reputations could be publicly rehabilitated, given that the circumstances of this case were so unusual. The very notion of tardecer enveloped innocent people in its legal embrace, given the leeway it provided for connecting dispersed events and intentions into a web of culpability. Marden Betancur was from the northern part of Jambaló, which had only recently joined the indigenous movement, in contrast to the inhabitants of Zumbico, who had been involved in land claims under the auspices of CRIC for decades and, for a time, worked with AICO. The investigators collected testimony going back to the early days of the movement, when the northern veredas were locked in a violent conflict with the militants of Zumbico, who accused them of furnishing the landlords with pájaros whose acts of violence rent the fabric of the community. In the logic of tardecer, such acts would be significant, given that the ELN assassinated Betancur as a presumed pájaro and paramilitary organizer. As the commission's report, read aloud at the assembly, stated: "The declarations, given their broad nature, forced witnesses to recount violent acts in the community for which the statute of limitations had already lapsed—the 1970s and 1980s—or which had been forgotten, converting into accomplices of many offenses those who should be considered guilty because of their silence. It is evident that all of this has contributed to the anxiety of the community." Some of those whose engagement in those long-forgotten events now prevented their participation in the proceedings were among the former governors to whom the cabildo was looking for assistance, men whose names appeared in decades-old political pamplets condemning the pájaros, pam-

phlets penned in the late 1970s, when a significant sector of Jambaló temporarily split from CRIC and allied itself with the precursor to AICO. Thus, the
trial of Francisco Gembuel was transformed into a space in which long-
standing rivalries between veredas were aired, bringing to the fore issues that
are missing from the court decisions but resonated among the inhabitants of
Jambaló as they deliberated over the future of the accused.

The regional actors who participated in the event brought other rivalries .
and conflicts to bear in the deliberations. Cristóbal Secue, called in from
Corinto to head the investigation, underlined the fact that such autonomous
cabildo decisions were essential to muting the influence of FARC in indigenous
territory:

> I, tomorrow, will not be here. I will leave tomorrow morning, because I realize
> that in the resguardo to which I belong and which is, currently, the resguardo
> where the most offenses are committed, we must whip some people who stole a
> vehicle in Santander and afterward, authorities from Guavito confiscated it and
> have evidence, and tomorrow were are going to punish those people as thieves.
> Why does the cabildo punish them? Why? If the cabildo doesn't punish them,
> an armed group will come and kill them. So we must punish them so that the
> armed group doesn't get involved.

While the Colombian justices who considered the Gembuel case framed their
decisions in terms of the relationship between Nasa uses and customs and the
national constitution, regional leaders consistently brought the ELN, FARC,
and guerrilla justice into the equation. For them, this was a pressing issue of
regional concern. In 1999 Jambaló hosted the signing by the cabildos of Cauca
of an accord repudiating the legitimacy of all armed actors, including not only
the guerrillas, but the paramilitary and the Colombian army as well, in their
territory and imposing sanctions on resguardo inhabitants who facilitated
their activities (ONIC 2002, 12–17), Gembuel's presumed contacts with the ELN
were consequently of interest far beyond Jambaló and had already provoked
regional responses, intensifying the necessity for ACIN's participation in what
would otherwise be considered a local dispute.

But the Gembuel case cannot be understood simply as an indigenous defense against the guerrillas as a force external to the indigenous community.
Northern Caucan resguardos have a long history of relationships with guerrilla organizations. At times, cabildos have resisted their encroachment and
have paid dearly for their acts of resistance. But at other times, resguardo
members, and indigenous leaders, have forged close relations with armed

organizations, to the point that many indigenous families in northern Cauca have members who have been in some way affiliated at some time in the past with FARC or other organizations, some as full-blown guerrillas, others as *milicianos* lending local support as the eyes and ears of FARC, and frequently as sympathizers. So when Cristóbal Secue points to the dangers of letting the guerrillas into the community, he sees them as much as an internal as an external threat to autonomy.

After Secue's speech, CRIC president Jesús Enrique Piñacué broke in, with an urgent plea to the representatives of the cabildos of Tierradentro to remain at the event. They were threatening to leave, angered by the Jambaló cabildo's insistence on tracing Gembuel's actions within the community and not beyond its boundaries; they, too, had allegations to make against Gembuel, but the net had not been cast widely enough to satisfy them. Remember that Tierradentro was, at the time, locked in bitter confrontation with the cabildos of northern Cauca and occupied the presidency of CRIC for the first time in the organization's history, placing them in a position to exert considerable influence. Piñacué was an active advocate of the cabildo, declining to retreat to the status of advisor, as former CRIC presidents had done in local controversies. His activism in the Gembuel case was, for the cabildos of Tierradentro, a mark of their ascendancy and not an indication that CRIC had overstepped its bounds. It also underlined the rivalries that had been brewing between CRIC's new political leadership, heralded by the Piñacué administration's advocacy of a discourse of peoplehood, and the old guard of the organization, represented by Francisco Gembuel, which endorsed a policy of situating the indigenous struggle as equivalent to the struggles of other oppressed classes. Thus, for CRIC and for the representatives from Tierradentro, this case was all about the future of the regional organization.

Translation and Intellectual Dialogue

The Gembuel case tells us a great deal about the genesis of indigenous political and legal discourse, as well as about how this discourse is negotiated both within a heterogeneous movement and with representatives of the state. In particular, I want to highlight the ways in which discourses of sovereignty and culture are wielded by a heterogeneous set of social actors, sometimes unlikely ones. In the process, I demonstrate that the development of indigenous discourses—in this case, concerning indigenous special jurisdiction—is a product of intercultural dialogue and confrontation and not simply a revival by indigenous actors of ancient lifeways. In this sense, the negotiation of autonomous indigenous cultural forms represents a strategy for engaging in pluralist politics.

Let me return momentarily to the process of translation through which Nasa notions of justice and the legitimacy of the state and its functionaries were defined. Ultimately, translation was a process involving profound reflection by and among Nasa speakers; it was also an intercultural process insofar as it brought together a disparate group of actors into a dialogue. On the one hand, nonindigenous lawyers and linguists entered into conversation with Nasa speakers, clarifying the nature of Colombian legal constructs so that they could then be reappropriated in a new form by the translators. But on the other hand, within the Nasa camp a dialogue was opened between indigenous culturalist intellectuals and the cabildo of Mosoco, a corporation concerned with the exercise of political, economic, and legal autonomy. The translation process also involved the juxtaposition and dialogue between culturally distinct sets of ideas and practices. Thus, academic linguistics became a tool for Nasa intellectuals intent on theorizing from a culturalist position. Consequently, the translation process afforded a methodology for making sense of ideas stemming from the dominant culture—in this case, legal concepts—and appropriating them in an indigenous philosophy of the state. The resulting translation can therefore best be thought of as a dialogue of ideas among heterogeneous actors that gave rise to a text that, after the fact, appears as homogeneously Nasa.

A similar process unfolds in the realm of indigenous special jurisdiction. In the Francisco Gembuel case, lines of dialogue between indigenous activists and nonnative colaboradores led to the drafting of documents that drew on academic studies of Nasa customary law as well as legal notions first made explicit in the constitutional translation. These documents are not examples of a "pure" Nasa voice but, instead, embody the deep-rooted intercultural attitudes that nourish the contemporary indigenous political project, whose search for autonomy is necessarily framed by the need to create new forms of democracy through which indigenous citizenship can be effectively expressed.

Ironically, although the cosmogonic referents drawn on in the Gembuel case originated in the investigations of indigenous researchers, native intellectuals did not wield them directly in this dispute. The Nasa politicians who played a central role in judging Gembuel and in defending the cabildo's autonomy before the Colombian justice system preferred, instead, to emphasize their right to sovereignty, in the face of both the Colombian courts and the guerrilla groups who sought to insert themselves into local life. Cosmovision was brought to the fore here by external actors: Magistrate Gaviria and the anthropological experts called to testify in support of Nasa customary law. This scenario appears unlikely at first glance, given that cosmovision is an expression of an indigenous worldview, not that of a Bogotá judge. Moreover, the magistrate in question did not explain cosmovision as an unchanging philosophical system, as modernist anthropology and other magistrates would have it, but saw it as a political utopia, in concordance with what culturalist intellectuals have expressed to me. Gaviria's intervention shows us quite clearly that the appeal to native uses and customs in a pluralist system is not exclusively the prerogative of minority actors, but is a major theme in the intercultural dialogue from which, ultimately, indigenous special jurisdiction springs. It also shows that such a dialogue is not about cultural essences but about proposals for the future of the nation.

The public meeting held in Jambaló was the last concerning Francisco Gembuel. Since then, he has been largely shunned by indigenous organizations and cabildos, retreating to his farm in Piendamó. The issues surrounding his trial have not disappeared, however. As local authorities endeavor to construct indigenous special jurisdiction in the Caucan countryside, they continue to confront disparities between the generation of Nasa legal theory and the capacity of local authorities to implement customary law and to maintain autonomy in their territory. Disputes between localities, and between localities and supralocal organizations, continue to impinge on the legal process, indeed, to constitute a vital part of it. Contradictions between the legal systems of armed actors and Nasa justice continue to flare. Cristóbal Secue, who became the first coordinator of the ACIN committee charged with implementing indigenous special jurisdiction in northern Cauca, was gunned down in 2001 by elements identified by CRIC as being allied with FARC. The leader who took his place, Aldemar Pinzón, was killed by guerrillas a year later.

EPILOGUE

The time I last saw Arquimedes Vitonás he was studying for an undergraduate degree in anthropology through IMA, the Missionary Institute of Anthropology, which Father Antonio had brought to Toribío and in which many of the region's most promising Nasa leaders, even those who criticized Consolata penetration of the indigenous movement, were enrolled. We exchanged our thoughts about indigenous control of mayoralties (alcaldías), the topic of the thesis that Arquimedes hoped to write in pursuit of his degree. He outlined his research problem by drawing a distinction between the relationship that a cabildo enjoys with its members and how an alcaldía relates to its constituents. The cabildo, he told me, is an integral part of the community, beholden to its constituents because it constitutes a microcosm of the resguardo. Arquimedes contrasted the cabildo with the alcaldía by pointing out that the latter represents the state, not the indigenous community. As the state's agent in the locality the alcalde is constrained by the bureaucratic rules that he or she must follow, even if they conflict with the goals of constituents, such as, for example, in how municipal funds must be disbursed. Thus, despite the fact that civic mayors, or even indigenous ones, are elected by the local community, they do not entirely represent it. Instead, they function as an extension of the state in the locality.

Phillip Abrams (1988) persuasively argues that social scientists mistakenly idealize the state, treating it as an all-encompassing structural ideal or an autonomous entity instead of grasping how it functions on the ground, where it operates within specific social structures and institutions. That is, scholars commonly mythify the state, treating it as an objective thing that is somehow separate from civil society. As a solution to this difficulty, Abrams suggests that "we should abandon the state as a material object of study whether concrete or abstract while continuing to take the *idea* of the state extremely seriously" (75). Ethnography provides a possible venue for teasing out how ephemeral and disparate relations of hierarchy and subordination come to be understood as constituting the state, which is how Abrams would have it. At the local level, the ways people experience the state can be abstracted out of the activities of its local practitioners, the bureaucrats who impact daily life with their procedures, their rules, and their encroachment on the activities of local people (Ferguson and Gupta 2002; Gupta 1995; Herron 2003). But, as Nancy Fraser (1997, chap. 3) suggests, it is equally crucial that we refrain from idealizing civil society as homogeneous and autonomous from the state. In practice, she points out, the bourgeois public sphere excludes subordinated groups from participation, silencing their voices and fostering the emergence of alternative and contestatory public spheres.

These theoretical points have been driven home in practice in Colombia, where indigenous organizations seek to remake the state in a new image and where popular organizations dispute who constitutes civil society, particularly with respect to how they might intervene in peace negotiations in a role that they feel has been largely usurped by the elite. Cauca is an exemplary case in point because of the strong presence of the indigenous movement, which has effectively led a contestatory public sphere that is attempting to redefine what a state should do for its constituents; they have begun, using electoral strategies, by taking over the state apparatus at the municipal and provincial levels. Under these circumstances, the role of movement intellectuals is magnified because their intervention as powerful actors in the public arena provides a significant space for making their utopias a reality. As indigenous organizations become increasingly successful in their mission, key scenarios have begun to emerge in which we can observe the negotiation of indigenous culture and the meaning of the state for native activists.

By way of a conclusion to this book, I examine a recent confrontation in which tensions over what constitutes the state and who represents civil society came to a head. At the turn of the millennium, an indigenous activist, Taita Floro Alberto Tunubalá, was elected to lead the provincial administration.[1] His victory was made possible by the emergence of an alternative public sphere growing out of a coalition of urban and rural social movements, with the indigenous movement at its vanguard. His administration reflected the diversity of the electoral coalition, bringing together in common cause indigenous activists, urban intellectuals, unionists, and peasant leaders. But what happens when traditional indigenous authorities, who are prominent members of the contestatory public sphere, come into conflict with an indigenous-led state? The case with which I close this book explores the antagonisms that flared when a group of cabildos attempted to impose what they called *derecho mayor*, their "greater right" as the original Americans, over the national law that the Tunubalá administration was bound by oath to uphold. This dispute, which erupted in the summer of 2002, magnifies the heterogeneity of the indigenous movement as well as amplifying the nature of the intertwined relationships of local and regional activists. This is an encounter between the culturalist vision of indigenous intellectuals and the expanded discourse of sovereignty of native politicians, but with a telling twist: it is almost impossible to separate out the threads of who is a politician, who is a cultural worker, who is affiliated with a regional apparatus, who is a local, who speaks in the cadences of sovereignty, and who can legitimately speak of cosmovision.

Taita Floro

Taita Floro Tunubalá, as most indigenous Caucans call him, using a Guambiano term of respect, is in his late forties and is married to a mestiza. A model of the new brand of indigenous leader who has assumed the reins of the indigenous movement, he has partially completed a university degree and has spent a great deal of time outside of Cauca, serving as a national senator and as a development consultant. But Taita Floro also enjoys local legitimacy, having been elected to two terms as governor of Guambía after having served in the Senate. Indeed, Taita Floro's affiliation with the cabildo of Guambía defies any easy distinction between local and regional actors, given that the provincial line of AICO is virtually generated from a single cabildo, as there are few other AICO affiliates in Cauca; AICO is strong in the south in neighboring Nariño and in the Putumayo, and in the Sierra Nevada de Santa Marta along the Caribbean coast. While Taita Floro is undoubtedly a politician of regional and national stature, he is also intimately associated with a locality, one that has a highly distinctive political line in comparison to other parts of Cauca. When in the public eye, Taita Floro's "Guambianoness" is accentuated, much to the consternation of the Popayán elite: he wears the trademark blue kilt, black poncho, and fedora hat of his ethnic compatriots, but in private, he is partial to blue jeans and leather jackets. He is equally fluent in Spanish and in Guambiano, although he speaks Spanish with a distinctive Guambiano accent.

Taita Floro came to the governor's palace in Popayán with the support of AICO and CRIC, who overcame their differences to join in an unprecedented alliance in the wake of a series of occupations of the Panamerican Highway. But his largest voting base was among nonindigenous urban dwellers who had tired of the stranglehold that the two mainstream political parties had on Caucan politics. Taita Floro made a mark on Cauca. His efforts at organizing the governors of surrounding provinces in opposition to the fumigation policies of Plan Colombia and his encouragement of the manual eradication of illicit crops attest to his broader political commitment beyond strictly indigenous issues. Similarly, the general development plan drafted by his administration (Cauca 2001) promoted community organizing in nonindigenous areas and in the cities in the hopes of dynamizing the mestizo and Afrocolombian populations. One of Taita Floro's central concerns was the paucity of participation in nonindigenous sectors. The proportion of community development proposals that his administration received from indigenous communities far surpassed the proportion of native people in Cauca's population. Yet, Taita Floro appropriated methods from his indigenous constituency, such as community assemblies and the notion of the *minga*, or Andean communal work party, as tools to revitalize the public sphere in nonnative rural and urban areas.

Thus, Taita Floro is a child of the indigenous movement, yet he also served as governor of Cauca, responding to a much broader constituency than the roughly 30 percent of the provincial population that identifies itself as indigenous. Hence, he felt a pull between two conflicting allegiances and sets of administrative priorities. Furthermore, as governor he was subject to the restrictions of the Colombian state and could not make decisions that contravened its rules and regulations. During his term of office Taita Floro regularly experienced, in the flesh, the contradictions of simultaneously leading an indigenous community and representing the state. In July 2002, one such contradiction flared when the indigenous authorities of the municipality of Caldono blocked the Panamerican Highway at La María, demanding that Taito Floro dismiss their municipal mayor.

Conflict in Caldono

Caldono is a large municipality encompassing six resguardos: La Aguada-San Antonio, La Laguna, Las Mercedes, Pioyá, Pueblo Nuevo, and San Lorenzo de Caldono. Located to the north of Popayán and to the east of the Panamerican Highway, Caldono is part of the cultural "inside," a space in which Nasa Yuwe is widely spoken and where some older women still dress in the traditional Nasa woven skirt and shawl. Several of the municipality's resguardos were home to intense land struggles in the early years of CRIC, and PEB set up experimental schools in their midst. These resguardos retain a vivid memory of Juan Tama and of the resguardo title he acquired in the early eighteenth century, a document that unites them into a single historical unit whose boundaries have been reinstated in the contemporary cabildo federation (Archivo Central del Cauca, Popayán [ACCP] 1881 [1700]). In recent years, as in Belalcázar, CRIC regional activists returned home to Caldono to run for cabildo office, but whereas the Tierradentro activists brought home a discourse of sovereignty acquired in their years working in CRIC's regional economic planning apparatus, the returnees to Caldono arrived in their cabildo positions armed with a militant culturalist position that they had developed in PEB.

Caldono's municipal seat was designated a *zona de población* under Law 89 of 1890, the law that, until the 1991 constitution, determined the nature of the resguardo system (Colombia 1970). The zona de población is an urban district established in the midst of resguardo territory, home to a mestizo settler population that is not subject to cabildo jurisdiction. The insertion of settlers into resguardo territory was meant, at the time the law was promulgated, to diffuse national culture within an indigenous hinterland and to form the core of a potential mestizo locality. As a result of this historical circumstance, the town of Caldono is still largely mestizo in character. Father Ezio Roattino used to be the parish priest there, until he was run out by townspeople opposed to his advocacy of the indigenous struggle, indicating that there is considerable hostility between urban center and resguardo. There are also various satellite towns with mestizo peasant populations and considerable Guambiano settlement throughout the municipality (Ulcué 1997), making this an ethnically heterogeneous area. Until the Indigenous Social Alliance (ASI) successfully ran Nasa candidates in municipal elections, the alcalde was mestizo, running a tight and ethnically segregated ship characterized by political patronage (Rojas 1993).

But in 1999, ASI lost out to a mestizo politician, Gerardo Iván Sandoval, whom the cabildos accused shortly thereafter of having usurped lands destined for purchase by the resguardo of La Laguna. They also charged him with misuse of municipal funds and of supporting an upstart cabildo in the locality of Plan de Zúñiga, which the other cabildos refused to recognize (Caldono 2002). Beginning in late May 2002, the cabildos sought Sandoval's resignation on the grounds that he was "unfit to govern them" (Tunubalá Paja and Tobar Mosquera 2002, 2). They convoked a "permanent assembly," a state of belligerency marked by constant public meetings, enlisting CRIC's executive com-

BLOQUEO INDÍGENA DE 14 HORAS

Más de 3.000 paeces de Caldono bloquearon ayer la carretera Panamericana, a la altura de Piendamó (Cauca), para exigir la destitución del alcalde Gerardo Sandoval. El bloqueo se levantó anoche, cuando los indígenas aceptaron esperar un fallo definitivo del Consejo de Estado sobre el caso. **1-3** Carlos Ortega / EL TIEMPO

13. Civic Guard at La María, June 2003. Carlos Ortega/ *El tiempo,* 27 June 2003.

mittee to assist them in persuading Taita Floro to remove the alcalde from office (3).

On 26 June the cabildos occupied the Panamerican Highway at La María, inviting their indigenous compatriots to join them in the struggle. Many cabildos from across Cauca sent representatives. La María was once again, as so many times in the past decade, the site of a tent city, fed by a huge communal kitchen and patrolled by an indigenous civic guard armed only with staffs and made up largely of teenagers, young adults, and elderly women. Hundreds congregated in the large public space overlooking the highway to listen to the addresses of cabildo representatives. The road below was blocked off by the civic guard and by hundreds of parked trucks, with Colombian soldiers lining the route. Before being allowed into the meeting space, visitors were subject to frisking by the guard and their identity papers were inspected (figure 13).

Cosmovision as a Route to Sovereignty

In the years before the 2002 highway occupation, regionally based cultural activists had made considerable inroads into the cabildos of the Caldono. One of the first was Luis Carlos Ulcué, who was elected to the governorship of Pueblo Nuevo in the late 1990s; he is originally from Caquetá, as I described him in the first chapter, but his parents were born in Caldono, permitting him to claim membership there. Luis Carlos came into conflict with the piously Catholic population when he advocated a return to reconstructed Nasa rituals meant to replace Christian practices. In the years since, members of PEB and their allies have been elected to high posts in local cabildos, to the zonal organization uniting Caldono's cabildos, and to CRIC's executive committee. The zonal cabildo federation became increasingly militant, barring all researchers from conducting investigations in the municipality; given that this is where CRIC's university program trains Nasa students to conduct research, such a militant posture opened a breach between region and zone. One of those students, Alicia Chocué, who also appears in the first chapter, the director of the CRIC high school in the municipality, assumed the lieutenant governorship of Pueblo Nuevo in 2002.

The influence of PEB activists is evident in the cabildos' cosmogonic discourse aimed against the municipal mayor. The cabildos pointedly affirmed their ethnic ascendancy and sovereignty by calling themselves the Indigenous Communities of the Ancestral Territory of the Nasa People of Caldono (Caldono 2002) and by asserting that they "affirm[ed] and ratif[ied] the teachings of the elders about our Laws of Origin [and] the Greater Right, founded in and lived through cosmovision" (2). Here, for the first time in a public and intercultural space, a group of indigenous politicians was employing the discourse of cosmovision in its purest form—which is no accident, as the cabildo rosters included PEB activists turned local authorities. In a widely circulated broadside they argued that the Greater Right (Derecho Mayor), whose hegemony they sought, was a law originating at the center of the earth, from the hearth, and was meant for all people because all living beings were born from the Mother Earth (Caldono 2002). They asserted that their territory was at once cosmic and earthly, harmonized by rituals that ensured equilibrium among its inhabitants and ruled by the laws of the creator ancestors. They couched their demand for political autonomy in a discourse that combined the political language of self-determination with an acceptance of the role played by the spirit world in orienting indigenous authorities. Their denunciation of the municipal mayor accused him of having violated ancestral law and of "trampling our dignity and integrity as Originary Peoples, charged with and pledged to the conservation and preservation of Harmonic Life in what we call planet Earth" (4). Their condemnation was delivered "in the name of the Earth, the Sun, the Water, the Moon, and the cosmic, earthly, and subterranean spirits" (4). The broadside was signed by the governors and captains of the six cabildos and by five councillors. Beside their signatures, the names of their offices were listed in both Nasa Yuwe and Spanish: the captains were called *sa't ne'jwe'sx*, combining the word for hereditary chief (*sa't*) with that of legitimate authority (*ne'jwe'sx*); the councillors were designated as *nasa ne'jwe'sx*, underlining the cosmic roots of their authority.

Merging Sovereignty and Cosmovision

Cosmovision has been a goal of the cultural activists who, for half a decade, have held cabildo office in the municipality, but the culturalist approach had never before received the overwhelming reception that it did in 2002, when a critical mass of the Caldono indigenous community followed its traditional authorities into confrontation over the alcaldía. The notion of the Greater Right that coalesced them was not part of the local discourse; in fact, although the Guambianos have articulated this notion in their political demands for the past twenty-odd years, it had never before been appropriated by CRIC-affiliated communities. The novelty of the discourse was indeed apparent in the speeches delivered at the gathering at La María. Most of the traditional authorities who spoke could say little about what constituted the Greater Right; they dwelled, instead, on how indigenous legislation, even the 1991 constitution, was an imposition by outsiders and indigenous activists who were accused of not having seen fit to show their faces at La María. In other words, they allowed culture to outflank sovereignty.

But the organizers knew little about the Greater Right and were forced to bring in speakers from the outside, most notably, Inocencio Ramos and, to my surprise, me. Our presentations were preceded by a brief, very self-conscious, and abbreviated shamanic cleansing ceremony consisting in chewing a small packet of herbs that, mixed with alcohol, we blew in the air, while two thê' walas mediated with the spirits; some participants criticized the ceremony as inappropriate, given that it was conducted in public and in broad daylight. I was first on the podium, taking the opportunity to speak about how the historical cacique Juan Tama had laid the basis for the Greater Right; I had been informed by Alicia Chocué that the cabildos wanted to know more about their resguardo title. Inocencio took the Nasa translation of "constitution," *eç ne'jwe'sx* or "the principal book," and proceeded to explain why the Greater Right was more primordial than the constitution. The Greater Right, Inocencio argued, could be translated as *mantey neesnxi*, which he cast in Spanish as an ancient ethical system that makes people *nasnasa*, or "very Nasa." The staff of office carried by cabildo members, Inocencio pointed out, was inhabited by the guardian spirit, or *ksxa'w*, thus transforming it into an object that embodies harmony and is emblematic of the cosmic roots of politics. He concluded that the language of the Greater Right is ritual in nature, aimed at redistributing energy to achieve equilibrium. Inocencio then went on to draw a diagram similar to Manuel Sisco's model of the cosmos, of three pairs of hierarchically ordered beings, with the primordial beings Uma and Tay at the top, followed by *Kiwe* (territory) and *Sek* (sun), and finally by *Yu'* (water) and *A'* (star). Out of the final pair spring the *nasa* (people). He concluded with a reminder of the Sakhelu, the harvest ritual that had been recently reintroduced in Caldono.

What was striking to me about this assembly was the tremendous discursive gulf that yawned between the indigenous politicians and the cultural activists-cum-traditional authorities. The politicians spoke in the cadences of sovereignty and the culturalists through the symbolism of cosmovision, both well-developed discourses whose narrative tropes did not resonate with one another in this context. As a result, although the presentations synthesized the theoretical foundations of the Greater Right and the political conditions that had made its introduction necessary, no one reached even the most preliminary of conclusions as to what implications this reasoning held for everyday political practice. It was as though two parallel intellectual and political projects had suddenly collided, the explosion propelling a community into action. The gulf between philosophy and practice was sensed by the representatives of other cabildos who had come to the assembly—people from Tierradentro, from the resguardos of northern Cauca, and from the Spanish-speaking Kokonuko communities of central Cauca—who, in a debate mediated by CRIC officers, attempted to persuade the cabildos of Caldono to retreat from the radically indefensible position they had assumed.

A Confrontation with Taita Floro

Taita Floro appeared at La María some six hours after the cabildos occupied the highway, accompanied by an entourage that included the Caucan secretary of government, Henry Caballero (a former Quintín), representatives of the regional legal apparatus, and close advisors. Unlike at earlier meetings in La María, where his electoral campaign held public events and where he was treated as an exemplary member of the indigenous movement, now Taita Floro found himself representing the Colombian state. He was invited into the large open-air public meeting space to address the assembly and then promptly banished to an exterior building while the cabildos mulled over their response to him. In his speech Taita Floro told the Caldonos that they had placed him in an untenable position. As a former governor of the cabildo of Guambía, he intimated, he understood and fully supported their demand for recognition of their Greater Right as originary peoples; in fact, he asserted that as a Guambiano he knew more about the Greater Right than they did. But as governor of Cauca he not only represented the indigenous communities that had propelled him into office but also was the governor of the mestizo town dwellers and peasants of Caldono, who, for the most part, supported the municipal mayor and feared the ascendancy of the cabildos. Taita Floro's quandary is precisely the point that Ernesto Laclau (1996, chap. 3) makes in his explication of the dynamics of the coalition politics of new social movements. Laclau reasons that the organization that assumes the leadership of a coalition is forced to place its own demands on the back burner in the interests of representing a communal platform. In the process, its organizational dynamic is muted and weakened. But the long-term unity of the coalition is also placed in danger because its survival is premised on the vitality of the component organizations and, in particular, of the coalition leadership. Were Taita Floro to take up the Greater Right as his banner—which is precisely what Guambiano resguardo governors do—he would risk alienating the peasant organizations in the coalition that elected him. When he showed reluctance to engage the cabildos to the exclusion of his peasant constituency, he was seen by the Caldonos as a sellout. The movement's very objective of refashioning the state, then, requires that the ethnic agenda must, necessarily, fall by the wayside.

But it is not only the exigencies of the coalition that forced Taita Floro to take the position he defended. So did the requirements of Colombian law. As he explained to an incredulous assembly, his options were limited by the office he held. He drew an apt comparison: a governor of a cabildo simultaneously fills executive, judicial, and legislative functions, but the governor of Cauca cannot encroach on the prerogatives of other branches of government. Thus, he could not force Iván Sandoval to resign from the alcaldía but was obliged to let accepted—and uncomfortably protracted—legal procedures take their course. What went unaddressed was the intense political pressure being exerted by Taito Floro's political opponents among the Popayán elite, who had lost the governorship to the popular coalition and who eagerly awaited his downfall as a result of the confrontation with Caldono (*El Liberal*, 25 July 2002 and 26 July 2002). This was what most concerned many influential colaboradores, who immediately deployed respected public figures, such as Carlos Gaviria, the magistrate in the Francisco Gembuel dispute, to evaluate the legality of the Caldonos' demands and defuse the situation.

In short, Taita Floro was about to become a casualty of the contradictions between community and state that Arquimedes Vitonás had explained to me several years before. He was *from* the community but no longer *of* it. At stake was his political future and that of the coalition that had backed him. At stake, also, was the legitimacy of the indigenous movement as the vanguard of a broader popular coalition and the extent to which its paired discourses of sovereignty and culture were at all relevant to other coalition members. Ultimately, and with the help of colaboradores, Taita Floro found a middle road. He persuaded the Caldonos to open the Panamerican Highway to traffic and assembled a commission to work with them at laying the groundwork for future legislation to establish indigenous territorial entities, the geoadministrative units of the Colombian state governed by indigenous people that are proposed in the 1991 constitution (Colombia 1991, Art. 287) but have never been legislated into existence (Rappaport 1996; E. Sánchez, Roldán, and Sánchez 1993). The cabildos of Caldono are now engaged in that process, attempting to harness the discourses of cosmovision and sovereignty into a new politics of indigenous citizenship. Thus, the 2002 confrontation at La María did not end in failure for any of the parties involved. Taita Floro effectively defused a dangerous conflict, the regional culturalist intellectuals ensconced in local cabildos were provided with a space in which to ground their utopias in political practice, and even the municipal mayor and his supporters were given a temporary lease on life (at least, until the ponderous state bureaucracy would make public its decision on his continued tenure in the alcaldía, which was obviated by the 2003 nationwide election of new municipal authorities).

Experiments with Culture, Experiments with Anthropology

The issues that emerge from this clash of indigenous political cultures at La María represent a microcosm of what I hope to have conveyed in this book. On the one hand, I have described the complex and creative field of contention that appears to outsiders as though it were a unified indigenous movement—which, in effect, it is when it comes to mobilizations in places like La María. On the other hand, I have juxtaposed the intersecting intellectual discourses that are deployed in political practice, those that generate a revitalized indigenous culture and those that are operationalized in the struggle to reform the state. The field research on which my writing is based was exhilarating, in the sense that it issued from exegetic exercises grounded in structures of collaboration that generated strong sentiments on my part and on the part of some of my interlocutors. But it was also a difficult book to write, because I did not want my role to be relegated to that of a CRIC cheerleader, which would contribute very little to our understanding of ethnic movements. Conversely, I did not want to undermine CRIC with ultracritical observations. Furthermore, I felt it imperative that I write myself into this ethnography, as it was only through collaborative analysis with Nasa intellectuals that I found I could adequately engage their ideas as more than ethnographic data. But I did not want the book to become a reflexive narrative whose center was the anthropologist when the people I was studying were locked in a heroic life-and-death struggle for survival in an excessively violent country.

To accomplish these goals, I have taken a number of tacks. First, I have chosen to look at how a group of people—whom I call intellectuals, although they do not think of themselves as such—has grappled with the kind of cultural innovation that Richard Fox (1989) calls "experiments with culture," and used it toward political ends. That is, they have engaged in deep and empirically based reflection that has led them to instrumentalize certain cultural forms in a self-conscious and pragmatic way. I have conceptualized their understanding of culture (and, correspondingly, their political project) as a utopia, a projection toward the future. In this sense, the ethnography they create represents the inverse of traditional anthropology, because although they speak in the guise of cultural essences, they are in fact projecting cultural potentialities. But they do not always succeed in their experimentation, for a variety of reasons.

The pitfalls that indigenous intellectuals encounter in the process of cultural innovation stem in part from the fact that they are constantly attempting to appropriate new ideas and conceptual models that do not always fit the reality in which they are working. In this sense, they are not so different from anthropologists who grapple with theory in the production of ethnography. However, we generally appropriate theory out of our own sociocultural milieu, in the case of Euro–North American anthropologists. In the case of Latin

American anthropologists, the provenance of theory is problematized by the unequal relationships between the academies of north and south, which has led to the development of distinct research agendas in many Latin American anthropologies. This issue is intensified for nonacademic minority researchers who are intertwined in a problematic relationship with both the academy and nonindigenous colaboradores. The theories that indigenous intellectuals produce are frequently marginalized as insufficiently rigorous by their academic opponents. Such asymmetries are magnified, moreover, by the breakneck pace at which activists, who are constantly juggling research with political practice, engage in their work. Their lack of time to dedicate to prolonged reflection is only exacerbated by the numerous meetings they are called on to attend, the time spent dealing with intense rivalries that brew within their organizations, and the crises that come up repeatedly in the violent terrain in which they operate.

But lack of success is a relative term that is apropos only if we constrain indigenous intellectuals to the mold of academics, seated alone before a computer and producing written work that reflects in a disinterested manner on the nature of culture and social life. In reality, indigenous cultural innovation is an intensely active process, at once interculturally collaborative, in which appropriation and cultural creation flow *between* regional and local venues, and along the contrasting discursive axes of sovereignty and culture. All of this results in a multiplicity of unforeseen appropriations of a single idea. It is this second line of reasoning that has guided my writing: I am not so much looking to critique the production of CRIC's regional intellectuals as to trace the ramifications of their constructs in a variety of settings and among a range of social actors. They are not successful in the sense that they produce a coherent document based on theoretical reflection and empirical research; instead, their accomplishment can be measured by how effectively they engage communities to bring projects to fruition in the local sphere.

I do not think that I would have been capable of doing ethnographic research on such topics if I had not worked in a collaborative relationship with CRIC and our interethnic research team, which facilitated my participation in meetings and mobilizations, alerted me to important events, and protected me from the obvious dangers that lurk in the Colombian countryside. More important, collaboration afforded me a venue in which I could share my ideas with indigenous intellectuals and, conversely, could begin to absorb their guiding concepts and incorporate them into my work. I tried to accomplish the latter goal by engaging in writing projects with CRIC intellectuals in which the guiding concepts grew out of joint discussion but adhered more closely to their categories than to mine. I also attempted to organize my writing agenda around issues brought to the fore in our collaborative research group and I shared the results with them. Participation observation, therefore, was more than a process of abstracting out concepts and metaphors from the discourse of movement intellectuals for the purpose of presenting them in my own ethnographic account—although, in some respects, this is what I do in this book. I was also trying to gain a feel for their ideas to merge them with my own models and paradigms culled from the anthropological literature and to employ this hybrid theoretical package in my writing. That is, I hoped to continue our very fruitful dialogue on the written page. In this sense, I trust that my CRIC interlocutors do not appear in these pages as mere ethnographic informants, but as thinkers whose very original analytical methods and interpretations are as valuable for making sense of Colombian reality as are the ruminations of anthropologists. And I can only hope that they find of value what I have shared with them in the course of our joint endeavors.

Durham, North Carolina
May 2003

GLOSSARY

Terms in Spanish are indicated by italics. Terms in Nasa Yuwe and other indigenous languages are indicated by bold italics. Terms in English are in roman.

cabildo	The elected council administering the *resguardo*.
cacique	Hereditary chief.
colaborador	Nonindigenous activist working in CRIC (see list of abbreviations for indigenous organizations).
compañero	Comrade.
cosmovision	Worldview, understood by Nasa activists as an approach to everyday experience that inserts human beings into a broader cosmos peopled by other types of beings and fosters a concern for cosmic harmony and balance (**fi'zenxi**, in Nasa Yuwe).
cultura propia	See *lo propio*.
derecho mayor	The primordial sovereignty of indigenous authorities by virtue of their being the first Americans.
desescolarización	Education that moves beyond the confines of the schoolhouse.
educación propia	Educational planning focusing on indigenous culture as the enveloping conceptual framework.
escuela propia	See *educación propia*.

ETI	*Entidad Territorial Indígena* (Indigenous Territorial Entity), an administrative unit proposed in the 1991 constitution to facilitate indigenous self-government parallel to other territorial administrative units.
fi'zenxi	Characteristically Nasa lifeway; see cosmovision and *vivencia*.
inculturation	Theological movement emphasizing the merging of indigenous with Christian beliefs as an evangelizing strategy.
indigenous movement	The public face presented by the various indigenous organizations operating regionally or nationally in Colombia.
indigenous special jurisdiction	The devolution of judicial functions to *cabildos* so that they can operate according to indigenous uses and customs.
integralidad	Interdisciplinary curricular planning.
interculturalism	Strategy for intercultural appropriation in the interests of cultural revitalization, political mobilization, and the achievement of social equality in an ethnically plural context.
ksxa'w	Guardian spirit.
mestizo	In the Colombian context, nonindigenous and non-Afrocolombian.
Nejwe	Primordial progenitors, Tay and Uma (pl. **ne'jwewe'sx**).
ne'jwe'sx	*Cabildo* authorities and the authority of the nation.
npiçthê'	Elected official.
pájaro	Hired assassin, generally in the pay of large landowners.

PEC	*Proyecto Educativo Comunitario*, or community-generated educational plan, adopted as an alternative to PEI.
PEI	*Proyecto Educativo Institucional*, institutional educational plan required by the Colombian Ministry of Education.
profesionalización	Movement- or government-sponsored normal school proficiency courses for rural teachers.
propio, lo	A politically grounded strategy for cultural revitalization and appropriation in which the indigenous culture provides the framework for reinterpreting other cultures.
qhip nayra	Aymara term meaning "to view the past through multiple eyes."
resguardo	Indigenous territorial unit comprising communal and inalienable lands administered by elected councils and legitimized by colonial title.
sabedor	An internal intellectual who articulates knowledge within the indigenous community on the margins of the dominant society; includes shamans and oral historians.
sa't	Hereditary chief or *cacique*; captain of a *cabildo*.
solidario	Nonindigenous activist organized in support of AICO (see list of abbreviations for indigenous organizations).
Tama, Juan	Historical and mythic hereditary chief of Vitoncó, Tierradentro.
tardecer	A Nasa juridical concept imputing guilt on a party because his or her actions, however divorced they were from a crime that has been committed, ultimately led to that act.
Tay	Male progenitor and primordial being; the Sun.

thê' wala	Nasa shaman.
Tierrafuera	Nasa lands on the western slopes of the Central Cordillera.
tul	House garden and microcosm of the universe.
tutela	Lawsuit brought to the national Constitutional Court, in which complainants attempt to justify that their rights as Colombian citizens have been violated by third parties. In the indigenous context, *tutelas* are most frequently complaints that the individual rights of the complainant have been violated by the communal nature of indigenous customary law.
Uma	Female progenitor and primordial being.
vivencia	Unconscious everyday lived experience (***fi'zenxi***, in Nasa Yuwe).

NOTES

Introduction

Unless otherwise noted, all translations are mine.

1 There is a plethora of books on the Colombian conflict. The most recent publications include Kirk (2003) and Leech (2002) in English and Pécault (2001) in Spanish. U.S. support for counterinsurgency through the Plan Colombia is examined in Estrada Álvarez (2001). Safford and Palacios (2002) have written the best general history of Colombia that is published in English.

2 The Kokonukos and Guambianos constitute a single linguistic family, although the Kokonukos lost their language in the nineteenth century, and inhabit the valleys and mountains surrounding the provincial capital of Popayán. The Nasa, who used to be called the Páez, live on both sides of the Central Cordillera and have expanded into the Western Cordillera and the Amazonian lowlands; Nasa is the term that is used in Nasa Yuwe, the Nasa language, and Páez is a hispanicized version of the name of a Conquest-era hereditary chief. The Yanacona are the large indigenous group inhabiting the Colombian Massif, where the three cordilleras meet in a vast mountainous knot. They chose their name roughly twenty years ago to reflect the fact that many of them were brought to Colombia from further south as *yanaconas* in the service of the Incas or the Spanish; Yanaconas are monolingual Spanish speakers. Although in Colombian administrative parlance Cauca is a *departamento*, akin to the departments of France in its subordination to a centralized national structure, I have translated it as "province" for the ease of an English-speaking readership.

3 I use "dialogue" to cover a multiplicity of communicative contexts, some of them (such as workshops or negotiations with the state) highly formalized, and some of them (informal conversations, working meetings) less structured and open to a more free exchange. In some instances, particularly in local contexts but also in meetings of Nasa-speaking regional activists, Nasa Yuwe and its particular dialogical forms are used, but on the whole, "dialogue" in the Caucan indigenous movement involves conversation in Spanish, given that at least half the Nasa population is monolingual in Spanish and almost none of the other indigenous groups or

colaboradores speak Nasa Yuwe. Nevertheless, at critical moments in conversation, Nasa Yuwe erupts through the Spanish-only barrier, as I describe at various points in this book. I participated in or observed a broad array of forms of dialogue during my work in Cauca.

4 Native identity in Colombia implies being a member of a legally constituted community (or of a community seeking official recognition). In other words, it is the community, and not the individual, who is recognized as indigenous. As native people have joined other rural inhabitants in migrating to cities, being indigenous has also come to include tracing descent to a family inhabiting a resguardo. Increasingly, deindianized groups and colonist populations are reclaiming indigenous identities as well. The latter two attempts at constructing indigenous identity are in continuous dispute with the state.

5 When I speak of community I am referring to a legal entity, generally a resguardo or part of one, and the practices that constitute it as a distinct social entity, such as cabildo activities, shamanic relationships to territory, and the building of schools by local people.

6 This is quite different from the emphases I have perceived in anthropological writings about the Maya (Montejo 2002; Nelson 1999; Warren 1998a), where violence is a central trope, just as it was a major focus of colonial-era prophecies handed down in the books of *Chilam Balam* and of indigenous chronicles such as the *Popol Vuh*.

7 There was no room in Gramsci's cosmology for peasants, for, like other Marxists, he felt that in the Italian case, they held no potential for confronting hegemonic classes, although history would prove the limitations of this vision (Feierman 1990). Anthropologist Kate Crehan (2002, chap. 6) provides a useful gloss on Gramsci's notion of the role of the intellectual, which I have used in this brief synthesis of his argument. Karabel (1976) has written an excellent analysis of the problems inherent in Gramsci's theory of intellectuals.

8 Subsistence agriculture has always been supplemented by short-term labor migration by men during the coffee harvest or by women who work as domestic employees in neighboring cities and towns. However, in recent years, these communities have entered the global economy through the cultivation of coca and opium poppies. The Nasa have a long history of struggle against their Spanish and Colombian overlords and thus brought to the indigenous movement a legacy of grassroots organizing. There is, moreover, a critical mass of speakers of Nasa Yuwe, which has resulted in a Nasa leadership in cultural affairs in the Caucan movement.

9 For the latter, indigenous identity is not a necessary part of their intellectual endeavor, but instead, is frequently a hindrance.

10 However, indigenous politicians also run the not inconsiderable risk of adopting dominant discourses when their locus of operations moves into the orbit of state institutions, such as the Senate or the provincial assembly (Luykx 1996).

11 However, indigenous intellectuals increasingly interact in academic venues with

scholarly researchers. They are students in undergraduate and graduate courses, they present papers at scholarly meetings, and they circulate their observations through publications aimed at both an academic and a nonacademic reading public. See, for example, Dagua Hurtado, Aranda, and Vasco (1998); Muelas Hurtado (1995); Nieves Oviedo and Ramos Pacho (1992); and Yule (1996). CRIC also publishes a broad range of books, pamphlets, and magazines that circulate among bilingual teachers as well as in pedagogical circles in Colombia and in the NGO community throughout Latin America.

12 I have chosen to focus in this book on the fruitful tensions across local and regional venues and between different groups of intellectuals. But the turbulent rivalries that take place between the various indigenous organizations in Cauca are equally significant as sites of the creation of movement politics (Gow and Rappaport 2002), and I consider these as they come up in the ethnographic scenarios I will be examining.

13 The ø is used in the Guambiano alphabet for vowels originating at the center of the tongue, like the French *u*. The rules of Nasa orthography are outlined in the frontmatter to this book.

14 Governors may serve for only a single term in Colombia.

Chapter 1. Frontier Nasa

1 Similar statements are made by Indians in the United States. I purposely use the word "Indian" in this case because it is the terminology of preference among the authors of the volume I am citing. Crow Creek Sioux writer Elizabeth Cook-Lynn (1998, 124) criticizes popular mixed-blood authors (Gerald Vizenor, Michael Dorris, and others), whose experience of Indianness, she argues, is rooted in nostalgia: "[Their] . . . main topic is the discussion of the connection between the present 'I' and the past 'They,' and the present pastness of 'We.' "

2 Many of the indigenous activists I met through CRIC's bilingual education program expressed an intense desire to shift their focus away from the regional sphere and onto local areas in an effort to diminish such elitist associations. A growing number have done so, in the process weakening the regional program. CRIC's political leadership voices similar concerns, although many of the intellectuals feel that the indigenous politicians who control the organization are more interested in sending current program staff to the countryside to insert their own allies into regional programs than they are in fostering a closer relationship with localities.

3 Some examples of coauthored publications include the work of the Guambiano History Committee (Dagua et al. 1998; Tróchez Tunubalá, Camayo, and Urdaneta Franco 1992; Vasco, Dagua, and Aranda 1993) and sociologically oriented work on Nasa domestic servants in Cali (Unigarro 2000). The publications of political leaders (for example, Morales Tunubalá 1997; J. Piñacué 1997) are public addresses, some of them coauthored by nonindigenous collaborators.

4 For years, Latin American intellectuals have agonized over the foreign origins of many of the ideas that have historically formed the core of their discourses (Krotz 1997). Brazilian literary critic Roberto Schwarz (1992) calls this phenomenon one of "misplaced ideas," a concept later taken up by sociologist Renato Ortiz (1998) in his characterization of Brazilian modernity. Brazilian anthropologist Roberto Cardoso de Oliveira (1995) characterizes the work of Latin American scholars in terms of the creation of "styles" of anthropology, in which metropolitan concepts are rethought in peripheral locations. However, such exercises take place within academic networks, in professional venues, and in publications aimed at educated readers. What Colombian anthropologist Myriam Jimeno (2000, 176) calls *antropología comprometida*, or socially committed anthropology, is more similar to the work of indigenous intellectuals, in the sense that it is transmitted within nonacademic networks and is not published in standard academic form. Notwithstanding the genres in which it is produced, however, its proponents are academically trained and are not engaged in the autoethnography of indigenous researchers.

5 I employ "mestizo" in a cultural sense, to convey identification with rural popular sectors, as opposed to indigenous or Afrodescendant identities, and not with any connotation of racial mixing. Among such individuals, mestizo is a form of self-identification. Although mestizos and Afrocolombians can and do participate in cabildo activities, in the resguardo of Belalcázar there is also a separate administrative structure within the Afrocolombian community, called the *capitanía*, which functions parallel to the cabildo; individuals may participate in both institutions.

6 Isolation does not, however, suffice in the making of an "inside." In the second half of the twentieth century, Nasas fleeing violent armed conflict joined other landless and disenfranchised peasants in colonization zones in the tropical lowlands of the Caquetá and the Putumayo. Far from isolating themselves from the dominant society, these Nasa colonists were swiftly integrated into the dominant peasant culture, despite their geographic distance from major population centers.

7 Mary Roldán (2002) has recently published a highly perceptive historical study of La Violencia in the province of Antioquia, one of the most hard-hit in Colombia. La Violencia in Tierradentro was documented by eyewitness Father David Gonzalez (n.d.).

8 I thank Myriam Amparo Espinosa for this insight. For an ethnographic study of Nasa poppy cultivation, see Gómez and Ruíz (1997). The number of Protestants in Tierradentro has increased in recent years in relation to the number of Catholics as a result of the exodus of several traditionally Catholic communities in the wake of the 1994 earthquake and landslide that destroyed numerous communities in the Moras River basin of Tierradentro.

9 The early ethnographies of Tierradentro are key to this process, including the work of Segundo Bernal Villa (1953, 1954a, 1954b, 1956) and Horst Nachtigall (1953, 1955) followed several decades later by Sutti Ortíz (1973). My own work (Rappaport

1980–81, 1982, 1988b), some of it translated into Spanish in published or un-published versions and some originally published in Colombia and hence available to indigenous activists, has also played a role in exoticizing Tierradentro.

10 I first discovered this intriguing concept used in reference to indigenous activists in Diane Nelson's (1999) ethnographic analysis of Maya intellectuals in Guatemala. Doris Sommer's (1996, 130–131) interpretation of Rigoberta Menchú's testimony is highly pertinent to Trinh's construct. Sommer argues that one of Menchú's ways of performing her ethnicity is by signaling certain "secrets" that she refuses to share with her audience as a way of distancing herself culturally from her readers and thus ensuring the continuity of her own subject position. Many Nasa activists interpret shamanism as one of their "secrets," despite the fact that few of them are privy to the esoteric knowledge of thê' walas.

11 In the course of this project I moved from a complete rejection of Spivak's argument to a partial acceptance of it, as will be illustrated in future chapters. I was initially made uncomfortable by her apparent negation of the voice of subordinated minorities. However, it is evident to me now that CRIC activists distance themselves from their political base precisely through the use of external discourses. But on the other hand, their interlinked goals of culture and sovereignty are premised on an acceptance of their position, not as "subaltern," but as "different," suggesting that what is at stake in native Cauca is not subalternity.

12 "Taita" is an honorific formerly used in Guambía for recognizing elderly men and now employed in recognition of the contributions of considerably younger political leaders, many of them in early middle age.

13 I thank César Maldonado, S.J., for clarifying this last point for me.

14 In fact, among the differences between the CRIC of Father Álvaro's period and the organization today are the current acceptance of the possibility of indigenous authorship in lieu of the projection of a unified organizational line and the recognition of the utility of academic scholarship in activist contexts.

15 Lesley Gill (1994, chap. 5) narrates similar experiences among indigenous domestic workers in La Paz, Bolivia, emphasizing the formation of an alternative view of the female condition that has arisen as a result of the loss of traditional family authority, economic independence, and the creation of broader and more heterogeneous social networks on the part of urban indigenous women.

Chapter 2. Colaboradores

1 I employ the Spanish term *colaborador* in an attempt to avoid the implications of "collaborator" in English.

2 The fall of the Soviet Union generated profound crises in Latin America, as it did worldwide (Castañeda 1993). However, the crisis of the Colombian left owes even more to the concerted effort of the armed right to literally kill off its leadership, the

most blatant example being the fall of the Patriotic Union (UP), a broad-based socialist organization that grew out of the Communist Party. The UP's national and local leaders were murdered, one by one, in the 1980s.

3 However, as I demonstrate later on in this book, this very function inhibits indigenous organizations from privileging their own demands over those of coalition partners.

4 Nicola Miller (1999, 2000) argues, to the contrary, that twentieth-century Latin American intellectuals were never effective mediators between civil society and the state because they were encompassed by the state through containment, co-optation, or suppression. She reasons, moreover, that their voices, whether in favor or in opposition, were muted by the anti-intellectual policies of most Latin American states because they were relegated to the lower rungs of the bureaucracy, on the one hand, and because they implicitly accepted the modernizing discourse of the state, on the other. Thus, they were encapsulated as specialists, not generalists. However, the same is not true for less encompassing spheres of action, such as villages in the hinterland, where intellectuals working in humble surroundings successfully articulated national concerns in local arenas (Lomnitz 1992; Mallon 1995).

5 The position of colaboradores has been threatened to some extent, given the growing number of indigenous professionals who can assume the responsibilities once covered by nonindigenous activists. However, the pluralist aims of the movement militate against the disappearance of colaboradores from the ranks of indigenous organizations.

6 Nevertheless, the solidarios of AICO saw part of their mission as mediating between the indigenous movement and Colombian civil society.

7 It is at this time that Nasa linguists suggested that the name of the ethnic group be changed from "Páez" to "Nasa," in keeping with the new orientation to peoplehood. "Páez" was a hispanization of the name of a hereditary chief in Tierradentro at the time of the Spanish invasion. "Nasa" means a living being in Nasa Yuwe and, more specifically, a member of the ethnic group.

8 The distancing of expert supporters from the indigenous movement's political base is a continentwide phenomenon, fueled in large part by the emergence of a professional sector within the indigenous population, which could replace outside experts in many areas. Friends in CRIC also intimated to me that the progressive Catholic Church in northern Cauca supported the shift from colaboradores to asesores, as it effectively reduced the competition for influence that they faced within the movement.

9 AICO turned much earlier than CRIC to an ideology that focused on cultural difference and the expression of peoplehood. In its early years, AICO accused CRIC of advocating land claims through official governmental channels that did not recognize cabildo sovereignty (Caviedes 2000). The positions of both organizations began to coincide in the 1990s, although Vasco (2002) accuses AICO of having

recently espoused an assimilationist line, in which indigenous leaders run for public office, essentially becoming part of the state.

10 I use the term *solidario* in the past tense because this organization, operating parallel to AICO, is largely inactive.

11 The *municipio* (municipality) is the most local unit of public administration in Colombia in which officials have been elected since the mid-1980s; before then, they were appointed by departmental governors. Similar to the county in the United States, the municipio has an elected executive (the *alcalde*, or mayor) and a municipal council. At the time of the FARC threat, several municipios with large Guambiano, Nasa, or Totoró populations had indigenous alcaldes; those communities who were part of CRIC elected alcaldes affiliated with the CRIC-supported Indigenous Social Alliance (ASI), while the municipio of Silvia elected a Guambiano alcalde who ran on the AICO ticket.

12 Perhaps Ezio's homily on Moses was also meant to draw me, a Jew, into spiritual dialogue. The catechist movement hosts workshops quite similar to those of CRIC, and their discourse is equally steeped in references to the autonomous aboriginal past. For this reason, it was not unusual for Ezio to invite me to organize a workshop that I had already facilitated on various occasions for CRIC.

13 I explore the implications of inculturation in northern Cauca in further detail in chapter 6.

14 La Gaitana is a mythicohistorical figure, a Conquest-era chieftainess who rallied indigenous groups against the Spaniards. Her deeds are documented by the Spanish chronicler Juan de Castellanos (1944 [1589]), are part of the general national mythology, and have been incorporated into Nasa oral tradition (Rappaport 1998b).

15 Not all of the indigenous participants in CRIC activities are Nasas, necessitating the use of Spanish as a lingua franca. Kokonukos and Puraceños are monolingual in Spanish. Some Totoróes speak a variant of Guambiano (although they see themselves as closer culturally to the Nasa). A small number of Guambianos, almost all of whom are bilingual in Guambiano and Spanish, participate in CRIC; the vast majority of Guambianos adhere to AICO.

Chapter 3. Risking Dialogue

1 This is not to say that there weren't some activists afraid I would "steal" information from them. My good fortune was to have entered into a collaborative relationship with several key individuals, among them Graciela Bolaños, Abelardo Ramos, and Inocencio Ramos, who welcomed my desire to enter into coanalysis, which meant sharing my own writings with them; almost all of the first drafts of these chapters have been in Spanish, or, as an alternative, I made oral translations in meetings with my friends. For Graciela, Abelardo, and Inocencio, the fact that I wrote scholarly articles did not imply that I was furtively extracting information

from them, but instead, provided an opportunity for entering into a dialogue substantiated by written work.

2 *Rosca* in Colombian Spanish refers to a kind of donut and is also used to speak of an in-group. Such collaborations are more the rule in North America, where the workings of the nation-state have forced non-Indian scholars to engage in more decisively politicized research than in Latin America, a process that in great part is related to the broader base of Native American scholars and the organic link of research to indigenous political activism (Field 2002, in press b).

3 The nature of the theorizations developed by the Guambiano History Committee are examined in detail in chapter 5.

4 I thank Rob Albro for bringing to my attention the need to consider in detail the nature of the kind of dialogue I am describing.

5 Julia Paley (2001), a North American anthropologist working on urban movements in Chile, was forced by the people with whom she was studying—whom she calls *pobladores* because their political identity is bound into their residence in a shanty-town, or *población*—to develop her research in a workshop format. She discovered that her embracing of this methodology involved an epistemological shift in her relationship to the pobladores: "The fact that *poblador* leaders routinely theorized the political processes shaping their lives means that as much of the theory in this book takes place in their voices as my own. Rather than objects of study, *pobladores* became intellectual colleagues; rather than a researcher of them, I became someone with and through whom the traditional objects of anthropological study reflected on the political processes they shaped and faced. How each of us—anthropologist and community leaders—was situated varied significantly. We had different things at stake, and we have generated different products through our work. But our process of analyzing and the uses to which our work was put intertwined and overlapped" (16).

6 The translation project, coordinated by CCELA, the Colombian Center for the Study of Aboriginal Languages (Universidad de los Andes), included other indigenous languages as well, among them Cubeo, Guambiano, Ika (Arhuaco), Ingano, Kamsáa, and Wayúu (formerly Guajiro); native speakers of all these languages had studied ethnolinguistics at CCELA, constituting a team of indigenous professionals. Nasa goals for the translation project were different from those of the other ethnic groups that participated in the process, as Rojas Curieux (2000, 367–368) describes. The Guambianos translated the entire constitution, not just preselected articles relating to indigenous issues, calling it all "our Constitution." The Ika, members of the Arhuaco confederation, understood the Colombian constitution to be a manifestation of the law of the dominant society, which they contrasted with their own legal system, which, from their point of view, is primordial and hence superior; for them, the project was a simple exercise in translation. The Cubeo, a tropical forest group that has been considerably more isolated than the others, grasped the trans-

lation project as an opportunity to become acquainted with the dominant society, with which they were unfamiliar.

7   This approach resonates with that of Native American scholars in the United States who also look to language as a source of alternative theory (King 1997).

8   This and other quotations of Adonías, Susana, and Tulio are taken from transcripts of our team meetings, which are available for citation by all team members, as are transcripts of the interviews conducted by individual team members.

9   I thank Bruce Mannheim for clarifying this argument for me. Jackson (1999) writes about a related issue, where she questions whether it is possible to communicate in the same way to multiple audiences—indigenous and academic, organizational and local—given the rivalries and conceptual differences that extend across these spheres.

10   In her paper, Susana simply provides a Spanish gloss on the Nasa categories. The nuances of her analysis were arrived at in a collective discussion in the summer of 2003 with Abelardo Ramos, graduate students in anthropology at the Universidad del Cauca, and Herinaldy Gómez, the coordinator of the seminar.

11   I derive the notion of urgency from literary analyses of testimonial literature (Beverley 1993), which emphasize the practical and political intent of *testimonio* in an attempt to contrast it with other forms of autobiography.

12   The stakes may be higher in this sense for Adonías, Susana, and their comrades than for the Maya intellectuals that Kay Warren (1998a) describes, whose writings are widely disseminated in Guatemala and have been translated into other languages (Fischer and Brown 1996). As I discuss in further detail below, in spite of their discomfort with their liminal position (or, perhaps, thanks to it), Nasa intellectuals are much more closely associated with local communities than are their more cosmopolitan Maya colleagues, whose professional degrees, employment, class position, and residence in the capital city all confer on them a safety of distance that my Nasa friends not only do not enjoy but would categorically reject. I thank Victoria Sanford for clarifying my understanding of this comparison.

13   I do not refer here to risks related to personal safety, which, though they are considerable for any researcher working in Colombia, be she indigenous, a Colombian national, or foreign, were to some degree ameliorated by the protection given us by CRIC and community authorities. Nevertheless, David and I have not conducted research in rural areas since 2001, except for sporadic trips, confining our work to the relatively safe haven of Popayán, and we no longer take our daughter with us to the field. Despite many of the fears foreigners have of conducting research in Colombia, it is also important to point out that Colombian nationals face the gravest dangers, which are only intensified if they belong to popular movements such as indigenous organizations.

14   Chapter 1 is a revised version of this presentation.

15 The term "ethnolinguistics" is used in Colombia to distinguish the structural analysis of indigenous languages from more traditional forms of Spanish linguistics.

Chapter 4. Interculturalism and Lo Propio

1 A normal school is akin to a teacher's college, but at the secondary level—a distant memory in North America, embodied in such place-names as Normal, Illinois, but a lived reality in Colombia. Until the Colombian government began to require that all teachers have university degrees, a *normalista* degree was sufficient to retain a teaching post. CRIC's *profesionalización* program awarded its participants with normal school degrees.

2 As an example of the bidirectional exchange that our collaborative research team entailed, I heard about Giroux's work from Susana Piñacué.

3 This is not to say that small NGOs do not intervene in the organizations they support. Terre des Hommes, in particular, has repeatedly called CRIC's attention to the need to incorporate the gender dimension into their projects. The German funder has also required that CRIC adequately compensate its staff in terms of salaries and fringe benefits, thus allying themselves with PEB activists against the CRIC leadership. I also observed the active and critical intervention of a representative of Mugarik Gabe in a PEB workshop, suggesting that this organization is not a passive donor either. Both of these NGOs deal with highly political issues, ranging from the defense of children in conflict zones (Terre des Hommes) to support work in Chiapas, Mexico (Mugarik Gabe); both are concerned with questions of gender. Further information on Terre des Hommes-Germany can be found at http://www.tdh.de and on Mugarik Gabe at http://www.nodo50.org/mugarik/.

4 Although technically, Colombia never experienced a transition from dictatorship to democracy in the twentieth century, the National Front that ensured the hegemony of the two major political parties after the civil war of the 1950s constituted a type of dictatorship for many popular sectors. The presidential election in 1974 was the first time the political pie was not evenly divided between Liberals and Conservatives alternating in the presidency and sharing in equal portions of cabinet positions (Safford and Palacios 2002, chap. 14). However, only with the advent of the Constituent Assembly that drew up the 1991 constitution did nontraditional political parties achieve any significant representation in public legislative bodies beyond the municipal level or in executive positions at any administrative level.

5 However, interculturalism has been appropriated by national governments, who replace its contents with those of multiculturalism, retaining only the name, such as occurred in the Bolivian educational reform (Luykx and Bustamante 2000). In an astute rumination on the challenges of multiculturalism for Latin American indigenous movements, Hale (2002) suggests that official neoliberal multiculturalism is poised to co-opt indigenous leaders, directing them toward constructions of plu-

ralism that are less threatening to hegemonic interests. As Christian Gros (1997, 2000) argues, the realities of Colombian ethnic pluralism have to some extent fostered the integration of national indigenous actors into what might be better appreciated as "politics as usual," isolating them from the grassroots and forcing them to incorporate themselves into the networks of mainstream political parties, what Colombians call *politiquería*, or machine politics. Povinelli (2002) critiques the similar instance of Australian multiculturalism's encapsulation of Aboriginal peoples.

6 An internationally funded university-level bilingual education program for Latin American indigenous students, PROEIB-Andes (Program for Training in Inter-cultural Bilingual Education) is based in Cochabamba, Bolivia (www.proeibandes. org; Sichra 2001). Several Nasa educators have been trained or are currently studying in the program. The influence of educators associated with PROEIB has stretched to Central America, given that its promoters are in dialogue with the Maya movement and other ethnic organizations, publishing their treatises there (López 1995; Muñoz Cruz 1996), attending conferences, and participating in educational exchanges.

7 On a technical level, such assertions imply the rejection of what is called transitional bilingualism, in which vernacular literacy is taught only as a bridge on the road to immersion in the national language, in favor of maintenance bilingualism, where both minority languages and the national language come into continuous dialogue throughout the curriculum (Hornberger 1988).

8 Adonías Perdomo was one of the informants of the SIL linguists. Ultimately, the CRIC alphabet was superseded by a new orthography developed in 2000 that unified the various alphabets being used by CRIC, church-affiliated teachers in Tierradentro, and Protestants, who had continued to adhere to the SIL proposal (Comisión de Alfabeto Nasa 2001; Abelardo Ramos 2000).

9 For example, the community school in López Adentro was called Êeka Thê', or Thunder, and the cabildo association for the municipality of Páez, Tierradentro, was named Nasa Çxhâçxha, or Fierce Nasa. Many CRIC militants are beginning to give their children names in Nasa Yuwe instead of Spanish, generally constructed using words of cosmological significance. For example, Inocencio Ramos's son is called Taynas, combining an archaic term for "the Sun" (*tay*) with "man" (*nas*). I have never heard of local community members following the militants' lead in this respect. However, neither have I heard of local people rejecting Nasa names for community institutions.

10 The same tack is taken by the 2001 governor of the resguardo of Jambaló, himself a university graduate with a degree in ethnoeducation. In a discussion with PEB members he described interculturalism as a means of extending the gains of the indigenous organization to the other oppressed peoples in his municipality, including mestizos.

Chapter 5. Second Sight

1 Not only minority scholars but feminists as well have begun to make such calls. Donna Haraway (1988) argues for epistemologies that are "situated," that is, based on specific contexts, not universal conditions; she calls this "partiality." Nancy Hartsock (1990, 34–35) looks to subjectivity as the source of such situatedness, calling for the construction of an epistemology based on everyday life (35–36) and forged in political struggle (36). With this move, women's awareness of themselves as subjects is not only heightened but is placed center stage, creating "an account of the world which treats our perspectives not as subjugated knowledges, but as primary" (34). What Hartsock is arguing for is of critical importance. By focusing on feminist epistemology as primary knowledge, as opposed to subjugated knowledge, she not only opens the way for an acceptance of situated theories as equivalent to mainstream academic theory, but also implicitly acknowledges the possibility of their use by groups other than those in which they originated.

2 As is, of course, the question of whether there is a single, monolithic thing called "Western thought." For this reason, I have opted instead for opposing "indigenous" to "academic," the second category being slightly more circumscribed than "Western."

3 For lack of space, I do not dwell here on the archaeological work of the committee (Tróchez Tunubalá et al. 1992). The pamphlets it produced for local consumption organize chronology and topography according to Guambiano categories.

4 In the years following the publication of this work, the cabildo of Guambía organized massive communal interventions in which poppy plants were uprooted by hand. This strategy of manual eradication was championed by Taita Floro Alberto Tunubalá, the governor of Cauca, when he was governor of Guambía, and became a powerful argument that Taita Floro wielded in his condemnation of U.S.-supported aerial fumigation of illicit crops in southern Colombia.

5 The erasure of the literate memory is most apparent in Thomas Abercrombie's (1998) reconstruction of the trajectory of Aymara memory in K'ulta, Bolivia, where contemporary oral tradition completely neglects the rich documentary foundations created by colonial caciques. Ironically, although the Nasa implicitly acknowledge the literate basis of their oral tradition in their constant reappropriation through time of resguardo titles and their conversion into oral narrative (Rappaport 1998b), CRIC also equates "indigenous" with orality and "European" with literacy.

6 On the problems inherent in academic genres of writing, see Beverley (1999). In contrast, grassroots publications, handwritten in comic book form and composed in native vernaculars—with all of the grammatical errors they exhibit from the point of view of the "lettered city"—depart more radically from the generic model. This point was brought home to me by Nasa university students, who embraced the history of Cohana that I mentioned earlier (Mamani Quispe 1988) as more "au-

thentic" and potentially liberatory to them than academic writings (Rappaport 2000).

7 I thank Gyan Pandey for alerting me to these issues.

8 I thank Gerardo Tunubalá, a member of the new generation of university-trained Guambiano historians conversant with archival materials and interested in reading documents in light of oral history, for alerting me to this new development, which I have been unable to visit under the current conditions of violent confrontation in Silvia.

9 Nevertheless, the Cátedra has produced an impressive series of pamphlets centered on the best of the narratives that were collected.

10 Unfortunately, the video is marred by intrusive voice-over narration, which adds nothing particularly useful, but does not succeed in superseding the organizing model either.

11 At the Congress of Indigenous People of Colombia, held in November 2001 in response to heightened attacks by all of the armed groups against native communities, cultural education, and ritual participation in particular, was repeatedly emphasized as a strategy for indigenous survival in the face of violent attacks.

12 Inspired by the history project's guiding concepts, the PEB collective voted recently to change the program's name to Bilingual Intercultural Education Program (PEBI).

Chapter 6. The Battle for the Legacy of Father Ulcué

1 In correct Nasa usage, the plural of thê' wala would be *thê' walawe'sx*. For the ease of an English-speaking readership, I have chosen instead to pluralize with an addition of *s*, which is a common adaptation in Spanish-language discussions of Nasa shamanism by CRIC militants.

2 Gayatri Spivak's (1988) argument that the subaltern cannot speak except in the hegemonic discourse is relevant here. The first stage of cosmovision—the transmission of reinterpreted shamanic lore to local activists—is quite clearly bound up with pervasive Western discursive forms. But the second stage—its transformation into a vivencia that refashions everyday life—must necessarily break with the terms of the dominant society.

3 This is somewhat of a simplification, as there are thê' walas like Ángel María Yoinó who have always been great narrators and who have for years been familiar with such foundational documents as the resguardo titles written by Juan Tama. These exceptional individuals, who have played a key role in encouraging the cosmovision project, have always merged shamanic forms of interpretation with what we might call ethnography. Furthermore, individuals like Ángel María who have always functioned simultaneously as sabedores and as organic intellectuals spur activists to imagine how a more autonomous Nasa society must have operated.

4 Kokonuko and Puracé, Spanish-speaking communities that once were part of the Guambiano-Coconuco language family, are the resguardos of origin of some of the most important regional leaders.

5 That is, until 2003, when CRIC effectively wrested control over indigenous education in Tierradentro from the Apostolic Vicariate.

6 Cosmovision is a particularly salient buzzword in the movement to promote respect for the biodiversity of native landscapes and the territorial autonomy of indigenous peoples, providing a framework for arguing that Fourth World peoples effectively conserve their environments because they view their ecosystem as existing within a broader cosmic balance. This generalization is under dispute by revisionist scholars (Krech 1999) but, nonetheless, supplies a discursive framework for the grassroots organizations that fund alternative rural development (Bilbao 2001) and the scholars who collaborate with them (Serrano 1993).

7 My own reading of the importance of Juan Tama (Rappaport 1998b) revolves around the translation into oral narrative of the contents of the resguardo titles that he left Pitayó and Vitoncó. I see the two readings as complementary because they differ largely in the points emphasized, not in the plot structure.

8 Jackson (1995) has studied meetings of shamans funded by the Ministry of Health that were convoked by anthropologists and attended by teachers in the Vaupés in the early 1980s. Unlike in the Nasa case, the objective of the Vaupés shamanic workshop was neither systematic research on the part of the shamans themselves nor the construction of a new and unified knowledge base. Moreover, the project reduced shamanic expertise to traditional medicine, seeking ways of incorporating local knowledge into the Western medical system, thus standing in contrast to the Nasa objectives, which were meant to explode this commonly held assumption and forge a modern shamanic strategy for cosmic redemption. Jackson's analysis of the failure of the Vaupés project to achieve its goals dovetails nicely with this distinction.

9 Susana Piñacué recently asked me to go over a draft of a pamphlet on gender that she is preparing for PEB. Like Manuel, Susana sees complementarity as a hallmark of Nasa cosmovision. She argues that with the adoption of Christianity and with colonial domination, gender roles among the Nasa were skewed, fostering the appearance of machismo. Nevertheless, Susana does not construct Nasa and Christian cosmovisions as polar opposites, as Manuel does, and she does not use a Christian model as a homologue through which Nasa cosmovision can be described.

10 I am indebted to Andrew Orta for sharing this insight with me and for alerting me to an article by Webb Keane (1996, 160), in which Indonesian non-Christians justify their practices in the face of converts to Christianity by appealing to Christian discourse: "*Marapu* people also seek to appropriate the language of functional equivalents (the purification *ratu* is like Christ, chicken entrails are like the Book), but in doing so leave themselves vulnerable to the claim . . . that Christianity provides a more encompassing language into which their local speech can be translated."

11 I must admit that I had never heard of the fire ritual before.

12 At the time of my dissertation research, cabildos were afraid to visit such sacred precincts for fear that Juan Tama would unleash the elements against them, as they observed had occurred when people visited these places without adequate spiritual preparation.

13 A similar ceremony is described for the mid-eighteenth century by Father Eugenio del Castillo y Orozco (1877 [1755], 58–59), but activists who contributed to the reintroduction of the Sakhelu told me they were not aware of this source. Instead, as I already mentioned, they learned of the ceremony from an elderly shaman; they also knew of a place in Tálaga called Tä' Fxnu (these days, occupied by a soccer field). A Sakhelu is being repeated annually, each year in a different location.

14 However, as will become evident, they do maintain a distinction between inside and outside when it comes to economic systems, such as capitalism.

15 Father Ulcué's diaries are in the hands of the Missionary Sisters of Mother Laura and unfortunately have not been available for consultation for many years.

16 David Gow (2005) has analyzed these drawings in his study of indigenous planning activities in northern Cauca. I thank David for making the images available to me. Unfortunately, the photocopies he made in Toribío are not of sufficient quality for reproduction here.

17 There were originally forty-one *maestros en sabiduría*, but Jesús Piñacué's name was removed from the rolls after his public announcement of support for the Liberal Party. How seriously those named to this lofty office take their appointments varies. In the north, where leaders are intimately enmeshed in the extensive political apparatus, people received the honor quite seriously; they explained to me that they felt it was given them in recognition of their community service and would encourage them to redouble their efforts. Some of the regional politicians take a quite pragmatic approach; they know that they need the support of the north to be elected to CRIC's executive board, and so they diligently participate in events when invited. Some PEB members acknowledge the title with humor but take advantage of the vantage point that it confers to keep tabs on northern activities by transforming meetings into a bully pulpit from which they can criticize the Consolatas.

18 Much of this was due to the fact that it was hard to digest the lengthy public speeches at the huge assemblies that went on for several days. Moreover, many of the young people did not have the reading skills necessary to pore over the extensive interview transcripts that were collected. FUCAI took it upon itself to coordinate the analysis of the data, chopping up interviews into fragments that were reclassified according to themes, thus breaking the flow of the narratives. Fortunately, in the end FUCAI's *sistematización*, which is what they called the process, was abandoned in favor of the publication of a series of accessible pamphlets recounting the lives of key northern militants. I have no knowledge of how they are being used, however.

Chapter 7. Imagining a Pluralist Nation

1 The administrative decentralization of the mid-1980s that preceded constitutional reform provided for the public election of municipal mayors, who had heretofore been appointed by provincial governors, as well as for the election of governors, who, before, were appointed by the president. Indigenous communities quickly jumped into the political arena, electing mayors in a number of municipalities, particularly in northern Cauca, under the rubric of ASI, the Indigenous Social Alliance, a political party founded by CRIC and the former Quintín Lame guerrillas. In Toribío, as in other localities, ASI allied itself with progressively minded mestizos, forming civic movements, a move that exemplifies how pluralism has taken hold at the local level. Guambianos and their allies in other parts of the country ran, and won alcaldías, under the umbrella of AICO. Arquimedes Vitonás and several other indigenous and civic leaders were kidnapped in 2004 by FARC as they travelled to the Caquetá region to facilitate development workshops among the Nasa who had organized resguardos there. In an unusual turn of events, a commission of over three hundred indigenous people from northern Cauca met with the guerrillas and obtained the liberty of the hostages, testimony to the effectiveness of the indigenous movement on the national stage.

2 A report by CRIC's executive committee presented at a meeting in 2000 described a survey conducted in the northern resguardo of San Francisco, which demonstrated that there was great ambivalence among members of the younger generation regarding their support of the militant cabildo, while among middle-aged people there was outright opposition. The only consistent base of support was among the oldest generation. This suggests that communities are considerably more heterogeneous than the indigenous movement has projected in public, although the San Francisco data contrast with the overwhelming support of cabildos that I have seen in Tierradentro.

3 All of the antigovernment armed organizations, including the paramilitary, pay recruits the equivalent of a monthly minimum wage, which provides a hefty incentive for local people to join them. Resguardo members are exempted by law from obligatory military service in the Colombian army, although the older generation served before this law was introduced.

4 Nevertheless, ACIN, the cabildo federation in northern Cauca, has gained the tentative support of the national Superior Court of the Judiciary to undertake an Indigenous Juridical School (Escuela Jurídica Indígena) in which customary law procedures would be standardized for general use among the Nasa (Gómez López 2003, 15).

5 Sometimes this process is accompanied by the production of written evidence to determine whether a defendant is guilty or innocent. The entire process is chronicled in a written record. Sometimes parts of the procedure take place in Spanish, with the participation of representatives of the complainants, who are aptly called

palabreros, underlining the centrality of the word (*palabra*) to the event, even though plaintiffs and defendants may be only marginally fluent in that language (Perdomo 2002).

6 Electronic mail message, 21 May 2004.

7 "Nation" is translated as *çxab wala kiwe* (Abelardo Ramos and Cabildo Indígena de Mosoco 1993, 118). There is little distinction between "nation" and "state" in the Nasa version. "State" is glossed as *çxab wala kiwete ikahsa*, with the final word meaning "power" or "rule." In other words, "state" is the enactment of the idea of "nation." I thank Alejandro Lugo for prodding me on how the Nasa translators made this distinction. There is a fascinating double meaning to the phrase *çxab wala kiwete npiçthê'* ("the authority of the territory of the greater people") given that *çxab wala* means not only the "greater people" or the nation, but is also the name in Nasa Yuwe for Vitoncó, the capital founded by Juan Tama, the Nasa mythic hero. I asked Abelardo about the possible identification of "nation" with Vitoncó. He responded that this was an issue discussed in the Mosoco workshops and he supposed that when Nasa speakers first hear the name *çxab wala* being used in this new context, they undoubtedly think of Juan Tama's capital but that they would quickly comprehend the more expansive usage. Nevertheless, the fact that two such disparate entities carry the same name invests the newly coined Nasa term for nation with a pointedly mythic quality that resonates with their equating of the legitimate authority of the constitution and of cabildos with the primordial beings Uma and Tay, in distinction to petty politicians.

8 Electronic mail message, 21 May 2004.

9 Note that *fxi'ze* was also the root of the term Susana Piñacué used to refer to *vivencia* in her classification of different types of Nasa women; she called older women "*nasa u'y dxihk fxi'zesa,*" or "Nasa women who live actively." There are thus profound connections being made in the neologism for justice between the conditions under which knowledge of a situation is acquired and the celebration of Nasa cultural practices.

10 Note, however, that in the case of Francisco Gembuel, which I take up later in this chapter, the magistrate ruled that the constitution's understanding of exile was confined to banishment beyond Colombia's borders, not within them (Gaviria Díaz 1997).

11 Henry Caballero, formerly secretary of government under Taita Flora Alberto Tunubalá, told me that Gembuel had allied himself with the local Liberal Party, a political choice that led him into a polar opposition in relation to local cabildo authorities and the regional organization, CRIC, that he had once led. Reference to mainstream political parties is muted in the documentation of the court case and its local settlement, although in later disputes, the cabildos of northern Cauca did accuse the indigenous senator Jesús Enrique Piñacué of such transgressions.

12 I am indebted to Donna Lee Van Cott for providing me a copy of this document.

13 Of course, this is a very idealized exposition, a utopia, as it were. Confession is

frequently extracted quite violently from the accused by means of the stocks, as I have already argued.

14 The letter quotes the governor of neighboring Pioyá, who ratifies the didactic function of confession: "If he is guilty, he should pay, and if he is not guilty, he should pay to provide an example" (Passú and Fiscué 1997, 17).

15 I am beholden to Carlos Ariel Ruiz for lending me a copy of a tape of this session. The quotes I reproduce from this meeting are excerpted from the transcript I made of Carlos Ariel's tape-recording.

Epilogue

1 Taita Floro's administration ended in January 2004. The coalition he had led to victory was unable to name an equally charismatic candidate and lost the election to one of the traditional political parties.

WORKS CITED

Interviews

All interviews were conducted by Joanne Rappaport, unless otherwise indicated.

Angucho, Hermes, Alvaro Cabrera, Inocencio Ramos, and Luis Yonda. Popayán, 20 May 2001. Interview conducted by Joanne Rappaport and Abelardo Ramos.

Angucho, Hermes, Luz Mery Niquinás, and Adonías Perdomo. N.d., n.p. Interview conducted by Abelardo Ramos.

Atillo, Alejandro. Tóez-Caloto, 3 August 1996.

Ávila, Floraldine. La María, Piendamó, 2 July 2002. Interview conducted by Joanne Rappaport, Graciela Bolaños, and Abelardo Ramos.

Bolaños, Graciela, Alicia Chocué, Rosalba Ipia, Yamilé Nene, and Susana Piñacué. La María, Piendamó, 3 July 2001. Interview conducted by Joanne Rappaport and Abelardo Ramos.

Bolaños, Graciela, and Abelardo Ramos. Bogotá, 9 June 2001.

Bonanomi, Antonio. N.d., n.p. Interview conducted by Graciela Bolaños.

Caballero, Henry. Popayán, July 1997.

Campo, José Manuel. San José del Guayabal, 28 July 1996.

Chepe, Roberto, Jorge Penagos, and Juan Peña. Las Delicias, Buenos Aires, 8 August 2001. Interview conducted by Abelardo Ramos.

Chocué, Alicia. Popayán, 26 July 1999.

Claudia (MAQL nom de guerre). Popayán, 2 July 1996. Interview conducted by Joanne Rappaport, Dalila, and Myriam Amparo Espinosa.

Cortés, Pedro, and Graciela Bolaños. Bogotá, 8 April 2001. Interview conducted by Graciela Bolaños.

Cortés, Pedro, and William García. Bogotá, 7 July 2001. Interview conducted by Joanne Rappaport, Graciela Bolaños, and Abelardo Ramos.

Dalila (MAQL nom de guerre). Popayán, 1 July 1996. Interview conducted by Joanne Rappaport, Luis Alberto Escobar, Myriam Amparo Espinosa, and David Gow.

Hurtado Mulcué, Stella. Tóez-Caloto, 4 June 1997.

Inseca, Jorge Eliécer. Tóez-Caloto, 4 August 1996.

Ipia, Eliceo. Jambaló, 13 June 2001. Interview conducted by Graciela Bolaños.

Ipia, Rosalba. Popayán, 14 June, 1999. Interview conducted by Joanne Rappaport and Susana Piñacué.

Medina, Omaira. Jambaló, 6 June 1999.

Montoya, Sol Beatríz. Popayán, July 1996.

Morales Paja, Felipe. Tóez-Caloto, 5 August 1996.

Mulcué, Adela. Tóez-Caloto, 5 August 1996.

Mulcué, José Miller. Mosoco, Tierradentro, 10 August 2001. Interview conducted by Abelardo Ramos.

Musse, Lucía. San José del Guayabal, 25 December 1996. Interview conducted by Tone Wang.

Niquinás, Luz Mery, Benilda Tróchez, and Julio Tróchez. La María, Piendamó, 3 July 2001. Interview conducted by Joanne Rappaport and Abelardo Ramos.

Pabón, Germán. Jambaló, 12 June 2001. Interview conducted by Graciela Bolaños.

Peña, Alfonso. Popayán, July 1997.

Perdomo, Adonías. Popayán, 30 July 1996. Interview conducted by Joanne Rappaport and the sixth-semester students, Licenciatura en Etnoeducación, Universidad del Cauca.

Perdomo, Griserio. Popayán, July 1996.

Piñacué, Daniel. Popayán, July 1997.

Piñacué, Susana. Popayán, 23 December 1997.

Ramos, Abelardo. Popayán, 5 September 2000 and Bogotá, 3 July 2002.

Ramos, Inocencio. Popayán, July 1997.

Roattino, Ezio. Santander de Quilichao, 15 July 1999.

Rojas, Tulio. Bogotá, 11 November 2001. Interview conducted by Joanne Rappaport, Graciela Bolaños, and Abelardo Ramos.

Serrano, Javier. Bogotá, 20 October 2001. Interview conducted by Graciela Bolaños.

Simmonds, Cristina. Popayán, 18 June 1998.

Sisco, Manuel. Popayán, 28 June 2001. Interview conducted by Joanne Rappaport, Graciela Bolaños, and Abelardo Ramos.

Sodemann, Ute. Bogotá, n.d. Interview conducted by Graciela Bolaños.

Tattay, Pablo. Popayán, 11 August 1996. Interview conducted by Joanne Rappaport, Graciela Bolaños, Luis Alberto Escobar, Myriam Amparo Espinosa, and David Gow.

Tróchez, Julio. López Adentro, Corinto, 9 April 2001. Interview conducted by Graciela Bolaños.

Tumbo, Samuel. Popayán, 12 July 1996.

Ulcué, Luis Carlos. Popayán, July 1997.

Vitonás, Arquimedes. Toribío, July 2000.

Yoinó, Angel María. Juan Tama, Santa Leticia, 11 August 2001. Interview conducted by Abelardo Ramos.

Yule, Marcos. Tóez-Caloto, 28 May 2001. Interview conducted by Graciela Bolaños.

Published Sources, Documents by Indigenous Organizations, and Films

Abercrombie, Thomas A. 1998. *Pathways of Memory and Power: Ethnography and History among an Andean People.* Madison: University of Wisconsin Press.

Abrams, Philip. 1988. "Notes on the Difficulty of Studying the State." *Journal of Historical Sociology* 1(1), 58–89.

Abu-Lughod, Lila. 1991. "Writing Against Culture." In Richard G. Fox, ed., *Recapturing Anthropology: Working in the Present*, pp. 137–162. Santa Fe: School of American Research Press.

Aguilera Peña, Mario. 2001. "Justicia guerrillera y población civil, 1964–1999." In Boaventura de Sousa Santos and Mauricio García Villegas, eds., *El caleidoscopio de las justicias en Colombia*, vol. 2, pp. 389–422. Bogotá: Siglo de Hombre Editores.

Albert, Bruce. 1995. *O ouro canibal e a queda do céu: Uma crítica xamânica da economia política da naturaleza.* Brasília: Série Antropologica no. 174, Departamento de Antropología, Universidade de Brasília.

Alberti, Giorgio, and Enrique Mayer, eds. 1974. *Reciprocidad e intercambio en los Andes peruanos.* Lima: Instituto de Estudios Peruanos.

Allen, Catherine J. 2002. *The Hold Life Has: Coca and Cultural Identity in an Andean Community.* Washington, D.C.: Smithsonian Institution Press.

Allen, Chadwick. 2002. *Blood Narrative: Indigenous Identity in American Indian and Maori Literary and Activist Texts.* Durham, N.C.: Duke University Press.

Alvarez, Sonia, Evelina Dagnino, and Arturo Escobar, eds. 1998. *Cultures of Politics, Politics of Cultures: Re-visioning Latin American Social Movements.* Boulder, Colo.: Westview.

Appadurai, Arjun. 1996. *Modernity at Large: Cultural Dimensions of Globalization.* Minneapolis: University of Minnesota Press.

Archivo Central del Cauca, Popayán (ACCP). 1881 [1700]. "Titulo de las parcialidades de Pitayo, Quichaya, Caldono, Pueblo Nuevo y Jambalo." *Protocolos Notariales*, partida 843.

———. 1883 [1708]. "Titulo de resguardo de Vitoncó." *Protocolos Notariales*, partida 959.

Archivo de la Casa Cural de Toribío, Cauca (ACCT). 1980–81. "Seminarios realizados con los cabildos de Toribío, San Francisco, Tacueyó, 1. Del 8 al 12 de Septiembre de 1.980, 2. Del 27 al 29 de Abril de 1.981." Papers of Fr. Álvaro Ulcué Chocué.

———. 1982. "Carta de los estudiantes indígenas del Instituto Misionero de Antropología al P. Marcos Zambrano." 20 January. Papers of Fr. Álvaro Uluce Chocué.

———. n.d. "Estatutos de la Organización de Rescate de Valores Autóctonos y Campesinos." Papers of Fr. Álvaro Ulcué Chocué.

Ari Chachaki, Waskar (Juan Félix Arias). 1994. *Historia de una esperanza: Los apoderados espiritualistas de Chuquisaca 1936–1964: Un estudio sobre milenarismo, rebelión, resistencia y conciencia campesino-indígena.* La Paz: Ediciones Aruwiyiri.

Arrupe, P. 1978. "Lettre et document de travail sur l'inculturation." *Acta Romana Societatis Jesu* 17(2), 282–309.

Asad, Talal. 1986. "The Concept of Cultural Translation in British Social Anthropology." In James Clifford and George E. Marcus, eds., *Writing Culture: The Poetics and Politics of Ethnography*, pp. 141–164. Berkeley: University of California Press.

Avirama, Jesús, and Rayda Márquez. 1995. "The Indigenous Movement in Colombia." In Donna Lee Van Cott, ed., *Indigenous Peoples and Democracy in Latin America*, pp. 83–105. New York: St. Martin's Press.

Bakhtin, M. M. 1981 [1975]. *The Dialogic Imagination.* Austin: University of Texas Press.

Barrera Carbonell, Antonio. 1997. *Derechos fundamentales de comunidad indígena.* Sentencia no. SU-039/97, Corte Constitucional, Bogotá.

Beltrán Peña, Francisco, and Lucila Mejía Salazar. 1989. *La utopía mueve montañas: Álvaro Ulcué Chocué.* Bogotá: Editorial Nueva América.

Benjamin, Walter. 1968. "The Task of the Translator." In Hannah Arendt, ed., *Illuminations*, pp. 69–82. New York: Schocken.

Berichá. 1992. *Tengo los pies en la cabeza.* Bogotá: Los Cuatro Elementos.

Bernal Villa, Segundo E. 1953. "Aspectos de la cultura páez: Mitología y cuentos de la parcialidad de Calderas, Tierradentro." *Revista Colombiana de Antropología* (Bogotá) 1(1): 279–309.

——. 1954a. "Economía de los páez." *Revista Colombiana de Antropología* (Bogotá) 3, 291–309.

——. 1954b. "Medicina y magia entre los paeces." *Revista Colombiana de Antropología* (Bogotá) 2(2), 219–264.

——. 1956. "Religious Life of the Páez Indians of Colombia." M.A. thesis, Columbia University, New York.

Beverley, John. 1993. *Against Literature.* Minneapolis: University of Minnesota Press.

——. 1999. *Subalternity and Representation: Arguments in Cultural Theory.* Durham, N.C.: Duke University Press.

Bilbao, Jorge, ed. 2001. *Cosmovisión indígena y biodiversidad en América Latina.* Cochabamba: COMPAS/AGRUCO.

Bishop, Russell. 1994. "Initiating Empowering Research?" *New Zealand Journal of Educational Studies* 29(1), 175–188.

Bodnar C., Yolanda. 1989. "El proceso de etnoeducación en Colombia: Una alternativa para el ejercicio de la autonomía." In Luis Enrique López and Ruth Moya, eds., *Pueblos indios, estados y educación*, pp. 71–86. Lima: PEB-Puno/Proyecto EBI/Programa ERA.

Bolaños, Graciela, Patricia Cerón, Martha Mendoza, Mélida Camayo, Isidro Fernández, Vaila Osnás, and River Chate. 1998. *Educación para comunidades indígenas: Hacia una secundaria integral: Centro de Formación Integral Luís Angel Monroy, Pueblo Nuevo, Caldono.* Popayán: PEB-CRIC.

Bolaños, Graciela, Abelardo Ramos, Joanne Rappaport, and Carlos Miñana. 2004. *¿Qué pasaría si la escuela . . . ? Treinta años de construcción educativa.* Popayán: PEBI-CRIC.

Bolaños, Graciela, and Peter Strack. 2001. "Parientes del Cauca: Entrevista con Graciela Bolaños." *Terre des Hommes 2000/2001*, 27–37.

Bonilla, Víctor Daniel. 1977. *Historia política de los paeces*. Bogotá: Carta al CRIC, 4.

———. 1982. "Algunas experiencias del proyecto 'Mapas Parlantes.'" In Juan Eduardo García Huidobro, ed., *Alfabetización y educación de adultos en la región andina*, pp. 145–161. Pátzcuaro, Mexico: UNESCO.

———. 1995. "Itinerario de una militancia paralela: La lucha por los derechos indígenas y la lucha por la democratización en Colombia." In Alicia Barabas, Miguel Bartolomé, and Salomón Nahmad, eds., *Articulación de la diversidad: Pluralidad étnica, autonomía y democratización en América Latina, Grupo de Barbados*, pp. 323–345. Quito: Abya-Yala.

Bonilla, Víctor Daniel, Gonzalo Castillo, Orlando Fals Borda, and Augusto Libreros. 1972. *Causa popular, ciencia popular: Una metodología del conocimiento científico a través de la acción*. Bogotá: La Rosca de Investigación y Acción Social.

Borque, Jesús, and Consejo Regional Indígena del Cauca (CRIC). 1996. *Nasa tul/La huerta nasa*. Popayán: CRIC. Video.

Bourke, Paul. 1996. "Klein Bottle." http://astronomy.swin.edu.au/~pbourke/surfaces/klein.

Briggs, Charles L. 1996. "The Politics of Discursive Authority in Research on the 'Invention of Tradition.'" *Cultural Anthropology* 11(4), 435–469.

Brown, Elsa Barkley. 1989. "African-American Women's Quilting: A Framework for Conceptualizing and Teaching African-American Women's History." *Signs: Journal of Women in Culture and Society* 14(4), 921–929.

Brysk, Alison. 2000. *From Tribal Village to Global Village: Indian Rights and International Relations in Latin America*. Stanford: Stanford University Press.

Caiza, José. 1989. "Hacia un modelo de educación bilingüe autogestionario." In Luis Enrique López and Ruth Moya, eds., *Pueblos indios, estados y educación*, pp. 309–325. Lima: PEB-Puno/Proyecto EBI/Programa ERA.

Caldeira, Teresa P. R. 2000. *City of Walls: Crime, Segregation, and Citizenship in São Paulo*. Berkeley: University of California Press.

Caldono, Autoridades Tradicionales del Territorio de. 2002. "Nuestra posición cultural y política: Resolución de la Asamblea Permanente del Territorio Ancestral del Pueblo Nasa (Indígena) de Caldono." Caldono, Cauca. Mimeo.

Camayo, Mélida. 2001. "Sakhelu: El despertar del espíritu de las semillas/Sakhelu's yu'skhewnxi." *Çxayu'çe* (Popayán) 5, 4–10.

Campbell, Howard. 1994. *Zapotec Renaissance: Ethnic Politics and Cultural Revivalism in Southern Mexico*. Albuquerque: University of New Mexico Press.

———. 1996. "Isthmus Zapotec Intellectuals: Cultural Production and Politics in Juchitán, Oaxaca." In Howard Campbell, ed., *The Politics of Ethnicity in Southern Mexico*, pp. 77–98. Nashville, Tenn.: Vanderbilt University Publications in Anthropology, no. 50.

Campisi, Jack. 1991. *The Mashpee Indians: Tribe on Trial*. Syracuse, N.Y.: Syracuse University Press.

Cardoso de Oliveira, Roberto. 1995. "Notas sobre uma estilística da antropologia." In Roberto Cardoso de Oliveira and Guillermo Raul Ruben, eds., *Estilos de antropologia*, pp. 177–189. Campinas: Editorial da Unicamp.

Castañeda, Jorge G. 1993.*Utopia Unarmed: The Latin American Left after the Cold War.* New York: Knopf.

Castellanos, Juan de. 1944 [1589]. *Elegías de varones ilustres de Indias.* Madrid: Biblioteca de Autores Españoles.

Castillo-Cárdenas, Gonzalo. 1971. "Manuel Quintín Lame: Luchador e intelectual indígena del siglo XX." In Manuel Quintín Lame, *En defensa de mi raza*, pp. xi–xlv. Bogotá: Comité de Defensa del Indio.

———. 1987. *Liberation Theology from Below: The Life and Thought of Manuel Quintín Lame.* Maryknoll, N.Y.: Orbis.

Castillo y Orozco, Eugenio del. 1877 [1755]. *Diccionario páez-castellano . . .* Transcribed by Ezequiel Uricoechea. Paris: Collection Linguistique Américaine, no. 2.

Castrillón Arboleda, Diego. 1973. *El indio Quintín Lame.* Bogotá: Tercer Mundo.

Cauca, Departamento del (Consejo del Gobierno Departamental). 2001. " 'En minga por el Cauca': Plan de desarrollo departamental 2001–2003." Popayán. Manuscript.

Caviedes, Mauricio. 2000. "Antropología y movimiento indígena." Tesis de grado, Universidad Nacional de Colombia, Bogotá.

Chakrabarty, Dipesh. 2000. *Provincializing Europe: Postcolonial Thought and Historical Difference.* Princeton, N.J.: Princeton University Press.

Chandler, Nahum Dimitri. 1996. "The Economy of Desedimentation: W. E. B. Du Bois and the Discourses of the Negro." *Callaloo* 19(1), 78–93.

———. 2000. "Originary Displacement." *Boundary* 2 27(3), 249–286.

Chocué Guasaquillo, Ana Alicia. 2000. "Nuestra doble conciencia." *C'ayu'ce* (Popayán) 4, 14–15.

Choque, Roberto, Vitaliano Soria, Humberto Mamani, Estéban Ticona, and Ramón Conde. n.d. *Educación indígena ¿Ciudadanía o colonización?* La Paz: THOA.

Chow, Rey. 1995. *Primitive Passions: Visuality, Sexuality, Ethnography, and Contemporary Chinese Cinema.* New York: Columbia University Press.

Cifuentes Muñoz, Eduardo. 1994. *Comunidad indígena-naturaleza/indefensión frente a comunidades indígenas.* Sentencia no. T-254/94, Corte Constitucional, Bogotá.

———. 1998. *Resguardo indígena ike o arhuaco—características generales.* Sentencia no. SU-510/98, Corte Constitucional, Bogotá.

Clandfield, David, and John Sivell. 1990. *Cooperative Learning and Social Change: Selected Writings of Célestin Freinet.* Toronto: Our Schools/Our Selves, OISE Publishing.

Clifford, James. 1986. "On Ethnographic Allegory." In James Clifford and George Marcus, eds., *Writing Culture: The Poetics and Politics of Ethnography*, pp. 98–121. Berkeley: University of California Press.

———. 1988. *The Predicament of Culture: Twentieth-Century Ethnography, Literature, and Art.* Cambridge, Mass.: Harvard University Press.

Cojtí Cuxil, Demetrio. 1997. *Ri maya' moloj pa iximuleu/El movimiento maya (en Guatemala).* Guatemala City: Editorial Cholsamaj.

Collier, George A., and Lynn Stephen, eds. 1997. *Ethnicity, Identity, and Citizenship in the Wake of the Zapatista Rebellion.* Special issue, *Journal of Latin American Anthropology* 3(1).

Collins, Patricia Hill. 1991. *Black Feminist Thought: Knowledge, Consciousness, and the Politics of Empowerment.* New York: Routledge.

Colombia, República de. 1970. *Legislación Nacional sobre indígenas.* Bogotá: Imprenta Nacional.

———. 1991. *Nueva Constitución política de Colombia.* Pasto: Minilibrería Jurídica Moral.

Colombia, República de, Dirección General de Asuntos Indígenas. 1997. *"Del olvido surgimos para traer nuevas esperanzas"—la jurisdicción especial indígena.* Bogotá: Ministerio de Justicia y del Derecho/Ministerio del Interior, Dirección General de Asuntos Indígenas.

Comisión de Alfabeto Nasa. 2001. *Somos patrimonio: El diseño técnico y la socialización de un alfabeto unificado para el "nasa yuwe," un paso importante hacia la unidad del pueblo "nasa" (páez) alrededor de su lengua y cultura.* Bogotá: Premio Nacional de Cultura y Medio Ambiente.

COMPAS Partners. 1996. "Joint Learning about Cosmovisions." *ILEIA Newsletter* 12(2), 26–27.

Comunidad Indígena de Juan Tama. 2000. *Cxa' kutya'/Volver a nacer.* Popayán: Consejo Regional Indígena del Cauca (CRIC). Video.

Condori Chura, Leandro, and Esteban Ticona Alejo. 1992. *El escribano de los caciques apoderados/kasikinakan purirarunakan qillqiripa.* La Paz: THOA/Hisbol.

Consejo Regional Indígena del Cauca (CRIC). 1990a. "Elaboración de currículo en comunidades indígenas paeces." Popayán: PEB-CRIC. Manuscript.

———. 1990b. *Etapas del desarrollo del niño nasa.* Popayán: PEB-CRIC.

———. 1991. *Sa't üus: Libro de comunicación oral y escrita, en Nasa Yuwe para primero y segundo grado de primaria, de las escuelas de Educación Intercultural Bilingüe.* Popayán: CRIC.

———. 1993. *Generalidades del nasa yuwe: Material de trabajo.* Popayán: PEB-CRIC y Asuntos Indígenas Cauca del Ministerio de Gobierno.

———. 1996. "Proyecto: Educación bilingüe en las comunidades indígenas del Cauca, años 1.992–1.995." Popayán: PEB-CRIC. Manuscript.

———. 1997. *Propuesta de formación superior: Licenciatura en Pedagogía Comunitaria.* Popayán: PEB-CRIC. Manuscript.

———. 2000. "Informe final, Profesionalización Consejo Regional Indígena del Cauca." Popayán: PEB-CRIC. Manuscript.

———. 2002. "Consolidación del sistema educativo de los pueblos indígenas del departamento del Cauca." Popayán: PEB-CRIC. Manuscript.

——. n.d.a. *Conociendo nuestra vida: Kwe's' u'hun'is hiyuna.* Popayán: PEB-CRIC.

——. n.d.b. *Escuela, comunidad y trabajo: Kwe's' hiyun'i's akiahn'i kwe's' üsn'i kiwe; kwe's' mahin'i.* Popayán: PEB-CRIC.

——. n.d.c. *Nasa Yuwete pissan f'i'n'i: El alfabeto Nasa Yuwe.* Popayán: PEB-CRIC.

——. n.d.d. *Representando nuestro mundo: Kwe's' fi'zen'i kiwe.* Popayán: PEB-CRIC.

Cook-Lynn, Elizabeth. 1998. "American Indian Intellectuals and the New Indian Story." In Devon A. Mihesuah, ed., *Natives and Academics: Researching and Writing about American Indians,* pp. 111–138. Lincoln: University of Nebraska Press.

Crehan, Kate. 2002. *Gramsci, Culture and Anthropology.* Berkeley: University of California Press.

Dagua Hurtado, Abelino, Misael Aranda, and Luis Guillermo Vasco. 1998. *Guambianos: Hijos del aroiris y del agua.* Bogotá: Los Cuatro Elementos.

Damen, Franz. 1989. "Hacia una teología de la inculturación." *Yachay* (Cochabamba) 10, 41–78.

de Certeau, Michel. 1986. *Heterologies: Discourse on the Other.* Trans. Brian Massumi. Minneapolis: University of Minnesota Press.

De la Cadena, Marisol. 2000. *Indigenous Mestizos: The Politics of Race and Culture in Cuzco, Peru, 1919–1991.* Durham, N.C.: Duke University Press.

Dover, Robert V. H. 1998. "Fetichismo, derechos e identidad en el pensamiento político indígena." In María Lucía Sotomayor, ed., *Modernidad, identidad y desarrollo: Construcción de sociedad y re-creación cultural en contextos de modernización,* pp. 41–50. Bogotá: Instituto Colombiano de Antropología.

Du Bois, W. E. B. 1989 [1903]. *The Souls of Black Folk.* New York: Bantam.

Dumont, Jean-Paul. 1992. *The Headman and I: Ambiguity and Ambivalence in the Fieldworking Experience.* Prospect Heights, Ill.: Waveland.

Edelman, Marc. 1999. *Peasants against Globalization: Rural Social Movements in Costa Rica.* Stanford: Stanford University Press.

——. 2001. "Social Movements: Changing Paradigms and Forms of Politics." *Annual Review of Anthropology* 30, 285–317.

Escobar, Arturo, and Sonia Alvarez, eds. 1992. *The Making of Social Movements in Latin America: Identity, Strategy, and Democracy.* Boulder, Colo.: Westview.

Escuela del Pensamiento Nasa. 1996. *Memorias del Primer y Segundo Encuentro.* Pitayó. Manuscript.

——. 1997. *Cue'sh uus yaatyni: Encuentro de socialización, Reubicación de Tóez, Caloto, noviembre 15 y 16 de 1997.* Popayán: Fundación para la Comunicación Popular.

Espinosa, Myriam Amparo. 1996. *Surgimiento y andar territorial del Quintín Lame.* Quito: Abya-Yala.

Estrada Álvarez, Jairo, ed. 2001. *Plan Colombia: Ensayos críticos.* Bogotá: Universidad Nacional de Colombia, Facultad de Derecho, Ciencias Políticas y Sociales.

Fabian, Johannes. 1983. *Time and the Other: How Anthropology Makes Its Object.* New York: Columbia University Press.

Fahim, Hussein, and Katherine Helmer. 1980. "Indigenous Anthropology in Non-Western Countries: A Further Elaboration." *Current Anthropology* 21(5), 644–663.

Fals Borda, Orlando. 1979a. *El problema de como investigar la realidad para transformarla: Por la praxis.* Bogotá: Ediciones Tercer Mundo.

———. 1979b. *Mompox y Loba: Historia doble de la Costa 1.* Bogotá: Carlos Valencia Editores.

———. 1981. *El Presidente Nieto: Historia doble de la Costa 2.* Bogotá: Carlos Valencia Editores.

———. 1984. *Resistencia en el San Jorge: Historia doble de la Costa 3.* Bogotá: Carlos Valencia Editores.

———. 1986. *Retorno a la tierra: Historia doble de la Costa 4.* Bogotá: Carlos Valencia Editores.

Fanon, Frantz. 1963. *The Wretched of the Earth.* New York: Grove Weidenfeld.

Feierman, Steven. 1990. *Peasant Intellectuals: Anthropology and History in Tanzania.* Madison: University of Wisconsin Press.

Ferguson, James, and Akhil Gupta. 2002. "Spatializing States: Toward an Ethnography of Neoliberal Governmentality." *American Ethnologist* 29(4), 981–1002.

Fernández, María Stella, and Freddy Osorio. 1994. *Amapola: ¿Solución o destrucción?* Popayán: Consejo Regional Indígena del Cauca (CRIC). Video.

Fernández Osco, Marcelo. 2000. *La ley del* ayllu: *Práctica de* jach'a *justicia y* jisk'a *justicia (justicia mayor y justicia menor) en comunidades aymaras.* La Paz: PIEB.

———. 2002. "Mirando con ojos de pasado y presente: Un mecanismo de descolonización del conocimiento." Paper presented at the annual meeting of the American Anthropological Association, New Orleans, November.

Field, Les. 1999. "Complicities and Collaborations: Anthropologists and the 'Unacknowledged Tribes' of California." *Current Anthropology* 40(2), 193–209.

———. 2002. "Blood and Traits: Preliminary Observations on the Analysis of Mestizo and Indigenous Identities in Latin vs. North America." *Journal of Latin American Anthropology* 7(1), 2–33.

———. in press. a. "Abalone Tales: Natural Histories, Pristine Moments, Native Voices in California." In Kevin Yelvington and Maximilian Fortes, eds., *Indigenous Identities and World Capitalism: Anthropologies of the Past and Future.* Manuscript.

———. in press. b. "From Applied Anthropology to Applications of Anthropology for Tribal Goals: Examples from Indian Country." In Thomas Bilosi, ed., *A Companion to the Anthropology of North American Indians.* Oxford: Blackwell.

Findji, María Teresa. 1992. "From Resistance to Social Movement: The Indigenous Authorities Movement in Colombia." In Arturo Escobar and Sonia Alvarez, eds., *The Making of Social Movements in Latin America: Identity, Strategy, and Democracy,* pp. 112–133. Boulder, Colo.: Westview.

Findji, María Teresa, and José María Rojas. 1985. *Territorio, economía y sociedad páez.* Cali: Editorial Universidad del Valle.

Fischer, Edward F. 2001. *Cultural Logics and Global Economies: Maya Identity in Thought and Practice*. Austin: University of Texas Press.

Fischer, Edward F., and R. McKenna Brown, eds. 1996. *Maya Cultural Activism in Guatemala*. Austin: University of Texas Press.

Foucault, Michel. 1977. *Power/Knowledge: Selected Interviews and Other Writings 1972–1977*. Ed. Colin Gordon. New York: Random House.

Fox, Richard G. 1989. *Gandhian Utopia: Experiments with Culture*. Boston: Beacon Press.

Fraser, Nancy. 1997. *Justice Interruptus: Critical Reflections on the "Postsocialist" Condition*. New York: Routledge.

Freire, Paulo. 1993. *Pedagogy of the Oppressed*. Trans. Myra Bergman Ramos. New York: Continuum.

Friedman, Jonathan. 1994. *Cultural Identity and Global Process*. London: Sage.

Fuss, Diana. 1989. *Essentially Speaking: Feminism, Nature, and Difference*. New York: Routledge.

García Bravo, William. 1992. "Elementos históricos para la comprensión del fenómeno educativo en zonas indígenas del nororiente caucano." Paper presented at the Primer Congreso Iberoamericano de Docentes e Investigadores en la Historia de la Educación en Latinoamérica, Bogotá, 2–5 September.

——. 1996. "Tendencias de la educación indígena en Colombia: 1985–1995." Paper presented at the Tercer Congreso Iberoamericano de Historia de la Educación Latinoamericana, Caracas, 9–14 June.

——. 1998. "The Teaching Profession in the Multicultural Educational Framework: A Case Study in Native Communities of Cauca, Colombia." M.A. thesis, Concordia University, Montreal, Canada.

García Canclini, Néstor, Alejandro Castellanos, and Ana Rosas Mantecón. 1996. *La ciudad de los viajeros: Travesías e imaginarios urbanos, México, 1940–2000*. México, D.F.: Universidad Autónoma Metropolitana Iztapalapa/Grijalbo.

García Isaza, Mario. 1996. *Gramática páez: Nasa yuwe's ew jiyuwa'j fi'jni'*. Bogotá: Prefectura Apostólica de Tierradentro.

Gaviria Díaz, Carlos. 1997. *Diversidad étnica y cultural-reconocimiento constitucional*. Sentencia no. T-523/97, Corte Constitucional, Bogotá.

Gill, Lesley. 1994. *Precarious Dependencies: Gender, Class, and Domestic Service in Bolivia*. New York: Columbia University Press.

Gilly, Adolfo. 1995. *Discusión sobre la historia*. Mexico City: Taurus.

Gilroy, Paul. 1987. *"There Ain't No Black in the Union Jack": The Cultural Politics of Race and Nation*. Chicago: University of Chicago Press.

——. 1993. *The Black Atlantic: Modernity and Double Consciousness*. Cambridge, Mass.: Harvard University Press.

Giroux, Henry A. 1988. *Teachers as Intellectuals: Toward a Critical Pedagogy of Learning*. Westport, Conn.: Bergin and Garvey.

Gómez, Herinaldy. 1995. "El derecho étnico ante el derecho estatal." *Convergencia* (México) 3 (8–9), 295–316.

———. 1999. "Crisis de la justicia y la jurisdicción indígena en Colombia." *Convergencia* (México) 6 (18), 285–308.

———. 2000. *De la justicia y el poder indígena*. Popayán: Editorial Universidad del Cauca.

Gómez, Herinaldy, and Carlos Ariel Ruiz. 1997. *Los paeces: Gente territorio: Metáfora que perdura*. Popayán: FUNCOP/Universidad del Cauca.

Gómez López, Ana María. 2003. "Legitimacies of Justice: Nasa Communities, the State, and Legal Pluralism in Northern Cauca, Colombia." Undergraduate thesis, University of Pennsylvania, Philadelphia.

González, Fr. David. n.d. *Los paeces o genocidio y luchas indígenas en Colombia*. N.p.: La Rueda Suelta.

González Echevarría, Roberto. 1990. *Myth and Archive: A Theory of Latin American Narrative*. Cambridge, England: Cambridge University Press.

Gottret, Gustavo. 1999. "Interculturalidad en el aula." In Nora Mengoa, ed., *Interculturalidad y calidad de los aprendizajes en ámbitos escolares urbanos*, pp. 31–39. La Paz: Centro Boliviano de Investigación y Acción Educativas.

Gould, Jeffrey. 1998. *To Die in This Way: Nicaraguan Indians and the Myth of Mestizaje, 1880–1965*. Durham, N.C.: Duke University Press.

Gow, David D. 1997. "Can the Subaltern Plan? Ethnicity and Development in Cauca, Colombia." *Urban Anthropology* 26(3–4), 243–292.

———. 2005. "Desde afuera y desde adentro: Planificación indígena como contra-desarrollo." In Joanne Rappaport, ed., *Retornando la mirada: Una investigación colaborativa interétnica sobre el Cauca a la entrada del milenio*, pp. 67–100. Popayán: Editorial Universidad del Cauca.

Gow, David D., and Joanne Rappaport. 2002. "The Indigenous Public Voice: The Multiple Idioms of Modernity in Indigenous Cauca." In Kay B. Warren and Jean Jackson, eds., *Indigenous Movements, Self-Representation, and the State in Latin America*, pp. 47–80. Austin: University of Texas Press.

Gramsci, Antonio. 1971. *Selections from the Prison Notebooks*. New York: International Publishers.

Grandin, Greg. 2000. *The Blood of Guatemala: A History of Race and Nation*. Durham, N.C.: Duke University Press.

Gros, Christian. 1991. *Colombia indígena: Identidad cultural y cambio social*. Bogotá: CEREC.

———. 1993. "Derechos indígenas y nueva Constitución en Colombia." *Análisis Político* (Bogotá) 19, 8–24.

———. 1997. "Indigenismo y etnicidad: El desafío neoliberal." In María Victoria Uribe and Eduardo Restrepo, eds., *Antropología en la modernidad*, pp. 15–59. Bogotá: Instituto Colombiano de Antropología.

———. 2000. *Políticas de la etnicidad: Identidad, Estado y modernidad*. Bogotá: Instituto Colombiano de Antropología e Historia.

Grueso, Libia, Carlos Rosero, and Arturo Escobar. 1998. "The Process of Black Community Organizing in the Southern Pacific Coast Region of Colombia." In Sonia Alvarez, Evelina Dagnino, and Arturo Escobar, eds., *Cultures of Politics, Politics of Cultures: Re-visioning Latin American Social Movements*, pp. 196–219. Boulder, Colo.: Westview.

Guambía, Cabildo, Taitas y Comisión de Trabajo del Pueblo Guambiano. 1994. *Diagnóstico y plan de vida del Pueblo Guambiano*. Territorio Guambiano/Silvia: Cabildo de Guambía/CENCOA/Corporación Autónoma Regional del Cauca/Visión Mundial Internacional.

Guambía, Comunidad Indígena de. 1980. *Manifiesto guambiano*. Silvia. Mimeo.

Gupta, Akhil. 1995. "Blurred Boundaries: The Discourse of Corruption, the Culture of Power, and the Imagined State." *American Ethnologist* 22(2), 375–403.

Gutiérrez, Natividad. 1999. *Nationalist Myths and Ethnic Identities: Indigenous Intellectuals and the Mexican State*. Lincoln: University of Nebraska Press.

Gwaltney, John L. 1981. "Common Sense and Science: Urban Core Black Observations." In Donald A. Messerschmidt, ed., *Anthropologists at Home in North America: Methods and Issues in the Study of One's Own Society*, pp. 46–61. Cambridge, England: Cambridge University Press.

——. 1993. *Drylongso: A Self-Portrait of Black America*. New York: New Press.

Hale, Charles R. 1997. "Cultural Politics of Identity in Latin America." *Annual Review of Anthropology* 26, 567–590.

——. 2002. "Does Multiculturalism Menace? Governance, Cultural Rights and the Politics of Identity in Guatemala." *Journal of Latin American Studies* 34, 485–524.

Hall, Stuart. 1996 [1989]. "New Ethnicities." In David Morley and Kuan-Hsing Chen, eds., *Stuart Hall: Critical Dialogues in Cultural Studies*, pp. 441–449. London: Routledge.

Haraway, Donna. 1988. "Situated Knowledges: The Science Question in Feminism and the Privilege of Partial Perspective." *Feminist Studies* 14(3), 575–599.

Hardman, Martha. 1988. "Jaqi aru: La lengua humana." In Xavier Albó, ed., *Raíces de América: El mundo aymara*, pp. 155–205. Madrid: Alianza.

Harris, Olivia. 2000. *To Make the Earth Bear Fruit: Essays on Fertility, Work and Gender in Highland Bolivia*. London: Institute of Latin American Studies.

Harrison, Regina. 1989. *Signs, Songs, and Memory in the Andes: Translating Quechua Language and Culture*. Austin: University of Texas Press.

Hartsock, Nancy. 1990. "Rethinking Modernism: Minority vs. Majority Theories." In Abdul R. JanMohamed and David Lloyd, eds., *The Nature and Context of Minority Discourse*, pp. 17–36. Oxford: Oxford University Press.

Heise, María, Fidel Tubino, and Wilfredo Ardito. 1994. *Interculturalidad: Un desafío*. Lima: Centro Amazónico de Antropología y Aplicación Práctica.

Hernández, R. Aída. 2002. "Indigenous Law and Identity Politics in Mexico: Indigenous Men's and Women's Struggles for a Multicultural Nation." *Political and Legal Anthropology Review* 25(1), 90–109.

Hernández de Alba, Gregorio. 1963. "The Highland Tribes of Southern Colombia." In

Julian Steward, ed., *Handbook of South American Indians*, vol. 2, pp. 915–960. New York: Cooper Square.

Hernández Díaz, Jorge. 1996. "The Bilingual Teachers: A New Indigenous Intelligentsia." In Howard Campbell, ed., *The Politics of Ethnicity in Southern Mexico*, pp. 41–58. Nashville, Tenn.: Vanderbilt University Publications in Anthropology, no. 50.

Herron, James. 2003. "The Embodied State: Discourse Genres in the Caja Agraria, Guambía, Colombia." Ph.D. dissertation, University of Michigan, Ann Arbor.

Hobsbawm, Eric, and Terence Ranger, eds. 1983. *The Invention of Tradition*. Cambridge, England: Cambridge University Press.

Hornberger, Nancy H. 1988. *Bilingual Education and Language Maintenance: A Southern Peruvian Quechua Case*. Dordrecht, Netherlands: Foris Publications.

Houghton, Juan. 1998. "¿A dónde apunta la educación en los pueblos indígenas?" In María Trillos Amaya, ed., *Educación endógena frente a educación formal*, pp. 51–67. Bogotá: Centro Ediciones CCELA-UniAndes.

Howard-Malverde, Rosaleen. 1990. *The Speaking of History: "Willapaakushayki" or Quechua Ways of Telling the Past*. London: University of London, Institute of Latin American Studies, Research papers 21.

Isbell, Billie Jean. 1978. *To Defend Ourselves: Ecology and Ritual in an Andean Village*. Austin: University of Texas Press.

Jackson, Jean E. 1995. "Preserving Indian Culture: Shaman Schools and Ethno-Education in the Vaupés, Colombia." *Cultural Anthropology* 10(3), 302–339.

——. 1999. "The Politics of Ethnographic Practice in the Colombian Vaupés." *Identities* 6(2–3), 281–317.

——. 2002. "Contested Discourses of Authority in Colombian National Indigenous Politics: The 1996 Summer Takeovers." In Kay B. Warren and Jean E. Jackson, eds., *Indigenous Movements, Self-Representation, and the State in Latin America*, pp. 81–122. Austin: University of Texas Press.

Jacoby, Russell. 1987. *The Last Intellectuals: American Culture in the Age of Academe*. New York: Basic.

Jimeno, Myriam. 1996. "Juan Gregorio Palechor: Tierra, identidad y recreación étnica." *Journal of Latin American Anthropology* 1(2), 46–77.

——. 1999. "Desde el punto de vista de la periferia: Desarrollo profesional y conciencia social." *Anuario Antropológico* (Rio de Janeiro) 97, 59–72.

——. 2000. "La emergencia del investigador ciudadano: Estilos de antropología y crisis de modelos en la antropología colombiana." In Jairo Tocancipá, ed., *La formación del Estado-nación y las disciplinas sociales en Colombia*, pp. 157–190. Popayán: Editorial Universidad del Cauca.

Jolicoeur, Luis. 1994. *El cristianismo aymara: ¿Inculturación o culturización?* Cochabamba: Universidad Católica Boliviana.

Jones, Delmos J. 1970. "Towards a Native Anthropology." *Human Organization* 29(4), 251–259.

Karabel, Jerome. 1976. "Revolutionary Contradictions: Antonio Gramsci and the Problem of Intellectuals." *Politics and Society* 6, 123–172.

Keane, Webb. 1996. "Materialism, Missionaries, and Modern Subjects in Colonial Indonesia." In Peter van derVeer, ed., *Conversion to Modernities: The Globalization of Christianity*, pp. 137–170. New York: Routledge.

Kieft, Johan. 1999. "Farmer's Decisions and Cosmovision." COMPAS *Newsletter*, February, 18–19.

King, Cecil. 1997. "Here Come the Anthros." In Thomas Biolsi and Larry Zimmerman, eds., *Indians and Anthropologists: Vine Deloria, Jr., and the Critique of Anthropology*, pp. 115–119. Tucson: University of Arizona Press.

Kirk, Robin. 2003. *More Terrible Than Death: Massacres, Drugs, and America's War in Colombia*. New York: Public Affairs.

Krech, Shepard, III. 1999. *The Ecological Indian: Myth and History*. New York: Norton.

Krotz, Esteban. 1997. "Anthropologies of the South: Their Rise, Their Silencing, Their Characteristics." *Critique of Anthropology* 17(3), 237–251.

Kymlicka, Will. 1995. *Multicultural Citizenship: A Liberal Theory of Minority Rights*. Oxford: Clarendon.

Laclau, Ernesto. 1996. *Emancipations*. London: Verso.

Laclau, Ernesto, and Chantal Mouffe. 1985. *Hegemony and Socialist Strategy: Towards a Radical Democratic Politics*. London: Verso.

Lame, Manuel Quintín. 1971 [1939]. *En defensa de mi raza*. Ed. Gonzalo Castillo Cárdenas. Bogotá: Comité de Defensa del Indio.

——. 2004 [1939]. *Los pensamientos del indio que se educó dentro de las selvas colombianas*. Cali: Editorial Universidad del Valle/Popayán: Editorial Universidad del Cauca.

Landsman, Gail. 1997. "Informant as Critic: Conducting Research on a Dispute between Iroquoianist Scholars and Traditional Iroquois." In Thomas Biolsi and Larry Zimmerman, eds., *Indians and Anthropologists: Vine Deloria, Jr., and the Critique of Anthropology*, pp. 160–176. Tucson: University of Arizona Press.

Laurent, Virginie. 2001. *Pueblos indígenas y espacios políticos en Colombia: Motivaciones, campos de acción e impactos (1990–1998)*. Final report, Convocatoria Becas Nacionales, Ministerio de Cultura, República de Colombia.

Leal Buitrago, Francisco, and Marc W. Chernick, eds. 1999. *Los laberintos de la guerra: Utopías e incertidumbres sobre la paz*. Bogotá: Universidad de los Andes, Facultad de Ciencias Sociales.

Lee, William B., and John Sivell. 2000. *French Elementary Education and the Ecole Moderne*. Bloomington, Ind.: Phi Delta Kappa Educational Foundation.

Leech, Garry M. 2002. *Killing Peace: Colombia's Conflict and the Failure of U.S. Intervention*. New York: Information Network of the Americas.

León, Jorge. 1994. *De campesinos a ciudadanos diferentes*. Quito: CEDIME/Abya-Yala.

León, Jorge, and María Eugenia Quintero. 1989. "Simiatug: Autogestión en la escuela." In Luis Enrique López and Ruth Moya, eds., *Pueblos indios, estados y educación*, pp. 327–351. Lima: PEB-Puno/Proyecto EBI/Programa ERA.

Lévi-Strauss, Claude. 1963. *Structural Anthropology*. New York: Basic Books.

Limón, José. 1994. *Dancing with the Devil: Society and Cultural Poetics in Mexican-American South Texas*. Madison: University of Wisconsin Press.

Liu, Lydia H. 1995. *Translingual Practice: Literature, National Culture, and Translated Modernity, China, 1900–1937*. Stanford: Stanford University Press.

Lomnitz, Claudio. 1992. *Exits from the Labyrinth: Culture and Ideology in the Mexican National Space*. Berkeley: University of California Press.

———. 2001. *Deep Mexico, Silent Mexico: An Anthropology of Nationalism*. Minneapolis: University of Minnesota Press.

López, Luis Enrique. 1991. "Educación bilingüe en Puno-Perú: Hacia un ajuste de cuentas." In Madeleine Zúñiga, Inés Pozzi-Escot, and Luis Enrique López, eds., *Educación bilingüe intercultural, reflexiones y desafíos*, pp. 173–217. Lima: FOMCIENCIAS.

———. *La educación en áreas indígenas de América Latina: Apreciaciones comparativas desde la educación bilingüe intercultural*. Guatemala City: CECMA, Centro de Estudios de la Cultura Maya.

———. "No más danzas de ratones grises: Sobre interculturalidad, democracia y educación." In Juan Godenzzi Alegre, ed., *Educación e interculturalidad en los Andes y la Amazonía*, pp. 23–80. Cusco: Centro de Estudios Regionales "Bartolomé de Las Casas," Serie Estudios y Debates Regionales Andinos, 93.

———. 1999. "El lenguaje en el desarrollo de los conocimientos en ámbitos escolares urbanos con diversidad cultural." In Nora Mengoa, ed., *Interculturalidad y calidad de los aprendizajes en ámbitos escolares urbanos*, pp. 47–70. La Paz: Centro Boliviano de Investigación y Acción Educativas.

López, Luis Enrique, and Ingrid Jung. 1988. *Las lenguas en la educación bilingüe: El caso de Puno*. Lima: GTZ, Deutsche Gesellschaft für Technische Zusammenarbeit/Sociedad Alemana de Cooperación Técnica.

López Adentro, Centro Educativo Comunitario Intercultural Bilingüe (CECIB). 1999. *Propuesta curricular, área: Territorio y sociedad*. Corinto. Manuscript.

López Hernández, Eleazar. 1992. "Teología india hoy." In *Teología india: Primer encuentro taller latinoamericano*, pp. 5–16. México: CENAMI.

Luykx, Aurolyn. 1996. "Bolivia's 'Campesino' Vice-President: International Activism and Post-Indigenous Identity." Paper presented at the annual meeting of the American Anthropological Association, San Francisco, November.

———. 1999. *The Citizen Factory: Schooling and Cultural Production in Bolivia*. Albany: State University of New York Press.

———. 2000. "Gender Equity and *Interculturalidad*: The Dilemma of Bolivian Education." *Journal of Latin American Anthropology* 5(2), 150–178.

———. n.d. "Theory into Practice: Indigenous Educators, Intercultural Pedagogy, and Anti-Anti-Essentialism." Manuscript.

Luykx, Aurolyn, and Martha Bustamante. 2000. "Reconceptualizing Interculturalism: Working Social Conflict from the Bottom Up." Paper presented at the annual meeting of the American Ethnological Society, Montreal, May.

Mallon, Florencia. 1995. *Peasant and Nation: The Making of Postcolonial Mexico and Peru.* Berkeley: University of California Press.

Mamani Quispe, Alejandro. 1988. *Historia y cultura de Cohana.* La Paz: Hisbol/Radio San Gabriel.

Mamdani, Mahmood. 2001. *When Victims Become Killers.* Princeton, N.J.: Princeton University Press.

Manzanera, Miguel. 1989. "Inculturación, evangelización y liberación: Reflexión teológica." *Yachay* (Cochabamba) 10, 81–112.

Martínez Caballero, Alejandro. 1994. *Servicio militar-exenciones/servicio militar prestado por indígenas.* Sentencia no. C-058/94, Corte Constitucional, Bogotá.

McNeil, Linda M. 1986. *Contradictions of Control: School Structure and School Knowledge.* New York: Routledge and Kegan Paul.

Medicine, Beatrice, with Sue-Ellen Jacobs. 2000. *Learning to Be an Anthropologist and Remaining "Native."* Urbana: University of Illinois Press.

Mejía Dindicué, Luis Ángel. 1989. *Quintín Lame: La caida del coloso colombiano.* Popayán. Manuscript.

Melià, Bartomeu. 1997. *El Paraguay inventado.* Asunción: Centro de Estudios Paraguayos "Antonio Guasch."

Mengoa, Nora. 1999. "Diversidad y procesos pedagógicos, lineamientos para una propuesta de educación intercultural en escuelas urbano-populares de la región andina en Bolivia." In Nora Mengoa, ed., *Interculturalidad y calidad de los aprendizajes en ámbitos escolares urbanos,* pp. 11–20. La Paz: Centro Boliviano de Investigación y Acción Educativas.

MENMAGUA. 1999. *Situación de pobreza del pueblo maya de Guatemala.* Guatemala City: MENMAGUA.

Merry, Sally Engle. 1988. "Legal Pluralism." *Law and Society Review* 22(5), 869–896.

Michaels, Eric. 1994. *Bad Aboriginal Art: Tradition, Media, and Technological Horizons.* Minneapolis: University of Minnesota Press.

Mignolo, Walter. 2000. *Local Histories/Global Designs: Coloniality, Subaltern Knowledges, and Border Thinking.* Princeton, N.J.: Princeton University Press.

Miller, Nicola. 1999. *In the Shadow of the State: Intellectuals and the Quest for National Identity in Twentieth-Century Spanish America.* London: Verso.

———. 2000. "The Anxiety of Ambivalence: Intellectuals and the State in Twentieth-Century Argentina, Chile, and Mexico." In Mariano Plotkin and Ricardo González Leandri, eds., *Localismo y globalización: Aportes para una historia de los intelectuales en Iberoamérica,* pp. 133–169. Madrid: Consejo Superior de Investigaciones Científicas, Instituto de Historia.

Molano, Alfredo. 2001. "La justicia guerrillera." In Boaventura de Sousa Santos and Mauricio García Villegas, eds., *El caleidoscopio de las justicias en Colombia,* vol. 2, pp. 331–388. Bogotá: Siglo de Hombre Editores.

Montejo, Víctor. 1987. *Testimony: The Death of a Guatemalan Village.* Willimantic, Conn.: Curbstone Press.

———. 2002. "The Multiplicity of Mayan Voices: Mayan Leadership and the Politics of Self-Representation." In Kay B. Warren and Jean E. Jackson, eds., *Indigenous Movements, Self-Representation, and the State in Latin America*, pp. 123–148. Austin: University of Texas Press.

Montejo, Víctor, and Q'anil Akab'. 1992. *Brevísima relación testimonial de la continua destrucción del Mayab' (Guatemala)*. Providence, R.I.: Maya Scholars Network.

Montoya, Rodrigo. 2001. "Límites y posibilidades de la educación bilingüe en el Perú." In Maria Heise, ed., *Interculturalidad: Creación de un concepto y desarrollo de una actitud*, pp. 165–179. Lima: Programa FORTE-PE/Ministerio de Educación.

Moore, Sally Falk. 1992. "Treating Law as Knowledge: Telling Colonial Officers What to Say to Africans about Running 'Their Own' Native Courts." *Law and Society Review* 26(1), 11–46.

Morales Tunubalá, Álvaro. 1997. "Sistema tradicional de juzgamiento en el pueblo guambiano." In República de Colombia, Dirección General de Asuntos Indígenas, ed., *"Del olvido surgimos para traer nuevas esperanzas"—la jurisdicción especial indígena*, pp. 73–85. Bogotá: Ministerio de Justicia y del Derecho/Ministerio del Interior.

Moreno B., Martha. 1998. "La educación popular en CINEP, un camino que deja huellas." In Fernán González, ed., *Una opción y muchas búsquedas: CINEP 25 años*, pp. 233–265. Bogotá: CINEP, Centro de Investigación y Educación Popular.

Mouffe, Chantal. 1995. "Democratic Politics and the Question of Identity." In John Rajchman, ed., *The Identity in Question*, pp. 33–45. London: Routledge.

Muehlebach, Andrea. 2001. "'Making Place' at the United Nations: Indigenous Cultural Politics at the U.N. Working Group on Indigenous Populations." *Cultural Anthropology* 16(3), 415–448.

Muelas Hurtado, Bárbara. 1995. "Relación espacio-tiempo en el pensamiento guambiano." *Proyecciones Lingüísticas* (Popayán) 1(1), 31–40.

Muelas Hurtado, Bárbara, et al. 1994. *Nupirau nu wamwan trek køntrai isua pørik: Apartes de la Constitución política de Colombia 1991 en guambiano*. Bogotá: CCELA-UniAndes.

Muñoz Alvear, Leoxmar Benjamín. 1997. *Acción de tutela impetrada por el señor Francisco Gembuel Pechené, en contra de los señores Luis Alberto Passú, Gobernador del Cabildo Indígena de Jambaló y Luis Alberto Fiscué, Presidente de la Asociación de Cabildos de la Zona Norte del Departamento del Cauca*. Sentencia del Juzgado Primero Penal Municipal, Santander de Quilichao (Cauca), 8 January.

Muñoz Cruz, Héctor. 1996. "Experiencias sociales y comunicativas como factores de la enseñanza/aprendizaje del lenguaje en contextos indoamericanos." Paper presented at the Taller Internacional "El Aprendizaje de Lenguas en Poblaciones Indígenas en América Latina: El Caso del Castellano," Santa Cruz de la Sierra, Bolivia, April.

Muratorio, Blanca. 1981. "Protestantism, Ethnicity, and Class in Chimborazo." In Norman E. Whitten Jr., ed., *Cultural Transformations and Ethnicity in Modern Ecuador*, pp. 506–534. Urbana: University of Illinois Press.

Nachtigall, Horst. 1953. "Shamanismo entre los indios paeces." *Revista colombiana de Folclor* (Bogotá) 2(2), 223–241.

——. 1955. *Tierradentro: Archeologie und Ethnographie einer Kolombianischen Landschaft*. Zurich: Otto Verlag.

Narayan, Kirin. 1993. "How Native Is a 'Native' Anthropologist?" *American Anthropologist* 95, 671–686.

Nash, June. 2001. *Mayan Visions: The Quest for Autonomy in an Age of Globalization*. New York: Routledge.

Nelson, Diane M. 1999. *A Finger in the Wound: Body Politics in Quincentennial Guatemala*. Berkeley: University of California Press.

Ng'weno, Bettina. 2002. "The State in Question: Afro-Colombians, Ethnic Territories and Governing in the Andes." Ph.D. dissertation, Johns Hopkins University, Baltimore.

Nieves Oviedo, Rocío, and Abelardo Ramos Pacho. 1992. "Expresión del espacio en nasa yuwe." In *Lenguas aborígenes de Colombia: Memorias 2 (II Congreso de CCELA)*, pp. 175–183. Bogotá: Universidad de los Andes.

Ocampo, Gloria Isabel. 1997. "Diversidad étnica y jurisdicción indígena en Colombia." *Boletín de Antropología* (Medellín) 11(27), 9–33.

Ohnuki-Tierney, Emiko. 1984. "'Native' Anthropologists." *American Ethnologist* 11, 584–586.

Ong, Walter J., S. J. 1982. *Orality and Literacy: The Technologizing of the Word*. London: Methuen.

Organización Nacional Indígena de Colombia (ONIC). 2002. *Los indígenas y la paz: Pronunciamientos, resoluciones, declaraciones y otros documentos de los pueblos y organizaciones indígenas sobre la violencia armada en sus territorios, la búsqueda de la paz, la autonomía y la resistencia*. Bogotá: Ediciones Turdakke.

Orta, Andrew. 1995. "From Theologies of Liberation to Theologies of Inculturation: Aymara Catechists and the *Second Evangelization* in Highlands Bolivia." In Satya R. Pattnayak, ed., *Organized Religion in the Political Transformation of Latin America*, pp. 97–124. Lanham, Md.: University Press of America.

——. 1998. "Converting Difference: Metaculture, Missionaries, and the Politics of Locality." *Ethnology* 37(2), 165–185.

——. 2000. "Syncretic Subjects and Body Politics: Doubleness, Personhood, and Aymara Catechists." *American Ethnologist* 26(4), 864–889.

——. 2005. *Catechizing Culture: Missionaries, Aymara, and the "New Evangelism."* New York: Colombia University Press.

Ortiz, Renato. 1985. *Cultura brasileira e identidade nacional*. São Paulo: Editoria Brasiliense.

——. 1998. *A moderna tradição brasileira: Cultura brasileira e indústria cultural*. São Paulo: Editoria Brasiliense.

Ortiz, Sutti R. 1973. *Uncertainties in Peasant Farming: A Colombian Case*. London School of Economics, Monographs on Social Anthropology, vol. 19. London: Athlone Press.

Osorio, Freddy Nelson, Fundación Sol y Tierra, and Daniel Piñacué. 1994. *Yu'up'hku/ Han parido las aguas*. Popayán: Fundación Sol y Tierra. Video.

Pabón Triana, Martha Lucía. 1986. "Maestros del Consejo Regional Indígena del Cauca-CRIC: Socialización y cambio cultural." Tesis de grado, Universidad de los Andes, Bogotá.

Page, Helan E. 1988. "Dialogic Principles of Interactive Learning in the Ethnographic Relationship." *Journal of Anthropological Research* 44(2), 163–181.

Paley, Julia. 2001. *Marketing Democracy: Power and Social Movements in Post-Dictatorship Chile*. Berkeley: University of California Press.

Pallares, Amalia. 2002. *From Peasant Struggles to Indian Resistance: The Ecuadorian Andes in the Late Twentieth Century*. Norman: University of Oklahoma Press.

Parra Sandoval, Rodrigo. 1996. *Escuela y modernidad en Colombia*, vol. 2, *La escuela rural*. Bogotá: Fundación FES/Fundación Restrepo Barco/Colciencias/IDEP/Tercer Mundo.

Passú, Luis Alberto, and Luis Alberto Fiscué. 1997. "Letter to Dr. Leodxmar [*sic*] Benjamín Muñóz Alvear, Juez Primero Municipal de Santander de Quilichao." 13 January. Manuscript.

Pécault, Daniel. 2001. *Guerra contra la sociedad*. Bogotá: Editorial Planeta.

Penagos, Jorge Eliécer. 2000. "Cómo pensaba Benjamín Dindicué sobre la educación propia." *C'ayu'ce* (Popayán) 4, 28–30.

Peñaranda, Ricardo. 1998. "Historia del Movimiento Armado Quintín Lame." M.A. thesis, Universidad Nacional de Colombia, Bogotá.

Perafán Simmonds, Carlos César. 1995. *Sistemas jurídicos paez, kogi, wayúu y tule*. Bogotá: Colcultura/Instituto Colombiano de Antropología.

Perdomo Dizú, Adonías. 1999. "Autonomía, autoridad y justicia interna en los resguardos de Pitayó Silvia, Pioyá Caldono y Pat Yu' Cajibío." Pitayó. Manuscript.

——. 2002. "La justicia interna y sus prácticas en el resguardo indígena de Pitayó." Pitayó. Manuscript.

——. 2005. "Actores de autoridad: Una mirada desde el pueblo nasa de Pitayó." In Joanne Rappaport, ed., *Retornando la mirada: Una investigación colaborativa interétnica sobre el Cauca a la entrada del milenio*, pp. 101–122. Popayán: Editorial Universidad del Cauca.

Piñacué, Jesús Enrique. 1997. "Ampliación autonómica de la justicia en comunidades paeces (una aproximación)." In República de Colombia, Dirección General de Asuntos Indígenas, ed., *"Del olvido surgimos para traer nuevas esperanzas"—la jurisdicción especial indígena*, pp. 31–52. Bogotá: Ministerio de Justicia y del Derecho/Ministerio del Interior.

Piñacué Achicué, Susana. 2005. "Liderazgo, poder y cultura de la mujer nasa (páez)." In Joanne Rappaport, ed., *Retornando la mirada: Una investigación colaborativa interetnica sobre el Cauca a la entrada del milenio*. pp. 57–66. Popayán: Editorial Universidad del Cauca.

Povinelli, Elizabeth. 2002. *The Cunning of Recognition: Indigenous Alterities and the Making of Australian Multiculturalism*. Durham, N.C.: Duke University Press.

Pratt, Mary Louise. 1991. "Arts of the Contact Zone." *Profession* 91, 33–40.

———. 1992. *Imperial Eyes: Travel Writing and Transculturation*. London: Routledge.

Price, Richard. 1990. *Alabi's World*. Baltimore: Johns Hopkins University Press.

Rama, Angel. 1996. *The Lettered City*. Durham, N.C.: Duke University Press.

Ramón Valarezo, Galo. 1993. *El regreso de los runas: La potencialidad del proyecto indio en el Ecuador contemporáneo*. Quito: Comunidec/Fundación Interamericana.

Ramos, Abelardo. 2000. "Acerca de la unificación del alfabeto Nasa Yuwe." *C'ayu'ce* (Popayán) 4, 52–53.

Ramos, Abelardo, Graciela Bolaños, Susana Piñacué, Luz Mary Niquinás, and Benjamín Ramos. 2000. "El area de comunicación y lenguaje en el proceso educativo del CRIC." Paper presented at the Segundo Congreso Nacional Universitario de Etnoeducación, Popayán, July.

Ramos, Abelardo, and Cabildo Indígena de Mosoco. 1993. *Ec ne'hwe's': Constitución política de Colombia en nasa yuwe*. Bogotá: CCELA-UniAndes.

Ramos, Abelardo, and Emiluth Collo. 2000. *Nasa Yuwe*. Popayán: CRIC.

Ramos, Abelardo, Ruben Ary Ulcué, Susana Piñacué, Joaquín Viluche, Aura María Ospina Gómez, and Humberto Muenala. 1996. *Hacia una sistematización de los CECIBS: Informe evaluativo CRIC.PEB*. Popayán: PEB-CRIC.

Ramos, Alcida Rita. 1990. "Ethnology Brazilian Style." *Cultural Anthropology* 5(4), 452–472.

———. 1998. *Indigenism: Ethnic Politics in Brazil*. Madison: University of Wisconsin Press.

Rappaport, Joanne. 1980–81. "El mesianismo y las transformaciones de símbolos mesiánicos en Tierradentro." *Revista Colombiana de Antropología* (Bogotá) 23, 365–413.

———. 1982. "Territory and Tradition: The Ethnohistory of the Páez of Tierradentro, Colombia." Ph.D. dissertation, University of Illinois at Urbana.

———. 1992. "Reinvented Traditions: The Heraldry of Ethnic Militancy in the Colombian Andes." In Robert Dover, Katharine Seibold, and John McDowell, eds., *Andean Cosmologies through Time: Persistence and Emergence*, pp. 202–228. Bloomington: Indiana University Press.

———. 1994. *Cumbe Reborn: An Andean Ethnography of History*. Chicago: University of Chicago Press.

———, ed. 1996. *Ethnicity Reconfigured: Indigenous Legislators and the Colombian Constitution of 1991*. Special issue, *Journal of Latin American Anthropology* 1(2).

———. 1998a. "Hacia la descolonización de la producción intelectual indígena en Colombia." In María Lucía Sotomayor, ed., *Modernidad, identidad y desarrollo: Construcción de sociedad y recreación cultural en contextos de modernización*, pp. 17–45. Bogotá: Instituto Colombiano de Antropología.

———. 1998b. *The Politics of Memory: Native Historical Interpretation in the Colombian Andes*. Durham, N.C.: Duke University Press.

———. 2000. "Hacia la construcción de una historia propia." *C'ayu'ce* (Popayán) 4, 10–13.

———. 2003. "Innovative Resistance in Cauca." *Cultural Survival Quarterly*, winter, 39–43.

——. ed. 2005. *Retornando la mirada: Una investigacion colaborativa interétnica sobre el Cauca a la entrada del milenio.* Popayán: Editorial Universidad del Cauca.

Rappaport, Joanne, and David D. Gow. 1997. "Cambio dirigido, movimiento indígena y estereotipos del indio: El Estado colombiano y la reubicación de los nasa." In María Victoria Uribe and Eduardo Restrepo, eds., *Antropología en la modernidad,* pp. 361–399. Bogotá: Instituto Colombiano de Antropología.

Reed-Danahay, Deborah E. 1997. Introduction to Deborah E. Reed-Danahay, ed., *Auto/Ethnography: Rewriting the Self and the Social,* pp. 1–17. Oxford: Berg.

Reichel-Dolmatoff, Gerardo. 1971. *Amazonian Cosmos: The Sexual and Religious Symbolism of the Tukano Indians.* Chicago: University of Chicago Press.

Restrepo, Eduardo. 1997. "Afrocolombianos, antropología y el proyecto de modernidad en Colombia." In María Victoria Uribe and Eduardo Restrepo, eds., *Antropología en la modernidad,* pp. 279–319. Bogotá: Instituto Colombiano de Antropología.

Riaño-Alcalá, Pilar. 1999. "Recuerdos metodológicos: El taller y la investigación etnográfica." *Estudios sobre las Culturas Contemporáneas* 5(10), 143–162. Universidad de Colima, Mexico.

Riles, Annelise. 2000. *The Network Inside Out.* Ann Arbor: University of Michigan Press.

Rivera Cusicanqui, Silvia. 1986. *"Oprimidos pero no vencidos": Luchas del campesinado aymara y qhechwa, 1900–1980.* La Paz: Hisbol.

——, ed. 1992. *Educación indígena ¿Ciudadanía o colonización?* La Paz: Ediciones Aruwiyiri.

Roattino, Ezio, I. M. C. 1986. *Álvaro Ulcué,* nasa pal: *Sangre india para una tierra nueva.* Bogotá: Editorial CINEP.

Rojas, José María. 1993. *La bipolaridad del poder local: Caldono en el Cauca indígena.* Cali: Universidad del Valle, Colección de Edición Previa.

Rojas Curieux, Tulio. 1997. "La traducción de la Constitución de la República de Colombia a lenguas indígenas." In República de Colombia, Dirección General de Asuntos Indígenas, ed., *"Del olvido surgimos para traer nuevas esperanzas"—la jurisdicción especial indígena,* pp. 229–244. Bogotá: Ministerio de Justicia y del Derecho/Ministerio del Interior.

——. 2000. "Transportar la cosa hablada a otra lengua: La experiencia de la traducción de la Constitución de la República a lenguas indígenas." In Felipe Castañeda and Matthias Vollet, eds., *Concepciones de la Conquista: Aproximaciones interdisciplinarias,* pp. 361–388. Bogotá: Ediciones UniAndes.

Roldán, Mary. 2002. *Blood and Fire: La Violencia in Antioquia, Colombia, 1946–1953.* Durham, N.C.: Duke University Press.

Roldán Ortega, Roque. 2000. *Pueblos indígenas y leyes en Colombia: Aproximación crítica al estudio de su pasado y su presente.* Bogotá: COAMA/The Gaia Foundation/OIT.

Santos, Boarentura de Sonsa. 2001. "El significado político y jurídico de la jurisdicción indígena." In Boaventura de Sousa Santos and Mauricio García Villegas, eds., *El caleidoscopio de las justicias en Colombia,* vol. 2, pp. 201–216. Bogotá: Siglo de Hombre Editores.

Sarlo, Beatriz. 2001. *Scenes from Postmodern Life.* Minneapolis: University of Minnesota Press.

Schwarz, Roberto. 1992. *Misplaced Ideas: Essays on Brazilian Culture.* London: Verso.

Selverston-Scher, Melina. 2001. *Ethnopolitics in Ecuador: Indigenous Rights and the Strengthening of Democracy.* Miami, Fla.: North-South Center Press.

Serrano, Vladimir, ed. 1993. *Economía de solidaridad y cosmovisión indígena.* Quito: Abya-Yala.

Sevilla Casas, Elías. 1986. *La pobreza de los excluidos: Economía y sobrevivencia en un resguardo indígena del Cauca–Colombia.* Quito: Abya-Yala.

Shostak, Marjorie. 2000 [1981]. *Nisa: The Life and Words of a !Kung Woman.* Cambridge, Mass.: Harvard University Press.

Sichra, Inge. 2001. "Huellas de interculturalidad en un ámbito intercultural de educación superior." In Maria Heise, ed., *Interculturalidad: Creación de un concepto y desarrollo de una actitud,* pp. 193–202. Lima: Programa FORTE-PE/Ministerio de Educación.

Sierra Sierra, Silvio. 1998. "Piñacué, al borde del fuete." *El País,* 8 July, p. E1.

Silverblatt, Irene. 1987. *Moon, Sun, and Witches: Gender Ideologies and Class in Inca and Colonial Peru.* Princeton, N.J.: Princeton University Press.

Sisco, Manuel. 2000. "El mito de La Gaitana/u'sxa Wey Tana wejxa." *C'ayu'ce* (Popayán) 4, 33–35.

——. n.d. *Despertar y uso de la palabra tradicional: Trabajo realizado en Tierradentro 1994/1999.* Popayán: CRIC.

Slocum, Marianna C. 1972. *¿Cómo se dice en páez? Gramática pedagógica páez-castellano.* Lomalinda, Colombia: Editorial Townsend.

Smith, Linda Tuhiwai. 1999. *Decolonizing Methodologies: Research and Indigenous Peoples.* Dunedin, New Zealand: University of Otago Press.

Sodemann, Ute. 2001. "Treinta años de trabajo en Colombia." *Terre des Hommes 2000/2001,* 21–25.

Sommer, Doris. 1996. "No Secrets." In Georg M. Gugelberger, ed., *The Real Thing: Testimonial Discourse and Latin America,* pp. 130–157. Durham, N.C.: Duke University Press.

Spivak, Gayatri Chakravorty. 1988. "Can the Subaltern Speak?" In Cary Nelson and Lawrence Grossberg, eds., *Marxism and the Interpretation of Culture,* pp. 271–313. Urbana: University of Illinois Press.

Spivak, Gayatri Chakravorty, and Elizabeth Grosz. 1990. "Criticism, Feminism, and the Institution." In Sarah Harasym, ed., *The Post-colonial Critic: Interviews, Strategies, Dialogues,* pp. 1–16. London: Routledge.

Stephen, Lynn. 2002. *Zapata Lives! Histories and Cultural Politics in Southern Mexico.* Berkeley: University of California Press.

Stephenson, Marcia. 2002. "Forging an Indigenous Counterpublic Sphere: The Taller de Historia Andina in Bolivia." *Latin American Research Review* 37(2), 99–118.

Stoller, Paul. 1997. *Sensuous Scholarship.* Philadelphia: University of Pennsylvania Press.

Strathern, Marilyn. 1987. "The Limits of Auto-anthropology." In Anthony Jackson, ed., *Anthropology at Home*, pp. 16–37. A.S.A. Monographs, no. 25. London: Tavistock.

Suess, Paulo. 1993. "Culturas indígenas y evangelización: Presupuestos para una pastoral inculturada de liberación." In Paulo Suess, ed., *Hacia una teología de la inculturación*, pp. 7–48. Quito: Abya-Yala.

"Sxabwes/El ombligo": El juego didáctico de las matemáticas." 2000. *C'ayu'ce* (Popayán) 4, 42–43.

Tedlock, Dennis, and Bruce Mannheim, eds. 1995. *The Dialogic Emergence of Culture.* Urbana: University of Illinois Press.

Tello Lozano, Piedad Lucía. 1982. "Vida y lucha de Manuel Quintín Lame." Tesis de grado, Universidad Nacional de Colombia, Bogotá.

Ticona Alejo, Esteban. 2000. *Organización y liderazgo aymara, 1979–1996.* La Paz: Universidad de la Cordillera.

Ticona A., Estéban, Gonzalo Rojas O., and Xavier Albó C. 1995. *Votos y wiphalas: Campesinos y pueblos originarios en democracia.* La Paz: Fundación Milenio/CIPCA.

Tocancipá, Jairo, ed. 2000. *La formación del Estado-Nación y las disciplinas sociales en Colombia.* Popayán: Taller Editorial Universidad del Cauca.

Trinh T. Minh-ha. 1991. *When the Moon Waxes Red: Representation, Gender and Cultural Politics.* London: Routledge.

Tróchez, Benilda, and José Fidel Secue. 2001. "CECIB Lopez Adentro Êeka'the: Algunas entrevistas trabajadas para la historia del programa educacíon del CRIC." Corinto. Manuscript.

Tróchez, Idalia, Benilda Tróchez, Diego Maya, and Floraldine Ávila. 1997. "López Adentro: aprendemos para vivir mejor." *C'ayu'ce* (Popayán) 1, 4–8.

Tróchez Tunubalá, Cruz, Miguel Flor Camayo, and Martha Urdaneta Franco. 1992. *Mananasrik wan wetøtraik køn.* Bogotá: Cabildo del Pueblo Guambiano.

Tunubalá Paja, Taita Floro Alberto, and José Julio Tobar Mosquera. 2002. "Carta a Armando Estrada Villa, Ministro del Interior, Bogotá." Photocopy.

Turner, Terence. 1993. "Anthropology and Multiculturalism: What Is Anthropology That Multiculturalists Should Be Mindful of It?" *Cultural Anthropology* 8(4), 411–429.

——. 2002. "Representation, Polyphony, and the Construction of Power in a Kayapó Video." In Kay B. Warren and Jean E. Jackson, eds., *Indigenous Movements, Self-Representation, and the State in Latin America*, pp. 229–250. Austin: University of Texas Press.

Ulcué Chocué, Álvaro. 1981. "Fundación de los pueblos paeces: Un relato mitológico en lengua páez." Research paper, Instituto Misionera de Antropología, Universidad Pontificia Bolivariana, Medellín, in Archivo de la Casa Cural de Toribío (ACCT).

——. 1983–84. "Educación bilingüe: Síntesis." Archivo de la Casa Cural de Toribío (ACCT).

——. 1984. "Legislación indígena nacional e idioma páez." Proposal, Tesis de Licenciatura, Instituto Misionero de Antropología, Universidad Pontificia Bolivariana, Medellín, in Archivo de la Casa Cural de Toribío (ACCT).

Ulcué, Luis Carlos. 1997. "El yu'kh 'monte' y la política de conservación en los nasa de Pueblo Nuevo, municipio de Caldono–Cauca." M.A. thesis, Universidad del Cauca, Popayán.

Ulcué, Luis Carlos, Inocencio Ramos, Graciela Bolaños, Abelardo Ramos, Mauricio Parada, Álvaro Tombé, and Ingrid Jung. 1994. "Evaluación, Programa de Educación Bilingüe, Consejo Regional Indígena del Cauca–CRIC." Popayán: CRIC.

Unigarro, María Helena. 2000. "Las jóvenes nasa migrantes en Cali." In Diana Castillo, ed., *Respetando mis derechos . . . otros serán mis pasos: La situación de la niña y la joven en la región andina*, pp. 126–146. Bogotá: Terre des Hommes.

Urdaneta Franco, Martha. 1988. "Investigación arqueológica en el resguardo indígena de Guambía." *Boletín del Museo del Oro* (Bogotá) 22, 54–81.

Urton, Gary D. 1981. *At the Crossroads of the Earth and the Sky: An Andean Cosmology.* Austin: University of Texas Press.

Valbuena, Armando. 2003. "There Can Be No Peace without Indians at the Table: A Narrative from Armando Valbuena as Told to David Edeli and Zachary Hurwitz." *Cultural Survival Quarterly* 26(4), 13–17.

Van Cott, Donna Lee. 2000a. *The Friendly Liquidation of the Past: The Politics of Diversity in Latin America.* Pittsburgh: University of Pittsburgh Press.

——. 2000b. "A Political Analysis of Legal Pluralism in Bolivia and Colombia." *Journal of Latin American Studies* 32, 207–234.

Van den Berg, Hans, and Norbert Schiffers, eds. 1992. *La cosmovisión aymara.* La Paz: Universidad Católica Boliviana/Hisbol.

Various. n.d. *Unificación del alfabeto de la lengua páez: Primer seminario.* Bogotá: Instituto Colombiano de Antropología.

Vasco Uribe, Luis Guillermo. 2002. *Entre selva y páramo: Viviendo y pensando la lucha indígena.* Bogotá: Instituto Colombiano de Antropología e Historia.

Vasco Uribe, Guillermo, Abelino Dagua Hurtado, and Misael Aranda. 1993. "En el segundo día, la Gente Grande (Numisak) sembró la autoridad y las plantas y, con su jugo, bebió el sentido." In François Correa, ed., *Encrucijadas de Colombia amerindia*, pp. 9–48. Bogotá: Instituto Colombiano de Antropología.

Vega Cantor, Renán. 2002. *Gente muy rebelde. 2. Indígenas, campesinos y protestas agrarias.* Bogotá: Ediciones Pensamiento Crítico.

Vengoechea, Alejandra de. 1998a. "Entre dos aguas." *Cambio16 Colombia* 266, 44–46.

——. 1998b. "Veinte fuetazos por Serpa." *Cambio16 Colombia* 265, 28.

Viluche, Joaquín. 2001. "¿Por qué una organización social como CRIC asume un proceso de investigación y construcción de la educación alternativa?" Popayán. Manuscript.

Wade, Peter. 1995. "The Cultural Politics of Blackness in Colombia." *American Ethnologist* 22(2), 341–357.

Wang Mingming. 2002. "The Third Eye: Towards a Critique of 'Nativist Anthropology.'" *Critique of Anthropology* 22(2), 149–174.

Warren, Kay B. 1998a. *Indigenous Movements and Their Critics: Pan-Maya Activism in Guatemala.* Princeton, N.J.: Princeton University Press.

——. 1998b. "Indigenous Movements as a Challenge to the Unified Social Movements Paradigm for Guatemala." In Sonia Alvarez, Evelina Dagnino, and Arturo Escobar, eds., *Cultures of Politics, Politics of Cultures: Re-visioning Latin American Social Movements*, pp. 165–195. Boulder, Colo.: Westview.

Yúdice, George. 1996. "Intellectuals and Civil Society in Latin America." *Annals of Scholarship* 11(1–2), 157–174.

Yule, Marcos. 1995. "Avances en la investigación del Nasa Yuwe (lengua páez)." *Proyecciones Lingüísticas* (Popayán) 1(1), 23–30.

——. 1996. *Nasa üus yaht'n u'hun'i/"Por los senderos de la memoria y el sentimiento Paez": Nasa yuwete twehn'i/"tradicion oral Nasa (Paez)."* Toribío: Programa de Educación Bilingüe Intercultural/PEBIN/Proyecto Nasa Toribío.

Zambrano, Carlos Vladimir. 1989. "Cultura y legitimidad: Proyectos culturales y política cultural." In Doris Lewin, José Eduardo Rueda, and Miguelangel Roldán L., eds., *Descentralización*, pp. 201–219. Bogotá: ICFES, Serie Memorias de Eventos Científicos.

Zambrano, Marta, ed. 1996. *Antropología en Latinoamérica*, special issue, *Maguaré, Revista del Departamento de Antropología, Universidad Nacional de Colombia* (Bogotá) 11–12.

Zamosc, León. 1986. *The Agrarian Question and the Peasant Movement in Colombia: Struggles of the National Peasant Association, 1967–1981.* Cambridge, England: Cambridge University Press.

Zuidema, R. T. 1964. *The Ceque System of Cuzco.* Leiden: E.J. Brill.

——. 1990. *Inca Civilization in Cuzco.* Austin: University of Texas Press.

INDEX

Joanne Rappaport is a professor in the Department of Spanish and Portuguese at Georgetown University.

Library of Congress Cataloging-in-Publication Data
Rappaport, Joanne.
Intercultural utopias : public intellectuals, cultural experimentation, and ethnic pluralism in Colombia / Joanne Rappaport.
p. cm. — (Latin America otherwise)
Includes bibliographical references and index.
ISBN 0-8223-3561-1 (cloth : alk. paper)
ISBN 0-8223-3599-9 (pbk. : alk. paper)
1. Indians of South America—Colombia—Cauca (Dept.)—Intellectual life. 2. Indians of South America—Colombia—Cauca (Dept.)—Social conditions. 3. Indians of South America—Colombia—Cauca (Dept.)—Politics and government. 4. Multiculturalism—Colombia—Cauca (Dept.) 5. Pluralism (Social sciences)—Colombia—Cauca (Dept.) 6. Cauca (Colombia : Dept.)—Cultural policy. 7. Cauca (Colombia : Dept.)—Ethnic relations. 8. Cauca (Colombia : Dept.)—Social life and customs. I. Title.
II. Series.
F2269.1.C375R36 2005
305.8′009861′53—dc22   2005002697

p29 Auto etnography
Reed- panehay

p40 Discursos hibridos gue
auti
41-42 Inappropriate others

Meterologies
p60-61